The Korean War
Challenges in Crisis, Credibility, and Command

❦ AMERICA IN CRISIS

A series of books on American Diplomatic History

EDITOR: *Robert A. Divine*

The Korean War

Challenges in Crisis, Credibility, and Command

Burton I. Kaufman
Kansas State University

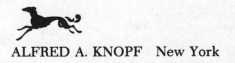

ALFRED A. KNOPF   New York

First Edition
987654321
Copyright © 1986 by Newbery Award Records, Inc.

Manufactured in the United States of America

Library of Congress Cataloging-in-Publication Data

Kaufman, Burton Ira.
  The Korean War.

  (America in crisis)
  Bibliography. p.
  Includes index.
  1. Korean War, 1950–1953—United States.
2. United States—Politics and government—1945–1953.
I. Title. II. Series.
DS919.K38 1986b   951.9′042   85–30054
ISBN 0-394-34154-6

To the
KSU History Faculty

Introduction

President Harry S. Truman wrote in his *Memoirs* that he regarded his decision to send American troops into Korea in June 1950 as his most important as president.[1] Certainly the Korean War was a turning point in the Cold War that has dominated international diplomacy since 1945. According to State Department expert Charles E. Bohlen, ". . . [i]t was the Korean War and not World War II that made [the United States] a world military-political power." The historian John Gaddis has commented that "the real commitment to contain communism everywhere originated in the events surrounding the Korean War."[2]

This is a history of the United States' involvement in the Korean War, including the reasons behind Truman's fateful decision to commit American troops to Korea after North Korean forces invaded South Korea on June 25. The book covers the major military decisions and events of the war, but it is primarily a study of foreign policy and not a military history. To the extent that it deals with the military side of the war its emphasis is on the nexus at which foreign policy decision making in Washington and military decision making in Korea and Tokyo interacted with each other. Thus, its focus is more on the White House, the Pentagon, and the negotiating tables at Kaesong and Panmunjom than in the foothills and mountains of Korea.

[1]Harry S. Truman, *Memoirs by Harry S. Truman: Years of Trial and Hope, 1946–1952* (New York, 1956), 390.

[2]Charles E. Bohlen, *Witness to History, 1929–1969* (New York, 1973), 303; John Lewis Gaddis, "Was the Truman Doctrine a Real Turning Point?," *Foreign Affairs,* 52 (January, 1974), 386.

By placing the conflict in a broad domestic and international setting and by discussing the various political pressures on the White House, both at home and abroad, I have also tried to provide the necessary context for understanding the decision making and diplomacy associated with the war. In this respect, I have attempted to make clear the constraints under which the Truman administration operated, first in terms of its initial decision to commit American troops to the war, then in its determination to cross the 38th parallel and "roll back" Communist expansion, and, finally, in its resolve to fight a limited war following the entry of the Chinese Communists into the conflict in November 1950. Similar considerations continued to influence American policy for the remainder of the war, and they are also discussed at considerable length.

The three basic themes of the book are those of crisis, credibility, and command. The first two are interrelated. The White House's decision to send troops into Korea and then to continue fighting a war there for almost three years can be fully appreciated only in terms of the crisis atmosphere that was so apparent in Washington during the late 1940s and early 1950s, an atmosphere underscored by the Red Scare and McCarthyism at home and by the fear of Communist expansion abroad. Likewise, the Truman administration committed American forces over an extended period in a country little known to most Americans prior to the summer of 1950 because it viewed the conflict in terms of maintaining American credibility abroad and its own credibility at home.

The third theme of the book has to do with what D. Clayton James has called a "crisis of command," and it relates to the problems of command in the first major conflict of any consequence (barring perhaps the War of 1812) in which the United States had to accept terms of settlement less than those of total victory. This was a bitter experience for many of America's military leaders, and I attempt to provide the reader with a sense of the problems they faced and the frustrations they endured in trying to conduct such a war. Without trying to rehabilitate the common image of General Douglas MacArthur as a military leader obsessed with his own sense of destiny and by a reckless disregard for higher authority, I try to view the war from his perspective and that of his two successors in Tokyo,

Generals Matthew Ridgway and Mark Clark. I argue the need for a more sympathetic understanding on the part of foreign policy-makers in Washington of the military imperatives of fighting a war.

There are a number of people who gave me sage advice while I wrote this book whom I would like to thank. Naomi Schneider, formerly with Alfred A. Knopf, did an expert job in editing the first half of this book, always forcing me to be clear and precise. The series editor, Professor Robert Divine of the University of Texas at Austin, was extremely helpful and sympathetic in his remarks to me. My former colleague Professor Joe Hawes now at Memphis State University, read the entire manuscript carefully and told me to move from merely writing a competent book to writing one that was also interesting. I have tried to follow his advice. My colleague and good friend Professor Al Hamscher, a true craftsman, helped me through some rough organizational and stylistic hurdles. But I dedicate this book to the entire history faculty at Kansas State University, as fine a group of dedicated teachers, scholars, and just good colleagues and friends as anyone could want. The reader will forgive me if I mention them by name: Kent Donovan, Clyde Ferguson, Marsha Frey, Buddy Gray, Al Hamscher, Robin Higham, Ken Jones, Jake Kipp, George Kren, Bob Linder, John McCulloh, Don Mrozek, Don Nieman, Roy Page, Homer Socolofsky, Lynn Stoner (now at Arizona State University), Dent Wilcoxon, and Sue Zschoche.

Contents

List of Maps

The Korean War

Challenges in Crisis, Credibility, and Command

CHAPTER 1

The Outbreak of Hostilities

The Korean conflict of 1950–1953 involved a great power struggle between the United States and the Soviet Union superimposed on a civil war between North and South Korea. It came amid a climate of crisis in the United States highlighted by fear of Communist aggression throughout the world and compounded by apprehension about internal Communist subversion reaching the highest levels of government. In the five years preceding the outbreak of hostilities in Korea, relations between the United States and the Soviet Union had soured and then become poisoned. Misperceptions and misunderstandings of one superpower by the other had hardened into myths that aggravated real grievances. Fearful of a worldwide Communist conspiracy, the United States had been sucked into the vortex of Asian politics, and American officials had formulated policy for Korea that badly estimated the consequences of their actions and failed to comprehend fully the political implications of Korea's social and political structure. Out of similar anxiety Washington responded to news of the North Korean invasion of South Korea on June 25 with deliberate speed and even relief now that it believed the Soviet Union had shown its true intentions in terms of world domination.

Relations between Washington and Moscow had never been good since the Communists first came to power in 1917. Along with other Western countries, the United States had intervened in the Russian Civil War in 1918, and Washington had not even recognized the Soviet Union until 1933. For its part Moscow made repeated calls in the 1920s and 1930s for world revolution

1

and the destruction of American capitalism. Americans were also shocked by news of purges within the Soviet Union in the 1930s and by the Nazi-Soviet Pact of 1939, which led to Germany's invasion of Poland the next month.[1]

Out of the expediency of needing to defeat a common enemy after Germany turned on Russia in 1941, the two powers had fought together during World War II, and for a time in early 1945, when the leaders of the wartime coalition met at the Crimean resort of Yalta on the Black Sea, it seemed possible that a lasting friendship might develop between capitalist America and communist Russia. In fact, Yalta marked the high point of wartime unity and goodwill. President Franklin Roosevelt based his vision for the postwar world on maintaining the Grand Alliance, which, along with the United States and the Soviet Union, included England and China. He also had great confidence in his ability to deal with the Soviet leader, Joseph Stalin, who, from all indications, rather liked and admired the American President.

With Germany facing imminent defeat, the leaders of the Grand Alliance—Roosevelt, Stalin, and Prime Minister Winston Churchill of England—concentrated on planning for the peace that would follow the war. Among the agreements they reached at Yalta was the Declaration of Liberated Europe, in which the Allies pledged to hold free elections in countries freed from the Axis powers. The Soviet Union also promised to reorganize the pro-Communist government of Poland along more democratic lines and to enter the war against Japan within three months after the Germans surrendered in Europe. In return for Stalin's pledge to join the war in the Far East, the United States agreed that the Soviet Union should receive a number of territorial concessions at the expense of Japan, including the Kurile Islands north of Japan along with the southern half of Sakhalin Island and Port Arthur, both of which Russia had lost in the Russo-Japanese War of 1904.

Even at Yalta, however, there were some very substantial differences between the United States and the Soviet Union, which were either left unresolved or glossed over with unstable compromises. In brief, there was a basic incompatibility between America's internationalist vision of an open world after the war, characterized by its interdependence and a commitment to democratic processes, and the Soviet vision of a world divided into strategic spheres of influence, including, in its case, a sphere of influence in eastern Europe. Beyond this, wartime cooperation against Germany had failed to dispel entirely the years of distrust between Moscow and its wartime partners. The lack of a second front in Europe until 1944, despite much earlier promises from Roosevelt that another front would soon be opened, also caused Soviet leaders to wonder whether the United States and Great Britain were not trying to bleed the Soviet Union to death by forcing it to bear the brunt of the war at a staggering cost in terms of lives (an estimated 20 million casualties) and physical damage.

Unquestionably the most serious differences between the wartime partners concerned the future of eastern Europe, particularly the status of Poland. Despite the Declaration of Liberated Europe Stalin was determined to maintain tight control over the region and to prevent Poland from being used as a corridor of invasion from the west. Having established a Communist government in Poland, he refused to expand it to include representatives of a rival pro-western government or to hold elections in Poland, despite promises to the contrary. He also insisted on moving Poland's boundaries to the west, annexing territory along the Russo-Polish boundary in the east and compensating Poland by taking territory from Germany in the west.

Americans felt betrayed by Stalin's determination to carve out a sphere of influence in eastern Europe and by his refusal to carry out the promises he had made at Yalta. This was particularly true of the country's large ethnic population from eastern Europe, many of whom still had families there. Very quickly there began to develop an image in the United States of an untrustworthy former ally, not all that different from Nazi Germany in terms of its totalitarian government and expansionist ambitions, and needing to be treated with a combination of toughness and deep suspicion. Without such a policy, a growing number of Americans believed, Moscow would attempt aggression throughout the world.

Certainly Harry Truman, who succeeded to the Presidency on Roosevelt's death in April, shared much of this view of the Soviet Union. Although he did not fully abandon Roosevelt's

policy of seeking accommodation with Moscow in favor of a
"get tough" policy until early 1946, he disliked and distrusted
the Soviets. Never having been taken into Roosevelt's confidence as vice-president, he also entered the White House ill-
informed on foreign policy and heavily dependent for advice on
the State Department, where a small group of Soviet experts
was already advocating a hard-line policy toward Moscow. An
indication of Truman's attitude toward the Russians was his
famous meeting on April 23 with Soviet Foreign Minister Vya-
cheslav Molotov, who was on his way to the opening of the
United Nations in San Francisco. In their meeting Truman allegedly berated Molotov "in terms of one syllable" and responded to Molotov's protests that he "had never been talked
to like that in [his] life" with the comment, "Carry out your
agreements and you won't get talked to like that [again]."

From the point of view of Moscow, however, the American
position was both unfriendly and hypocritical. Americans
talked about an open world and the elimination of spheres of
influence, but maintained their own sphere of influence in the
Western Hemisphere. They spoke of free elections in eastern
Europe but supported dictatorships in Central and South America. They sought to dictate the form of government in Poland,
which bordered on the Soviet Union, but had not consulted
Moscow or made much of an issue about representative government when administrations were being established for Greece
and Belgium. From all this it was easy for the Russians to conclude that the United States was pursuing the same policy of
hostility toward the Soviet people that it had always pursued
and that the capitalist nations of the West were seeking to
"encircle" the Soviet Union for the purpose of eventually over-
throwing its communist form of government.

In other words, within a very short time after the western
coalition had met at Yalta to map out the peace that would
follow the war, the coalition had begun to unravel. Traditional
distrusts had surfaced once more, and new misperceptions had
developed about Soviet aggression, on one hand, and American
counterrevolutionary activity, on the other. Some of the drift
away from wartime partnership to peacetime confrontation
was already evident at the Potsdam Conference of July. At this,
the last of the "Big Three" wartime meetings, held after Ger-

many had surrendered but before the Japanese had been defeated, President Truman made clear his anger at the Soviet Union for not abiding by the Yalta agreements on eastern Europe. He also disagreed with Stalin on a number of other issues, including a common policy for Germany, and he left Potsdam determined not to allow the Soviets to participate in the control of Japan. During the course of the conference, Truman learned that an atomic bomb had been successfully tested in New Mexico. According to Winston Churchill, this caused the President to become significantly more assertive in negotiating with the Soviet leader.

One of the issues that Truman discussed with Stalin was the postwar status of Korea. This was not the first time the Allied leaders had considered this matter. For forty years, ever since the Russo-Japanese War of 1904, Korea had been under the complete control of the Japanese, who had attempted to destroy all semblance of its national identity. But at the Cairo conference of November 1943, President Roosevelt, Prime Minister Churchill, and Generalissimo Chiang Kai-shek of China had stated their determination "that in due course Korea shall become free and independent." The Soviet Union adhered to this agreement at the Teheran conference the same month, and at Potsdam the wartime partners reaffirmed the Cairo statement, making it clear that Japan would not be allowed to retain Korea.[2]

What Roosevelt had anticipated at Cairo, however, was a multipower trusteeship, including the United States, the Soviet Union, China, and Great Britain, which might last as long as forty years. He believed that Korea needed to go through a period of apprenticeship before receiving full independence. At the same time, the American President opposed occupation of Korea by a single nation, fearing that this might lead to the same kind of great power rivalry for the control of Korea that had contributed to the Russo-Japanese War in 1904 and, for that matter, to the Sino-Japanese conflict ten years earlier. Washington wanted to avoid the mistakes of the 1930s when no checks were placed on Japanese expansion in Asia and German aggression in Central Europe. Also, Roosevelt was not naïve in dealing with the Russians, and while he stressed the importance of Soviet-American cooperation, he realized at the same time that Soviet occupation of Korea might threaten the American position in the Pacific and further enhance Soviet power in Northeast Asia at a time when Japan could no longer act as an effective counterweight to Soviet influence. As for the United States, it was simply not willing to assume the responsibility of a single trustee.[3]

In retrospect, the United States might have been wiser to have let the Soviet Union occupy Korea unilaterally. A real question exists as to how much the Soviet Union could have exploited its enhanced position in Northeast Asia. As an historian, William Stueck, Jr., has argued, "[t]he Asian people, so numerous and so nationalistic, were poor prospects for long-term exploitation by a foreign power, no matter how strong." Beyond this, it is quite reasonable to suppose that the Soviet Union might have accepted a neutralized Korea headed by a coalition government that included non-Communists as well as Communists. Notwithstanding growing American perceptions to the contrary, Stalin was far more concerned with the security of the Soviet Union than with the spread of international communism. He insisted on a tightly controlled sphere of influence along his borders, but rather than encouraging Communists outside the Soviet Union, he urged them to cooperate in coalition governments in Czechoslovakia, Hungary, Italy, and France. There is no reason to believe he would have done otherwise in Korea. Certainly there is no evidence that during the war Stalin saw any overriding strategic interest in Korea.[4]

However, the United States failed to make concrete arrangements for the postwar occupation of Korea, in part because of Roosevelt's policy of postponing decisions on postwar political matters so long as the fighting continued and in part because of his tendency to procrastinate over difficult problems. This was particularly regrettable, given the deterioration in Soviet-American relations that soon took place. In fact, by the time the war ended on August 15, hard-liners within the State Department were already arguing that Soviet occupation of the peninsula would threaten American security interests in the Far East. By no means did everyone within the State Department share this view, and America's military leaders at the Pentagon consistently maintained that Korea would have no strategic value in case of a general world conflict and that American forces could be better used elsewhere.[5]

Nonetheless, Truman listened to the hard-liners in the State Department. Surprised by the suddenness of Japan's surrender, still overwhelmed by the duties of his office, and faced with a surfeit of foreign policy problems, particularly the growing strain in relations with Moscow, the President agreed to a proposal aimed at preventing a Soviet take-over of Korea by accepting a zone of occupation in the country south of a line at the 38th parallel. The line would divide Soviet and American occupation forces. Now the two superpowers would face each other across a divided land.[6]

In reaching this decision to divide Korea into two zones of occupation, the White House failed to appreciate fully the internal social and political disorder in Korea at war's end or the aspirations of the Korean people themselves. For four thousand years prior to World War II, Korea had possessed a homogenous society with a single language, national heritage, and political culture. Forty years of Japanese occupation had not changed traditional behavior patterns, but Japan's colonial enterprise had upset Korea's delicately balanced economic and social structure. Decentralization of administration, industrialization, the development of commerce, and the mobilization of the population, all by Japan, had produced fractured and fragmented development, uprooting the sedentary peasant population, for example, causing a mass movement of peasants from their villages into the country's towns and cities, casting them in the role of workers, miners, and soldiers, and exposing them to the outside world, but never completely tearing them from their native roots.[7]

As a result, at war's end, Korea was in a state of political chaos and locked in an internal social struggle. Forces on the political left, demanding fundamental change in Korean society, clashed with political elites seeking to maintain privileges enjoyed under Japanese rule. Workers and peasant unions mushroomed, and Communist strength grew. The Korean People's Republic (KPR), an anti-Japanese coalition of Korean nationalists, organized just before American troops arrived in Korea in September but after the Soviets had entered the country a month earlier, failed to bridge the differences between

right and left. Instead, the KPR oriented itself increasingly toward radical change, including land confiscation and redistribu-
tion and nationalization of major industries. It also established
people's committees in most of Korea's provinces. Except for
foreign intervention, it probably would have triumphed politically throughout the peninsula within a few months.[8]

News that the United States would occupy Korea, however,
proved the critical factor in organizing the right to ward off
leftist attacks on existing privileges. Landowners, manufacturers, and other businessmen (including Japanese collaborators)
formed the Korean Democratic Party (KDP), which became
the pillar of the right and would remain the single strongest
rightist party throughout American occupation. Offering no
well-articulated program of its own, focusing its efforts in Seoul,
and having little support in the countryside, the KDP's principal purpose was to resist the groups and programs associated
with the KPR.[9]

In addition to the KPR and the KDP there were dozens of
other affiliated and nonaffiliated groups that sprang up all over
Korea after the war. Radicals, Communists, and other revolutionary factions, seeking to bring about a general restructuring
of Korean society and claiming the mantle of Korean leadership
on the basis of their support among the countryside, clashed
with rightist and conservative groups whose primary claim to
legitimacy lay in the fact that they had ruled before. In between
were more moderate elements seeking gradual economic and
social reform.[10]

All political factions were in agreement, however, on the
fundamental issue of immediate independence for Korea. Forty
years of Japanese rule had failed to suppress patriotic fervor.
Exiled or imprisoned by the Japanese, nationalist leaders had
continued to speak out and protest against Japanese authority.
In 1919 a group of Korean exiles in Shanghai, meeting with the
leaders of the underground movement in Korea, had formed a
Korean Provisional Government, and in the 1920s and 1930s
several centers of nationalist activity had developed in China,
the United States, and the Soviet maritime provinces. But the
nationalist movement as a whole lacked leadership, unity, and
a coherent program.[11]

Among those who had fled their country to work for Korean

independence, the best known was Syngman Rhee. Born in 1875, Rhee had spent most of his life working almost single-mindedly in the cause of Korea nationalism. In 1898 he had been imprisoned for antigovernment activities, including leading a demonstration against the employment of Russian advisers because they interfered with the exercise of national sovereignty. Released from prison in 1904, Rhee had come to the United States, where he received a Ph.D. in international law from Princeton in 1910. He returned to Korea and was almost arrested again, this time by the Japanese for his work with the Christian Youth movement. He managed to escape back to the United States, where he remained for the next thirty years. But by 1919 he was identified so closely with the cause of Korean nationalism that he was named head of the Provincial Government that had been formed at Shanghai. For the remainder of the Japanese occupation he badgered, pleaded, and begged as he traveled throughout the United States and elsewhere, speaking and writing and promoting the cause of Korean independence. The large sums of money he needed to finance his travels and activities he raised from Koreans in the United States, from contributions from sympathetic Americans, and from American businessmen to whom he promised lavish investment opportunities in Korea after independence. Proud, obstinate, and obstreperous, Rhee was also deeply religious and self-righteous, rather in the tradition of Woodrow Wilson, whom Rhee had met while at Princeton and with whom he had pictures taken that later circulated throughout Korea. In addition, he was a political conservative and a strident anti-Communist who had argued as World War II drew to a close that recognition of the Provisional Government was the only effective means of blocking the Soviet seizure of Korea. But perhaps more than anyone else he came to represent the cause of Korean nationalism.[12]

When American occupation forces landed in Korea in September 1945, therefore, the country was united in its demand for immediate independence. Also, it had in Syngman Rhee a much-venerated elder statesman who was prepared to return to Korea from the United States in order to assume the responsibilities of power. But Korea was also in the midst of political and social upheaval, and leftists, Communists, and other radical groups, who had penetrated the countryside, were intent on making their own claim to the mantle of Korean sovereignty.

The thrust of the American occupation was to contain the forces of social and political change within its zone of occupation. Officially, American policy was not to recognize any group as Korea's legitimate government but to proceed with the establishment of an American Military Government (AMG). The commander of the American troops, Lieutenant General John Hodge, was thus given few instructions other than that "no organized political groups, however sound in sentiment, should have any part in determining the policies of military government." Because of his advocacy of immediate independence for Korea and his ties to the Provisional Government, the State Department even delayed Syngman Rhee's return to Korea. Not until friends in the War Department interceded in his behalf was he allowed to proceed home in October.[13]

In fact, though, Hodge had been impressed with the political chaos in Korea even before taking up his new assignment, and after he arrived in Korea in September, he quickly established ties with what he regarded as the forces of political order and stability, including Japanese collaborators and members of the KDP. The Japanese had released thousands of political prisoners after August 15, and they radioed to Hodge in Okinawa that Communists and other political agitators were seizing weapons and creating a situation of near anarchy. An unsophisticated and politically insensitive midwesterner who understood the imperatives of the occupation in terms of containing Soviet expansion, Hodge failed, however, to grasp the wider social ferment at the heart of the political disorder in Korea. In his view the American occupation was menaced by an internal as well as external Communist threat that included the KPR, and both had to be contained. Beyond this, the ordinary functions of government required working with those who accepted American authority and who had administrative experience and knowledge. This meant business and professional men, educators, government bureaucrats, and property owners, most of whom had ties with the KDP.[14]

Very quickly, therefore, the American occupation established close relations with the KDP and other rightist and anti-Communist elements, while it refused to accept assistance from the KPR in handling the volatile situation in Korea. In October Hodge welcomed Rhee to Seoul in lavish ceremonies during which Rhee condemned "the slavery" of North Korea under the Soviets. In subsequent months Hodge staffed the Korean bureaucracy, including the police and justice systems, with members of the KDP or with those who had served under the Japanese or been prominent during the period of colonial rule. He also established a national defense force whose purpose was to aid the police in the cities and provinces in disbanding private armies linked to the KPR and in otherwise engaging in counterinsurgency activities. Most important, he made the first moves toward instituting a separate southern government under Rhee and other rightists associated with him.[15]

By December the polarization of Korean politics south of the 38th parallel had gone far. But a chance still existed that a unified and neutralist state could be established in Korea involving a broad coalition of Korean nationalists both north and south of the 38th parallel. An analogue of the leftist movements in the south, such as the peasant unions and people's committees of the KPR, existed above the 38th parallel. The difference was that the Soviet Union nurtured their development and gave them a great degree of autonomy. Accordingly, they offered the foundation on which a coalition government for all of Korea could be based.

In formulating policy for Korea, the Soviets almost certainly intended that any regime be "friendly" to its interests, which meant maintaining close ties to Moscow, and they sponsored the development of the Korean Communist Party (KCP). Also, they encouraged their own form of socialist revolution in the north and placed their own people in positions of power and responsibility. Among these was Kim Il-sung, a resistance fighter who had participated in anti-Japanese activities since the early 1930s and had received military training from the Soviets during the war. Only thirty-three years old in 1945, Kim was cultivated by Soviet officials, and in December he was named to head the northern branch of the KCP.[16]

But the Soviet Union was stretched dangerously thin in eastern Asia. It also did not regard Korea (or, for that matter, Manchuria) as of the same importance as it regarded eastern Europe. It was faced with huge reconstruction problems at home, and it lacked the resources to create a full satellite state in Korea, even if that had been its purpose. Within the operating assumption of a dependable regime in Korea, therefore, Moscow left it pretty much to the northern Koreans to carry out their own internal revolution, mainly through the people's committees and other groups that had been organized on the local and regional levels. The result was a degree of political participation not seen in southern Korea, and a complete restructuring of society above the 38th parallel.[17]

At the Moscow foreign ministers' conference in December, moreover, the Soviets agreed to an American proposal for a joint Soviet-American commission to prepare Korea for the election of a provisional government. The election would be followed by a four-power trusteeship lasting as much as five years. The foreign ministers of the three wartime partners—the United States, Great Britain, and the Soviet Union—had decided to meet in Moscow in an effort to resolve a number of postwar problems and to restore the faltering relationship that had developed among them. Korea was high on the agenda discussed at Moscow, and the fact that the Soviets accepted the American proposal for a joint commission contributed to what most observers agreed was a highly successful meeting.

According to the American proposal, the Joint Commission was to consult with democratic parties and social organizations throughout Korea. Any provisional government truly representative of the Korean people and satisfactory to the Soviet Union would have to involve representatives of leftist groups, including the KPR and Communists. But this did not mean Soviet domination of Korea. It did not even mean that the political left would act as a united bloc in a unified and neutralized country. Although the KPR was moving increasingly to the political left and included a number of Communists within its leadership, it still represented Koreans of many political persuasions. As for the Communists, they were far from united as a political bloc. The Soviet-sponsored KCP led by Kim Il-sung met considerable resistance from two other Communist groups —the domestic Communists and a group trained in Yenan, China, where Mao Tse-tung and the Chinese Communists had their headquarters. In the south the Communists were headed by Pak Hon-yong, perhaps the leading Communist figure in

Korea in 1945 and a potential rival to Kim. Nor was the Yenan faction prepared to subordinate itself to Kim's leadership. In March it even formed its own faction, the New People's Party, with the purpose of surpassing the KCP in membership and prestige.[18]

A unified and neutralized Korea was not to be, however. In the first place, strikes, work stoppages, and demonstrations by Koreans of all political persuasions broke out in Seoul and elsewhere in the south against the Moscow agreement because of its proposal of a five-year trusteeship. The proposal itself became part of a domestic power struggle with a variety of participants of all political persuasions vying for power. Also, Soviet-American relations, which remained strained despite the success of the Moscow meeting, were aggravated further— and, in the process, the Moscow accords undermined—by the AMG's effort to attribute responsibility for the trusteeship proposal to the Soviets and by Hodge's open support of the movement against the trusteeship. Almost certainly Moscow viewed this as an act of American perfidy, all the more so because the political left in the South, at the risk of appearing in collusion with the Russians and against immediate Korean independence, decided to follow the Soviet line in standing by the highly unpopular Moscow agreement.[19]

Also, Hodge and other officials of the American Occupation continued their efforts to limit the leftist thrust south of the 38th parallel. At the beginning of 1946 they helped organize the Representative Democratic Council (RDC) to facilitate the establishment of the provisional government for Korea provided for by the Moscow agreement. Supposedly intended as a coalition of all important groups and factions in Korea, the RDC consisted almost exclusively of political representatives from rightist parties led by Rhee. One observer put it bluntly when he remarked that the RDC "was neither representative, nor democratic, nor did it ever counsel."[20]

By the spring of 1946, furthermore, relations between the Soviet Union and the United States had deteriorated to the point where the chances of cooperation between the two powers over such places as Korea had become virtually nil. Any success that might have been achieved at Moscow in repairing Soviet-American relations was effectively nullified in March

1946 when the Soviets refused to follow the British and Americans in withdrawing their troops from oil-rich Iran, despite a 1942 occupation treaty requiring the Russians to leave the country six months after the end of the war. Seeking oil concessions from the Teheran government, the Russians even started tanks toward the border and supported a revolt in northern Iran. Not until Washington sent a strong note to Moscow demanding immediate withdrawal and the Iranians agreed to establish a joint operating company with the Russians (in a treaty later rejected by Parliament) did the Soviets agree to pull out their forces.

Meanwhile, in an effort to mobilize the Soviet people for the task of reconstruction after the United States rejected a Soviet request for a one-billion-dollar loan, Stalin delivered a speech in which he talked about the incompatibility of communism and capitalism. About the same time, George Kennan, a State Department expert on the Soviet Union, sent a long telegram from Moscow to Washington warning that the United States was confronted with "a political force committed fanatically to the belief that with [the] U.S. there can be no permanent modus vivendi." And in Washington the State Department came under increasingly heavy attack from Republican leaders in Congress for allegedly following an appeasement policy toward the Soviets.[21]

All this led President Truman to adopt a "get tough" policy with the Russians. By January he concluded that it was necessary to treat Moscow with an iron fist if another war was to be avoided. "We should rehabilitate China and create a strong central government there," he said. "We should do the same for Korea." The next month he reached much the same conclusion. As the situation in Iran became explosive and reports from Korea indicated a lack of agreement on fundamental issues between the United States and Russia, the President remarked that America was going to war with the Soviets and there were two fronts, one of which was Korea. Similarly, the administration more and more conceived of Korea as an ideological battleground on which America's entire success in Asia might depend. In early 1946 Ambassador Edwin C. Pauley, who made an inspection tour of the Far East, told President Truman that it was in Korea that a test would be made "of whether a democratic competitive system can be adapted to meet the challenge of defeated feudalism, or whether some other system, i.e., Communism, will become stronger."[22]

Under these circumstances, chances for Korean unification dimmed and then diminished altogether. On one hand, the administration supported Hodge's program of limiting leftist activity in the south as its purpose became increasingly one of containing Soviet expansion in Korea and less one of providing for Korea's eventual unification and independence. Occasional voices in the State Department were still heard against Occupation policy, but criticism was muted. On the other hand, the Soviet Union refused to consult with rightist and moderate elements in Korea about the election of a provisional government for the country, using as a pretext their opposition to a trusteeship. The United States rejected the Soviet position, and although the Joint Commission to oversee the election of a provisional government met a number of times throughout the first half of 1946, it failed to resolve differences between Moscow and Washington. Finally it disbanded altogether on May 6.[23]

During the next two years Soviet and American positions on Korea hardened even more, and the partition of the country became permanent. The Occupation's policy of working closely with the right came back to haunt it. In the spring it launched a campaign to bring more moderate leaders into the governing process in the south, and in the fall it held elections for an interim legislature. The Occupation hoped to end its dependence on the right by creating a centrist coalition. Along with a broad program of economic and social reform (particularly land reform), it would appeal to the majority of Koreans and, in the process, isolate extremists of both the right and left while providing the basis for a new middle class. Even Hodge grew tired of the carping demands by Rhee and his group for immediate independence, and he became annoyed at their hostility toward any major economic and social change. He agreed with a State Department directive that by appealing to the vast majority of Koreans, basic land and fiscal reform would be a means of containing the leftist (Communist) threat in the south.[24]

A coalition was, in fact, organized that included moderate

leftists and rightists, and it agreed to a set of basic principles, one of which was the establishment of an interim legislative assembly. But the coalition failed to bridge the important differences that remained even among its own members. Also, Hodge stayed distrustful of the political left, and he continued to tolerate rightist control of the police and most of the governing bureaucracy, a power which the right used to help assure a victory in the October elections.[25]

After the assassination, in the summer of 1947, of one of its most prominent members, Lyuh Woon-hyung, a moderate leftist with important political ties to the north, the coalition fell apart. By this time, however, the Soviet Union had tightened its grip on the north, establishing a Communist Provisional People's Committee led by Kim Il-sung. A second Soviet-American Joint Commission, which had been formed in the spring of 1947, also ended in failure, having been unsuccessful in resolving the dispute over consultation with groups opposed to trusteeship. By this time, too, the AMG had given up its effort to establish a consensus government in the south and was once more backing the extreme right led by Rhee.[26]

In fact, the United States had already begun to consider ways of gracefully withdrawing from Korea without turning it over entirely to Communist control. Washington was clearly in the throes of a dilemma with respect to Korea in the winter and spring of 1947. Basic to American foreign policy by this time was the theory of "containment." Closely associated with the name of George Kennan, who first used the term in an article he wrote for *Foreign Affairs* in June 1947 under the pseudonym, "Mr. X," the United States had in fact been following a policy of containment since at least 1946. Indeed, Kennan had outlined his ideas on the need to contain *further* Soviet expansion in a lengthy telegram he had sent to the State Department from Moscow more than a year earlier, and President Truman had accepted his arguments in the crisis over Soviet troop withdrawal from Iran. In terms of the containment doctrine, the United States could not easily risk a Communist takeover of Korea.[27]

At the same time, however, Washington was faced with acute political and economic crises in Europe and the Middle East. A brutal winter in Europe threatening total economic

paralysis and collapse was accompanied by a British announcement that it could no longer furnish economic and military aid
either to Greece, whose British-backed government was
fighting a Communist-led insurgency, or to Turkey, which
many foreign policy experts considered a likely target for Soviet
aggression. Together these two developments created an emer-
gency-like situation in Washington. In 1947 the administration
responded by pushing through Congress the $400-million Tru-
man Doctrine and making an open-ended pledge to protect
friendly nations from subversion and aggression. A few months
later Secretary of State George Marshall proposed a massive
program of economic assistance to Europe, which was later
incorporated into the $12-billion Marshall Plan.

In simplest terms, funds were not available to meet the
needs of Europe and the Mediterranean areas and at the same
time pay for the expensive occupation in Korea. This was especially true since the Republican-controlled and budget-
conscious Congress was insisting that Truman cut his budget,
and the United States had to consider the possibility that it
might be called on to aid Chiang Kai-shek in his struggle against
the Chinese Communists.[28]

Then, too, there was the question of the military value of
Korea. The Joint Chiefs of Staff would shortly determine that
from a military and strategic standpoint Korea was of little
value; an American offensive on the Asian mainland in time of
war would bypass Korea, and the two divisions in Korea of
approximately 45,000 men could better be used elsewhere. But
this view was already widely shared in the War Department.
Like the State Department, War Department planners recognized the political value of Korea in terms of containing the
Soviet threat in Asia, but in their minds military imperatives
loomed larger. Besides, the occupation was a thankless task for
which the War Department paid the entire cost.[29]

In April 1947, therefore, before the second Joint Commission had even met, Secretary of War Robert Patterson wrote
Acting Secretary of State Dean Rusk that "the United States
should pursue forcefully a course of action whereby we get out
of Korea at an early date." In June, while the Second Joint
Commission was still meeting, Secretary of State Marshall informed the political adviser in Korea, Joseph E. Jacobs, that if

the Joint Commission failed to reach an agreement soon for a general election of a provisional government for Korea, the United States would insist upon an agreement by the four powers adhering to the Moscow agreement that an election date be held for a provisional government at the earliest practicable date. A month later an Ad Hoc Committee on Korea recommended that if no agreement could be reached between the four powers regarding the election of a provisional Korean government, the United States should announce its intention to turn the whole Korean problem over to the UN General Assembly.[30]

The Ad Hoc Committee's report ably summarized Washington's Korean policy as it had developed by August. The United States, the committee made clear, would not withdraw from Korea under circumstances that would eventually lead to Communist domination of the entire country. That would be damaging to American prestige in the Far East and throughout the entire world and would discourage smaller countries relying on American support to resist Communist pressure. In the event of early failure of the Joint Commission negotiations, however, the Committee worried that extremist groups of the right or left might create such internal political chaos in Korea that the American public would demand the withdrawal of American forces from the country, which would almost certainly result in complete Soviet domination. The committee felt it was imperative, therefore, that the United States expedite a solution to the Korean problem; turning the matter over to the next session of the UN General Assembly seemed the best alternative.[31]

In September Acting Secretary of State Robert A. Lovett informed Jacobs that it was "extremely unlikely" that the Soviets would take part in four-power conversations on Korea. Two weeks later he told the Soviet Union that in view of the failure of the Joint Commission, the United States was referring the matter to the UN. In October Washington presented its resolution for elections to the General Assembly. The resolution called for the Soviet Union and the United States to hold elections in their respective zones no later than March 31, 1948, for the formation of a national assembly and a national government. A United Nations Temporary Commission on Korea (UNTCOK) would be established to supervise the elections and report to the General Assembly. In November the General Assembly approved the American proposal.[32]

The United States now threw its entire support behind Syngman Rhee. Although unstated at the time, the administration's policy was clearly one of holding elections in anticipation of establishing a separate South Korean government. Washington realized that the Soviet Union, having refused to participate in four-power discussions on Korea, would never go along with an American-sponsored plan under the auspices of the United Nations, which at the time was dominated by the United States. Time was on the side of the Communists. In the south Communist strength was continuing to grow as politics there became increasingly polarized. In September Jacobs reported from Seoul that "at least thirty percent of the people in South Korea [were] Leftists, following the Comintern Communist leaders who would support the Soviets behind the United States lines." Lieutenant General Albert Wedemeyer, who led a mission to Korea, pretty much confirmed what Jacobs had said when he commented the same month on the growing strength of the political left below the 38th parallel. Once the United States was effectively removed from Korea, all kinds of possibilities existed for Communist domination of the entire peninsula within a relatively short period.[33]

Policy makers in Washington considered it all the more imperative, therefore, that the United States establish a separate regime in the south resistant to Communist infiltration and subversion and supportive of America's overall foreign policy aims. Given the polarization of Korean politics, the large following that Rhee still commanded on the right, and the fact that he was the only major political leader in the south to favor the establishment of a separate government, the administration felt it had little alternative but to support him despite its previous reservations about his leadership. By the end of December the reconciliation between the United States and Rhee was complete. On December 17 General Hodge issued a special message warning the Korean people of a Communist threat. The next day Rhee replied by declaring that Hodge's statement "dispelled, once and for all, the doubts which had been created by statements and official documents issued previously by the American military government." From then on the United

States remained rigidly committed to Rhee and to the establishment of a separate anti-Communist government for South Korea.[34]

Other members of the UN's Temporary Commission on Korea (UNTCOK), including even America's own allies, Australia and Canada, believed that no elections should be held in Korea unless they could be administered throughout the entire peninsula. But the AMG bitterly assailed this "British bloc" for its "leftist leanings," and in February the UN General Assembly approved an American-sponsored resolution giving UNTCOK authority to supervise elections "in such parts of Korea as might be accessible to the Commission." Canada and Australia continued to oppose separate elections. They also objected to the activities of the Rhee-controlled police and saw in a proposed conference of northern and southern leaders a remaining opportunity to bring about Korean unification. Again, however, they were overruled. UNTCOK decided to observe elections in South Korea provided there existed a "reasonable degree of free atmosphere in the South." Elections were held in May, and although UNTCOK divided once more over their fairness, Rhee won an impressive, if not overwhelming, victory. During the next several months separate regimes were established in North and South Korea. In the North a new constitution was drafted, and the Democratic People's Republic was proclaimed, headed by Kim Il-sung, who took office as premier.[35]

In the South Rhee and his supporters moved rapidly to form their own separate government. At the end of May the new legislative assembly overwhelmingly elected Rhee as its chairman. A special committee then drafted a constitution, which the assembly adopted in July. Eight days later it elected Rhee as the first president of the Republic of Korea (ROK). Although several members of UNTCOK still held out against recognizing the new government, Secretary of State Marshall made the United States' position clear. In a letter to diplomatic and consular officers abroad he stated that "[a]ny weakening of prestige and authority of new government in south would inevitably redound to advantage of Soviet puppet regime in north, with consequent lessening of chances of unification of Korea on anything but Soviet satellite basis." In December the UN General Assembly adopted a resolution declaring the South Korean government the lawful government in that part of Korea where UNTCOK was able to observe elections and stating that it was the "only such Government in Korea."[36]

Conditions in South Korea remained very unstable and chaotic, however, and Rhee instituted a program of repression that included the imposition of martial law. Even during the election campaign there had been widespread violence and disorder, especially on the island of Cheju-do, off the southern coast of Korea, where guerrilla units associated with the political left attacked towns, burned villages, and kidnapped and killed a number of rightists and police. The situation became so serious that a U. S. destroyer was sent off the coast of Cheju-do to prevent guerrilla infiltration from the mainland, and planes flew over the island in a show of force.[37]

After Rhee had been in office for a few months, the fighting flared up again and became even more widespread and violent. Before it ended in January, it claimed 30,000 lives, or about 10 percent of the island's population. Meanwhile the rebellion spread to other regions. Two thousand members of the South Korean constabulary mutinied in October as they were about to embark for Cheju-do. Leaders of the mutineers explained that they "refused to murder the people of Cheju-do [fighting] against imperialist policy." The next month Rhee imposed martial law over about one-fourth of Korea. But reports of sporadic violence continued to be received in Seoul, the capital of South Korea. The rebellion undermined public confidence in the security forces and widened the gulf between the police and the army. So, too, it showed how weak the Rhee government was to deal with such a crisis. Rhee himself was reported by some observers to be suffering from "incipient senility," while his cabinet was badly torn by political dissension and personal rivalry. Without American support the South Korean leader may not have been able to remain in political power.[38]

Nevertheless, the United States decided to go ahead with its plans for the withdrawal of American forces. Not everyone agreed with this decision. The State Department demurred, pointing not only to the instability of the Rhee regime but to the military danger from the north. The North Koreans built a large army fully supplied with Soviet arms. Military intelligence estimates of North Korean armed strength concluded that the

North was capable of victory if civil war broke out. In the opinion of the State Department, therefore, only the continued presence of American occupation forces could give the Korean government the period needed to improve internal conditions.[39]

Weighted against this view, however, was a combination of budgetary restraints and the continued insistence by the military that in a war in Asia Korea had no military or strategic value. On numerous occasions since 1947 the Joint Chiefs of Staff (JCS) had warned the administration that it was extending America's diplomatic commitments beyond the nation's existing military means. They recommended a doubling of military spending to meet the requirements of a war emergency. But Truman remained committed to trimming the military budget, not increasing it, and in 1949 he appointed as secretary of defense Louis Johnson, who promised to cut defense spending.[40]

Coupled with the scarcity of resources was the relative military insignificance of Korea. In October 1949 Mao Tse-tung's forces in China finally drove the Nationalist regime of Chiang Kai-shek from the mainland to the island of Formosa after a twenty-five-year civil war in which the United States had poured billions of dollars into China in an unsuccessful effort to prop up Chiang's faltering regime. Mao's victory, when added to this lack of resources, left the Pentagon even more leery of making military commitments on the Asian mainland. On one hand, most military leaders shared the administration's view that Europe and not Asia was the main area of confrontation with the Soviet Union. On the other hand, they were convinced that the resources obligated to the Far East should be limited to a few secure military positions. Because of what one writer has called "the high-technology/low-manpower orientation of the American military," this almost certainly meant islands. General Douglas MacArthur, head of the American government in Japan, and the JCS both emphasized the need to avoid military commitments on the Asian mainland while keeping such important islands as Japan, Okinawa, Formosa, and the Philippines out of hostile hands. At the same time, they believed that the United States should rely on economic assistance to prevent South Korea and other mainland nations from going Communist.[41]

The military pressed its view before the National Security Council (NSC), and in March 1949 it won a significant victory when the NSC issued its latest directive. Although it recognized that the withdrawal of American troops from Korea, even with the substitution of military and technical assistance, might be followed by a North Korean attempt to overthrow the South Korean government, the NSC stated that this risk existed at all times and that the final withdrawal of American troops should be completed no later than June 30, 1949. Prior to the final withdrawal of these forces, Korea should be given a stockpile of equipment and maintenance supplies adequate to cover six months' replacement and consumption requirements, together with an emergency reserve.[42]

Syngman Rhee, who was determined to reunify Korea under his government, was clearly unhappy with the purely defensive nature of American military aid. Instead, he wanted airplanes, combat ships, and arms to equip an additional 100,000 troops. The United States agreed to the establishment of a Korean Military Advisory Group (KMAG) to help train ROK military forces, but Washington was not prepared to give Rhee the military assistance he needed to attack North Korea. Aware of the risks involved in terms of an invasion from the North, the United States had decided, nonetheless, to withdraw its forces from Korea and to build up South Korea's own military forces only to the point of giving the South Korean government a reasonable chance of survival. In short, the United States tried to follow much the same policy in Korea that it would follow in Vietnam twenty years later, when in a program known as Vietnamization it attempted to hand more and more of the ground war over to South Vietnamese troops while removing American forces from combat.[43]

As in its program of phased withdrawal from South Vietnam in the 1960s, however, the United States in the 1940s was not easily able to extricate itself from Korea. Even though it had written off Korea from a military or strategic standpoint and was unwilling to commit American forces to the peninsula, the administration still regarded the country as of major symbolic importance. In fact, after the Communist victory in China, Korea became the only symbol left of America's willingness to contain Communist expansion in Asia. Washing its hands of Korea would be a signal to other Asians that the United States had abandoned them as well.[44]

At the same time, the administration recognized that its Korean policy depended on public support in the United States as well as the backing of the United Nations. In particular the Rhee government had to prove that the American experience in Korea would not be a repeat of what had happened in China. Neither Congress nor the American public was prepared to offer assistance to a government that lacked the support of its people or could not manage its own affairs.

But in Korea opposition to the Rhee regime mounted. One by one, his cabinet officials were forced to resign by the National Assembly, which clashed with the administration over issues of political authority and legitimacy. In the Assembly Rhee's own former party, the KDP, joined with another group to form the Democratic Nationalist Party (DNP), which together held more than two-thirds of the seats in the legislature. The South Korean leader retaliated, using the police and military forces to put down internal dissension and to arrest dissident politicians and newspaper editors.

Also, as a result of his government's practice of deficit spending and the printing of paper money, the country was faced with spiraling inflation. If this was not bad enough, Rhee infuriated administration officials in Washington by his caustic remarks about the insufficiency of American aid and by his strident demands for an American pledge of protection for the ROK. Secretary of State Dean Acheson warned the South Korean leader that his criticism of the United States could have "serious adverse consequences" on his request for economic and military aid, while he and other American officials made similar threats if Seoul did not alter its political practices or take measures to stabilize its economy.[45]

By the beginning of 1950, therefore, the United States was following a policy that was internally consistent but that rested on a shaky premise. Preoccupied with Europe, the administration was concerned with avoiding overinvolvement on the Asiatic mainland. Also, Korea did not warrant the stationing of

American forces. However, South Korea remained an important symbol of democracy to the rest of Asia that needed to be saved from Communist expansion. Toward that end the United States would rely on a program of military and economic assistance while pressing South Korea to avoid the mistakes that had led to disaster in China. Underlying this policy was the assumption that an invasion from North Korea was not likely in the near future and that with sufficient American assistance South Korea could take care of any trouble started solely by North Korea, although it could not repel an invasion started by the Chinese Communists or supported by them or the Soviet Union.[46]

In the context of this commitment to South Korea, Secretary of State Dean Acheson delivered a major address in January to the National Press Club in which he outlined a defense perimeter in-the Far Pacific that extended only so far as the Aleutian Islands, Japan and the Ryukyu Islands, and the Philippines, thereby excluding South Korea. Acheson was later blamed for having encouraged North Korea to attack South Korea by his speech. But the secretary of state maintained that he had no more "excluded" Korea as essential to American interests than he had any other area on the Asiatic mainland. More to the point, in making his statement, Acheson merely reaffirmed the administration's position that South Korea—and, for that matter, all the Asiatic mainland and Formosa—could be saved from Communist expansion without the use of military force.[47]

Administration policy toward South Korea changed remarkably little in the six months prior to the North Korean invasion in June. During this time the political and economic problems plaguing the Rhee regime worsened and government coercion intensified. Rhee's internal bases of political support almost completely disintegrated. In the May elections for a new National Assembly, his political organization won only 48 seats as opposed to 120 seats for all other parties, despite the fact that Rhee arrested thirty political opponents in "anti-Communist" raids just before the elections. Nor were economic conditions in the country encouraging. The problem of rising rice prices was compounded by continued fighting in the countryside and by rumors of a coming invasion from the North, which led to hoarding and still higher prices.[48]

The administration continued to speak out against Rhee's repressive policies, and it was instrumental in preventing him from postponing the general elections from May to November. Assistant Secretary of State Dean Rusk warned the Korean ambassador to the United States, Dr. John M. Chang, that postponement of the elections would be widely interpreted as an arbitrary action inconsistent with the principles according to which South Korea was established. At the same time, State Department officials in Washington and Korea continued to press the Rhee government for internal reforms—especially for more stringent measures to bring inflation under control.[49]

Also of growing concern to some American officials in the months prior to June was the infiltration of guerrilla forces from the North, causing a reexamination of the relative military strengths and capabilities of both sides. At the end of April the American chargé in Korea, Everett Drumwright, reported that South Korean army units had broken up a band of more than 6000 North Korean guerrillas who had infiltrated below the 38th parallel. "They were far and away the best-equipped guerrillas yet to come south," Drumwright remarked. A few weeks later Drumwright estimated North Korean forces at 103,000, including a contingent of troops that had fought in Manchuria alongside the Chinese Communists.[50]

Yet to most observers in Washington the situation in South Korea on the eve of the North Korean invasion did not seem particularly critical, certainly not measurably worse than before 1950 or as serious as the situation elsewhere. In the first place, while the elections of May had represented a setback for Rhee, the composition of the new legislature was not entirely clear on the eve of the war. Many successful independent candidates had actually been encouraged to run by Rhee, who recognized the weakness of his own organization and the lack of an alternative leader around whom the opposition could coalesce. In fact, Rhee's supporters lost fewer seats than the main conservative opposition group, and the South Korean leader was able to piece together a coalition government that had a reasonable chance of survival.[51]

In the countryside the spring of 1950 was relatively tranquil. Notwithstanding the fighting reported by Drumwright and other military incidents, as both North and South Korea sent probes across the border, guerrilla activity and border clashes actually fell off markedly in the months before the war, and the ROK army enjoyed considerable success in wiping out those bands that did come across the 38th parallel. So, too, the government was increasingly successful in its ongoing struggle to eliminate armed subversion from within.[52]

Most important, although a number of American officials expressed growing apprehension about the North's military superiority over the South, particularly in terms of having an air force and better equipment, and although by June intelligence reports indicated a gradual concentration of North Korean tanks and troops along the 38th parallel, the consensus remained that North Korea would not invade South Korea. A memorandum by the Central Intelligence Agency (CIA) a week before the North invaded the South stated that despite the North's apparent military superiority, it was "not certain that the northern regime, lacking the active participation of Soviet and Chinese Communist military units, would be able to gain effective control over all southern Korea." Similarly, a paper prepared by Army Intelligence concluded that "South Korea can maintain itself, unless the Soviets openly support North Korea in an armed invasion." As for the possibility that the Soviets would support a North Korean attack on South Korea, this was generally regarded as unlikely. As late as June 19 John Foster Dulles, a prominent Republican spokesman on foreign policy who had recently been appointed to negotiate a Japanese peace treaty, told President Rhee that it was the opinion of the best-informed minds in Washington that Moscow did not for the present wish to become involved in a shooting war.[53]

In contrast to conditions in Korea, the situation elsewhere seemed critical. Mao's success in China encouraged the tide of nationalist revolution throughout Asia, including Indochina and Indonesia, as well as an insurrectionary movement in the Philippines. In Indochina, in particular, a war that the French had been waging against Communist-led Vietminh guerrillas fighting for independence from France had turned against the French, and the administration was convinced that if the French colony fell to the Communists, the rest of Southeast Asia would be imperiled. In February, therefore, the United States made its first commitment in Indochina by recognizing the

nominally independent states of Laos, Cambodia, and Vietnam
and by initiating plans to support them with economic and
technical assistance. In May the administration formally extended military assistance to the French in Indochina.[54]

But from the White House's perspective danger existed
throughout the world. At any moment the Soviet Union might
strike against Berlin, Iran, Greece, Turkey, or a number of
other trouble spots, any of which could imperil the free world
and bring on a new war. Indeed, the Cold War had entered its
most perilous phase in 1950. In April the National Security
Council sent to President Truman a report, NSC-68, that became one of the key documents in American foreign policy for
the next twenty years. Intended as a comprehensive review of
American policy following the news in 1949 that the Soviet
Union had successfully tested an atomic bomb, NSC-68 became
the United States' field manual for waging the Cold War. Delivered to President Truman just a few months before the outbreak of hostilities in Korea, NSC-68 spelled out the danger to
the United States even as it prescribed its remedy. "The assault
on free institutions is worldwide," it said, "and in the context of
the present polarization of power a defeat of free institutions
anywhere is a defeat everywhere." "Soviet efforts are now directed toward the domination of the Eurasian land mass," and
any further extension of the area under the domination of the
Kremlin "would raise the possibility that no coalition adequate
to confront the Kremlin with greater strength could be assembled." In order to meet the threat of Soviet aggression, the
United States would have to increase substantially its defense
spending. Although NSC-68 offered no specific figures, the report stated that as rich as America was, it could afford to spend
up to 20 percent of its Gross National Product (GNP) for military purposes instead of its current level of about 5 percent. In
1950 that would have been about $50 billion.[55]

It was not that the leaders in Washington were ignorant of
Korea (although most Americans were) or that they did not
regard an attack by North Korea on South Korea as a serious
threat to American interests in the world. In the equation of the
Cold War as it had developed by 1950, any Communist gain
anywhere was a serious setback everywhere. Most certainly it
was not that they failed to anticipate the possibility—even prob-

ability—of a Soviet-directed military initiative somewhere. It was simply that the administration expected that if a war came, it would not come in Korea. Indeed, Washington had received reports in the spring of 1950 of a Communist military thrust in Asia, but it anticipated the probable target would be Indochina or Formosa.[56]

Part of the reason for this breakdown in intelligence was also the fact that so many reports had circulated since 1945 of a Soviet-supported North Korean invasion that it made proper evaluation of them difficult. So, too, did the division of responsibility for intelligence gathering between Washington and General Douglas MacArthur's command in Tokyo. Also, most American military strategists did not think that Korea ranked high among Soviet priorities. Even in the case of a limited war, Soviet experts in the Department of State anticipated military action somewhere along the periphery of the Soviet sphere of influence. Because of its substantial army and close relationship to the United Nations, they regarded South Korea as among the least likely targets.[57]

Yet on Sunday, June 25 (Korean time), North Korea invaded South Korea, and the United States responded almost immediately. During the next five days, as the situation in Korea continued to deteriorate rapidly, the White House increased the stakes involved in the invasion. Step by step, it broadened America's commitment in the conflict while bringing the invasion before the United Nations and turning its own military involvement into an international police action. What took place during these five days is fairly clear. Why North Korea invaded South Korea in the first place and why the United States reacted as it did are not as simple to explain.

The size of the forces which the North Koreans sent across the border was formidable and distinguished the attack from the numerous border crossings and skirmishes that had become common by the summer of 1950. Nearly 110,000 soldiers, more than 1400 artillery pieces, and 126 tanks were committed to the invasion. Once word was received in Washington that a full-scale invasion was indeed under way—it took about four hours before the American ambassador to Korea, John Muccio, could confirm the attack and cable Washington—key officials from the Departments of State and Defense gathered at the State Department. Secretary of State Acheson also conferred with President Truman, who was at his home in Independence, Missouri. Preliminary steps were then taken to call for a special session of the UN Security Council. The next day the President gave his final approval of an emergency meeting at the UN and, after receiving additional news of the deteriorating situation in Korea, flew back to Washington.[58]

The Security Council met on Sunday afternoon, June 25 (New York time), and approved an American-sponsored resolution calling for the cessation of all hostilities and a withdrawal of North Korean forces behind the 38th parallel. That same evening President Truman, having returned to Washington, met at Blair House with members of his cabinet, the Joint Chiefs of Staff, and other senior officials to map out America's response to North Korea's attack. At the meeting Truman approved recommendations by the State and Defense departments ordering General MacArthur in Tokyo to send supplies and a survey team to Korea and U. S. air and naval forces to prevent the North Korean army from interfering with the evacuation of American dependents from the Seoul-Inchon area. Put off for the moment was a third recommendation to send the Seventh Fleet to the Formosa Strait in order to prevent an attack on or from Formosa. In thus deciding to employ American military forces to maintain the Seoul-Inchon area, the President acted without reference to the United Nations. Implicit in his decision was the possibility of combat with North Korea. The decision also established a precedent for the later use of American ground forces.[59]

The fighting in Korea soon outpaced these preliminary steps. By the third day of hostilities the defenses of Seoul had nearly fallen and a general evacuation was ordered. Because of the rapidly deteriorating situation, Truman called a second Blair House meeting in which he agreed to lift all restrictions on air and naval operations in South Korea but not to permit attacks north of the 38th parallel. The President also consented to place the Seventh Fleet in the Formosa Strait. Of greater importance for the future, he agreed as well to accelerate aid to Indochina and the Philippines, where the government of Elpidio Quirino was fighting the Hukbalahap, a Communist-led guerrilla organization, and to increase American military forces in the Philippines.[60]

The next day, Tuesday, June 27, the Security Council placed its imprimatur on America's action in Korea by adopting an American-sponsored resolution calling for military sanctions against the invaders of the Republic of Korea. Even as this was happening, however, North Korean forces captured Seoul. During the next two days the military situation worsened even more. On June 28 General John Church, whom MacArthur had sent to Korea with a survey team, reported that the United States would have to commit ground forces to the fighting if the 38th parallel was to be restored. The next day, at the request of the Joint Chiefs, Truman authorized military targets in North Korea and the use of American troops to secure the area around Pusan. Twenty-four hours later, on the recommendation of General MacArthur, who had gone to Korea himself after receiving Church's report, the President approved the sending of a regimental combat team to Korea. Finally, following another meeting with his advisers at Blair House, Truman authorized MacArthur to engage whatever Army forces were available to him, subject only to Japan's security.[61]

Why, then, had North Korea invaded South Korea on June 25, and why did the Truman administration decide on military action in a part of the world that it had just a few months earlier dismissed as having no military or strategic importance? In this respect, what were the political pressures that Truman was under and what influence did they have in his final decision to commit ground forces to Korea? Did he have other choices, and why, during the days of decision, was each action that he took less than what was needed but his basic determination of what was necessary went unchallenged? Finally, why was the fateful decision regarding Formosa and Indochina made so quickly and with so little debate?

The reasons for North Korea's invasion of the South are still not entirely clear. Some writers have even hypothesized that it was the South that invaded the North or at least prodded the North into beginning the war by its own buildup of military forces and by its aggressive declarations of reunification under the Rhee regime.[62] But such interpretations are difficult to square with the military imbalance that existed between the two sides or with the way in which the North Korean offensive was carried out. As Stephen Ambrose has pointed out, "The North Korean offensive was too strong, too well-coordinated, and too successful to be a counterattack."[63] Its army consisted of approximately 135,000 well-trained and highly organized troops, including 29,000 combat-hardened forces from Manchuria. It also benefited from 150 tanks, 110 combat planes, and a large supply of heavy artillery. In contrast, the South Korean (ROK) armed forces consisted of about 100,000 poorly organized and poorly equipped troops plus a 25,000-man constabulary. Not only was there no equipment or weaponry for about a third of South Korea's armed forces; there were no tanks, no medium artillery, and no fighter aircraft or bombers. While the Soviet Union had sponsored the buildup of North Korean forces, the United States had carried through with its program of giving only limited supplies to the Rhee government.[64]

Nevertheless, the motives behind North Korea's decision to attack South Korea seem to do as much with internal Korean politics, both north and south of the 38th parallel, as with the larger Cold War struggle between the United States and the Soviet Union, for the conflict between North and South Korea was a true civil war and not merely part of the global confrontation between Washington and Moscow. In contrast to the view widely shared by American officials after the attack that North Korea invaded South Korea at the behest of the Soviet Union and with the tacit approval of the People's Republic of China (PRC), the North apparently attacked the South unilaterally and without the knowledge of either the Soviet Union or the PRC. Although Moscow expected a war, the evidence indicates that it anticipated an invasion sometime in August, which was one reason it was still boycotting the United Nations over the seating of the PRC when the attack occurred. As for the PRC, it was interested in maintaining communications with the United States in the hope of taking Formosa unopposed by Washington, which had indicated that the island was also not included in America's defense perimeter. An invasion of Formosa after the Korean War began was more likely to draw some form of military response from the United States.[65]

Nor was the North Korean leader, Kim Il-sung, merely the puppet of the Soviet Union, as leaders in Washington liked to believe. Although Kim undoubtedly owed his power and position to Soviet support, he had learned from his struggle with the leaders of other Communist factions that he could not rely totally on Soviet goodwill, that one of the reasons the Soviets had backed him in the first place was his ability to organize his cadres on the local and regional levels, and that his credentials of legitimacy rested as much on his nationalist claims as on his ties to the Soviet Union.[66]

In 1950 these claims were being challenged by a political rival, Pak Hon-yong, formerly the leader of the South Korean Communist Party, who had fled north in 1949 to escape arrest by Rhee's police. In 1949 Pak organized the Democratic Front for the Unification of the Fatherland (DFUF) in response to calls from leftist groups in the South. In simplest terms, it behooved Kim to "outnationalize" Pak and to undermine his position in the South by appearing himself as the champion of Korean unification.[67]

But there seem to have been other reasons as well why Kim ordered the invasion of South Korea. Secretary of State Acheson's speech to the National Press Club in January must have led Kim to expect that the United States would not intervene in the struggle, while he could anticipate continued Soviet military support. At the same time, the border incidents in which both sides had been involved since the spring of 1949, and Rhee's own martial pronouncements, may have persuaded the North Korean leader of a long-term threat from South Korea, which would be eliminated only by a preemptive strike southward. Finally, the continued inflation and growing anti-Rhee sentiment in the South, as evident by the results of the 1950 elections, seemed to augur well for a successful invasion from the North.[68]

The reasons behind the American response to the attack are also complex, although, in the final analysis, they can be reduced to one fundamental consideration. In the first place, bringing the invasion to the UN appeared the only reasonable course of action. The United States had earlier acted within the framework of the UN, and taking the matter to the Security Council was a way of serving notice to the world as to how seriously the United States viewed the fighting in Korea. It was also a way of achieving a collective response to the invasion, which seemed preferable to unilateral American action.

Yet almost from the time they first received news of the invasion, American officials both in South Korea and in Washington responded in a way that made a unilateral American response likely. Most important, they perceived the North Korean move across the border as a Soviet-sponsored and Soviet-controlled attack against free world interests in Asia and elsewhere. In their minds, the invasion was a test of American resolve to resist Communist expansion that would have serious consequences throughout the Far East and Southeast Asia. As a State Department intelligence estimate put it, the elimination of South Korea would influence both Soviet and Chinese moves in Indochina, Formosa, Malaysia, and Burma. The Soviet Union, it said, would "make much of American inability or unwillingness to support effectively those who cast their lot with the U. S. and [would] stress the line that the American imperialists are willing to fight only to the last Korean, Formosan, etc."[69]

Indeed, a very real concern existed in Washington, almost as soon as North Korea crossed the 38th parallel, that the Korean invasion might be the first of several Soviet thrusts in other parts of the world. At the very least, the failure of the United States to take any action in Korea would cause significant damage to America's prestige in Europe and the Middle East. Very much on the minds of America's leaders, including President Truman and Secretary of State Acheson, was the need to avoid another case of appeasement, such as had characterized the diplomacy of the late 1930s and had been responsible for the ill-fated and notorious Munich Conference of 1938 in which the French and British had tried to appease Adolph Hitler by giving Germany part of Czechoslovakia.[70]

Domestic considerations also weighed heavily on the Truman administration's decision to intervene in Korea. As the historian Stephen Pelz has remarked, Truman "was vulnerable to serious charges from his domestic critics if he did not intervene." If Korea fell to the Communists so soon after the fall of China, this might very well lead to a congressional investigation into the military reasons why. Such an investigation would show that the administration had left the United States badly weakened militarily. A cutback in conventional forces as a result of budget restrictions, the lack of an adequate atomic deterrent to a Soviet attack in Europe or elsewhere, and inadequate war planning would be some of the charges made by administration critics and confirmed by a congressional investigation. The insufficiency of America's military aid to South Korea would be another charge.[71]

Beyond this, Truman also had to contend with the general climate of fear and crisis that gripped the nation in the spring and early summer of 1950. At the time that North Korea invaded South Korea, the United States seemed to many Americans imperiled by the threat of Communism both at home and abroad. Events of the previous year hardly augured well for the future. First there had been the news in September 1949 that the Soviet Union had successfully tested an atomic bomb several years ahead of schedule. A month later Americans had learned that the Chinese civil war was over and that China had been "lost" to the Communists. The following January Alger Hiss, a former State Department official, who, in testimony before a congressional committee, had denied charges that he had been a Communist in the 1930s, was found guilty of perjury. About the same time, Klaus Fuchs, a high-level atomic scientist, confessed in England to giving atomic secrets to the Soviet Union. And in February Senator Joseph McCarthy of Wisconsin announced before a group of Republican women in Wheeling, West Virginia, that he had a list of 205 officials of the State Department who were members of, or loyal to, the Communist Party.[72]

Taken together, these developments suggested to many Americans that the tide of the Cold War was running in favor of the Communists. More than that, they seemed to support charges of conspiracy even within Washington itself. Americans felt particularly betrayed by the "fall" of China, with which, it was widely believed, the United States had always had a special relationship. It mattered little that Chiang Kai-shek had been thoroughly corrupt or that his regime lacked popular support. For a large number of Americans, China could have been saved from Communism had the administration been more resolute and forthcoming in its support of Chiang. A powerful China lobby closely associated with the right wing of the Republican Party railed against the administration's Far East policy, attributing the Communist victory in China to the traitorous actions of diplomatic officials employed by Roosevelt and Truman.

Much of the bipartisanship that had characterized American

foreign policy in recent years and had been responsible for approval of the Truman Doctrine and the Marshall Plan vanished amid partisan wrangling over the China issue and the priority the administration gave to affairs in Europe. Senator McCarthy became headline news as he continued to make charges of internal subversion and espionage, and a new word, "McCarthyism," was introduced into the language to describe unsupported accusations of disloyalty and demagoguery. But for many Americans McCarthy's accusations offered a convincing explanation of why China had been lost to the Communists or why the Soviet Union had developed a nuclear capability so fast.[73]

American politics was infected by this sense of betrayal and by a national mood of ugliness in a period which the London *Economist* referred to as America's "months of degradation," and which *Commonweal* described as "a time of confusion and general suspicion such as must exist in the always-threatened police state." Observing the mood of America in the spring of 1950, Michael Straight remarked that what struck him from his ten-thousand-mile trip across and through America was "the prevalence of fear." "There is growing fear among merchants, businessmen, and bankers about the future," Straight wrote. "Freedom forums are conspiring up horrid apparitions of socialism among civic organizations. Hundreds of thousands of Americans are being persuaded to resist change, in the belief that all progress leads eventually to Communism." A Minnesota poll taken in the spring of 1950 showed that 41 percent of those interviewed believed McCarthy's charges of Communist infiltration in the State Department, while only 29 percent did not. Similarly, a Gallup poll revealed that 39 percent of those questioned felt that McCarthy's charges were "a good thing," while again only 29 percent thought they were harmful.[74]

As these polls indicated, the conspiratorial mentality that existed in America in 1950 was not limited to the anti-Communist hysteria and antics of Joseph McCarthy and those beholden to him. It was widespread and growing, and it intruded itself most forcibly in the national debate over the administration's Far Eastern policy. The shattering loss of China continued to sting and unsettle many Americans. Senator Robert Taft blamed the defeat of the Chinese Nationalists on "Communist influence" in the State Department. Senator Styles Bridges declared that American reverses in the Cold War were "no accident," that Joseph Stalin was no "superman," and that the Soviet leader must have had "help from inside our ranks." Even many Democrats joined the chorus suggesting internal betrayal. "What our young men have saved," Congressman John F. Kennedy of Massachusetts contended, "our diplomats and our President have frittered away." The loss of Korea so soon after the Communist victory in China, therefore, would almost certainly have added to the storm of protest over the administration's Asian policy, raised additional accusations of internal subversion (which happened anyway), and, at the very least, furthered the already existing charges that the President was "soft" on communism.[75]

Under these circumstances the administration would have been hard-pressed to respond decisively to the North Korean invasion of South Korea even if there had not been other compelling reasons to do so. In fact, to the extent that it lifted the uncertainty surrounding Moscow's world aims and ambitions, news of the North Korean invasion actually brought a feeling of relief to many Americans. As Joseph C. Harsch, chief of the *Christian Science Monitor*'s Washington bureau for twenty years, added: "Never before in that time have I felt such a sense of relief and unity pass through the city."[76]

In other words, the credibility of the administration's foreign policy was at issue in the Korean War, both abroad and at home, both among America's allies and its adversaries. In such a situation of crisis as seemed to face the United States in the summer of 1950, furthermore, the President had to act forthrightly and unequivocally. Anything less would be an indication of weakness on his part, which the enemies of the United States and the foes of the administration could use to their benefits. Once Truman and his closest advisers accepted these basic assumptions—as they did almost immediately after receiving news of the fighting in Korea—there really seemed no course open to them other than the one they followed.

Significantly, Truman did not actually commit ground forces to the defense of Korea until the fifth day of fighting, after Seoul had fallen and after General Church had reported that only American troops could reestablish the 38th parallel. Even then

their function was limited to protecting military facilities in
Pusan and helping supply ROK forces at the front. The administration's whole purpose, in fact, was to try to contain the war
in Korea and, above all, to avoid a military showdown with the
Soviet Union and China. Thus, on the third day of fighting,
while Truman lifted restrictions on air and naval operations in
South Korea, he prohibited attacks north of the 38th parallel in
order to minimize the possibility of direct Soviet or Chinese
intervention and to avoid letting the fighting turn into a general
war elsewhere. And on the fifth day, although he authorized
strikes against military targets in North Korea, he ordered that
special care be taken to insure that operations in North Korea
were in fact limited to military targets and stayed well clear of
the Manchurian and Soviet frontiers.[77]

At the same time, the United States could not allow Korea
to fall to the Communists by default. The stakes were too high
and the consequences too grave. As the military situation continued to deteriorate, therefore, the options that were open to
the administration seemed to come down to one, until, finally,
on the sixth day of fighting, Truman released ground forces
stationed in Japan for combat use in Korea. But even then he
anticipated that America's military mission would be limited in
scope and duration.[78]

One option that might have been pursued more discreetly
was direct negotiations with the Soviet Union. In order to avoid
a confrontation with Moscow and to probe its position, Secretary of State Acheson asked the Soviets to disclaim responsibility for the attack and to press the North Koreans to withdraw
their forces north of the 38th parallel. But before Moscow could
respond to this note, Acheson made it public. By thus denying
the Soviets an opportunity to save face, he effectively undermined any small chance that might have existed that Moscow
would cooperate with Washington to end the war. Instead, the
Soviets responded on June 29 by accusing South Korea of provoking the hostilities and warning that it regarded foreign interference "in the internal affairs of Korea" unwarranted. With
the United States holding the Soviet Union ultimately responsible for the war and with Moscow thus accusing the United
States of aggression against North Korea (and China), the likeli-

hood of a meaningful dialogue between the two powers seemed negligible, and no effort was made to preserve it.[79]

As for Truman's decisions to increase aid to Indochina and the Philippines and to send the Seventh Fleet into the Formosa Strait, they followed logically from Washington's perception of the Korean War as only the initial thrust of a much larger Communist offensive in the Far East. After all, earlier intelligence reports had raised the probability of a Communist military initiative somewhere in Asia, with the likely target being Indochina or Formosa. Also, Washington had already emphasized the strategic importance it attached to Indochina by its commitment of military and economic assistance to the French. As for Formosa, its loss would have serious foreign and domestic repercussions, particularly in terms of endangering the security of Japan and unleashing a tremendous barrage of political flak at home. The neutralization of Formosa would also prevent an extension of the Asian war, something which the administration was most anxious to avoid.

Washington's decision to intervene in Korea, then, was made deliberately and with consideration of the risks of a Soviet response either in Korea or elsewhere. Its action in expanding aid to Indochina and the Philippines and neutralizing Formosa was also in large measure a product of this warped perception of a worldwide Communist threat. It is true that the course it followed, particularly its commitment of combat forces to Korea, was made easier by the lack of military action or even preparation for a military attack by Moscow or Peking, either in Korea or some other danger spot. But irrespective of other considerations, the Truman administration felt it had no alternative except to prevent South Korea from falling to the Communists. In simplest terms, American credibility in the world and its own credibility at home were at issue.

Throughout most of the period after World War II, the United States had attempted a policy of disengagement from Korea and all the rest of the Asian mainland. But the imperatives of the Cold War, the conviction that the world was in peril, that the tide of events was not going well for the United States, and that in the global confrontation with the Soviet Union America had to support any country and any regime threatened by communism, led the United States by 1950 into military involvement in a part of the world few Americans knew anything about and in a country which only a short time earlier had been deemed to lie outside America's defense perimeter.

NOTES

1. For this and the next seven paragraphs consult especially John Lewis Gaddis, *Russia, the Soviet Union, and the United States: An Interpretive History* (New York, 1978), 72–138; Gaddis, *The United States and the Origins of the Cold War, 1941–1947* (New York, 1972); Walter LaFeber, *America, Russia, and the Cold War, 1945–1980* (New York, 1980), 1–29; Stephen E. Ambrose, *Rise to Globalism: American Foreign Policy Since 1938* (London, 1971), 102–35; Ralph B. Levering, *The Cold War, 1945–1972* (Arlington Heights, Ill., 1982), 1–10.
2. Soon Sung Cho, *Korea in World Politics, 1940–1950: An Evaluation of American Responsibility* (Berkeley, Calif., 1967), 13–15.
3. William Whitney Stueck, Jr., *The Road to Confrontation: American Policy Toward China and Korea, 1947–1950* (Chapel Hill, N.C., 1981), 19–20.
4. *Ibid.*, 20; Bruce Cumings, *The Origins of the Korean War: Liberation and the Emergence of Separate Regimes, 1945–1947* (Princeton, N. J., 1981), 113.
5. Cumings, *The Origins of the Korean War*, 117–22.
6. *Ibid.;* Mark Paul, "Diplomacy Delayed: The Atomic Bomb and the Division of Korea, 1945," in Bruce Cumings (ed.), *Child of Conflict: The Korean-American Relationship, 1943–1953* (Seattle, Wash., 1983), 88–91.
7. Gregory Henderson, *Korea: The Politics of the Vortex* (Cambridge, Mass., 1968), 1–9 and 72–112.
8. Cumings, *The Origins of the Korean War*, 68–91.
9. *Ibid.*, 91–100.
10. *Ibid.*
11. Henderson, *Korea: The Politics of the Vortex*, 84–86
12. Robert T. Oliver, *Syngman Rhee: The Man Behind the Myth* (New York, 1954), 1–213; Joungwon A. Kim, *Divided Korea: The Politics of Development* (Cambridge, Mass., 1975), 34–39.
13. Henderson, *Korea: The Politics of the Vortex*, 125; Edward Grant Meade, *American Military Government in Korea* (New York, 1951), 58; Lisle A. Rose, *Roots of Tragedy: The United States and*

the *Struggle for Asia, 1945–1953* (Westport, Conn., 1976), 34–36.

14. Cumings, *The Origins of the Korean War,* 122–31; Stueck, Jr., *The Road to Confrontation,* 22–33.

15. Cumings, *The Origins of the Korean War,* 135–78.

16. *Ibid.,* 382–427. See also Kim, *Divided Korea,* 86–101; Dae-Sook Suh, *The Korean Communist Movement, 1918–1948* (Princeton, N. J., 1967), 253-95.

17. Max Beloff, *Soviet Policy in the Far East, 1944–1951* (London, 1953), 156.

18. Ipyong J. Kim, *Communist Politics in North Korea* (New York, 1975), 25–34.

19. Kim, *Divided Korea,* 60–62; Cumings, *The Origins of the Korean War,* 217–27.

20. Cumings, *The Origins of the Korean War,* 231–35.

21. LaFeber, *America, Russia, and the Cold War,* 35–39; Thomas G. Paterson, *On Every Front: The Making of the Cold War* (New York, 1979), 52–54.

22. *Foreign Relations of the United States,* 1946, VIII, 706–709. Hereafter cited as *FR* with date and volume number; Robert H. Ferrell (ed.), *Off the Record: The Private Papers of Harry S. Truman* (New York, 1980), 80; Cumings, *The Origins of the Korean War,* 226.

23. Cumings, *The Origins of the Korean War,* 223–27.

24. *FR,* 1946, VIII, 692–99; Henderson, *Korea: The Politics of the Vortex,* 131–34; Kenneth R. Mauck, "The Formation of American Foreign Policy in Korea, 1945–1953" (unpublished Ph.D. dissertation, University of Oklahoma, 1978), 90–102.

25. Stueck, Jr., *The Road to Confrontation,* 27; Cumings, *The Origins of the Korean War,* 252–62.

26. Okonogi Masao, "The Domestic Roots of the Korean War," in Yonosuke Nagai and Akira Iriye (eds.), *The Origins of the Cold War in Asia* (New York, 1970), 308.

27. Levering, *The Cold War, 1945–1972,* 29–31; "X," "The Sources of Soviet Conduct," *Foreign Affairs,* XXV (July 1947), 566–72.

28. Stephen Pelz, "U.S. Decisions on Korean Policy, 1943–1950: Some Hypotheses," in Cumings (ed.), *Child of Conflict,* 110.

29. *FR,* 1947, VI, 817–18 and 832–33; Stueck, Jr., *The Road to Confrontation,* 86–88.

30. *FR,* 1947, VI, 625–28, 675–76, and 738–41.

31. *Ibid.,* 738–41. See also Leland M. Goodrich, *Korea: A Study of U.S. Policy in the United Nations* (New York, 1956), 28–29.

32. *FR,* 1947, VI, 776, 790, 817–18, and 832–33.

33. *Ibid.,* 1947, VI, 803–807; Stueck, Jr., *The Road to Confrontation,* 86–87.

34. Masao, "The Domestic Roots of the Korean War," 309.
35. *FR*, 1948, VI, 1093–95, 1101–13; Cho, *Korea in World Politics*, 184–97; Stueck, Jr., *The Road to Confrontation*, 96–98; Kim, *Divided Korea*, 196–207.
36. *FR*, 1948, VI, 1164–69.
37. John Merrill, "Internal Warfare in Korea, 1948–1950: The Local Setting of the Korean War," in Cumings (ed.), *Child of Conflict*, 142–45.
38. *Ibid.*
39. *FR*, 1948, VI, 1325–27.
40. Pelz, "U.S. Decisions on Korean Policy," 114–15.
41. John Lewis Gaddis, "Korea in American Politics, Strategy, and Diplomacy, 1949–1950," in Nagai and Iriye (eds.), *The Origins of the Cold War in Asia*, 284.
42. *FR*, 1949, VII, 944–46, 958–59, and 969–78.
43. Gaddis, "Korea in American Politics, Strategy, and Diplomacy, 1949–1950," 283.
44. U.S. Congress, Senate, *Economic Assistance to China and Korea: 1949–1950.* Hearings Held in Executive Session Before the Committee on Foreign Relations, 81st Congress, 1st and 2d Sessions, 120–21, 128–29, and 157.
45. *FR*, 1949, VII, 1003–1005, 1010, 1014, 1041–43, and 1063; *ibid.*, 1950, VII, 6–11 and 26–29; James Irving Matray, "The Reluctant Crusade: American Foreign Policy in Korea, 1941–1950" (unpublished Ph.D. dissertation, University of Virginia, 1977), 421–23 and 481–82.
46. U.S. Congress, Senate, *Review of the World Situation: 1949–1950.* Hearings Held in Executive Session Before the Committee on Foreign Relations, 81st Congress, 1st and 2d Sessions, 191.
47. Dean Acheson, *Present at the Creation: My Years in the State Department* (New York, 1969), 691.
48. Kim, *Divided Korea*, 115–29.
49. *FR*, 1950, VII, 40–41.
50. *Ibid.*, 47–48 and 84–85.
51. Merrill, "Internal Warfare in Korea, 1948–1950," 156.
52. *Ibid.*
53. Memorandum of Conversation with President Rhee, June 19, 1950, Box 4262, Records of the Department of State, RG 59, 795.00/6–1950; *FR*, 1950, VII, 109–12; Stueck, Jr., *The Road to Confrontation*, 164–65; Glenn D. Paige, *The Korean Decision* (New York, 1968), 75.

54. George C. Herring, *America's Longest War: The United States and Vietnam, 1950-1975* (New York, 1979), 9-13.
55. *FR*, 1950, I, 237-92. See also LaFeber, *America, Russia, and the Cold War*, 97-100; Levering, *The Cold War, 1945-1972*, 29-31.
56. *FR*, 1950, VII, 95-96.
57. Gaddis, "Korea in American Politics, Strategy, and Diplomacy, 1945-1950," 286-287.
58. *FR*, 1950, VII, 125; Paige, *The Korean Decision*, 81-124.
59. Mauck, "The Formation of American Foreign Policy in Korea," 192; Paige, *The Korean Decision*, 125-41.
60. *FR*, 1950, VII, 178-83; Roy Appleman, *South to the Naktong, North to the Yalu* (Washington, D.C., 1961), 31.
61. *FR*, 1950, VII, 428-53; Paige, *The Korean Decision*, 145-270.
62. I. F. Stone, *The Hidden History of the Korean War* (New York, 1952), 1-66; Joyce and Gabriel Kolko, *The Limits of Power: The World and United States Foreign Policy, 1945-1954* (New York, 1972), 565-78.
63. Ambrose, *Rise to Globalism*, 196.
64. Appleman, *South to the Naktong, North to the Yalu*, 8-18.
65. Robert R. Simmons, *The Strained Alliance: Peking, Pyongyang, Moscow and the Politics of the Korean Civil War* (New York, 1975), 102-30.
66. *Ibid.*, 25-26.
67. *Ibid.*, 104-10; Merrill, "Internal Warfare in Korea," 150-53. See also Robert R. Simmons, "The Korean Civil War," in Frank Baldwin (ed.), *Without Parallel: The American-Korean Relationship Since 1945* (New York, 1973), 146-47.
68. Merrill, "Internal Warfare in Korea," 150-53; Simmons, *The Strained Alliance*, 102-30; Stueck, Jr., *The Road to Confrontation*, 170-71.
69. *FR*, 1950, VII, 148-55.
70. Harry S. Truman, *Years of Trial and Hope: Memoirs, 1946-1952* (New York, 1965), 377-86; Acheson, *Present at the Creation*, 405; David Rees, *Korea: The Limited War* (New York, 1964), 31.
71. Pelz, "U.S. Decisions on Korean Policy," 112-27.
72. Ambrose, *Rise to Globalism*, 184-88; LaFeber, *America, Russia, and the Cold War, 1945-1980*, 89-97; Thomas C. Reeves, *The Life and Times of Joe McCarthy* (New York, 1982), 198-233.
73. *Ibid.*
74. Reeves, *The Life and Times of Joe McCarthy*, 283; *Commonweal*,

51 (April 7, 1950), 675; *New Republic,* 122 (April 10, 1950), 4; *ibid.* (April 17, 1950), 3–4; *ibid.* (June 26, 1950), 10–12.

75. Lawrence S. Wittner, *Cold War America: From Hiroshima to Watergate* (New York, 1974), 89.
76. *Time,* 56 (July 10, 1950), 9.
77. *FR,* 1950, VII, 178–83.
78. *Ibid.,* 248–53; Paige, *The Korean Decision,* 145–270.
79. Stueck, Jr., *The Road to Confrontation,* 192. See also Gaddis Smith, *Dean Acheson* (New York, 1972), 190.

CHAPTER 2

War and the Climate of Crisis and Conspiracy

The sense of despair and crisis in the United States during the first half of 1950 was only exacerbated during the first few months of the Korean War as North Korean troops moved relentlessly southward, meeting small pockets of resistance. On one hand, the war heightened, not diminished, the anti-Communist hysteria in America. On the other hand, the Truman administration, perceiving the war as part of a global struggle whose principal actors were the United States and the Soviet Union, expanded its scope to include not merely the containment of Soviet aggression, but the rollback of Communist forces from territory they had occupied prior to the outbreak of hostilities.

Similarly, Washington broadened the United States' commitments worldwide. Not only did the administration accelerate aid to Indochina, offer assistance to the Philippine government fighting the Hukbalahap insurrection, and neutralize Formosa, it used the opportunity afforded by the war to promote numerous measures in Europe earlier regarded as improbable because of American and European opposition. These included the arming of West Germany and its integration firmly into the western alliance, the commitment of American troops to the North Atlantic Treaty Organization (NATO), and the establishment of a unified command structure for NATO under General Dwight D. Eisenhower.

The conflict had important domestic consequences as well. In the first place, the power of the executive branch over the conduct of foreign policy was reinforced in a battle between the

45

JUNE TO SEPTEMBER, 1950

U.S.S.R.
Vladivostok

C H I N A
(MANCHURIA)

Tumen R.

Chongjin

Hyesanjin

Yalu R.

Chosan

Iwon

Sinuiju

Hungnam

SEA OF
JAPAN

Pyongyang ★

Wonsan

Start of North Korean Offensive
June 25, 1950

NORTH
KOREA   38th parallel

Ongjin

Chunchon

SOUTH
KOREA

Seoul ★

Inchon

Controlled by U.N.
Communist advances
Controlled by
Communists

Taejon

Kunsan

Pohang

YELLOW

Taegu

Pusan Perimeter
September 14, 1950

SEA

Mokpo

Sunchon

Pusan

JAPAN

0   300
Miles

White House and the chief military officer in Korea, General
Douglas MacArthur. Second, important decisions had to be
made regarding the war's effects on the domestic economy and
on executive-congressional relations. Finally, by seeming to
confirm many of NSC-68's assumptions about the bipolarity of
world power and the determination of the Soviet Union to
achieve world domination, the outbreak of hostilities in Korea
made the implementation of its spending recommendations
among the nation's highest priorities. By mid-July Truman's

military budget requests had grown to approximately $30 billion. By December they would approach the $50 billion level.

The UN resolution of June 27 providing for military sanctions against North Korea requested member states to assist the Republic of Korea (ROK). Eventually sixteen nations, including the United States, provided armed forces. Another UN resolution of July 7 by the Security Council established a unified command under the UN flag and delegated the authority for the command to the United States. President Truman appointed General MacArthur as the Supreme United Nations Commander, and the United Nations Command (UNC) became the official title of the force.

For all of July and part of August the military situation in South Korea for United Nations forces remained bleak. Not only were North Korean troops able to capture Seoul within four days after their invasion of South Korea, they destroyed more than half of the ROK army. As the North Koreans moved south in July, moreover, they enjoyed considerable popular support. The CIA reported that more than 50 percent of Seoul's students were actively aiding the Communist invasion, with many voluntarily enlisting in the Northern army. Much of the working class also backed the North Koreans.[1]

A military defeat of the UNC remained a real possibility at this point. An American task force, which arrived from Japan on July 1, 1950, consisted of only two understrengthed rifle companies. Although more troops arrived by the second week in July, the best they were able to do was to carry out an orderly retreat to a perimeter around Pusan at the southeastern end of the peninsula. Meanwhile the enemy continued to advance southward. On July 13 two North Korean divisions crossed the Kum River and enveloped U. S. troops holding positions near Konji and Taejon, a key railroad center about 100 miles south of Seoul. A week later Taejon fell after an intense two-day struggle in which American casualties approached 30 percent. Most of the survivors, including Major General William F. Dean, withdrew into the hills, where Dean was later taken prisoner.[2]

In all, American and ROK forces in the first weeks of the war were too ill-equipped to stop the North Koreans. The first American troops had nothing better against their heavily ar-

mored T-34 tanks than howitzers and bazookas of World War
II vintage, which, for the most part, were incapable of penetrat-
ing the T-34's armor. Under these circumstances the job of
holding off the Communist tanks devolved largely on the Air
Force, and here also problems existed. Although America's control of the air eventually proved decisive in stopping the enemy
advance, the Air Force at first relied on its World War II tactic
of strategic bombing, striking beyond the area of ground
fighting and hitting such enemy installations as factories, ware-
houses, oil refineries, and communication facilities with B-29
medium bombers. Lieutenant General George E. Stratemeyer,
who controlled air operations, commanded his bombers to operate only north of the 38th parallel. On several occasions in
mid-July General MacArthur had to overrule him by ordering
his planes to strike against enemy troop concentrations and
other tactical targets.[3]

The net result was, as one observer commented, that American ground troops in Korea were "fighting a World War III
army with World War II weapons," and for much of the time
with very little of the kind of air support they really needed.
The F-51 Mustangs that might have helped were still in the
United States, as were the 3.5 rockets needed to take out the
Soviet-made tanks. Similarly, the Sherman and Patton tanks,
which might have stood up against the T-34s, were in the factory, and the antitank weapons that could dispose of any armored vehicle were still on the drawing board.[4]

By the beginning of August, when the numerical advantage
in terms of troop deployment began to shift against the enemy,
UN forces had established a perimeter around Pusan that extended in rectangular fashion about eighty miles from north to
south and fifty miles from east to west. Even then it was uncertain that the UN forces could maintain this position. On the east
coast, for example, a North Korean division was approaching
Yongdok only ninety miles north of Pusan. At the southern end
of the perimeter a North Korean force ambushed an American
infantry division sent to intercept it and then broke to strike the
Pusan perimeter near Chinju. Without American air superiority it is quite possible that the North Korean forces would have
overrun the entire peninsula.[5]

Only toward the middle and latter parts of August did the

situation within the perimeter improve. By the end of August the number of ground troops had increased to about 180,000, including 92,000 ROK personnel, as opposed to about 133,000 North Koreans, many of whom were ill-trained conscripts. Tanks and vehicles had also begun to arrive in substantial numbers, so that by the end of the month U.S. troops had about 500 Pershing and Sherman tanks against the 100 or so T-34s that the enemy was estimated still to have in operating order. Control of the air over Korea had also been largely accomplished, and the UN Air Force was engaged in both tactical and strategic operations, providing close air cover for UN forces on the ground and hitting at targets well inside North Korea.

As a result, UN forces were able to beat back a major offensive that the enemy opened on the last day of August. Although the North Koreans were able to break through the perimeter in a number of places, they were unable to exploit their opportunity. Short of fuel, ammunition, and food, forced to rely on local conscripts to carry supplies, and the target of close air support by American planes, the North Koreans quickly spent themselves. By September 7 the offensive was over, and the Communists had suffered their first major defeat of the war. Soon UN forces would launch their own counteroffensive.

It had been a trying and difficult eleven weeks for many Americans, however, and one of the ramifications of the war was to intensify the shrill debate in the United States over an alleged Communist conspiracy inside government. The war afforded Senator McCarthy and a number of other Republicans an ideal topic for campaign oratory in an election year against the administration. Indeed, by heightening the fears and doubts of many Americans, the first few months of the conflict helped precipitate what some have referred to as America's second great Red Scare (the first having taken place just after World War I).

McCarthy and other Republicans were quick to exploit the war for their own purposes. For the previous three months the Wisconsin senator's charges that there were "card-carrying Communists" in the State Department had been the subject of a special Senate investigation headed by Millard E. Tydings of Maryland. On July 14 the Tydings Committee issued a majority report dismissing McCarthy's accusations as a fraud and a hoax.

Instead of silencing McCarthy and his supporters, however, the report had just the opposite effect, for by arousing Cold War passions, the conflict in Korea also intensified popular anti-Communism in the United States. Sensing that they had an issue that could finally bring them back to power after twenty years of Democratic control, Republicans in Congress came to McCarthy's defense and joined in the swirling chorus of anti-Communist hyperbole. Even many Democrats, including some noted for their libertarianism and commitment to free speech and free expression, felt obliged to vote for antisubversive legislation.[6]

McCarthy's first remarks on Korea came only a week after the war began. In a television interview on July 2, he charged that "American boys [were] dying in Korea" because "a group of untouchables in the State Department" had sabotaged the aid program Congress had voted for South Korea. In a Senate speech a few days later, he made similar charges and spoke of "highly placed Red Counselors" who were "far more deadly than Red machine gunners in Korea." In a talk to his constituents he again repeated his accusation of State Department infamy and warned, "If you want more of that, keep them in office. But if you vote for them, remember this. When the Communist trap to conquer this nation is sprung, it will be your votes that pulled the trigger."[7]

Just as charges of an internal conspiracy had offered a ready explanation to many Americans of why China had fallen to the Communists in 1949, so the same accusation now seemed to explain why, in McCarthy's words, American boys were dying in Korea. Americans responded not only by attacking the alleged Communists in government but by seeking to eliminate the Communist threat wherever it was thought to exist. A veritable witch-hunt took place in many parts of the United States as suspected Communists were ferreted out of employment and exposed to public damnation. A number of municipalities went even further. In Detroit, for example, the Common Council forbade sidewalk news vendors to sell "subversive literature" and gave the commissioner of police the responsibility for determining what was subversive. In Birmingham, Alabama, Police Commissioner "Bull" Connor, who would gain notoriety in the 1960s for unleashing vicious dogs and using fire hoses against civil rights demonstrators, pushed a new ordinance through the city commission banishing Communists from Birmingham. And in Columbus, Ohio, police juvenile officers warned teenage clubs to beware of "Communist agitators" and to be suspicious of any new member of a group whose background was "not an open book."[8]

Republicans in Congress sought to capitalize on this swell of anti-Communist emotion. Not only did the entire Republican membership of the Senate reject the Tydings Committee report, which Senator William Jenner called the "most scandalous and brazen whitewash of treasonable conspiracy in our history," but the Republican Party Policy Committee made passage of the McCarran Internal Security Bill one of its highest priorities. This legislation, which was a new version of an earlier bill, required all Communist organizations to register with the government and to publish their records. Americans were also subject to prosecution on grounds as vague as "fomenting revolution," and Communists were barred from working in defense plants or receiving passports. Emerging from a meeting of the Policy Committee, Republican Senator Karl E. Mundt of South Dakota told reporters, "The climate is certainly conducive for Congressional passage of this right now. If we are asking our boys to die fighting in Korea and other areas, we certainly should protect them from sabotage behind their backs at home."[9]

In fairness to the Republicans in Congress, a large number of Democrats, for purposes of self-preservation, also felt compelled to vote for the McCarran bill, so strong was the public demand for anti-Communist and antisubversive legislation. Among those Democrats who voted for the measure were such well-known liberals as Paul Douglas of Illinois, Harley Kilgore of West Virginia, Herbert Lehman of New York, and Hubert Humphrey of Minnesota. As Lehman later explained, "the fever of fear was on my colleagues." With such bipartisan support the legislation was passed in September by lopsided votes in both the House and the Senate, and later it was approved again, this time over the President's veto.[10]

By September both parties had begun to map out campaign strategy for the 1950 elections, and the Korean War figured prominently in the Republican plans to unseat the Democrats in Congress. At the end of August the Republican members of the Senate Foreign Relations Committee issued a paper analyzing American foreign policy since 1945 in which they blamed the administration for its "failure in 1945 to recognize the true aims and methods of the rulers of Soviet Russia." This lack of firmness on the part of the Democrats they referred to as "the major tragedy of our time." Along with similar statements by other Republican members of Congress, the paper became part of a fifty-six-page news release, "Background to Korea," which the chairman of the Republican National Committee, Guy Gabrielson, prepared for use by Republican candidates and workers in the campaign.[11]

Democrats responded by accusing such Republican notables as Senator Robert Taft of Ohio of isolationalism and by maintaining that the nation would have been much worse off if the Republicans had had their way on military and foreign policy issues since the end of World War II. Senator Tydings charged that if the country had accepted the GOP platforms for the last five years, which generally called for lower taxes and economy in government, "we should be impotent today," and he even went so far as to compare the Republican voting record on Korea with the course recommended by the Communist *Daily Worker.*[12]

Nevertheless, the Republican charges against the administration of internal subversion and the exposed position of its Far Eastern policy, first with respect to China and now in Korea, weighed heavily in the formulation of its foreign policy in the summer of 1950. On one hand, the administration rejected initial peace efforts by England and India while it reviewed plans to cross the 38th parallel and carry the war into North Korea once the tide of battle turned. On the other hand, it expanded the scope of the war by using the conflict as a fulcrum to achieve policy objectives elsewhere, particularly in Europe. Korea thus became a "war for both Asia and Europe" in the words of the historian Walter LaFeber.[13] By broadening the aims and purpose of the conflict in this way, the administration was less vulnerable to domestic criticism from the "primitives," as Secretary of State Acheson called the right wing, or Old Guard, of the Republican Party, and presumably was in a stronger position to deal with the Communists over Korea.[14]

The British and Indian peace initiatives began early in July, soon after President Truman committed combat troops to Korea, when the British ambassador to Moscow, Sir David Kelly, met with Soviet Foreign Minister Andrei Gromyko. After assuring Kelly that the Soviet Union wanted a peaceful settlement to the war, Gromyko asked the British ambassador for specific proposals to end the conflict.[15] About the same time, the Indian government attempted to act as an informal mediator by making separate overtures to Moscow, Washington, and Peking, which involved recognition of the People's Republic of China (PRC) by the United States in return for ending the war. In China the Indian ambassador, K. M. Panikkar, simply proposed that the Korean problem be solved in the Security Council with Peking "taking her legitimate place." To Moscow and Washington India offered a somewhat different proposal that included two points. First, Washington would support the admission of the PRC to the UN with a seat on the Security Council. Second, the Security Council, with the PRC and the Soviet Union represented, would support an immediate cease-fire in Korea and the withdrawal of North Korean forces to the 38th parallel.[16]

The United States showed mild interest in the British attempt at mediation but strongly disdained the Indian effort. In simplest terms, the administration was unwilling to link the China question—which, in addition to the matter of the PRC's admission into the UN, involved the problem of whether Formosa should be returned to the Peking government—to a settlement of the Korean War. The administration was prepared, for example, to discuss the future status of Formosa under the auspices of the United Nations or some other forum, but not as a precondition for ending the war in Korea. To do otherwise, it maintained, would constitute blackmail and extortion and would, in the opinion of Secretary Acheson, "whet communist appetites and bring on other aggressions elsewhere."[17]

Since the Indian mediation effort rested on a linkage between the China question and a Korean settlement, the United States was openly hostile to it. In the Soviet Union the Indian effort was being promoted by its ambassador to Moscow, Sarvepalli Radhakrishnan. Acheson instructed America's ambassador to Moscow, Alan G. Kirk, to tell Radhakrishnan that the

United States would "probably oppose" any settlement to the Korean War "which directly or indirectly meant payment or reward to [the] aggressor." Despite this rejection, India persevered. The Indian Foreign Office opened talks with America's ambassador to India, Loy W. Henderson, while it maintained channels of communication with Moscow and Peking. But the United States squashed India's efforts by continuing to insist that there could be no exchange between ending the war in Korea and settling the China question.[18]

As for the British peace initiative, that too failed, and largely for the same reasons. Acheson did follow up on Kelly's meeting with Gromyko by telling the British that he tended to view Gromyko's statement as a "serious approach" at ending the conflict without undue loss of prestige to the Soviet Union. But Acheson also made it clear to London that a resolution of the China question would not be the price paid by the United States for a settlement of the Korean War. Although England believed that the Peking government should be seated on the Security Council and that its claim to Formosa was valid, it accepted the American position. Denied this *quid pro quo*, however, the Soviets failed to pursue the British initiative, and chances for ending the war disappeared. Although India made another attempt at mediation in the middle of August, that too failed for lack of interest on the part of both Washington and Moscow.[19]

Should the United States have been more forthcoming in its response to the British and Indian peace initiatives? It would seem so. At the very least, by responding more positively to their efforts, Washington might have shifted more of the responsibility for the war's continuation onto the Communists. Doing so could have been particularly important in terms of America's relations with India, a nation which the United States hoped would play an important role in offsetting Communist China's influence in Asia. As it was, America's response to mediation only irritated the New Delhi government and had an unsettling effect among other Asian and neutralist nations as well.[20]

To have been more receptive to the British and Indian initiatives, the United States would have had to be more flexible on the twin questions of PRC representation at the UN and the future status of Formosa, and that would have meant a willingness on its part to link the China question to a Korean settlement. Although the administration remained adamantly opposed to such a linkage, it might have had a number of advantages. Most obviously, by bringing an end to the Korean War and settling the thorniest questions separating the PRC and the United States, it might have avoided twenty dangerous years of the most extreme bitterness and hostility between any two nations not actually at war. Conceivably, a solution could even have been worked out that included the unification of Korea. Although this was highly unlikely under existing circumstances, at least there would have been opportunity for discussion of the issue. By linking the problem of Korea (which most concerned the Soviets) with the China question (which most interested the Peking government), the administration might also have revealed important differences between the Soviet Union and the PRC that could later be used to America's advantage.[21]

Considering the prevailing political climate in the United States, however, any effort by the administration to resolve the China question as part of a bargain to end the Korean War almost certainly would have been wrought with the most serious political consequences. Acheson's "primitives" would have been up in arms against the administration. Charges of conspiracy and internal subversion would have proliferated, and demands for Acheson's resignation would have soared.[22] Undoubtedly the administration would have been able to ride out this storm of anguish and anger, just as it was doing with respect to the fall of China, but its task in this regard would have been much more difficult. Most important, as John Foster Dulles told Secretary Acheson, and as Acheson himself agreed, even U. S. abstention at the UN on the question of admitting Communist China to that body (a position favored only by George Kennan of the State Department's Policy Planning Staff) would have confused the American public and weakened support for the administration's crash program of increased military spending. As it was, public opinion in the United States almost universally supported Washington's rejection of the Indian peace initiative. Although most news commentators believed that India was motivated by good intentions and good faith, they generally agreed that to negotiate on the terms offered by India would be appeasement in its most despicable form.[23]

Indeed, neither much of the American public nor the administration was in the mood to negotiate with the Communists in the summer of 1950. A widespread conviction existed that negotiations with the Soviet Union would be fruitless and that before sitting down with the Communists to discuss peace, the United States would have to turn the war around and be able to bargain from a position of strength. A number of Americans even talked of a preventive war, or preemptive nuclear strike, against the Soviet Union, and within the administration serious consideration was already being given to the possibility of carrying the war into North Korea at some future date.

One should not make too much of the talk about launching a preventive nuclear war against the Soviet Union. Such a view was certainly not new. There had been similar talk during almost every crisis since the Cold War began, and there would continue to be the same talk long after the Korean War was over. Yet there does seem to have been an unusual increase in public sentiment for a preventive war following the outbreak of hostilities in Korea. Instead of deterring such talk, knowledge that the Soviet Union had developed its own nuclear capability appears to have had just the opposite effect, the rationale being that the United States had better take out the Russians while it still enjoyed nuclear superiority. The sentiment for a preventive war was quite pervasive. In Washington and "everywhere else in the country, too, you can hear lots of 'preventive war' talk," one news writer thus reported toward the end of August. "It is something for the Russians to think about in assessing the mood of the American people." A month later *Time* devoted a full-page spread weighing the advantages and disadvantages of a preventive war against Moscow. "When a man knows he has a good chance to be A-bombed," *Time* commented, "nothing can stop him from considering whether there isn't something he can do to prevent it. That is why talk of 'preventive war' by the U. S. against the U. S. S. R. stays on the tongues of the American people." Nor was such talk limited to those outside government. Secretary of the Navy Francis Matthews even commented that Washington should consider "instituting . . . a war of aggression for peace." Although Matthews' views were by no means those of the administration, there was enough of that kind of talk for President Truman to order an official stop to it.[24]

Of far greater significance, however, was the consideration that the administration gave to the question of what to do after the tide of battle had turned in Korea. Ultimately this boiled down to the issue of whether to contain Communist expansion by driving the North Koreans back above the 38th parallel or to seize the chance to roll back Soviet aggression (the North Koreans being regarded as agents of Moscow) by carrying the war into North Korea itself. In fact, by the time the decision was made in September to send UN forces across the 38th parallel, the administration had engaged in an extensive dialogue over a period of several months, weighing all the public ramifications of such an action, and had moved almost inexorably to the conclusion that the opportunities of taking the initiative in the Cold War outweighed the dangers of escalating the conflict into a yet larger war, possibly even into a nuclear confrontation with the Soviet Union.

As early as July 1 the director of the Office of Northeast Asian Affairs in the State Department, John Allison, spoke out against a report that President Truman intended to announce in a speech that American and ROK forces would limit their military mission to driving the North Koreans back above the 38th parallel. In a memorandum to Assistant Secretary of State Dean Rusk, Allison argued that such a statement would be the height of folly and that there could be no permanent peace in Korea so long as the artificial division at the 38th parallel continued.[25] Others like John Foster Dulles and General Douglas MacArthur made much the same argument. According to Dulles the North Koreans should be destroyed even if this required pursuit beyond the 38th parallel. For his part, General MacArthur informed the Defense Department that he intended not only to drive the North Koreans back above the 38th parallel, but also to destroy all North Korean forces and to occupy all of North Korea if necessary.[26]

But advocates of not moving beyond the 38th parallel were equally vigorous. Herbert Feis of the State Department's Policy Planning Staff urged that the United States disassociate itself from remarks by Syngman Rhee that North Korea had obliterated the 38th parallel. Feis did not believe that the Soviets would allow substantial American armed units to reach the Soviet frontier. He was also convinced that relations with America's allies would be harmed by any association with Rhee's remarks. Similarly, Charles Bohlen, minister to France and an expert on Soviet affairs, warned of the danger from the Soviet Union if the United States moved aggressively across North Korea.[27]

This concern as to what the Soviet Union would do if the UN forces moved north of the 38th parallel was central to the entire debate over Korea. Opponents of moving across the 38th parallel argued that would increase the chances both of Soviet intervention in Korea and of global war. In contrast, advocates of crossing into North Korea admitted the risks involved but held that the risks of doing nothing were even greater. It would be impossible, they claimed, to achieve the terms of the June 27 resolution of the Security Council, which were to restore "international peace and security" in Korea, as long as Korea was divided at the 38th parallel. At the very least, the United States should wait until UN troops approached the 38th parallel before deciding on whether to cross it.[28]

By the middle of July the debate over breaching the 38th parallel had become so heated that Secretary of State Acheson ordered the American embassy in Korea to avoid official statements on the subject. But while the administration agreed that the issue should not be argued publicly, substantial differences remained, particularly between the Departments of State and Defense and, within the State Department, between the Policy Planning Staff (PPS) and the Office of Northeast Asian Affairs.

At the Pentagon, Defense Department planners had grown increasingly confident by the end of July and beginning of August that the Soviet Union would not intervene in North Korea if UN forces moved beyond the 38th parallel. The Soviet threat remained real, and it was global in nature. Soviet troops could attack across Europe or into the Middle East if the United States and its allies became bogged down in Korea. The prospects of a united Korea under UN auspices might also lead the Soviet Union to try to prevent its total loss. But Moscow's "uncompleted strategic position in the Far East" was more likely to keep the Kremlin leaders from risking a general war over Korea. In any case, not to advance beyond the 38th parallel would result in the same military instability as before the outbreak of hostilities in June and would require a huge outlay of funds to reconstruct and secure South Korea. For these reasons the Defense Department felt the UN command should try to defeat North Korean forces north and south of the 38th parallel.[29]

In contrast to the Defense Department, the State Department was divided over crossing the 38th parallel. For the most part the split was between the PPS and the Office of Northeast Asian Affairs. Under the influence of George Kennan, the PPS favored a return to the *status quo ante bellum.* In contrast, the Office of Northeast Asian Affairs, headed by Allison, wanted to roll back Communism beyond the 38th parallel. Allison thus objected strongly to a recommendation by the PPS that the United States issue a statement of its intention not to allow American or ROK forces to advance across the 38th parallel. No statement should be made, he argued, "which in any way commits this government not to proceed beyond the 38th parallel or implies that we will agree to any settlement which merely restores the *status quo ante bellum.*"[30]

Considerable internal bickering took place before the two sides finally compromised their differences. On July 22 the PPS issued a lengthy draft memorandum, the gist of which was the strategic importance of the Korean peninsula to the Soviet Union and the likelihood of Soviet or Chinese intervention should a regime be established in North Korea which Moscow would not dominate or control. Allison labeled these conclusions "appeasement" and said they implied that the North Korean regime had legal status and that the area north of the 38th parallel was, in fact, a separate nation.[31]

In an effort to compromise its differences with Allison, Dean Rusk, and others of similar mind, however, the PPS agreed to revise its memorandum. The new document still emphasized the danger from the Soviet Union if UN troops crossed the 38th parallel, but it recommended that no final decision on the matter be made "until military and political developments provide additional information." Although this was less than Allison and others wanted, at least it left open the option of crossing into North Korea. On this basis they endorsed the PPS statement, which then became State Department policy. About the only high State Department official who continued to take a strong stand against a UN move into North Korea was Kennan, and at the end of August he left the foreign service to assume a position at the Institute for Advanced Study in Princeton, New Jersey.[32]

Still, this was not the same as advocating an actual crossing of the 38th parallel, and on this question there remained considerable disagreement with the Pentagon. In fact, at the time the UN forces began their counteroffensive on September 15, a final decision on crossing the 38th parallel had not been made. In an effort to resolve the differences that remained within the administration, the National Security Council issued a study in September (NSC-81), which seemed to authorize at least the limited conduct of military operations north of the 38th parallel. But those who favored a less adventurous policy were able to revise the study so that the new version (NSC-81/1) merely stated that it would "be expected" that such authority to cross into North Korea would be given to the UN commander. The new version also contained a revised paragraph requiring the commander to receive Presidential authority before putting any such plan into operation.[33]

In effect, NSC-81/1 amounted to a web of ambiguities strung along a fog of uncertainties. Nonetheless, by the middle of September the clouds of disagreement had begun to clear and the administration had moved significantly closer to a decision to carry the war into North Korea by sending combat troops across the 38th parallel. So it was that despite the changes from NSC-81, NSC-81/1 concluded that the UN's purpose in Korea was to bring about "the complete independence and unity" of that country and that if this could be accomplished "without substantially increasing the risk of general war with the Soviet Union or Communist China, it would be in [the United States'] interest to advocate the pressing of the United Nations action to the conclusion." Such a position, while by no means a firm commitment, made a decision by the President to move north of the 38th parallel that much more likely.[34]

If the United States was moving toward broadening the war in Korea by shifting from the containment to the rollback of Communist aggression, it was taking additional steps that further expanded America's commitments worldwide. Having responded to the initial outbreak of hostilities in Korea by increasing aid to Indochina and the Philippines and neutralizing Formosa, the administration moved, in the critical summer months that followed, to increase its commitment to the defense of western Europe. Instead of vague promises of mutual assistance in case of attack, the United States offered the west European nations firm guarantees of military support and began to turn NATO into a military pact able to defend Europe against assault from the east. In doing so, it sought to achieve other political and economic objectives, including the full integration of West Germany into the western concert. Although only the very first steps toward strengthening that Atlantic alliance were actually started by September, the Korean War was critical in initiating this process.

After the initial shock of hostilities and throughout the remainder of the summer, Americans engaged in a wide ranging debate as to where the country's foreign policy priorities should lie. And the discussion did not always fit the neat prescription of earlier years, which pitted right-wing Republicans and other "isolationists," who argued that the administration was doing too much in Europe and too little in Asia, against "internationalists" of both the Democratic and Republican parties, who maintained that the nation's first priority had to be Europe. Even respected internationalist journals, like the *New Republic* and the *Nation,* which always emphasized that America's main interests were in close ties with a strong and united Europe, now began to stress the need for a foreign policy that struck a better balance between Asia and Europe. Writing in the *New Republic,* Harold Isaacs, author of *New Peace for Asia,* remarked about the Korean War, "The lesson, up to now stubbornly unlearned, is that our future and the future of the world are wrapped up primarily in Asia. We have been acting since 1945 as if the small European peninsula . . . was still the area of main decision."[35]

For many other internationalists, however, the war in Korea revealed just how vulnerable western Europe was to Soviet aggression from the east and how important it was to knit Europe into a tighter military, political, and economic fabric. The establishment of NATO in 1949 had been an important step in that direction, and in July 1950, even as the United

States was being flooded by the latest war reports from Korea, came the news that eighteen European nations had formed the European Payments Union for the exchange of currencies among Marshall Plan countries. This happened not too long after West Germany had decided to send delegates to the Council of Europe at Strasbourg and after talks had opened in Paris about the merger of Europe's coal and steel industries (the so-called Schuman Plan).[36]

NATO remained organizationally weak, however, and quite incapable of repelling a serious challenge from the Soviet Union. At the time war broke out in Korea, the rearming of Europe had scarcely started. Only $52 million of $1.3 billion in military assistance from the United States for America's NATO allies had been obligated, little had been done in the way of military planning, and only twelve divisions were at NATO's disposal in Europe. Nor had any decisions been made on such basic questions as whether to establish a unified command, or even on the size and construction of the NATO forces. One question, in particular, that was of crucial importance to NATO's prospects but that few of the NATO partners dared to raise publicly so soon after the defeat of the Nazis, was the rearming of Germany and its inclusion as a partner in NATO. Although it was widely recognized that German troops would be essential to the defense of Europe, most political leaders were loath to bring up such a sensitive issue.[37]

Along with the weakness of NATO went deep fears that the war in Korea would divert American interest away from Europe at the very time that the strengthening of the western community seemed most urgent. Remarking on the accomplishments of the previous few months in terms of affecting European solidarity, *Commonweal* warned, nevertheless, that "if we allow Korea to divert our attention from Europe, if we let our interest in these plans for unity flag, then we will have unwillingly let Korea become a bloody decoy." Columnist Michael Straight put matters more simply when he stated about the same time, "Among America, Western Europe, and the British Commonwealth, a far closer union is necessary and possible today. . . . In this war of ideas, Western Europe is still the key to the free world."[38]

Concern that the Korean War would deflect the United

States from its European responsibilities, however, proved needless. Instead, the outbreak of hostilities underscored for the administration the imperative of a united and strong Europe able not only to resist an attack from the east, but to resolve common political and economic problems. No one felt more strongly about this than Dean Acheson. Indeed, no secretary of state had worked more tirelessly to bridge the ocean between the United States and Europe than Acheson. His whole foreign policy was predicated on close ties with the major capitals of Europe, and both as undersecretary of state from 1945 to 1949 and then as secretary of state after 1949 he operated with that principle in mind. So, too, after the critical first few weeks of the war in Korea, he turned to evaluate the administration's European policy in light of what had taken place in Korea.[39]

More than ever the Korean conflict convinced Acheson of the need to strengthen the Atlantic alliance. As he later remarked about the summer of 1950, "it was time to consider our plans for European defense in the light of Korea." Immediately that raised the question of the rearming of Western Germany and its inclusion in the NATO pact. For a number of years the Department of Defense had maintained that Europe could not be defended without the active participation of Germany, and as late as April 1950 the Joint Chiefs of Staff had approved a German rearmament plan. Acheson had hitherto maintained a different position. In testimony over the ratification of NATO in 1949, the secretary had told Congress that under no circumstances would Germany be included in the NATO alliance and that the dismantling of German industry would be "complete and absolute." He gave similar assurances a year later when he remarked that the United States would continue its policy of German demilitarization. "There is no discussion of doing anything else," he said. "That is our policy and we have not raised it or revalued it."[40]

The outbreak of hostilities in Korea, however, caused Acheson to change his mind, and rather quickly. General Omar Bradley told the secretary simply that the defense of western Europe would be strengthened by the inclusion of Germany. In mid-July John J. McCloy, America's high commissioner in Germany, put matters more dramatically. Unless Germany was allowed to rearm and fight in an emergency, he said, that country would be lost to the west, politically and militarily, and a valuable reserve of manpower would be used by Moscow against the west.[41]

Acheson was persuaded by these arguments. "The idea that Germany's place in the defense of Europe would be worked out by a process of evolution was outmoded," said the secretary of state. As far as he was concerned, the two major requirements for making NATO work were the inclusion of Germany in Europe's defense arrangements and the acceptance by America's European partners of more of the burden for their own defense. Congress shared a similar position. In House and Senate hearings legislators demanded to know what the allies' contribution of troops and funds for their common defense would be. They also insisted that Germany be included in the rearming of Europe.[42]

Here was the rub. Would the European allies accept Germany into NATO and would they be willing to bear more of the costs of defending themselves? The outlook was far from clear. On one hand, the Korean War created a new mood in western Europe. Britain began a partial mobilization of its reserves, and France undertook to raise fifteen divisions with American aid. Most responsible military leaders in Europe also accepted the principle of a rearmed Germany as a partner in NATO, and, according to J. J. Servan-Schreiber of Paris' *Le Monde,* much the same was true of the European public.[43] On the other hand, by August fear of a Russian invasion and concern about American neglect of Europe had diminished considerably. At the same time the terrific costs of rearmament dulled the enthusiasm for a massive European defense effort, and, among most French, Dutch, and Belgian politicians at least, there remained strong opposition to the establishment of a German army. The economic and emotional costs of such a defense program reignited neutralist tendencies throughout Europe.[44]

At a meeting of the Big Three foreign ministers in New York on September 12, Secretary of State Acheson presented the American proposal for European defense as it had developed after weeks of discussion within the administration.[45] The plan called for the addition of four to six divisions of American forces in Europe, a substantial increase in British and French forces, the establishment of a supreme commander for NATO (most likely an American), and the inclusion of a ten-division German army in a European defense system.[46] Afterward one French delegate referred to the presentation as the "bomb in the Waldorf" because of its explosive impact. But it was not so much what happened in New York in September as what occurred in Europe during the next several months. The French were implacable in their opposition to German rearmament, and the British went along with the Americans largely because they did not believe the French would accept the plan. Without French support and with only the lukewarm backing of the British, the American proposal floundered and then fizzled. In December NATO approved the concept of a united command but accepted German participation only in principle.[47]

Nonetheless, the United States had taken several important incentives in response to the Korean War that extended America's commitment to Europe and strengthened the NATO alliance. In the first place, in cooperation with its European partners, Washington established a unified command structure for NATO. Although this would not happen officially until December, President Truman asked General Eisenhower in October to accept the appointment as supreme commander of NATO. Second, European rearmament, which had scarcely begun at the start of the Korean War, was well under way by the fall, and Truman had pledged to send four American divisions to Europe. While this commitment would get Truman into political hot water at home, forcing the President to tell a rebellious Congress that he needed to send no more than four divisions across the Atlantic, in April 1951 the House and Senate finally approved the administration's proposals for NATO. Third, the United States endorsed the principle of a German army as part of NATO's military force. Although this was the least successful—and, in many ways, the most important—of the administration's proposals for strengthening the western concert, the process was started at least that would make Germany a full-fledged NATO partner in 1955. Also, after the Korean War began, Germany ceased to be regarded in the west European capitals as a former enemy under Allied occupation, but, instead, obtained new status as a member of the council of Europe. In response to the Korean War, in other words, the

United States undertook obligations and helped define issues with respect to Europe that shaped the course of the Atlantic alliance for years to come.[48]

The commitments made by Washington in Europe and Asia, as well as the costs of the Korean War itself, meant an enormous increase in the nation's military budget. By confirming NSC-68's analysis of Communist aggression, the war also seemed to corroborate its estimate of the funds necessary to contain the Soviet threat. As Secretary Acheson put it, the dispatch of American troops to Korea "removed the recommendations of NSC-68 from the realm of theory and made them immediate budget issues."[49]

Until the outbreak of the Korean War the administration had taken no action on NSC-68's recommendations. Indeed, so much opposition existed in Congress to any major spending increases that President Truman had refused to allow publication of the report. His Defense Secretary, Louis Johnson, had been appointed to that position in order to cut the defense budget. Reflecting Johnson's tight budget policies, the Pentagon asked for only modest budget increases. Even after hostilities had begun, the Council of Economic Advisers assumed that the fighting would be localized and concluded that no standby economic controls were necessary. But all this changed within a matter of a few weeks. On July 19 President Truman delivered a report to Congress in which he asked for a substantial increase in military and defense spending, including an expanded program of military assistance for America's allies. He also requested a package of economic controls that included the allocation of essential raw materials, limits on consumer credit, and certain production incentives. "Under all the circumstances," the President told the House and Senate, "it is apparent that the United States is required to increase its military strength and preparedness not only to deal with the aggression in Korea but also to increase our common defense with other free nations, against further aggression."[50]

Congress responded by passing a series of appropriation and supplemental appropriation bills that doubled and then doubled again the defense budget and provided for a greatly expanded program of mutual defense assistance. At the end of August the House and Senate passed an omnibus bill that provided $13 billion for defense. A few weeks later they approved a supplemental measure that allowed for an additional $17 billion for emergency war and defense needs, and at the end of December they enacted a second supplemental bill of $20 billion, almost every cent of which was earmarked for the military. By the time that Truman signed the measure into law on January 6, the nation's military and defense spending approximated the recommendations of NSC-68.[51]

In addition, Congress approved legislation in September that gave the White House almost everything it asked for in the way of economic controls. The Defense Production Act (DPA), as the measure was known, granted the President various requisition and allocation powers for defense purposes, including a standby program of wages and price controls. The legislation also contained such other provisions as government loans and guarantees to expand the nation's productive capacity and funds for government purchases and development of strategic raw materials. Finally, it allowed the President in certain circumstances to exempt business arrangements deemed beneficial to the war effort from the antitrust laws. In sum, the DPA was a sweeping piece of legislation that vastly increased the power of the executive branch as it sought to mobilize the economy for wartime purposes.[52]

In fact, one of the indirect consequences of the war was to reinforce the power of the executive at the expense of the House and Senate. This came through the President's failure to consult with Congress on war-related matters and through an incident involving the President's authority as commander in chief. Although wartime has traditionally been a period when power gravitates to the White House, the Korean War was unusual in how quickly the question of executive-congressional conduct of the war was raised. It was also unusual in that the issue of the President's power as commander in chief was raised at all. The President might have handled the first of these matters differently, but as to the second, it is hard to imagine how he could have responded in any other way than he did after his authority as commander in chief was challenged in August by one of his generals, Douglas MacArthur. Correctly or not, Truman's failure to consult fully with Congress figured to be a major issue in the 1950 congressional elections (along with the administration's overall handling of the war), while the President's problems with MacArthur foreshadowed later difficulties that would help make the Truman administration among the least popular in American history.

The issue of consultation with Congress came up very early in the war. On June 28 Senator Taft told Truman that while he supported the President's actions with respect to Korea, there was "no legal authority" for the steps he had taken. Two days later, on the same day, in fact, that Truman consented to the sending of a combat force to Korea, the President met with his cabinet and a group of congressional leaders at Blair House to outline the actions he had already taken. For the most part, congressional leaders approved the President's program. However, Republican Senator Kenneth Wherry of Nebraska, the minority leader, asked the President if he was going to advise Congress before he sent ground troops into Korea. When Truman responded that some ground troops had already been ordered into Korea, Wherry replied that Congress should be consulted before the President made moves like this. Although Truman said he was faced with an emergency situation and that there was no time for a lot of talk, Wherry persisted and on several more occasions during the meeting repeated his belief that Congress should be consulted before any large-scale actions were taken again. Senator H. Alexander Smith of New Jersey also recommended that Truman request a joint resolution of Congress approving his actions. Truman replied that if any large-scale moves were to take place, he would tell Congress about them.[53]

Impressed by the arguments for full disclosure of the Korean situation, Acheson recommended to Truman on July 3 that he make a full report to a joint session of the House and Senate within the next several days. The secretary of state advised the President not to seek a resolution of approval but to rest his case for military action on his constitutional authority as commander in chief of the armed forces. However, he drafted a resolution commending the action taken by the United States that would be acceptable to the administration if proposed by Congress.[54]

Why, then, did Truman not ask for a declaration of war in Korea or at least for congressional approval of the steps he had already taken there? There appear to have been several reasons why. In the first place, other administration officials, particularly within the Defense Department, and at least one congressional leader (Scott Lucas of Illinois), believed that it would be a great mistake to rush into a speech, especially since the President might regret any hasty decision. The President himself pointed out that he could not possibly address a joint session on July 5 (the day proposed for the speech) inasmuch as the House had recessed for the week and would be holding only a token session that day. Second, Truman felt that a congressional resolution was simply not necessary since most of Congress already supported his actions. "They are all with me," Truman told Secretary of the Army Frank Pace in pointing to the backing he enjoyed in Congress on the Korean issue. But probably more important than either of these reasons, the President did not think at first that the conflict in Korea would lead to a world war, and he did not want to increase the stakes in Korea or unnecessarily alarm the American public or world opinion by asking for a declaration or anything resembling that. As Truman's biographer, Robert J. Donovan, has remarked, the President "seems not to have had a sense of a major war's blossoming in Korea, although he was ready to go 'all out,' if necessary to squelch the Communist invasion." And by the time it had become clear that Korea was a full-blown war, it was probably too late to get the kind of resolution unanimously approved by Congress that Truman would have wanted.[55]

As a result, Secretary Acheson's proposal for an immediate speech was dropped. Although White House officials, realizing that a Presidential address was inevitable, gathered materials for a speech, Truman delayed any action until June 19. Then he merely sent his message to Capitol Hill rather than address the full House and Senate. Nor did the President ask for a joint congressional resolution of approval. Instead, he outlined the steps the White House had taken with respect to Korea and the Far East and presented his program for increased defense spending and emergency power legislation that was incorporated into the DPA.[56]

Should the President have taken Congress more into his confidence by asking for a joint resolution of approval for the steps he had taken in Korea? In the long run it would probably not have made that much difference, although it might have been of some immediate benefit to the administration. Later criticism of the war had little to do with Truman's failure to consult Congress but was a result of the frustration of a limited war in which the United States failed to achieve a quick victory. According to Dean Acheson, the process of obtaining a resolution might even have been harmful, since criticism of the administration policy could have been injurious to troop morale and national unity at a time when UN forces were in retreat. But this argument seems specious since the conduct of the war was debated at home and abroad, and troops in Korea were hardly likely to be greatly affected by what was said in Congress at any given moment.[57]

If a resolution of approval would not have made that much difference in eventually having the war turned into "Truman's war" (a perjorative term reflecting America's growing displeasure with the conduct of the war), it is also hard to see what political harm it could have caused. Indeed, the advantage of stealing the thunder of the opposition by going to Congress for its approval could have been significant in the same way that President Lyndon Johnson was able in 1964 to line up congressional support for his Vietnam policies as a result of the Gulf of Tonkin Resolution—at least until the country finally turned against the conflict. A joint resolution of approval in July would have made it all that more difficult for Truman's opponents later to criticize the intervention.

Of much greater concern to the White House, however, than the constitutional issue of informing Congress before taking military action in Korea was another, related, constitutional matter having to do with the role of the President as commander in chief—of the armed forces. In what proved to be a portent of the administration's greatest domestic crisis, the President clashed with General Douglas MacArthur over a major policy question regarding the future of Formosa.

Appointed by President Truman on July 8 as commander of the UN forces in Korea, MacArthur was also commander in chief, Far East, and supreme commander, allied powers, Japan. Of heroic stature and great forcefulness, MacArthur was also deeply egotistical and vainglorious. Brilliant, austere, possessed of the gift of total recall, he "could never see another sun . . . in the heavens," as Eisenhower later said of him.[58] He was also a person of deep conviction and moral certitude, whose absolute views, arrogance, and personal rectitude made his vision sometimes narrow and parochial and incapable of fathoming the larger picture in which his own command had to be fitted. But so great was his personal fame, so overwhelming was his character, so eloquent was his rhetoric, that his views on military and nonmilitary matters alike were listened to with reverential respect by a broad cross-section of the American public.

Essentially MacArthur was one of those who believed in 1950 that the United States had shown too great an interest in European affairs and not enough in the Far East, whose "billions of inhabitants," he once said, "will determine the course of history for the next ten thousand years." More specifically, he believed in the summer of 1950 that the United States had the obligation to preserve Formosa and its leader, Chiang Kai-shek, against possible attack by Communist China. At the end of July he visited the island, allegedly to assess the military situation there. Returning to his headquarters in Tokyo, he ordered three squadrons of jet fighters to Formosa without the knowledge of the Pentagon. He also issued a statement in which he stressed the military nature of his talks with Chiang and remarked that plans had been formulated for the effective coordination of Chinese and American forces in case of an attack on the island. Shortly thereafter Chiang issued his own statement to the effect that his meeting with MacArthur had laid the basis for the joint defense of Formosa and "Sino-American military cooperation."[59]

Chiang's announcement caused considerable consternation in Washington, whose policy was as much to avoid an expansion of the conflict in Asia by keeping Chiang from launching an attack against the mainland as it was to prevent an attack from being launched against him. Averell Harriman was dispatched to Tokyo to explain America's China policy to MacArthur. The general denied that he had superseded his authority by going to Formosa, and he issued a caustic statement in which he said that the purpose of his trip had been "maliciously misrepresented to the public by those who invariably in the past have propagandized a policy of defeatism and appeasement in the Pacific."[60] MacArthur's words hardly satisfied the administration, which on August 14 tried to set the record straight by issuing a new directive to the general that he was not to authorize any attack from Formosa against the mainland. MacArthur wrote back that he understood the Presidential decision of June 27 "to protect the Communist mainland."[61]

This was the situation when MacArthur sent a lengthy message to the Veterans of Foreign Wars at the end of August in which he wrote about the "misconceptions currently being voiced concerning the relationship of Formosa to our strategic potential in the Pacific" and predicted dire consequences defensively if Formosa fell into hostile hands. To pursue any course other than defending Formosa, he said, "would be to turn over the fruits of our Pacific victory to a potential enemy. It would shift any future battle over 5,000 miles eastward to the coast of the American continent, our own home coast."[62]

On August 26, Averell Harriman took a copy of the press release containing MacArthur's statement to President Truman. The President was appalled by what he read. Modest where MacArthur was grandiloquent, folksy where MacArthur was ceremonious, Truman could, nevertheless, be as crafty as any political leader in Washington and as certain in his views of right and wrong as the general was in his. After discussing the news release with Harriman, therefore, Truman held his customary morning briefing on the military situation in Korea with the JCS, members of his cabinet, and White House aides. The President read to the group the full text of MacArthur's message. Then turning to Defense Secretary Johnson, he remarked that he "decisively repudiated" the statement MacArthur had made, that it directly contradicted the nation's foreign policy, and that he wished MacArthur's statement canceled.[63]

Johnson responded that he had no previous knowledge of the MacArthur statement and that he would immediately request him to cancel it. Army Chief of Staff J. Lawton Collins also denied having any previous knowledge of MacArthur's remarks. Truman, Harriman, and Acheson all agreed that they would have catastrophic implications for the nation's foreign policy. MacArthur's remarks rejected Truman's policy of neutralizing Formosa, it demanded more cordiality with Chiang Kai-shek than the administration was prepared to extend, and it wholeheartedly acknowledged the PRC as America's enemy when a firm policy toward China had still not yet been decided.[64]

After the meeting several of Truman's advisers saw the President in order to tell him that MacArthur should be ordered in writing—and not simply orally as Johnson proposed—to withdraw the statement on Formosa. The President agreed, and when the Defense Department appeared to procrastinate and was otherwise indecisive as to what to tell MacArthur, Truman called Johnson on the phone and virtually dictated the contents of the message sent to the general. "The President of the United States directs that you withdraw your message for the National Encampment of Veterans of Foreign Wars, because various features with respect to Formosa are in conflict with the policy of the United States and its position in the United Nations," read the message which Johnson transmitted to MacArthur on August 26. MacArthur complied with the directive at once.[65] Later Truman remarked that he "gave serious thought" to replacing MacArthur as military field commander in the Far East with General Omar Bradley but decided against such a step because it "would have been difficult to avoid the appearance of a demotion and [he] had no desire to hurt MacArthur personally." Undoubtedly Truman was also aware of the unpopularity of such a move and the backlash against the administration it would have generated.[66]

The first few months of the war, then, had been critical ones for the United States in a number of respects. Most important, of course, UN forces had been able to stabilize the war, successfully defend a perimeter around Pusan, and even make preparations for a counterattack, which would take place very shortly. Beyond that, the administration had taken under advisement the possibility of crossing the 38th parallel when the tide of battle should turn, and it had framed that issue in such a way that made an affirmative decision about crossing into North Korea more than likely. Third, it had expanded America's commitments in Europe as well as Asia. Having committed itself to containing Communism everywhere, the administration sought, nevertheless, to bolster the defenses of that part of the world, western Europe, that still meant the most to the United States. To meet the expenses of its new commitments as well as the cost of the war itself, the administration had asked for—and would receive before the year was out—almost a quadrupling of funding for defense purposes much along the lines set down by NSC-68. Finally, it had dealt with certain issues of a constitutional nature that also had long-term political implications. In all these respects the administration had acted out of a sense of urgency complicated by a domestic climate of crisis and conspiracy.

NOTES

1. CIA Memorandum: The Korean Situation, July 19, 1950, Box 58, President's Secretary File, Papers of Harry S. Truman, Harry S. Truman Library (Independence, Missouri).
2. James F. Schnabel, *Policy and Direction: The First Year* (Washington, D. C., 1972), 81–114; Edgar O'Ballance, *Korea: 1950–1953* (London, 1969), 36–40.
3. *Ibid.*
4. *New Republic,* 123 (July 24, 1950), 11–13.
5. O'Ballance, *Korea,* 40–44; David Rees, *Korea: The Limited War* (New York, 1964), 41–54.
6. Thomas C. Reeves, *The Life and Times of Joe McCarthy* (New York, 1982), 305–14.
7. *Ibid.*, 328–29.
8. *Time,* 56 (July 31, 1950), 13.
9. *New Republic,* 123 (July 17, 1950), 8; Reeves, *The Life and Times of Joe McCarthy,* 311 and 329–30.
10. Robert Griffith, *The Politics of Fear* (Lexington, Kentucky, 1970), 117–22.
11. *Commonweal,* 52 (July 21, 1950), 355–56; *Nation,* 171 (September, 12, 1950), 199–200; *New Republic,* 123 (August 28, 1950), 5; *ibid.* (September 11, 1950), 7.
12. *New Republic,* 123 (September 11, 1950), 7.
13. Walter LaFeber, *America, Russia, and the Cold War, 1945–1980* (New York, 1980), 101–27.
14. *Nation,* 171 (August 26, 1950), 181.
15. Clement Attlee, *Twilight of Empire: Memoirs of Prime Minister Clement Attlee* (New York, 1962), 230–31.
16. *FR,* 1950, VII, 327–28, 331–32, 337–79, 340–43, 355–60, and 365–67; Dean Acheson, *Present at the Creation: My Years at the State Department* (New York, 1969), 418–20.

17. Acheson, *Present at the Creation,* 418–20; *FR,* 1950, VII, 347–51 and 395–99; Acheson to American Embassy, London, July 10, 1950, Box 4262, Records of the Department of State, RG 59, 795.00/7-1050.
18. *FR,* 1950, VII, 359–60, and 426–27; William Whitney Stueck, Jr., *The Road to Confrontation: American Policy Toward China and Korea, 1947–1950* (Chapel Hill, N.C., 1981), 198–201.
19. *FR,* 1950, VII, 312–13, 315–16, and 327–28.
20. Stueck, Jr., *The Road to Confrontation,* 200–202.
21. *Ibid.*
22. *Nation,* 171 (July 22, 1950), 72–73.
23. Daily Opinion Summary, Department of State, July 21, 1950, Box 71, George M. Elsey Papers, Harry S. Truman Library (Independence, Missouri).
24. *New Republic,* 122 (August 21, 1950), 3; *Time,* 56 (September, 18, 1950), 30.
25. *FR,* 1950, VII, 272.
26. *Ibid.,* 386–87; Kenneth R. Mauck, "The Formation of American Foreign Policy in Korea, 1945–1953" (unpublished Ph.D. dissertation, University of Oklahoma, 1978), 214–15.
27. Charles E. Bohlen, *Witness to History* (New York, 1973), 292–94; *FR,* 1950, VII, 393.
28. *FR,* 1950, VII, 346, 393–95, 449–54, and 458–61.
29. *Ibid.,* 483–85 and 502–10.
30. *Ibid.,* 393–95; Stueck, Jr., *Road to Confrontation,* 203–204.
31. *FR,* 1950, VII, 449–54 and 458–61.
32. *Ibid.,* 393–95; Stueck, Jr., *Road to Confrontation,* 203–204.
33. *FR,* 1950, VII, 712–21.
34. *Ibid.*
35. *New Republic,* 123 (August 7, 1950), 14–16.
36. *Commonweal,* 52 (July 28, 1950), 380–81; *ibid.,* 52 (August 4, 1950), 410–11.
37. Robert McGeehan, *The German Rearmament Question: American Diplomacy and European Defense After World War II* (Urbana, Ill., 1971), 4–20; Lawrence S. Kaplan, "The Korean War and U. S. Foreign Relations: The Case of Nato," in Francis H. Heller (ed.), *The Korean War: A 25-Year Perspective* (Lawrence, Kans., 1977), 46–52.
38. *Commonweal,* 52 (July 28, 1950), 380–81.
39. Gaddis Smith, *Dean Acheson* (New York, 1972), 25–51 and 59–78.
40. Acheson, *Present at the Creation,* 435–37.
41. *Ibid.*

42. *Ibid.;* Harry S. Truman, *Years of Trial and Hope: Memoirs* (New York, 1965), 290–92; McGeehan, *The German Rearmament Question,* 25–39; Kaplan, "The Korean War and U. S. Foreign Relations," 51–53.

43. Quoted in *Commonweal,* 52 (August 4, 1950), 404–405.

44. Kaplan, "The Korean War and U. S. Foreign Relations," 53–54.

45. Acheson, *Present at the Creation,* 437–38.

46. *Ibid.,* 438–39; Truman, *Years of Trial and Hope,* 291–92; McGeehan, *The German Rearmament Question,* 39–49.

47. Acheson, *Present at the Creation,* 440; McGeehan, *The German Rearmament Question,* 49–93.

48. Kaplan, "The Korean War and U. S. Foreign Relations," 56–60; Stephen E. Ambrose, *Eisenhower: Soldier, General of the Army, President-Elect* (New York, 1983), 495–97.

49. Acheson, *Present at the Creation,* 420–21.

50. "Special Message to the Congress Reporting on the Situation in Korea," July 19, 1950, *Public Papers of the Presidents: Harry S. Truman,* 1950 (Washington, D. C., 1965), 527–37.

51. *Congressional Quarterly Almanac,* VI (1950), 104–109.

52. "The Defense Production Act of 1950," *Senate Reports,* 81st Congress, 2d Session (report no., 2250), 1–8, 11–12, and 52–53; "Defense Production Act of 1950," *House Reports,* 81st Congress, 2d Session (report no., 2759), 1–4, 13, 22–23.

53. "Unsigned Memorandum," [June 30, 1950?], Box 71, Elsey Papers; Arthur M. Schlesinger, Jr., *The Imperial Presidency* (Boston, 1970), 130–35; Acheson, *Present at the Creation,* 410 and 413.

54. *Ibid.*

55. Robert J. Donovan, *Tumultuous Years: The Presidency of Harry S. Truman, 1949–53* (New York, 1982), 219–24.

56. "Memorandum for the File," July 19, 1950, Box 71, Elsey Papers; "Special Message to the Congress Reporting on the Situation in Korea," July 19, 1950, *Public Papers of the Presidents: Harry S. Truman,* 1950, 527–37.

57. Acheson, *Present at the Creation,* 414–15.

58. Ambrose, *Eisenhower: Soldier, General of the Army, President-Elect,* 93–94.

59. John W. Spanier, *The Truman-MacArthur Controversy and the Korean War* (Cambridge, Mass., 1959), 67–71.

60. Quoted in Acheson, *Present at the Creation,* 422.

61. Spanier, *The Truman-MacArthur Controversy,* 72–73.

62. Quoted in *ibid.,* 74.

63. "Memorandum for the Files," August 26, 1950, Box 62, Elsey Papers.

64. *Ibid.*
65. *Ibid.*
66. Truman, *Years of Trial and Hope, 1946–1952*, 405–406; "From the President Personal for General MacArthur," Box 15, Selected Records Relating to the Korean War, Harry S. Truman Library (Independence, Missouri).

CHAPTER 3

The Period of the UN Offensive

On September 15, 1950, United Nations forces conducted a successful amphibious landing at Inchon, about twenty miles from Seoul and about 180 miles behind the North Korean lines at the Pusan perimeter. The next day the Eighth Army began a cautious offensive against the perimeter. A day later UN forces recaptured the Kimpo Airfield outside of Seoul. By September 19 enemy forces at Pusan had begun to collapse, and by September 28 Seoul was recaptured and UN forces were in full pursuit of North Korean armies fleeing behind the 38th parallel. Immediately the Truman administration was faced with the crucial decision of whether to move beyond the 38th parallel and to seek to reunite Korea by military force. Weighing the alternatives, the administration decided that so long as there was no evidence of a major Soviet or Chinese intervention in the war, the UN forces (which were composed largely of American and ROK troops) should pursue the North Koreans beyond the 38th parallel. So began the period of the UN offensive, which by October led General MacArthur to predict that American troops would be home by Christmas, but which ultimately resulted in the intervention on a massive scale of the Chinese Communists.

General MacArthur had conceived of an amphibious operation against the enemy during the first week of battle, even before the first clash of American and North Korean troops. Since his first counteroffensive against the Japanese in New Guinea in 1943, he had specialized in the amphibious end run. On July 3 he ordered 1200 specially trained operators for am-

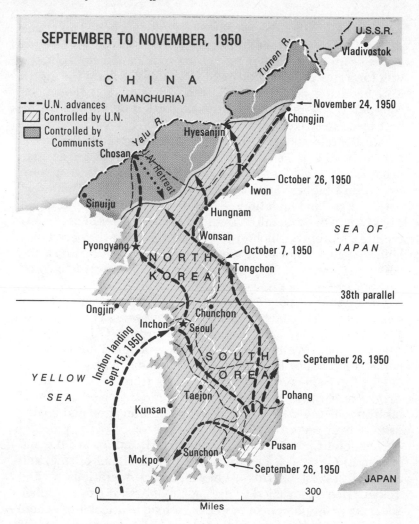

SEPTEMBER TO NOVEMBER, 1950

U.S.S.R.
Vladivostok

C H I N A
(MANCHURIA)

- - - U.N. advances
▨ Controlled by U.N.
▨ Controlled by Communists

Yalu R.
Tumen R.

November 24, 1950
Chongjin

Hyesanjin
Chosan
N. Retreat
Iwon
October 26, 1950

Sinuiju
Hungnam

Pyongyang ★
Wonsan

N O R T H
K O R E A
Tongchon
October 7, 1950

SEA OF
JAPAN

38th parallel

Ongjin
Chunchon
Inchon ★ Seoul

Inchon landing
Sept 15, 1950

YELLOW
SEA

S O U T H
K O R E A

September 26, 1950

Taejon
Pohang

Kunsan

Mokpo
Sunchon
Pusan

September 26, 1950

JAPAN

0   300
Miles

phibious landing craft. Two days later he requested an engineer special brigade trained in amphibious operations and an airborne regimental combat team "to participate in planned operations from 20 July to 10 August."[1]

Because of the exigencies of battle against an advancing enemy, no troops were available for an amphibious attack, and the operation was canceled on July 10. But the deterioration on the front strengthened MacArthur's determination to strike amphibiously. More specifically, MacArthur believed an attack against the enemy's rear on Korea's west coast would cut North Korea's supply lines and means of communication and open the way for a pincer operation with UN forces striking the North Koreans along both their front and their rear. Although he considered several landing sites, he settled on Inchon as the best place to strike.[2]

Most of the military's high command disagreed with MacArthur, believing, in fact, that he could not have selected a worse place for an amphibious operation. The tides at Inchon were the second highest in the world, averaging twenty-nine feet between low and high tides. The tides also moved rapidly, and a boat could become mired in the mud in a matter of only a few minutes. Moreover, Inchon was protected from the ocean by a high seawall, and invading troops would come ashore into a city with a population of 250,000 where each building could be used as a bunker by enemy troops.[3]

MacArthur responded to his critics by emphasizing the element of surprise, which would come about precisely because of the unlikelihood of an invasion against Inchon. On July 23 the general cabled Washington: "Operation planned mid-September is amphibious landing of a two-division corps in rear of enemy forces in conjunction with attack from south by Eighth Army. I am firmly convinced that early and strong effort behind his front will sever his main lines of communication and enable us to deliver a crushing blow."[4]

The Joint Chiefs of Staff (JCS) hesitated, and toward the end of August General J. Lawton Collins, Army chief of staff, and Admiral Forrest Sherman, chief of naval operations, visited Tokyo, where they tried to dissuade MacArthur from his plan. Sherman and Collins proposed that instead of attacking Inchon, MacArthur aim for the west coast port of Kunsan, which was much farther south and presented few of Inchon's physical obstacles. Again stressing the element of surprise in his plan and comparing it to Wolfe's famous attack on Quebec's precipitous but undefended riverbank in 1759, MacArthur replied that an attack on Kunsan would be largely ineffective and indecisive. It would not envelop the enemy or destroy his supply lines or distribution center.[5]

MacArthur's response was persuasive enough that on August 29, after Collins and Sherman had returned to Washington, he received the authority he wanted from the JCS to go ahead with his planned attack at Inchon. But this did not settle the matter entirely, for as the day planned for the invasion (September 15) drew closer, the JCS began to have second thoughts and sent a message to MacArthur asking him again to evaluate the feasibility and chances of success of the projected operation. There was no question in his mind on either score, MacArthur wrote back. "I go further," he added, "in belief that it represents the only hope of wrestling the initiative from the enemy and thereby presenting an opportunity for a decisive blow. To do otherwise is to commit us to a war of indefinite duration, of gradual attrition and doubtful results."[6] Reluctant to challenge a field commander so vigorous in defense of his strategy and so widely esteemed in political and military circles, the JCS gave their final consent to the Inchon invasion after obtaining President Truman's approval for the landing.[7]

As previously planned, the attack took place on September 15. The operation was as successful as MacArthur had predicted. The North Koreans were overextended and stretched thin. There were only about 2000 North Korean troops in the Inchon area to defend against a combined UN force of 70,000 personnel carried in 260 ships. The attack began early in the morning of September 15 when American Marines landed on the island of Wolmi, which protected Inchon Harbor. Meeting only light resistance, they secured the island in about two hours with only one man killed. There they remained while the tide ebbed and flowed, but in the late afternoon UN forces were able finally to strike at Inchon itself. One group of Marines landed on the northern edge of the city in an area designated Red Beach, while another went ashore just to the south at Blue Beach.[8]

Dazed by the tremendous firepower of the cruisers offshore, which had earlier blasted the city, and heavily outnumbered, the North Korean defenders offered some resistance, but by midnight Inchon had been taken, although there was still considerable mopping up to be done. The next morning X Corps, consisting of the First Marine Division and the Army's Seventh Infantry Division and commanded by Major General Edward M. Almond, headed east toward Kimpo Airfield and Seoul. Although the troops met stiff resistance, they took Seoul by September 28, and the next day Syngman Rhee moved his government back to the capital city. By this time, also, the Eighth Army under the command of General Walton H. Walker had broken through the Pusan perimeter and linked up with elements of X Corps advancing from the northwest. North Korean resistance had collapsed, and North Korean forces were in total disarray.[9]

For MacArthur the Inchon invasion was an object lesson of how to win a war with a minimum of casualties. In October, after it had been decided to carry the war into North Korea, the UN commander would try to repeat his tactic of an amphibious envelopment by withdrawing X Corps from South Korea and landing it at the port of Wonson on the east coast of North Korea. Only this time the evacuation of the First Marine Division through Inchon would badly hamper logistical support of the Eighth Army as it advanced from Seoul into North Korea. The Eighth Army would remain strapped of supplies for the remainder of the campaign, and ROK forces would actually capture Wonson before the First Marine Division had sailed from Inchon.[10]

The rapid and overwhelming success of UN forces following the Inchon invasion, however, made MacArthur into even more of a national hero than before and assured his lasting military fame. Admiral William F. Halsey telegraphed the UN commander to say, "The Inchon landing is the most masterly and audacious strategic stroke in all history."[11] The successful landing also boosted morale at home, colored political discourse, and led opinion makers to speculate on the course the administration should follow in the coming weeks and months.

Of particular note was the fact that the UN offensive took place just about the same time that George Marshall replaced Louis Johnson as defense secretary. Truman's appointment of the former secretary of state and Army chief of staff outraged a core of right-wing Republicans and other members of the China lobby, which had supported Chiang Kai-shek and his Nationalist forces in the civil war in China and was sharply critical of the administration for not providing more aid to Chiang. As Truman's representative to China from 1945 to 1947 and then as secretary of state from 1947 to 1949, Marshall was considered one of the principal architects of the policy that had led to the loss of China to the Communists. Senator William Jenner even attacked Marshall personally, suggesting that he was "eager to play the role of a front man, for traitors." Senator Robert Taft added that Marshall's appointment was a "reaffirmation of the tragic policy of the administration in encouraging Chinese communism which brought on the Korean War." These right-wing Republicans were joined by the other congressmen who, as a matter of principle, opposed legislation clearing the way for Marshall's appointment by setting aside a provision of the National Security Act of 1947 prohibiting military officers from serving as defense secretary.[12]

Nevertheless, Marshall's appointment was generally a popular one both in Washington and in most west European capitals. The new secretary of defense was widely respected for his judiciousness, broad-mindedness, and reasonableness. This was particularly important to those concerned by the loose talk of a preemptive nuclear strike against the Soviet Union. Also, Marshall was expected to work closely with Acheson in formulating and carrying out defense policy, and his appointment was seen by many as indicating American sensitivity both to European interests and to the rising tide of nationalism in Asia. On September 20 the Senate approved Marshall's nomination by a vote of 57 to 11.[13]

By this time the national mood had already begun to change from one of despair and even desperation to one of optimism. "With the Marines just outside Seoul and General Marshall already in the Pentagon," political columnist Richard Rovere reported from Washington, "many of the dark anticipations of a month ago are giving way to something approaching hope, and even confidence, here." Already, too, a national debate over the future conduct and direction of American foreign policy had begun that would continue well into October. On one level, previous demands were renewed for the resignation of Secretary of State Acheson, who was held responsible for the fall of China to the Communists because of his neglect of Asia and his emphasis on Europe. The editors of *Life,* a magazine closely identified with the China lobby, termed the secretary of state "the symbol of appeasement of Communism everywhere in Asia." By October the attacks against Acheson had become so intense and vituperative that rumors circulated throughout Washington about his pending resignation from office on the grounds that the time and effort required to defend himself and his policies had diminished his effectiveness as secretary of state.[14]

On another level, however, Washington observers considered the problem of what policy to follow in Korea (and Asia) after the North Koreans had been driven back above the 38th parallel. The most immediate question was whether to carry the war into North Korea in order to roll back Communist expansion and bring about Korean unification. Although there was a variety of opinion on these issues, the majority sentiment was to expand the war by crossing into North Korea. The editors of *Life* maintained, for example, that authority for UN forces to march above the 38th parallel was implicit in the 1943 agreement in Cairo that "in due course" Korea was to become free and independent and in the June 27 Security Council resolution instructing UN forces to restore security in Korea. Similarly, the *New Republic,* a liberal journal of opinion generally poles apart politically from *Life,* concluded that if, for no other reason than the UN's identification with Korean unification, "the restoration of the status quo ante [in Korea was] no longer a matter for negotiation with the USSR." Even the *Nation,* another liberal journal of opinion, which had serious reservations about expanding the war into North Korea, lamented the "growing sentiment" for incorporating North Korea into a republic under Syngman Rhee's leadership.[15]

Would the Soviet Union or Communist China intervene if UN forces moved above the 38th parallel? *Commonweal,* a Catholic journal of opinion, did not think so. "If it is correct to assume that no further Soviet intervention is forthcoming in Korea," it commented, "that 'little war' . . . is about over as far as the United States is concerned." *Life* reached a similar conclusion. "The danger of Chinese or Soviet intervention if the North Korean Communists are pressed close to the Manchurian border is, in our curbstone opinion, negligible." Even the *Nation* conceded that "if the Russians or Chinese should commit their own forces to the struggle [in Korea] they would do so knowing that they were inviting general war, and that is a price Moscow is not prepared to pay."[16]

Broad sentiment for crossing into North Korea also existed in Congress, which likewise felt that chances of Soviet or Chinese intervention were small. Democratic Senator Joseph O'Mahoney of Wyoming thus wrote Truman, "Let the United States . . . not be a party to the tragic error of permitting the Communists to retire in defeat beyond the 38th parallel, and, there, reestablishing the iron curtain which has now been destroyed, prepare anew for future aggression." Indeed, Republicans in the House and Senate made it clear that they would regard a decision *not* to carry the war above the 38th parallel an act of appeasement. Representative Hugh D. Scott, Jr., of Pennsylvania, former chairman of the Republican Party, went so far as to accuse the State Department of planning "to subvert our military victory by calling a halt at the 38th parallel."[17]

It is hard to imagine that these winds of war did not weigh heavily on the White House's decision to expand the war into North Korea, particularly with congressional elections just about six weeks away. The influential conservative journalist David Lawrence even warned Democrats that if UN forces were "not permitted to go beyond the 38th parallel to disarm the government which has committed the aggression," the Republicans would take political advantage of that policy. Surely Truman could not have been unaware of the political lightning and thunder a determination to contain the conflict to South Korea would generate against his administration.[18]

Yet the President had already decided to allow MacArthur's forces to cross into North Korea. On September 27 Defense Secretary Marshall presented him with a draft directive for MacArthur prepared by the JCS and based on NSC-81/1. Agreed to by both Marshall and Secretary of State Acheson, the directive instructed MacArthur to move beyond the 38th parallel if necessary to destroy North Korean armed forces, provided that there was no intervention or threat of intervention by major Soviet or Chinese forces. As a matter of policy, no non-Korean ground forces were to be used in the northeast provinces of Korea bordering the Soviet Union or in the area along the Manchurian border. In case of Soviet military intervention MacArthur was to assume the defense, report to Washington, and make no move to aggravate the situation. In the case of Chinese intervention MacArthur was to continue military action as long as it offered a reasonable chance of successful resistance.[19]

Truman approved the directive to MacArthur on the same day he received it. Two days later Marshall sent the UN commander a personal "eyes-only" message telling him that he should "feel unhampered tactically and strategically to proceed north of the 38th Parallel."[20] About the same time, the American delegation at the United Nations helped draft a resolution in the General Assembly (thereby avoiding a Soviet veto in the Security Council) that authorized UN forces to enter North Korea and to remain there until Korean unification was completed and stability in the country achieved. On October 7 the General Assembly easily approved the resolution by a vote of 47 to 5 with 7 abstentions. In effect the purpose of the war had been fundamentally altered. Hitherto the war aim had been to repel aggression. Now it was to produce a unified Korea that was also clearly intended to be non-Communist. The evolving military situation had altered foreign policy objectives.[21]

With the United States now committed to Korean unification through military means (since the North Koreans would hardly permit the entry of UN troops into North Korea), Washington might have lost a real opportunity to negotiate a peace settlement with the Soviet Union. At least in the General Assembly the Soviet delegation had softened its tirades against the United States and sponsored a resolution which, while unsatisfactory to the United States in several respects, called for elections supervised by the United Nations throughout Korea. Also, the Soviet foreign minister, Andrei Vishinsky, indicated a willingness to negotiate on the Korean question either through a UN committee or through private channels. But anxious to maintain the momentum generated by the Inchon landing and sensing total victory in Korea, Washington did little to encourage the Soviet initiative.[22]

The administration continued to be concerned, however, about Soviet and Chinese intentions should the United States cross the 38th parallel. On this issue intelligence reports were constantly changing. For example, on September 20 the American ambassador to India, Loy Henderson, reported that a conversation had taken place between the Indian ambassador to Peking, K. M. Panikkar, and the Chinese foreign minister,

Chou En-lai, the gist of which was that China had no intention of entering the Korean conflict short of a world war. Similarly, the American consul general at Hong Kong, James R. Wilkinson, reported two days later that he had received reliable evidence that the Chinese Communists did not intend to invade Formosa that year and that they might limit further aid to North Korea to token support. On the other hand, in a memorandum for the State Department, the director of the Office of Chinese Affairs, O. Edmund Clubb, and Assistant Secretary of State Dean Rusk concluded that if the Soviets determined that they could not prevent a movement of UN forces into North Korea, "they might plan an intervention of either Chinese Communists, Chinese and Soviet forces or Soviet forces in North Korea to restore the status quo ante Soviet withdrawal." More important, on October 2 the Chinese, acting through the Indian ambassador, Panikkar, warned the United States that they would not permit the American forces to cross the 38th parallel without taking some retaliatory measures. (They said nothing about the ROK forces crossing the parallel.)[23]

Neither these warnings nor others received by the administration kept it from giving MacArthur the go-ahead to advance beyond the 38th parallel. On October 4 Clubb concluded that if the Soviet Union or China was willing to accept the risk of a clash with the UN in Korea, it meant they were willing to risk World War III. "In such a case, we cannot avoid danger either by retreating from it or by surrendering to the Peiping threat; either move would increase, not diminish, the danger inherent in the situation for us."[24]

Difficulties of communication, misperceptions, and false calculations on the part of the administration complicated the problems of information and resulted in an image of Chinese intentions that amounted to a nether land of distortion and unreality. White House officials placed little faith in the credibility of Ambassador Panikkar, who only two weeks earlier had reported that Peking had no intention of intervening in Korea and whom President Truman regarded as little more than an agent of Chinese propaganda. Even if Panikkar's information could be trusted, however, the President believed that China's warning was probably only "a bald attempt to blackmail the United Nations," which was considering the resolution authorizing UN forces to cross the 38th parallel, by threatening to send troops into Korea should that happen.[25]

More important, the administration shared a curiously bifurcated image of China, which, on one hand, held the Peking government as little more than an agent provocateur of Moscow and, on the other hand, as an independent regime pursuing its own interests quite apart from those of the Soviet Union. Coexisting with this second image of the PRC was the conviction that Peking's motivation was more nationalist than Communist and that the traditional friendship between the United States and China could be resumed once the affair in Korea was settled. This led White House and State Department officials to the additional assumption that if the United States made clear to China's leaders that America harbored no ill will or aggressive designs against them, China would not intervene should UN forces advance above the 38th parallel.

These conflicting and often mistaken perceptions of the PRC were clearly evident in the public speeches and private correspondence of Secretary of State Acheson. One reason that Acheson had not expected China to enter the Korean War in August, when its intervention might have been decisive in defeating UN forces, was his conviction that the Soviet leader, Joseph Stalin, controlled Chinese movements and that he did not want to expand the conflict in Korea into a global war. At the same time, however, no one was more eloquent than the secretary of state in pointing to the substantial differences of interest between Moscow and Peking. In his famous speech to the National Press Club in January, in which he excluded Korea from the nation's defense perimeter in the Far Pacific, Acheson had spelled out the differences separating China from the Soviet Union, pointing out that for generations Russia had sought to dominate the peoples of Asia and none so much as those of northern China. Because Acheson and other administration leaders perceived significant disagreement between Moscow and Peking, and because they were convinced that China had nothing to fear from UN operations and realized that fact, it never occurred to them that Peking's conception of its national security might not be the same as their own.[26]

Despite the conflicting reports it received about Soviet or Chinese intervention, therefore, the administration concluded that neither Moscow nor Peking was likely to send troops into Korea, that the time for intervention would have come much earlier (well before UN forces reached the 38th parallel), and that Moscow and Peking were anxious to avoid hostilities with the United States. Accordingly, on the day after the UN passed its resolution authorizing UN forces to pursue the enemy beyond the 38th parallel, the first American troops began crossing the parallel. (ROK forces had already crossed the line on October 1, and General MacArthur had called on North Korea to surrender to UN forces.) The UN troops met relatively little resistance from the North Koreans, and on October 10 ROK forces captured Wonson before MacArthur could carry out his plan for an amphibious landing at the port. Nine days later the capital of Pyongyang fell to the UN troops. By this time the first Chinese troops—the People's Volunteers—had secretly entered Korea from Manchuria.[27]

The advance into North Korea by American troops represented a political decision to bring about the unification of Korea through military means. As such it was based on faulty intelligence to the effect that neither the Soviet Union nor Communist China would intervene militarily to save North Korea. Even after UN forces crossed into North Korea, the Central Intelligence Agency (CIA) determined that Chinese or Soviet intervention was highly unlikely. "While full-scale Chinese Communist intervention in Korea must be regarded as a continuing possibility," the CIA concluded, "a consideration of all known factors leads to the conclusion that, barring a Soviet decision for global war, such action is not probable in 1950." As for the chance of Moscow's intervention, the Soviets would "intervene in the Korean hostilities if they had decided, not on the basis of the Korea situation alone, but on the basis of over-all considerations, that it is to their interest to precipitate a global war at this time." The possibility of the Soviets opting for global war "exists now and hereafter at any time when the Soviet rulers may elect to take action which threatens, wholly or in part, the vital interests of the Western Powers." In case of a global war, however, it had already been determined that Korea would be strategically unimportant.[28]

If there still remained doubts about the possibility of intervention into Korea by Peking and Moscow, the Wake Island conference of October 15 between President Truman and General MacArthur served to dispel them. In his memoirs Truman claims that he made this 18,000-mile trip to the Far Pacific because he had never met MacArthur and thought that he and his Far East commander should get better acquainted. A second reason Truman made the trip was almost certainly to make clear to MacArthur that Korea and the entire Far East were only a part of America's larger global responsibilities and that statements like the general's August message to the Veterans of Foreign Wars were inappropriate because they falsely implied that Communist China could be overcome by force. Then, too, the President was concerned about an American air raid against a Soviet airfield sixty-two miles from the Korean border, for which the United States later apologized and offered to pay damages. He wanted assurances that no similar episode would happen in the future.[29]

More important than those other considerations, however, Truman appears to have gone to Wake Island for political reasons. Actually, the success of the UN offensive and the move across the 38th parallel had blunted the full fury of Republican charges against the administration, and in the months between the Inchon invasion and the Wake Island meeting there was a noticeable decline in the intensity and degree of Republican oratory against the administration's Korean policy. In fact, in several states, such as Connecticut, where two Senate seats were to be decided in November, Democrats seemed to be benefiting from the Korean issue. Before the Inchon landing Republicans had hoped to pick up one and possibly both seats in Connecticut. Now that UN forces had moved into North Korea, nobody was making any predictions; the race was that close.[30]

Yet while the military success of the previous few weeks had turned what promised to be a political liability for the Democrats into a possible political asset, Korea remained a campaign issue, and in states like Illinois, where former Republican Congressman Everett Dirksen was running for the Senate seat held by Democratic Majority Leader Scott Lucas, the GOP persisted in blaming the Korean War on the "appeasement, vacillation, and weakness" of the Truman administration. At the same time, Senator McCarthy continued to flail away at the administration for its "treasonable" Far East policy. President Truman's White House staff was also greatly concerned by the President's lack of visibility in recent weeks. In truth, while Truman cruised leisurely on Chesapeake Bay aboard the yacht *Williamsburg,* newspaper headlines were monopolized by stories of the General Assembly's vote authorizing UN forces to cross into North Korea, of MacArthur's surrender ultimatum to the North Koreans, and of the rapid advance up North Korea's east coast by ROK forces.[31]

To regain the political spotlight for the President and to strengthen Democratic chances in the coming elections, a group of Truman's closest political advisers approached him with the idea of meeting MacArthur somewhere in the Pacific, arguing that it would be "good election-year stuff." At first the President rejected the recommendation precisely because he thought it was too obviously political and because he did not believe there was any real need for him to confer with MacArthur. But he soon changed his mind, and arrangements were then quickly made for a meeting at Wake Island, after MacArthur turned down an alternate site at Honolulu, which had been Truman's first choice.[32]

Arriving on Wake Island, Truman was greeted by the general, whom he later described as "wearing a greasy ham and eggs cap that evidently had been in use for twenty years."[33] The meeting between the two men was short, lasting only ninety-six minutes. But during that time MacArthur stated that formal resistance in Korea would end by Thanksgiving, that he hoped to withdraw the Eighth Army by Christmas, and that there was little need to fear Soviet or Communist Chinese intervention. When Assistant Secretary of State Dean Rusk, who accompanied Truman on his trip, mentioned to the general that the Chinese had threatened privately to enter the Korean War if UN forces crossed the 38th parallel, MacArthur replied that he did not understand fully why the Chinese made such a statement and that they were probably greatly embarrassed by the predicament in which they now found themselves.[34]

Both Truman and MacArthur left the Wake Island conference confident they had made their respective positions clear to the other. Truman was satisfied that he had established a more cordial and harmonious relation with his field commander. MacArthur even apologized for his VFW message of August, and as Truman stated on his return to the United States, he had "never had a more satisfactory conference" since becoming President. For his part, MacArthur returned to Tokyo with a sense of greater freedom than when he arrived. The general had good reason to feel this way. MacArthur's personal sense of infallibility and invincibility was contagious, and he left the President and members of Truman's party fully expecting an early end to the Korean War.[35]

Illusion prevailed over reality. As Hanson Baldwin of *The New York Times* reported, Chinese troops were already beginning to mass along the Chinese frontier. Baldwin estimated that there were about 250,000 troops near the Korean frontier and 200,000 more elsewhere in Manchuria. Even the CIA concluded the Chinese would enter North Korea, albeit for the limited purpose of protecting the power plants along the Yalu River, which separated Korea from Manchuria.[36] Yet, until the time the Chinese Communists entered the fighting in Korea and the first Chinese prisoners were taken on October 26, the United States lacked a meaningful contingency plan with respect to Chinese intervention. The American position was contained in a vaguely worded October 9 directive of the JCS to MacArthur, which was intended as an amplification of their earlier September 27 directive. "Hereafter in the event of the open or covert employment anywhere in Korea of major Chinese units, without prior announcement," the JCS instructed MacArthur, "you should continue the action as long as, in your judgment, action by forces now under your control offers a reasonable chance of success." MacArthur was also to "obtain authorization from Washington prior to taking any military action against objectives in Chinese territory."[37]

The Truman administration continued to believe that as long as it made clear to Peking that the United States harbored no offensive intentions against China, the Chinese would not intervene militarily in Korea. For this purpose the administration kept up a major diplomatic effort at the United Nations and elsewhere even after passage of the October 7 resolution authorizing UN troops to enter North Korea. At the UN the United States had already agreed to a Security Council invitation to Peking to send a representative to the Security Council in order to discuss the issue of Formosa. Although the American delegation opposed any additional steps that might raise the unwelcome question of Peking's admission as a UN member, it also made clear that the United States was willing to listen to China's views on Korea. In India, Ambassador Loy Henderson even tried unsuccessfully to arrange a meeting with the Chinese ambassador to that country.

What influenced the PRC even more than America's proclaimed intentions of goodwill was the UN's uninterrupted march toward the Yalu River. Also, the often hostile and aggressive statements by the China lobby and others in Washington, including Navy Secretary Francis Matthews' talk of preventive war, reinforced Peking's worst suspicions of the United States. Even as China began massing troops in Manchuria for a possible invasion into Korea, therefore, Peking gave additional warnings that it would not tolerate an American advance toward its borders. China's foreign minister, Chou En-lai, made a statement to this effect in a sudden nighttime meeting with a group of ambassadors in Peking from neutralist countries. Similarly, the paper *Kung Jen Jih Pao* declared on October 13: "We cannot stand idly by when the American imperialist, a notorious enemy, is now expanding its war of aggression against our neighbor and is attempting to extend the aggressive flames to the borders of the country." While not dismissing these threats out of hand, Washington continued to believe that the most favorable moment for Chinese (and Soviet) intervention had passed and that if intervention did occur, it would be limited in scope and be nominally covert instead of overt.[38]

Indeed, in the United States the overwhelming assumption through at least the beginning of November was that the war in Korea would be over in a matter of weeks or, at the most, a few months. On this basis Democratic political fortunes continued to improve. Although opponents of the administration remained defiant and Senator McCarthy continued to receive more invitations to speak than all the other senators combined, in states like Pennsylvania where Democratic Senator Francis Myers was being challenged by Republican Governor James Duff, and in Ohio where Democratic candidate Joseph T. Ferguson was attempting to unseat Robert Taft, political analysts reported that Democratic chances remained in the upswing.

According to *Time,* by the beginning of November the Republican campaign slogan of "Bungling in Korea" had lost its appeal, and even the issue of Communists in government had waned.[39]

Now that victory in Korea seemed assured, Americans even tried to draw larger lessons from the war. For a number of these persons, the most important lesson to be learned from Korea was the need to be more responsive to the economic requirements and political wishes of the world's underdeveloped areas, particularly in Asia. A few commentators even made the point that since the Korean War had been fought under the aegis of the United Nations, the manner in which the UN responded to the reconstruction needs of Korea would determine its future effectiveness among Third World nations. On the other hand, Americans were reminded that Korea was not the only trouble spot in Asia, and they were warned that in the future the United States would need to be extremely leery of supporting undemocratic regimes or propping up colonial enterprises, such as the Bao Dai government in Vietnam. So, too, the Rhee government in South Korea came under strong criticism for being repressive, unpopular, and unrepresentative of all Koreans, and the fundamental question was raised whether his administration was to be tossed overboard as preparations were made to establish a government of national unification.[40]

By the beginning of November, all intelligence estimates agreed that Chinese forces had entered North Korea. But considerable differences still remained as to the size of these forces or their purpose. On November 1 the director of the Office of Chinese Affairs, O. Edmund Clubb, informed Assistant Secretary of State Dean Rusk that the presence of Chinese forces in North Korea was now confirmed. "It seems unlikely," Clubb added, "that the Chinese Communists would be prepared to venture into the Korean theater in such a limited manner as would confront them with the danger of being promptly bloodied and thrown out by the force which they themselves have constantly characterized as a 'paper tiger.' " Therefore, it was safe to assume that if the Chinese were intervening in Korea, they would be doing so in considerable numbers and at the behest of the Soviet Union. Indeed, Moscow might be planning to strike elsewhere, such as Berlin. "In sum," Clubb concluded, "there is to be considered the definite possibility that the Soviets plan at this juncture to extend the area of conflict." In contrast, the director of the CIA, Walter Bedell Smith, in a memorandum to the President, reported on the basis of his own intelligence estimates that while the Chinese forces had entered North Korea, they numbered only between 15,000 and 20,000 and that their main purpose was probably to establish a limited *"cordon sanitaire"* south of the Yalu River.[41]

Not until November 6 did the reality of the Chinese invasion figure into the calculus of decision making in Washington. The immediate question confronting the administration concerned General MacArthur's orders for a bombing mission to take out a bridge across the Yalu River from Sinuiju (Korea) to Antung (Manchuria). The Defense Department learned of MacArthur's orders only by chance and less than four hours before they were carried out. Deputy Secretary of Defense Robert Lovett, who believed that the bombing would not significantly interrupt traffic across the Yalu and might result in the accidental bombing of Antung and other points on the Manchurian side of the river, informed Secretary of State Acheson and Assistant Secretary of State Dean Rusk of the planned operation. Acheson then telephoned President Truman in Kansas City recommending that the mission be scrubbed until the reasons for it were more clearly known. Soon thereafter the Joint Chiefs of Staff, acting on the President's instructions, ordered MacArthur to postpone all bombing of targets within five miles of the Manchurian border.[42]

MacArthur objected strongly to these new orders. As late as November 4 he had expressed his doubts to the Joint Chiefs that the Communists intended in any direct way to intervene militarily in Korea. To do so "would represent a momentous decision of the gravest international importance," he said. Without being more explicit, he stated that there were "many logical reasons" against such an attack, and he recommended "against hasty conclusions which might be premature."[43]

Two days later, however, after he received his latest instructions from Washington, the general offered an entirely different scenario. He reported that materiel and personnel were "pouring across all bridges over the Yalu from Manchuria." The only way to stop this reinforcement of the enemy was "the destruction of these bridges and the subjection of all installations in the north area supporting the enemy" to American bombing. "Under the gravest protest that I can make," he told the Joint Chiefs, "I am suspending this strike and carrying out your instructions. . . . I trust that the matter be immediately brought to the attention of the President as I believe your instructions may well result in a calamity of major proportion for which I cannot accept the responsibility without his personal and dir-[ect] understanding of the sit[uation]."[44]

MacArthur's response might have been intended for the record should the enemy inflict a major defeat on his forces. Certainly in urging Presidential approval of the Joint Chiefs' orders, it bordered on insubordination. Nevertheless, the JCS felt they had little choice except to defer to their commander in the Far East. To a considerable measure they were responsible for their own dilemma. In the past, when the general had challenged accepted administration policy, they had voiced no objection. Only two weeks earlier MacArthur had ordered his troops to advance in some places to within thirty-five miles of the Manchurian border, ignoring Washington's acknowledged policy of using ROK troops to pacify the northern part of Korea, or that area beyond the peninsula's narrow waist. But the JCS made no protest. On October 24 the general ordered American troops to march to the Yalu River. Once again the JCS failed to countermand the order.[45]

The fact was that the situation in Korea, seen from Washington, was thoroughly confused. First there had been the standing instructions to MacArthur since the end of September to feel unhampered in proceeding north of the 38th parallel. Second was the broad latitude that the general took in carrying out those instructions. Third was the need to redefine policy now that the Chinese Communists had entered the war. On this matter the administration was indecisive and vacillating. "We all agree that if the Chinese Communists come into Korea, we get out," General Omar Bradley, the chairman of the JCS, had said on October 23 during a meeting of the American and British chiefs of staff. But matters were not as simple as that. To cede Korea to the Communists was to undermine the United States' whole position in the Far East. In this respect the administration's analysis of Chinese foreign policy abruptly changed; instead of nationalism being the motivating factor behind China's policy, now it was communism, and the Chinese were once more seen as puppets of Moscow. Under these circumstances it behooved the JCS (and the rest of the administration) to give MacArthur the necessary authority to beat back the Chinese and to bring the Korean War to a successful conclusion.[46]

Consequently, on November 6, the same day that they received MacArthur's blistering communication, the JCS reversed themselves and authorized MacArthur to hit targets at Sinuiju and the Korean side of the Yalu bridges "provided that at the time of the receipt of this message you still find such action essential to [the] safety of your forces." However, the general was to take extreme care to avoid violating Manchurian territory and airspace and to report promptly hostile action from Manchuria.[47]

By this time news of the Chinese invasion had filtered out from the White House, the State Department, and the Pentagon. Chinese forces had already penetrated up to seventy miles south of the Yalu River, and there were reports of four ROK divisions being "chopped up piecemeal" by the Red armies. *The New York Times* wrote of "Chinese Communist hordes, attacking on horse and on foot to the sound of bugle calls" and cutting up American and Korean forces "in an Indian style massacre." Similar reports had the Chinese offensive carrying to within fifteen miles of the vital UN transportation and supply center at Sinonju and threatening both the rear and the right flanks of the U. S. Twenty-fourth Infantry Division. According to *Time,* in northeastern Korea "the battle seemed everywhere at once."[48]

Almost certainly news of the Chinese invasion hurt Democrats at the polls on November 7, although in most instances local issues were more important. As a result of the elections, the Republicans picked up four Senate and twenty-eight House seats. At the time, Republican gains were attributed largely to the Red-baiting and smear tactics of Senator McCarthy and his followers. In California, Wisconsin, Illinois, Ohio, and Maryland, where either the issue of internal subversion was raised or McCarthy campaigned extensively, Democrats went down to defeat. "In every contest where it was a major factor," Marquis Childs pointed out, "McCarthyism won." Nowhere did this observation seem more true than in Maryland where McCarthy's people practically took over the campaign of the Republican candidate for the Senate, John Marshall Butler, and brought revenge against the incumbent, Millard Tydings, who as head of the Tydings Committee had earlier tried to disgrace McCarthy.[49]

In truth, Red baiting appears to have been only one issue and not always the most important in accounting for the election results. In Illinois the defeat of Scott Lucas seems to have been due more to scandals involving the powerful Cook County Democratic machine than anything else. In Ohio Taft's decisive victory over Joseph Ferguson was largely the result of Taft's views on labor and the ineptness of his Democratic opponent. In Wisconsin, McCarthy's home state, Democrats actually increased their overall strength and had their most impressive gains precisely in those counties where McCarthy had campaigned. And in Maryland dissension within Democratic ranks, Tyding's close association with an unpopular governor, and black opposition to the incumbent appear to have been decisive.[50]

Still, throughout the campaign charges had been pinned against the administration of "communism, confusion, and corruption," and to the extent that the latest news from Korea seemed to confirm these charges and to undermine the optimism about the war apparent just a few days earlier, it contributed to the Republican victory. Even Senator Tydings attributed his defeat in part to the most recent information from Korea, and as the *New Republic* later commented in analyzing the election results, "Everywhere the GOP [had] ranted about 'confusion' in the Government until the public seemingly believed that some other administration could have kept the threat of war further away." This was so much grist for the mill of the China lobby, which interpreted the election as a repudiation of State Department policy and predicted Secretary of State Acheson's imminent resignation.[51]

Almost as abruptly as they had entered the war in Korea, however, the Chinese cut off their attack. There then followed a three-week lull in the fighting. In effect, the United States was given an opportunity to redefine its policy and strategy with respect to Korea. During this time, the administration did reconsider its directives to MacArthur. In September the Far East commander had been instructed to continue military action against the Chinese so long as there was a reasonable chance of success. On October 9 Secretary of Defense George Marshall had told MacArthur that he should "feel unhampered tactically and strategically to proceed north of the 38th Parallel." But now on November 8 the JCS informed MacArthur that his objective of destroying North Korean armed forces might "have to be reexamined in the light of the Chinese intervention." What most troubled administration officials was the possibility that Chinese involvement in Korea was merely a prelude to a larger global war involving the Soviet Union, without whose encouragement, they believed, the Chinese would never have intervened. Both the JCS and the director of the CIA, Walter Bedell Smith, agreed with this analysis. So, too, did Secretary of State Acheson who, at a meeting of the National Security Council on November 9, offered a British proposal to establish a ten-mile buffer zone on either side of the Yalu River.[52]

Despite the anxiety caused by the Chinese intervention, however, nothing was done to limit MacArthur's advance to the Yalu River. The JCS continued to defer to the Far East commander. Responding to their communication of November 8 raising the possibility of reexamining the American mission in Korea, MacArthur stated his belief that "it would be fatal to weaken the fundamental and basic policy of the United States to destroy all resisting armed forces in Korea and bring that country into a unified and free nation." To give up any portion of North Korea to the aggression of the Chinese Communists, he added, "would be the greatest defeat of the free world in recent times."[53]

Faced with such a grim analysis of American options in Korea, the JCS, along with other members of the NSC, reaffirmed in November the discretionary power they had given to MacArthur in September and October. The CIA even concluded that while the commitment of Chinese Communist forces, with Soviet assistance, indicated that Moscow was willing to risk a general war in Korea, it "was not probable" that UN attacks south of the Yalu would alone trigger such action. MacArthur was thus instructed not to attack Manchuria; otherwise the participants agreed that no change would be made in the general directives. Except for attacking Manchuria, he would be free to act as he saw fit. At the same time, the Department of State would investigate the possibility of negotiating with the Chinese Communists.[54]

Following the NSC meeting of November 9, the administration tried again to reassure China that it had no hostile aims against that country. In the UN the United States joined Britain and France and three other countries in sponsoring a Security Council resolution stating that it was "the policy of the United Nations to hold the Chinese frontier inviolate and fully to protect legitimate Chinese and Korean interests in the frontier zone." Less than a week later President Truman remarked that the United States had no designs on China's border or any desire to expand the war. But with the Chinese having apparently withdrawn from the war and with MacArthur's discretionary power reaffirmed, there was nothing to prevent the Far East commander from resuming his drive northward, which he did toward the end of the month.[55]

A sense of despair hung over policy makers in Washington and among America's European allies as MacArthur made plans to resume the offensive. Few if any within the administration wanted to expand the war into a global confrontation involving the Soviet Union as well as Communist China. They realized that the entry of Chinese troops into the fighting could change the whole complexion of the war, and there was growing uncertainty as to what the Peking government (and Moscow) might do if the UN forces should advance to the Yalu. Also, the war diverted attention from the difficult task of rebuilding Europe and preventing the spread of communism on that continent. Yet the war had become a test of wills between the Communist and non-Communist worlds. America's standing in the Far East and its commitment to democratic forces everywhere were on the line.[56]

Of America's allies, the British were particularly anxious to bring about a quick diplomatic solution to the war. While London had gone along with the United States policy in Korea, it had preferred a different policy, one that would have exchanged recognition of the Peking government and its seating in the UN for an end to Korean hostilities. It had proposed a cease-fire along these lines in July, only to have its efforts rebuffed by Washington. In November it was concerned about the rapid escalation of the war now that the Chinese had evidently committed their armed forces into the conflict. It was also disturbed by the fact that the war might deflect the interests and resources of the West from the more urgent problem of European defense against Soviet attack. Newsman Howard K. Smith reported from London that British attitudes toward the United States had not been so testy and jaundiced for several years. Still recalling the saber-rattling and talk of preventive war by Navy Secretary Matthews and others, London had decided at the highest levels that Washington must avoid war with China at all costs. It thus opposed any action, such as a UN condemnation of Chinese aggression, that might make it more difficult for Peking to withdraw from the war without loss of face.[57]

In an effort to reassure England and America's other allies that it, too, wanted to contain the war and bring about an early end to hostilities, the administration rejected a proposal supported by the JCS that would have allowed American planes to pursue enemy aircraft across the Manchurian border. A number of administration officials, including Secretary of State Acheson, also supported the British plan to create a buffer zone on each side of the Yalu River. But as already noted, the National Security Council, at its meeting of November 9, took no action on the proposal, merely restating the discretionary power it had already given MacArthur. MacArthur was vehemently opposed to the concept of a buffer zone, comparing the plan to the agreement at the Munich Conference of 1938, where the British and French had tried to appease Adolph Hitler by ceding the Sudeten region of Czechoslovakia to Germany.[58]

Even though the plan and similar ones like it continued to receive considerable support in the United States during the next two weeks, Secretary of State Acheson tried to discourage London from pressing its proposal. He pointed out the difficulty of securing agreement on a demilitarized zone on both sides of the border, and he commented on the need to prevent the zone from being used as a staging area for the further buildup of Chinese forces. Moreover, Acheson told British Foreign Minister Ernest Bevin that while the United States would do nothing to provoke the Chinese, their invasion could not simply be ignored. "[I]t may become necessary, at an early date," he remarked, "to permit UN aircraft to defend themselves in the airspace over the Yalu River to the extent of permitting hot pursuit of attacking enemy aircraft up to two or three minutes' flying time into Manchurian airspace."[59]

The lull in the fighting, which continued until the last week in November, found the British still trying to gain American backing for the concept of a demilitarized zone between Manchuria and Korea. "I still feel most strongly," Bevin wrote Acheson on November 23, "that my suggestions for a demilitarised area offer the best chance of bringing the conflict to a speedy conclusion." But the next day MacArthur launched his "final offensive," which he promised would have American troops home by Christmas but which soon turned into a debacle.[60]

In effect the United States had lost the opportunity to prevent a dangerous escalation of the fighting. As Secretary Acheson later lamented, the White House "missed its last chance to halt the march to disaster in Korea."[61] This happened not because the administration officials were unfearful of the possibility of an escalation of the fighting involving, possibly, the Soviet Union as well as the Chinese. If there was one theme consistent throughout American policy following MacArthur's landing at Inchon in September, it was the uncertainty over Chinese (and Soviet) intentions with respect to Korea. On the same day that MacArthur launched his invasion, in fact, and before the Chinese began their massive attack, a National Intelligence Estimate prepared by the CIA concluded that available evidence "was not conclusive as to whether or not the Chinese Communists are as yet committed to a full-scale offensive effort."[62] The JCS, the Department of State, and the Department of Defense all sought some kind of political settlement to the war involving negotiations rather than a full-scale military effort. But no one in the administration was willing to push very hard for a demilitarized zone as proposed by Bevin or any other plan that might have reassured the Chinese of the UN's good intentions. To make such a proposal would have involved a fight with General MacArthur, which no one was yet prepared to make. Even more important, administration officials in Washington were just as guilty of hubris as was MacArthur in Tokyo. While

uncertain of Communist intentions in Korea and while preferring a political settlement to the war, the White House and the
Pentagon wanted to believe, and did believe, MacArthur's
statement that military victory was just a few weeks away.

NOTES

1. James F. Schnabel, *Policy and Direction: The First Year, The
   United States Army in the Korean War* (Washington, D. C., 1972),
   111–114.
2. *Ibid.*, 139–40; David Rees, *Korea: The Limited War* (New York,
   1964), 78.
3. Schnabel, *Policy and Direction*, 146–49.
4. Quoted in Courtney Whitney, *MacArthur: His Rendezvous with
   History* (New York, 1955), 343–44 and 348–50. See also Douglas
   MacArthur, *Reminiscences* (New York, 1964), 348–51.
5. Schnabel, *Policy and Direction*, 149–50; James F. Schnabel and
   Robert J. Watson, *The History of the Joint Chiefs of Staff*, III, *The
   Korean War* (unpublished manuscript, National Archives, 1978),
   213.
6. MacArthur to JCS, September 8, 1950, Box 15, Selected Records
   Relating to the Korean War. See also MacArthur, *Reminiscences*, 351–52.
7. Schnabel, *Policy and Direction*, 154; Joseph C. Goulden, *Korea:
   The Untold Story of the War* (New York, 1982), 198–99.
8. Schnabel, *Policy and Direction*, 173–77; Rees, *Korea: The Limited
   War*, 85–88.
9. *Ibid.*
10. Russell F. Weigley, *The American Way of War: A History of United
    States Military Strategy and Policy* (New York, 1973), 387–88.
11. *Ibid.*, 386–87.
12. David M. Oshinsky, *A Conspiracy So Immense: The World of Joe
    McCarthy* (New York, 1983), 197–98; James T. Patterson, *Mr. Re-
    publican: A Biography of Robert A. Taft* (Boston, 1972), 455; Ron-
    ald J. Caridi, *The Korean War and American Politics: The
    Republican Party as a Case Study* (Philadelphia, 1968), 65.
13. Caridi, *The Korean War and American Politics*, 65; *New
    Yorker*, 26 (September 30, 1950), 86–88; *Nation*, 171 (September
    23, 1950), 263; *New Republic*, 123 (September 25, 1950), 3.
14. *Life*, 29 (September 25, 1950), 34; *New Yorker*, 26 (September 30,
    1950), 86–93; *New Republic*, 123, (October 16, 1950), 3.

15. *New Republic,* 123 (September 25, 1950), 5–7; *New Yorker,* 26 (September 30, 1950), 86–93; *Life,* 29 (October 9, 1950), 38; *Nation,* 171 (September 23, 1950), 257.

16. *Commonweal,* 52 (October 6, 1950), 621; *ibid.,* 53 (October 13, 1950), 3; *Life,* 29 (October 9, 1950), 38; *Nation,* 171 (September 23, 1950), 257.

17. Robert J. Donovan, *Tumultuous Years: The Presidency of Harry S. Truman, 1949–1953* (New York, 1982), 277.

18. *Ibid.*

19. Directive to the Commander of the United Nations Forces in Korea, September 27, 1950, attached to Marshall to Truman, September 27, 1950, Box 243, President's Secretary File, Truman Papers; *FR,* 1950, VII, 781–82 and 792–93; Schnabel, *Policy and Direction,* 179–81.

20. *FR,* 1950, VII, 826; Dean Acheson, *Present at the Creation: My Years in the State Department* (New York, 1969), 453–55; Rees, *Korea: The Limited War,* 100.

21. *Yearbook of the United Nations,* 1950 (New York, 1951), 264–66; Schnabel and Watson, *The History of the Joint Chiefs of Staff,* III, *The Korean War,* 213.

22. William Whitney Stueck, Jr., *The Road to Confrontation: American Policy Toward China and Korea, 1947–1950* (Chapel Hill, N. C., 1981), 227–28 and 234–36; *Nation,* 171 (October 7, 1950), 303–304.

23. *FR,* 1950, VII, 742, 765, 791, 795–96, and 851.

24. *Ibid.,* 864–65.

25. Harry S. Truman, *Years of Trial and Hope: Memoirs* (New York, 1956), 462–63.

26. David S. McLellan, *Dean Acheson: The State Department Years* (New York, 1976), 211–12.

27. Rees, *Korea: The Limited War,* 111–12 and 123–28; Schnabel, *Policy and Direction,* 193–97, 202-10, and 215-32.

28. *FR,* 1950, VII, 933–38 and 980–91; Schnabel and Watson, *The History of the Joint Chiefs of Staff,* III, *The Korean War,* 258–59.

29. Truman, *Years of Trial and Hope,* 413–414; Caridi, *The Korean War and American Politics,* 77–78 and 93; John W. Spanier, *The Truman-MacArthur Controversy and the War* (Cambridge, Mass., 1959), 104–13.

30. *New Republic,* 123 (October 9, 1950), 3; *ibid.* (October 30, 1950), 7; *New York Times,* November 11, 1950; Caridi, *The Korean War and American Politics,* 94.

31. Thomas C. Reeves, *The Life and Times of Joe McCarthy: A Biography* (New York, 1982), 332–33.

32. Donovan, *The Tumultuous Years,* 284–85.
33. Robert H. Ferrell (ed.), *Off the Record: The Private Papers of Harry S. Truman* (New York, 1980), 200.
34. *FR,* 1950, VII, 948–62; Truman, *Years of Trial and Hope,* 416–18.
35. Truman, *Years of Trial and Hope,* 419–22; Stueck, Jr., *The Road to Confrontation,* 238–39; Spanier, *The Truman-MacArthur Controversy and the Korean War,* 114–228; *FR,* 1950, VII, 1025–26.
36. *FR,* 1950, VII, 915; Goulden, *Korea: The Untold Story,* 274–77.
37. *FR,* 1950, VII, 901–902 and 921; Acheson, *Present at the Creation,* 451–52.
38. Allen S. Whitney, *China Crosses the Yalu: The Decision to Enter the Korean War* (Stanford, Calif., 1960), 114–28; *FR,* 1950, VII, 944.
39. *Nation,* 171 (October 28, 1950), 385–88; *New Republic,* 123 (October 30, 1950), 7; *Time,* 56 (November 6, 1950), 19.
40. *Nation,* 171 (September 23, 1950), 257; *Atlantic Monthly,* 186 (September 1950), 4, 6, and 8: *New Yorker,* 26 (October 21, 1950), 23.
41. *FR,* 1950, VII, 1023–26; Clubb to Dean Rusk, November 7, 1950, Box 4262, Records of the Department of State, RG 59, 795a.5/11-750.
42. Acheson, *Present at the Creation,* 463–64; Truman, *Years of Trial and Hope,* 426–27.
43. Quotation in Schnabel, *Policy and Direction,* 240–41.
44. MacArthur to JCS, November 6, 1950, Box 15, Selected Records Relating to the Korean War.
45. Schnabel and Watson, *The History of the Joint Chiefs of Staff,* III, *The Korean War,* 274–76.
46. *FR,* 1950, VII, 1078–85 and 1101–1106.
47. *Ibid.,* 1075–76.
48. *Time,* 56 (November 13, 1950), 26–27.
49. Richard M. Fried, *Men Against McCarthy* (New York, 1976), 118–21; *New Republic,* 123 (November 20, 1950), 3; *Time,* 56 (November 13, 1950), 19; *ibid.* (November 20, 1950), 20–21.
50. *Nation,* 171 (November 25, 1950), 472–73; Fried, *Men Against McCarthy,* 110–40.
51. *New Republic,* 123 (November 20, 1950), 7.
52. *FR,* 1950, VII, 1097–98, 1101–1106, and 1117–22.
53. *Ibid.,* 1107–1108.
54. Schnabel and Watson, *The History of the Joint Chiefs of Staff,* III, *The Korean War,* 304–305; Truman, *Years of Trial and Hope,* 432–33.

55. Schnabel, *Policy and Direction,* 248–50.
56. *Nation,* 171 (November 25, 1950), 474; *New Yorker,* 26 (December 9, 1950), 67.
57. *FR,* 1950, VII, 1032–33, 1050–53, 1067, and 1138–40; Schnabel and Watson, *The History of the Joint Chiefs of Staff,* III, *The Korean War,* 306; *Nation,* 171 (November 18, 1950), 458.
58. Goulden, *Korea: The Untold Story of the War,* 312–16.
59. *FR,* 1950, VII, 1145–46 and 1205. See also Leon D. Epstein, *Britain —Uneasy Ally* (Chicago, 1954), 216–17.
60. *FR,* 1950, VII, 1217–18.
61. Acheson, *Present at the Creation,* 466–67.
62. *FR,* 1950, VII, 1220–22.

CHAPTER 4

The Chinese Communist Intervention

The Chinese invasion into North Korea, which began sometime between November 25 and 28—within days after MacArthur had begun his "home by Christmas" offensive—tore MacArthur's advance apart and led to an entirely new war. Instead of a conflict that had as its purpose the reunification of Korea under UN auspices, the war became a holding action, an effort to contain the Communist advance, or, at least, to give the UN forces an opportunity to withdraw from Korea with honor. While UN forces were eventually able to stop the Chinese and the war settled into one of attrition, roughly along the 38th parallel, the month of December was one of the grimmest for the United States and its allies since the end of World War II.

The first two days of MacArthur's offensive went well enough. The attack was planned so that the Eighth Army would strike on a broad front northward in the west and center while X Corps in the east would move in a northwest direction to cut off the enemy's supply lines. Between the two forces lay the high mountainous spine that cut vertically across the Korean peninsula. This meant a gap of as much as fifty air miles between the Eighth Army and X Corps, but MacArthur believed sufficient communication could be maintained between the two forces so as not to jeopardize them.

Almost without opposition the Eighth Army advanced up to eight miles in the far west, while elements of X Corps to the east advanced northward toward the Yalu River. But then the Chinese struck in force along both fronts, threatening to turn the Eighth Army's right flank in the west and cutting off the First

NOVEMBER, 1950 TO JANUARY, 1951

U.S.S.R.

Vladivostok

C H I N A
(MANCHURIA)

Tumen R.

Chongjin

Chinese Intervention
November, 1950

Hyesanjin

Yalu R. Chosan

Iwon

Sinuiju

N O R T H

K O R E A

Hungnam

SEA OF
JAPAN

Pyongyang ★

Wonsan

U.N. evacuations
Dec. 5-15, 1950

Tongchon

38th parallel

Ongjin

Jan 24,
1951

Seoul ★

☐ Controlled by U.N.
— Communist advances
▨ Controlled by
   Communists

S O U T H
K O R E A

YELLOW

SEA

Taejon

Kunsan

Pohang

0   300

Mokpo   Sunchon

Pusan

JAPAN

Miles

Marine Division at the Chosin Reservoir in the east. The Second
Infantry Division was cut to pieces, losing all its guns and most
of its transport and suffering 80 percent casualties. The ROK II
Corps also came under heavy fire in the area of Tokchon on the
Taedong River. Efforts by Turkish and British forces to relieve
the ROK troops were blocked by repeated Chinese ambushes
and concentrated Chinese fire.[1]

By December 4 UN forces were in full retreat. Plans to hold the North Korean capital of Pyongyang were abandoned, and the city was quickly recaptured by the Communists. Moving usually at night in human wave attacks, yelling and blowing bugles and loud whistles, the Chinese terrified the UN forces and inflicted heavy casualties even as they took enormous losses themselves. But the Marines at the Chosin River were able to break out of their trap and to join the rest of the X Corps at Hungnam on the east coast, where the evacuation of the corps was completed by Christmas. "For the first time in its military experience," *Life* reported while the evacuation was under way, "the U. S. faced a problem such as Britain faced in the historic withdrawal from Gallipoli, Dunkirk, and Greece."[2]

President Truman reacted to this sudden turn of events by convening a special meeting of the National Security Council at the White House on November 28. The session was as somber as any that one could recall. General Bradley read from a cablegram from General MacArthur in which MacArthur said that the Chinese invasion presented his command with an entirely new war. Secretary Acheson remarked that the Chinese attack had moved the United States very much closer to a general war. Everyone at the White House was troubled and angered by the fact that MacArthur had badly misjudged the capacity and willingness of China to invade Korea.[3]

As a result of the meeting, the administration all but abandoned its objective of bringing about the political reunification of Korea through military means. Instead, the NSC agreed that the White House should not allow itself to be pulled into any war with China and that no new directive should be given to MacArthur in addition to the one of the previous September that he continue fighting the Chinese Communists as long as feasible. Maintaining that the Soviet Union had always been behind every move of aggression, Acheson argued that the United States had to realize that it faced the Russians around the world. America's great objective in Korea, he concluded, must be to hold an area, terminate the fighting, turn over some region to the Republic of Korea, and get out so that it could go ahead with building up its own strength and that of Europe.[4]

Europe or Asia? This perennial question of Cold War diplomacy and American politics was thrashed out anew as Americans and Europeans sought to evaluate the short- and long-term consequences of the Chinese intervention and the subsequent UN military disaster. At home and abroad the collapse of MacArthur's offensive produced serious diplomatic and political problems. "There is no doubt that confidence in General Douglas MacArthur, even on Capitol Hill, has been shaken badly as a result of the events of the last few days," wrote James Reston of *The New York Times* on November 30. "Similarly, there is no doubt that the United States leadership in the Western world has been damaged by President Truman's acceptance of the bold MacArthur offensive."[5]

In the United States MacArthur was assailed mostly for the poor planning and lack of good intelligence behind his Thanksgiving offensive. Several of his sharpest critics made the point that had he concentrated his forces instead of dividing and then spreading them over a 350-mile front, the Chinese offensive might have been contained. Others blamed the problem of inadequate intelligence on the fact that since early in World War II MacArthur had relied on his own intelligence organizations rather than on regular intelligence services. The failure of MacArthur's own people to forecast the Chinese offensive, his critics pointed out, was their second big mistake, the first having been their failure to anticipate North Korea's original aggression.

In Europe MacArthur was regarded more as a symbol of what was wrong in American foreign policy. The UN commander was thus bitterly accused of wanting to plunge the United States and its allies into a major Asiatic war that would leave Europe virtually undefended. Europeans remained terribly afraid that the Korean War might balloon into a worldwide confrontation between East and West, most of which would be fought on their continent. They also nursed other grievances, mainly having to do with Washington's failure to consult them often enough.[6]

The rumblings of discontent in Europe became louder after MacArthur permitted Syngman Rhee to establish administrative authority in the liberated areas of North Korea in direct contravention of a UN decision that only the UN should control those areas. But they reached a crescendo on November 30, when President Truman raised the possibility of using nuclear weapons in Korea. The JCS had been studying this very question since at least November 20, even before MacArthur's Thanksgiving offensive and the Chinese counteroffensive. Although they had not reached any decision on the subject, at his regular press conference on November 30, Truman stated that the United States would use every weapon at its disposal to meet the military situation in Korea. When a reporter asked the President whether that would include the atomic bomb, he responded, "That includes every weapon we have." When asked again whether he meant that there was active consideration about using the atomic bomb, Truman replied that there had "always been active consideration of its use." Later in the news conference he even indicated that, as with other weapons, the military commander in the field would decide whether to employ nuclear weapons.[7]

Apparently Truman never meant what he said, intending his remarks merely as a warning to the Chinese and the Soviet Union not to escalate the war in Korea. Even so, western Europe was shocked and outraged. Newspapers in Stockholm, Rome, and Vienna joined others in London and Paris in condemning the President's statement. In Vienna the story had the lead spot in all the morning newspapers, while in Rome one paper even reported that the Tokyo bomber command was ready to take off with an atomic bomb within an hour after receiving the order from Washington. Newsman Howard K. Smith referred to the European reaction as "one of the most amazing political upheavals in Europe since the war."[8]

In England Prime Minister Clement Attlee was virtually forced to go to Washington in protest, so great was the public reaction against the President's press conference. The London *Times* best articulated the disaffection of the British—and, for that matter, most other western Europeans—when it lashed out against the White House for making momentous decisions on such matters as using atomic weapons without first consulting its allies. "The Administration has taken decisions based less on rightness of policy than to keep Republicans in a cooperative mood," the *Times* also remarked. "Misgivings of other countries about American policy in Korea have been largely muffled because the United States has supplied such a great proportion of the troops; but the time for silence has ended."[9]

In the House of Commons a debate on foreign policy was interrupted by the news of Truman's statement. Hurried conferences were called, and a Labor member of Parliament drafted a letter to Attlee demanding that British troops be withdrawn from Korea if the atomic bomb was used. Within two hours the letter was signed by 150 Laborites. But Conservatives also spoke out against American policy. "The voice of Britain must be heard with greater authority," one Tory member, R. A. Butler, called out to the government benches. "This country must exert its influence to avoid war with China." He and others proposed that Attlee proceed at once to see Truman. With his own party in revolt and the opposition party gaining momentum, the prime minister called an emergency meeting of his cabinet, after which he declared that he would go to the United States. The decision was widely hailed throughout Europe. The visit to London of French Prime Minister René Pleven, who had just received an overwhelming vote of confidence for his foreign policy of "preventing the [Korean] conflict from spreading," was taken by some observers to mean that Attlee would represent all of western Europe.[10]

By the time that Attlee arrived in Washington, the administration felt it had to offer some plan for extricating UN forces from Korea without appearing to be run out of the country by the Communists. The situation in Korea seemed even more dangerous than it had been three months earlier when the Pusan perimeter was under attack. The possibility of UN troops being driven off the peninsula with a large loss of life was real. In Tokyo General MacArthur began preparations for a possible evacuation by sea of American troops in North Korea, while in Washington Secretary of State Acheson proposed to General Bradley the possibility of a cease-fire—probably along the 38th parallel—which could form the basis for negotiations to end the conflict. Otherwise Acheson feared the Korean conflict might escalate into a larger conflict with China, in which case he was afraid that many of America's allies would desert the United States and deal directly with the Soviet Union in a bid to end hostilities.[11]

As a result of his talks with President Truman, conducted during the first two weeks of December, Prime Minister Attlee was able to straighten out some of the misgivings that had developed between the United States and its European allies over Korea. He was also able to moderate some of the passion that had been generated as a result of Truman's press conference. But the British prime minister returned to London with far less than he had hoped to achieve.

As soon as the talks started, the British made the argument that the UN's position in Korea was so weak and precarious that the United States had no choice but to negotiate with China. If the United States became involved with China, they claimed, it would have an adverse effect on opinion in the United States, Europe, and Asia. What Peking wanted was a diplomatic recognition by the United States, a settlement of the Formosa question, and a seat at the United Nations, none of which were unreasonable demands. Attlee also conveyed to Truman Europe's feeling that MacArthur was "running the show" in Korea and that the other partnership countries were generally being ignored. The British even proposed some sort of committee to direct the war, an idea that met a cold reception from the Americans.[12]

Responding to the British and keeping his own reservations about the war to himself, Acheson denied that the UN was defeated in Korea. He also warned that the United States would not accept a surrender in the Far East to satisfy its allies and then cooperate with them in Europe. Americans demanded that the United States be vigorous everywhere. Furthermore, if the United States accepted surrender, Japan could not be expected to stay with the West. If the United States surrendered, it would be conceding that the Soviet Union and China were the most powerful forces in the Far East, and, as a result, all Asians would hurry to make their best deal with the Communists.[13]

In the final communiqué of the summit conference, Truman stressed his hope that world conditions would never require the use of the atomic bomb, and he promised to keep the prime minister informed at all times if developments warranted a change. Attlee was thus able to take back with him assurances from Truman that he did not anticipate using nuclear weapons in Korea. But this was not the partnership Attlee had sought. Also, on the question of Washington's relations with Peking, the Americans and British remained far apart; the United States would not bargain recognition, Formosa, or a seat at the UN for a cease-fire in Korea. As far as the administration was concerned, there could be no thought of appeasement, which would amount to rewarding aggression.[14]

Certainly this was the policy the United States pursued at the United Nations, where efforts were already under way to bring about a negotiated settlement to the war. Even under allied coaxing the American delegation at Lake Success (the UN's temporary home on Long Island) refused to budge from its position that an acceptable cease-fire would have to precede negotiations on any other Far Eastern question. For their part the Chinese insisted that their claim to Formosa and a seat at the UN must be part of any cease-fire proposal. With both sides assuming intractable positions, no meeting of the minds was possible.[15]

The PRC was represented at the United Nations for the first time, having been previously invited to send a delegation in order to discuss the Formosan question. Arriving in New York almost at the same time that the Chinese halted MacArthur's offensive, the Chinese delegation, headed by General Hsui-ch'uan Wu, was greeted warmly at the airport by Soviet Ambassador Jacob Malik, but its presence at the UN caused considerable outrage among the China lobby and its spokesmen. "In one weekend," *Time* commented, "the Chinese Reds had punched a 20-mile hole in the U.N. line in Korea and an even bigger hole in the diplomatic front resisting the admission of Red China to the U.N." Nor did Wu's blistering language against the United States, which he accused of instigating the Korean War in order to conceal its invasion of Formosa and to further "its fanatical design of dominating Asia and the world," auger well for successful negotiations on Korea.[16]

The debate over Korea centered in two resolutions introduced on December 11 by a thirteen-member Asian–Arab bloc led by India. The first of these attempted to mollify the United States by establishing a three-man committee to seek a cease-fire without prior conditions, as the United States insisted. The second tried to appease the Communists by calling for a conference on Far Eastern affairs to deal with such matters as the China question.[17]

Unalterably opposed to the second resolution, which

smacked of appeasement, the administration even had reservations about the first. Many in Washington were afraid that a
cease-fire according to the terms of the proposal would give the
Chinese time to build up their forces for another thrust southward. As one State Department official put it, "[t]here was no
provision preventing movement of the Chinese Communist
units in North Korea in such a way as to regroup to strengthen
their position." The Pentagon distrusted the resolution for
much the same reason, fearing a buildup of Chinese personnel
along the front free of air or naval interdiction. On the day after
the Asia–Arab delegates introduced their resolutions, the JCS
listed their terms for a cease-fire. These included the establishment of a cease-fire commission by the UN with unlimited access to the whole of Korea, the creation of a twenty-mile
demilitarized zone with the southern line following generally
the line of the 38th parallel, and an exchange of prisoners on a
one-for-one basis. No cease-fire should be agreed to, the JCS
emphasized, that did not provide for a competent cease-fire
commission.[18]

In the end, however, the White House concluded that it had
little choice but to endorse the resolution establishing a cease-
fire committee while voting against the proposal calling for a
conference on Far Eastern affairs. Defense Secretary Marshall
understood the dilemma facing the United States. A cease-fire
could stop American air and naval activity and permit a Chinese buildup. "If we objected, they would say that we had not
lived up to the cease-fire. On the other hand, if we oppose a
cease-fire, our friends would think that we were objecting to a
peaceful solution." With American support the General Assembly overwhelmingly approved the cease-fire resolution. Only
Russia's Jacob Malik objected, insisting on the withdrawal of all
UN forces from Korea.[19]

The next day a three-man commission was appointed,
headed by the General Assembly's president, Nasrollah En-
tezam of Iran. The United States indicated it would be willing
to negotiate with the Chinese provided discussions were limited to Korea. A few days later Secretary Acheson laid down
conditions for a cease-fire very similar to those the Joint Chiefs
of Staff had approved earlier. Following a cessation of all hostilities, a demilitarized zone approximately twenty miles wide

would be established across all of Korea with the southern line following the 38th parallel. All ground forces would remain in position, and there would be no reinforcement or replacement units. An exchange of prisoners of war would take place on a one-for-one basis. A UN commission with free and unlimited access to the whole of Korea would be established to supervise the cease-fire.[20]

The Chinese maintained that the establishment of a three-member cease-fire commission was a hoax perpetrated by the United States, which substituted the establishment of a commission for a broader negotiating conference to consider all the problems of the Far East. General Wu refused even to meet with the commission and returned to Peking where, on December 21, the Chinese announced their rejection of the thirteen-power proposal, saying all actions taken by the United Nations without Chinese participation were illegal.[21]

By this time, UN forces had retreated to a defensive line approximating the 38th parallel, and the Truman administration had determined to remain in Korea as long as possible. It also had taken a number of steps to mobilize the economy and to prepare the American people for the fighting that lay ahead. Making full use of the Defense Production Act passed earlier, it sought additional legislation to put the economy on a wartime footing. On December 15 Truman delivered a radio and television address to the nation in which he announced his intention to declare a state of national emergency the following day. In addition, he announced plans to increase defense production, to expand the armed forces, and to establish wage and price controls. On December 16 the President issued his declaration of a national emergency, and the White House set up the Office of Defense Mobilization to direct and coordinate the government's mobilization effort.[22]

To shore up his support on Capitol Hill, the President also consulted with congressional leaders from both parties. At a White House meeting on December 13, Truman disclosed his plans to declare a state of national emergency and to mobilize the country for war, including the implementation of price controls and wage stabilization measures. The Republicans reacted coolly to these proposals. Truman tried to reassure Senator Robert Taft and other Republican leaders that he would not order an all-out mobilization so long as the United States did not become involved in an all-out war. But this failed to satisfy the Republicans, who also wondered why a proclamation of national emergency was necessary in the first place. What the country needed more than any declaration, Taft thought, was a definite program of military preparedness the American people could understand.[23]

Even as the administration was lobbying Congress and appealing to the American public, however, it continued to debate the next steps it should pursue under the changed circumstances of war. Although the White House had made clear its determination to remain in Korea as long as possible, a realistic assessment of the conflict by the middle of December revealed just how precarious the UN position was. Questions continued to be raised, therefore, about America's military commitment in Korea. Ironically, the State Department gave higher priority to continuing the fighting than the Pentagon. State Department officials believed that American prestige in the world would suffer a severe blow if the United States was driven from Korea, while the Defense Department and JCS were more concerned with saving enough troops from Korea to defend Japan.

At a high-level meeting of the Defense Department on December 19 that was also attended by Assistant Secretary of State Dean Rusk, Defense Secretary Marshall emphasized the extreme vulnerability of Japan in the event of a sudden Soviet attack. The American people, he commented, understood the ever-present Soviet danger in Europe, but they did not have the same appreciation of Japan's total inability to respond to Soviet aggression. In contrast, Rusk made the point that the United States could not abandon twenty million South Koreans to Communism. A withdrawal from Korea would also cast the United States as an unreliable ally, reduce America's military prestige, and increase Communist China's military and political prestige.[24]

In other words, both the Departments of State and Defense were in agreement as to cease-fire arrangements if they could be worked out with the enemy. But in the interim the State Department was for continuing the war at least at its present level, while the Defense Department wanted to wind it down and, perhaps, withdraw entirely from Korea. In effect, the two agencies of government had assumed positions remarkably similar to those prior to the war when the State Department had stressed the importance of Korea in terms of American credibility in the world and the Pentagon had favored a withdrawal from Korea on the basis of military imperatives. As of late December, the issues involved in the Korean War seemed much the same. But even in the case of the State Department, there was now no contemplation of absolute victory; that had disappeared with the Chinese invasion a month earlier.

In Japan, General MacArthur held a different view. He asked the JCS for all four of the National Guard divisions now in the United States in order to reinforce his position in Japan. It had been this request that had led to the meeting on December 19. Although no final decision was made at this meeting, on December 22 the Joint Chiefs informed MacArthur that no additional divisions would be sent to the Far East until the administration had decided on future courses of action. Less than a week later Marshall approved a JCS memorandum for MacArthur along much the same lines except that, in order to satisfy the State Department, language was included to emphasize the great political advantage of resisting in Korea as long as possible and inflicting maximum damage upon the enemy. The decision to evacuate Korea, the JCS stressed to MacArthur, "should not be based on political grounds; rather it should be based on our best military judgement as to whether or how long it is possible to maintain combat forces in Korea." Korea "is not the place to fight a major war," the JCS continued. Furthermore, the United States should not commit its "remaining available ground forces to action against Chinese Communist forces in Korea in face of the increased threat of general war."[25]

One can thus understand MacArthur's chagrin at the confusion of military and political considerations that went into his operational orders in Korea. The State Department wanted a stronger military effort in Korea than the Defense Department, and he was to maintain maximum military pressure, but no additional forces were to be assigned to him. He was not to win the war in any conventional sense, but neither was he to allow the enemy to claim victory in Korea.

MacArthur's reply to this latest directive was to ask for additional troops and other measures, which, he believed, could still bring about total victory. Specifically, he requested that he be allowed to blockade China, to destroy China's industrial capacity to wage war, and to employ Chinese Nationalist troops in Korea and for diversionary action against vulnerable areas of the Chinese mainland. "I believe that by the foregoing measures we could severely cripple and largely neutralize China's capabilities to wage aggressive war and thus save Asia from the engulfment otherwise facing it," MacArthur told the JCS. He understood completely the importance of preserving European security "but not to the point of accepting defeat anywhere else —an acceptance which I am sure could not fail to insure later defeat in Europe itself."[26]

During the next few weeks a sparring match took place between the JCS and the administration, on one hand, and MacArthur, on the other, that neither side won. On January 9 the JCS responded to MacArthur's message of December 30. The Joint Chiefs told the general that the retaliatory measures he recommended would be "given serious consideration," but they then went on to explain to him that most of them would not be adopted. First, there was little possibility of strengthening the UN effort in Korea. Second, a blockade of the Chinese coast, if undertaken, would have to await either a stabilization of the American position in Korea or an evacuation from Korea. Even then a naval blockade of China's coast would require negotiations with the British because of their extensive trade with China through Hong Kong. Third, no naval or air attacks on China would probably be authorized without a Chinese Communist attack on American forces outside of Korea. Lastly, it was against administration policy to employ Chinese Nationalist forces in Korea. Instead of being given authority to carry out retaliatory measures against China, MacArthur was thus instructed once more to defend against the enemy on successive positions, "inflicting maximum damage subject to primary consideration of the safety of your troops and your basic mission of protecting Japan."[27]

MacArthur was irate at his latest orders. He considered them a "booby trap" that offered two contradictory alternatives —successful resistance at some point in Korea would be desirable, but Korea was not the place to fight a major war. Respond-

ing again to the JCS, the general said that they could not have
it both ways. "As I have pointed out, under the extraordinary
limitations and conditions imposed upon the command in
Korea its military position is untenable, but it can hold for any
length of time up to its complete destruction if overriding political considerations so dictate." In his memoirs President Truman described himself as "deeply disturbed" by MacArthur's
communication. In effect the general told the President that
present policy as determined by the National Security Council
and the JCS and approved by Truman was not feasible. Secretary of State Acheson was even more upset. "[N]othing further
was needed," he later wrote, "to convince me that the General
was incurably recalcitrant and basically disloyal to the purposes
of his Commander-in-Chief."[28]

Yet MacArthur had not been given clear instructions. On
one hand, he was told that the world prestige of the United
States and the United Nations was at stake in Korea. It was
essential that he hold the line there as long as possible. On the
other hand, he was instructed that it was necessary for America's security interests to preserve his troops for use in Japan and
elsewhere. Which had higher priority? Nothing in the directives MacArthur received made this clear. To complicate matters even more, Truman emphasized to the JCS and members
of his administration that he was "unwilling to abandon the
South Koreans to be murdered."[29]

On January 12 the JCS gave MacArthur new instructions
approved by the President, which were hardly an improvement over earlier orders except that they were accompanied by
a series of actions that the UN Command might take against
China should it be forced to withdraw from Korea. Although
the list included three recommendations suggested by General
MacArthur in his December 30 message, only one, removal of
restrictions on Nationalist forces, was adopted without qualifica-
tion. Two others, a naval blockade and bombardment of Chinese territory, appeared as contingent possibilities; the fourth,
use of Nationalist forces in Korea, was omitted entirely. It cannot be emphasized too strongly that these were proposals only,
not directives, and had not even been approved by Defense
Secretary Marshall. Nevertheless, it is not too difficult to understand how MacArthur, given his world view and sense of priori-

ties, could interpret these recommendations as policy parameters within which he could still operate, even at this late date, to achieve a UN victory in Korea.[30]

Events of the previous two months, however, had changed the complexion of the war in a way that MacArthur could not understand. By the end of December and beginning of January the administration had firmly committed itself to a cease-fire and, for all practical purposes, had abandoned any thought of unifying Korea. But this decision had not been arrived at independent of the crosscurrents of public opinion and political pressures at home and abroad. Indeed, as UN forces had retreated southward in the icy month of December, Americans divided over foreign policy in a way they had not since Pearl Harbor. By the new year this "great debate" had been extended to include renewed consideration of the constitutional issues involved in formulating foreign policy and the related issue of stationing additional American forces in Europe. At the same time, the Truman administation had to contend with continuing and, indeed, growing European opposition to its conduct of foreign policy, particularly on the China question. Europeans fretted at what they regarded as the whimsical and mercurial nature of the American temperament and remained fearful that the Korean conflict would be expanded into a global war. The White House's efforts to placate public opinion at home, congressional opposition on Capitol Hill, and allied concerns in Europe strained the administration's political resources to their limits.

Almost all segments of American public opinion were shocked and disheartened by the tide of battle as winter approached in Korea. "[F]ew generations in the long history of Christendom have faced a darker prospect than our own," wrote *Commonweal.* "This prospect recalls the days of Augustine and 'The City of God,' written as the Roman Empire fell about him before the onslaught of the barbarians." For those who believed that President Truman and Secretary of State Acheson had courted disaster in Asia by their misdirected attention toward Europe, the retreat of UN forces toward the 38th parallel confirmed their worst fears. House and Senate Republicans overwhelmingly passed a resolution asking for Acheson's resignation and urging a thorough "housecleaning" of the State

Department. Senator McCarthy even spoke of impeaching President Truman.[31]

As in Europe, the figure of General MacArthur loomed large in the foreign policy debate that followed. Opponents of the general were accused of villifying him, and MacArthur's highly publicized views on the Communist threat were cited as gospel by those who would give him carte blanche to turn back the Red tide in Asia. *Life* even conducted a mock interview with the general to explain his views on Korea. "General MacArthur is not infallible—far from it," explained *Life*. "But his estimate of the actual situation in Korea, and his attitude toward the Communist aggressors, are in healthy contrast to the sick and fearful atmosphere of London, Washington and Lake Success."[32]

Liberal opinion could be just as harsh in condemning MacArthur as *Life* was in defending him. But the tide of sentiment in the United States deeply troubled the administration and was one reason it had taken such a firm stand in its earlier talks with the British on pursuing the war in Korea without concessions to the Peking government. As Acheson and Truman had told Prime Minister Attlee during their conversations, domestic political pressures had made it impossible for the United States to be "internationalist" in Europe and "isolationist" in Asia.[33]

In fact, there was influential sentiment in the United States to follow an isolationist policy both in Asia and Europe. Advocates of this view ranged from the right-wing publisher of the Chicago *Tribune,* Colonel Robert R. McCormick, who would defend the United States and possibly Canada and leave the rest of the world to its own fate, to former Ambassador Joseph P. Kennedy, who would add South America to the area he would protect. But the resurgent view that the United States should make itself as strong as possible at home and should be prepared to stand alone against foreign threats was most clearly articulated at the end of December in a speech by former President Herbert Hoover, in which Hoover outlined his "Gibraltar" concept of military defense based largely on air power. According to this view, the United States should strive for hemispheric and economic self-sufficiency, turning the Western Hemisphere into the "Gibraltar of Civilization," protected only by a cordon of ocean bases in the Pacific—Formosa, the Philippines, and Japan—and perhaps by England in the Atlantic.[34]

Dismissed by some as the mutterings of a failed leader rapidly growing senile, Hoover's remarks were, nevertheless, widely disseminated and received enormous press coverage, some critical, most favorable. The *New Republic* warned that if such a proposal as Hoover's was followed, it might lead Stalin to attack western Europe in 1951. "Just as our strategic abandonment of Korea led to the Korean War, so our strategic abandonment of Europe will lead at once to a world war." The highly respected editor of the Atlanta *Constitution,* Ralph McGill, stated that the former President's policy of "withdrawing nationally to an ivory tower over which he could hang armor plate . . . is national suicide." And the historian, Arthur Schlesinger, Jr., wrote in *The New York Times* that Hoover "merely demonstrate[d] once again his inability to learn by experience. On Oct. 27, 1917 he [argued] against sending American armies to France. He was clearly wrong in 1917 and 1940, and he is equally wrong now."[35]

What especially concerned these and other critics of Hoover's "Gibraltar" address was that it appeared to represent a much broader trend toward isolationism and against bipartisanship in foreign policy. Although President Truman referred to the former President's comments as nothing else but isolationism, the weight of public response to Hoover's remarks and those of others sharing similar views was overwhelmingly favorable, a fact that the *Nation* noted as representing "a widespread revival of blind isolationism" and *Commonweal* referred to as "a new surge of isolationism."[36]

Contributing to this growing isolationism was the speculation, which many Americans shared with Europeans, that the world was closer to a global conflict than at any other time since 1945. Not since the first days of the Korean conflict did so many Americans believe that World War III was imminent. Americans talked of being "A-bombed" and made civil defense preparations in case of war. Booklets were distributed on what to do if a nuclear attack took place. Bomb shelters were set up. Plans for evacuating city populations—and for feeding, clothing, and sheltering them—were started. Talk of "preventive war" was heard again, and sentiment grew for using nuclear weapons against the Communists. Two members of Montana's Roosevelt County draft board were even suspended by Selective Service Director Lewis B. Hershey after they announced that they would not draft any new men until the United States guaranteed to use the atomic bomb. The national commanders of the American Legion, Veterans of Foreign Wars, Disabled American Veterans, and Amvets wrote President Truman a joint letter urging him to give General MacArthur full authority to bomb Chinese bases in Manchuria, and Republican Presidential aspirant Harold Stassen called on the United Nations to demand that the Chinese agree to a cease-fire in Korea and to "A-bomb" targets in China if they refused.[37]

All this discourse was part of what *Life* labeled a "great debate on foreign policy that tugged at the nation's mind and soul." Stemming from America's involvement in Korea, the issues involved had built gradually over the summer and fall and had been joined in the November elections. But the current round of debate stemmed from remarks made soon afterward by Senator Taft, who asked, "Is Europe our first line of defense? Is it defendable at all?" and called for a thorough review of the Truman foreign policy. Widespread dismay at the latest war news from Korea after the Chinese invasion, the harping criticisms by America's west European allies, particularly on the China question, and their procrastination in rearming caused many Americans to ask similar questions and make similar demands. As a result, by the time Hoover delivered his "Gibraltar" address, he was assured a receptive audience.[38]

The great debate continued, however, long after Hoover made his statement. Throughout the winter and well into the spring of 1951 many of the same arguments that had been heard in December were still being made. The dialogue defied easy description. The administration was defended and attacked from the political left and political right; from those who agreed with Hoover's remarks in part, in whole, or not at all; from those who would orient the nation's foreign policy more toward Europe and those who would direct it more toward Asia; and from those who would avoid such a confrontation at almost any cost. Strange alliances sometimes appeared. The influential liberal journalist Walter Lippmann found himself sounding much like Hoover and Taft in writing about America's incapacity to defend against Soviet attack in the Eurasian heartland and about the need, therefore, to build up and defend the "North American citadel and arsenal workshop," a theory that the *New Republic*, which had helped launch his national career thirty-five years earlier, called "curious" and even dangerous.[39] In contrast, *Life*, which remained sharply critical of the administration's European-oriented policy, found kind words to say about President Truman and came to the White House's defense in speaking out against the drift in the United States toward isolationism, framing the essential question before Americans as being one of whether the country would support or abandon its allies.[40]

A new dimension was added to this dialogue when an earlier issue involving the constitutional powers of the President over foreign policy was raised once more by Republican opponents of the administration. This time, however, the doubts expressed had to do not only with the President's conduct of the war in Korea but with his authority to send American troops to Europe without congressional approval. The administration never equivocated from its position that the Executive had the requisite constitutional powers to order American troops abroad, whether it be to repulse aggression in Korea or to protect its interests and honor its obligations in Europe. But on both constitutional and strategic grounds Republicans in Congress, led by Senator Taft, challenged the White House and threatened to paralyze its conduct of foreign policy.

The son of former President and Chief Justice William Howard Taft, the Ohio senator was generally acknowledged in 1950 as the most powerful Republican in Washington. Highly respected by most of his Senate colleagues, he was regarded as a man of good sense and logical mind, who rejected the extremism of the Republican right, with which he was, nevertheless, closely associated. He frowned on "name-calling" against the Soviet Union by many of his fellow senators, which he thought was provocative and harmful to peace, and he often voted with more liberal Democrats and Republicans on key domestic issues, such as federal aid for housing and education.[41]

At the same time, Taft was a highly partisan politician who sought to make political capital out of the Red Scare in the United States. He also honestly believed that China had been lost to the Communists by the stupidity and treasonable actions of the State Department. He objected to the European orientation of Democratic foreign policy, and he argued that America's vital interests and moral obligations lay in Asia and the Far Pacific. Had the United States not withdrawn its troops from South Korea in 1949 and had it given ample warning to North Korea that it would repulse any invasion from above the 38th parallel, he was certain that "there never would have been such an attack by the North Koreans." Furthermore, he would rely on a navy and air force strong enough to deter Russians rather than send ground forces abroad.[42]

No less important than these other issues to Taft, however, was his commitment to defending what he considered the constitutional prerogatives of Congress in formulating and executing foreign policy. Although he had supported Truman's original decision to send American military forces to South Korea after the North Korean invasion, he also had serious reservations about the President's authority to do so without first consulting Congress. Even his initial support for American involvement had been couched in such a way as to make clear his assumption that Truman would act only with congressional approval. If the President would ask for a constitutional resolution approving the sending of air and naval forces into Korea, Taft had remarked on the Senate floor on June 28, he would vote for it. As the war continued, Taft became increasingly protective of Congress's place in formulating foreign policy. On January 5 he took the Senate floor to deliver a 10,000-word harangue against the administration in which he charged that Truman had "simply usurped authority—in violation of the laws and the Constitution—when he sent troops to Korea to carry out the resolution of the United Nations, in an undeclared war."[43]

In making his remarks, however, the Ohio senator was more concerned about the administration's plan to send additional American forces to Europe than he was about the war in Korea. Taft and other Republican congressmen were opposed to any large contingent of American soldiers going to Europe, much less without prior approval of Congress. Although the administration had decided in September to send more troops to Europe as part of a NATO army, Taft did not learn of this plan until November, and President Truman did not make the formal announcement until December 19. Having voted against the NATO pact in 1949, Taft reacted sharply to the proposal and took up his pen against it. To Arthur Vandenberg of Michigan he wrote, "the whole policy of building up very large land forces with the idea of throwing several million men into Europe in case of a Russian attack ought to be carefully studied." And to John Foster Dulles he added, "It seems to me that a large land force is of dubious value and that the defense of this country as well as the deterring of Russia rests far more on an all-powerful air force." Taft also argued, like Hoover and other critics of the administration, that since Europeans were unwilling to rearm, the United States should not assume the responsibility and cost of their defense.[44]

Taft's remarks to the Senate in January were an extension and refinement of these views except that the senator now also emphasized the constitutional issues involved in deploying American troops abroad without congressional authority. "The President has no power to agree to send American troops to fight in Europe," he argued in the Senate. "Congress by resolution . . . or by restriction in the appropriation bill providing the divisions required may finally determine the policy to be pursued."[45]

Taft's speech kept alive the foreign policy debate. Supporters of a strong NATO army and backers of Truman's policy in Korea came to the administration's defense. *The Nation* called Taft "a man without scruple" and an "isolationist" and noted that history was "replete" with more than a hundred cases where ground forces were used without prior congressional sanction, ranging from Thomas Jefferson's expedition against the Barbary pirates in 1802 to Woodrow Wilson's use of troops in Archangel more than a century later. Even critics of the administration took issue with Taft. Despite his serious reservations about the fighting in Korea, Walter Lippmann remarked, nevertheless, on Truman's decision to engage the North Koreans, "A 'usurpation' which the leader of the opposition offers publicly to legalize twenty-four hours later is not a heinous crime." Once again *Life* found itself also arguing the administration's case. Certain "fundamentals" of foreign policy must always be kept in mind, the popular weekly stated. "One of these fundamentals is the duty and power of the President to act for the U. S. in foreign affairs. His hands are America's hands. They must not be tied."[46]

Assuming the offensive, the White House prepared a lengthy memorandum on the powers of the President to send armed forces outside the United States. "Senator Taft's position," the statement read, "finds no support in the decided cases [on the issue of Presidential power as commander in chief], and none of the consequences in the practice of our Presidents from the time of George Washington down to the present day." The Taft position was contradicted by many authorities on the Presidency, including Taft's own father.[47]

Taft struck back, remarking that his father had noted the "power" of the President to send troops overseas, not his "right." Truman had lacked the constitutional authority in 1950 to commit American forces in Korea, just as he lacked the same authority now to send American troops to Europe. On this basis Taft gave his powerful support to a measure introduced by Kenneth Wherry of Nebraska on January 8 stating that it was the Senate's sense that no ground troops be sent to Europe for use by the North Atlantic Treaty Organization without congressional authority.[48]

Almost immediately the Wherry Resolution became the focal point of the foreign policy debate. Weeks and then months were taken up discussing the merits of sending American troops to Europe and arguing the constitutional questions involved. Not until April, when the Wherry Resolution was finally defeated and a compromise reached authorizing the sending of four American divisions to Europe, were these matters finally resolved. Even then there was included among the many provisions of the legislation one that stated that no additional ground forces should be sent to Europe "without further Congressional approval." Also, the Wherry Resolution was defeated only after two influential Democrats, Walter F. George of Georgia and Paul H. Douglas of Illinois, added their voices to the Republican demand that the President obtain congressional consent before sending any additional troops to Europe. Finally, while the issue of Korea was strangely absent from the debate over the Wherry Resolution, some of the sense of Congress on this subject was illustrated when Senator H. Alexander Smith of New Jersey and other Republicans almost succeeded in adding committee language to the resolution stating that "Congressional approval should be obtained of any policy requiring the assignment of American troops abroad."[49]

The entire debate over foreign policy, lasting from the end of 1950 into the spring of 1951, was watched closely in Europe and Canada. America's western allies were fearful of both the isolationist sentiment and talk of nuclear war that seemed to coexist in America. Many of them believed this reflected the capricious and unstable nature of the American character and the unreliability of American foreign policy. Apprehensive that the United States might retreat from its world responsibilities, just as it had after World War I, they remained even more afraid of a nuclear war between America and Russia in which, the Europeans believed, they would be its first victims. Seeking to resolve differences between East and West, they persisted in their protests against Washington's China policy. Although they continued to support the American position at the United Nations, they frequently did so reluctantly and made clear their strong objections to an American-sponsored resolution labeling China an "aggressor nation" even though they eventually voted for it. Lastly, they criticized American smugness and challenged the argument that the United States was carrying most of the responsibility for containing Communist expansion in the Far East.

James Reston of *The New York Times* sensed the attitude—and the frustration—of many of America's allies when he remarked in January that there "was something of a rebellion within the Western coalition against the past United States policy in the Far East."[50] The isolationist sentiments expressed by Hoover, Taft, and others were seen by America's coalition partners as indicating a lack of leadership on the United States' part. In England the *Manchester Guardian* thus reported that the British had "been thrown into sad depression by the tepid douches of Mr. Hoover and Senator Taft," while a correspondent for *The New Yorker* wrote from London that Hoover's remarks and similar "isolationist utterances" had "produced a wave of alarm here and across the channel," a statement borne out by press opinion throughout western Europe. At the same time, Europeans were disturbed that the constant beating of the American war drum and the careless talk of atomic warfare might put them at risk to a Soviet invasion or nuclear attack at a time when they were still unarmed. They also worried about General MacArthur's influence on American foreign policy, and they were afraid that Chiang Kai-shek on Formosa might be unleashed to attack the China mainland. "The Europeans are just plain scared," said a Parisian journalist, "that if the U. S. sent Chiang Kai-shek into the fight, Russia would introduce its air force and we would have a world war."[51]

Because of their concern about a world war largely fought on their soil, the west European governments encouraged a dialogue between Moscow and Washington. They were thus highly receptive to a Soviet proposal to hold Big Four talks involving the foreign ministers of Britain, France, the United States, and the Soviet Union. Plainly alarmed at the possibility of a rearmed West Germany, the Soviets had proposed such a meeting on November 3, and the western powers had replied with a counterproposal that the meeting be expanded to include all issues then in controversy. But while Secretary of State Acheson responded negatively to the Soviets' latest offer to "discuss other questions also, pertaining to Germany," the European reaction was much more positive. Both London and Paris interpreted the Soviet reply as encouragingly precise and more conciliatory than any other recent Russian statement. They were annoyed, therefore, at Washington's apparent unwillingness to try to resolve differences with Moscow. In contrast to many political leaders in Washington, who objected to the administration's foreign policy because it did not seem rigid enough, they protested that it was too rigid.[52]

European—and Canadian—displeasure with American policy became even more apparent when, at the United Nations, an open rift developed over an American resolution to brand China as an "aggressor nation" and to impose sanctions on it. The United States first proposed that the UN issue a strong resolution condemning the Chinese as aggressors shortly after that body reconvened at the beginning of January from a two-week recess. By this time the Cease-Fire Commission established in December had twice failed in its effort to negotiate a settlement of the Korean War. The Chinese simply refused to negotiate unless their claims to Formosa and a seat at the

United Nations were made part of any cease-fire proposal.[53] By this time also, the Chinese had launched another major offensive, driving across the 38th parallel, forcing UN forces into full retreat, and retaking Seoul on January 4. Maintaining that China obviously did not want a cease-fire and had "indicated its attitudes towards the efforts of the United Nations" by its offensive, the head of the American delegation, Warren Austin, announced that the United Nations should take the next logical step and formally charge Communist China with aggression. This might be followed by other measures, including the withdrawal of recognition by those countries still maintaining relations with Peking and even the imposition of sanctions.[54]

Every one of America's western allies objected to the American proposal, arguing that it would make negotiations with the Chinese even more difficult and might lead to Soviet involvement in the Korean War. The head of the Norwegian delegation told the Americans that the Asian nations would not support a resolution of aggression. The British and the French said much the same thing. In London a conference of Commonwealth prime ministers explicitly rejected the United States' China policy. "We must build a bridge between East and West," stated Canada's prime minister, Louis St. Laurent, and the other Commonwealth members agreed.[55]

Determined to avoid any action that might lead to sanctions and an expansion of the Korean War, the chief European nations, together with the British Commonwealth and an Asian–Arab group at Lake Success, backed another attempt at arranging a cease-fire, this time to be followed by an international conference on the Far East issues, as Peking had always demanded. Only if the PRC rejected this latest UN effort at ending the war would it be appropriate to consider a declaration of aggression. In principle the United States was against the latest proposal, which it considered to be fraught with great danger. To agree to a conference on Far East issues might suggest American willingness to accept Peking's claim to Formosa and a seat at the UN. Such apparent kowtowing to aggression would not only amount to appeasement, it would stir up domestic passions and lead to new charges that the administration was "soft" on communism.[56]

Still the White House could not simply ignore the advice of

its allies and the weight of opinion at the United Nations. Besides, Secretary of State Acheson anticipated that China might yet turn down another effort at peacemaking in the hope of gaining even greater concessions later, including prior admission to the UN and American withdrawal from Formosa. China's third rejection of a cease-fire, he believed, would strengthen allied solidarity and make it easier for Washington to brand China as an "aggressor nation." At the United Nations, therefore, the American delegation agreed to a formula for ending Korean hostilities that included an immediate cease-fire (which the United States wanted), to be followed by a conference on Far East problems (which Peking wanted).[57]

As the secretary of state had expected, domestic foes of the administration reacted to the news of the latest cease-fire proposal by accusing the White House "of ignominiously truckling" to the enemy. "The State Department seemed to see no opportunity for decisive action," *Time* added, "while the U. S. still had the big advantage of the atomic-bomb stockpile." In Congress the State Department was charged with having abandoned its announced position that the Chinese Communists would not "be rewarded for aggression" or be allowed to "shoot their way into the U.N." Even Democratic Senator Tom Connally of Texas, Chairman of the Senate Foreign Relations Committee, flayed the State Department because the American delegation at the UN had voted without consulting his committee.[58]

As Acheson had also anticipated, however, the Chinese—much to his relief—turned down the UN proposal. The secretary learned of the Chinese rejection while being questioned at a news conference about the administration's decision to participate in a Far East conference. In the middle of an embarrassing question over whether the administration's bowing to allied pressure on the meeting meant that the allies would control American policy when the conference took place, Acheson was handed the news of Peking's reply. Responding to the reporter asking the question, he said it now seemed to be academic. Then, smiling, he read aloud the wire service bulletin he had just received. Two hours later he issued a statement calling the counterproposals the Chinese had made totally unacceptable.[59]

China's rejection of the UN offer seemed firm enough. Peking stated that the UN proposal was still based on a cease-fire in Korea prior to negotiations on other essential questions. If a cease-fire came into effect before negotiations on these other matters had even been started, endless discussions might follow without any problems being resolved. Instead, China repeated earlier demands for negotiations prior to a cease-fire, which must include a seat for the PRC at the UN and the withdrawal of American armed forces from Taiwan (Formosa) and the Taiwan Straits. With China thus having apparently rejected the UN's latest effort at a cease-fire, England, France, Canada, and America's other allies, who, too, regarded Peking as being guilty of aggression, felt bound to follow the United States in branding China as an aggressor nation. With these countries voting in the affirmative, the General Assembly easily approved the American resolution on February 1 by a margin of 44 to 7 with 9 abstentions.[60]

Even so, Washington did not win at the UN without applying considerable pressure and without causing a wound within the western coalition requiring significant diplomatic healing. A few days after China's rejection of the cease-fire proposal, India received a communication from Peking in which the Chinese foreign minister, Chou En-lai, agreed to make a cease-fire in Korea the first order of business in an international conference on the Far East. Similar to an earlier Asian–Arab proposal that had never been acted upon, the Chinese counterproposal seemed to offer a workable compromise on a cease-fire. Very quickly, therefore, the Indian delegation moved for a delay in the UN's consideration of the American resolution of condemnation, which had already begun, in order to consider the Chinese proposal. Over American objections, India's motion passed by a narrow vote. What was significant about the vote, however, was that even such close American allies as Canada and England joined with the majority against the United States. Because of the encouraging nature of the Chinese reply, Canada argued that it would be premature and unwise to approve the American resolution. If that proposal was not accompanied by sanctions, as the United States intended, it would increase the danger of war with China and divide Asia even more from the West. The head of the British delegation, Sir Gladwynn Jebb, made many of the same points. "My government feels," he told the other delegates at the UN, "that until the situation [regarding China's latest communication] has been further clarified, until we have the answers to some . . . major questions, we should not do well to consider measures which in fact prejudge them. Such measures . . . might only result in further crises."[61]

The United States regarded such arguments as specious. To accept China's counterproposals would constitute an implicit declaration that neither North Korea nor Communist China had been guilty of aggression and that the Security Council and the General Assembly had been mistaken in defending the Republic of Korea. The White House would have none of this. Determined to brand China as an aggressor and to lay the groundwork for imposing sanctions, the administration flexed its political muscle. To the British and other allies it warned that their opposition to a resolution of condemnation might hurt their chances of obtaining congressional aid for rearmament, and it added that Congress would look askance at an open split in the UN since that was "exactly what the Soviets wan[ted]."[62]

By itself this type of diplomatic pressure did not assure the UN's approval of the American resolution. After debate was over, America's allies were willing to vote for a resolution of condemnation because, like the United States, they believed the fact of Chinese aggression in Korea should not go totally ignored by the United Nations. Also, as the American proposal was presented to the UN, it provided for a cessation of hostilities without precluding further discussions with China if Peking wanted them. The American resolution was a call to Peking to desist from aggression, but it was also a promise of a peaceful settlement if it did. Western powers could live with that.[63]

Yet there can be no denying that America's western allies had also been pushed and shoved into approving a resolution they did not fully support. What is more, they resented that fact. Political columnist Richard Rovere might thus have overstated the case when he reported from Lake Success that the American resolution had placed most delegates at the UN "in the odd, uneasy position of being on record of favoring an action they don't favor at all and that, indeed, they have said may lead to general war and the ruin of the United Nations." But the gist of his remarks was accurate. The British were especially upset at the treatment they received. Although they voted for the American resolution, they remained strongly opposed to Washington's persistent hard line toward China. They also remained miffed at the administration's habit of ignoring allied advice. The *New Statesman and Nation* expressed this British feeling when it remarked on the UN debate on China. "The real issue of this week's events is whether the Western alliance is to be a pact of equals or the suzerainty of one over all the rest."[64]

In fairness to the administration it must be said that it was under intense domestic pressure to follow a hard line toward Peking, including labeling China as an aggressor. Not only had White House critics attacked President Truman and Secretary of State Acheson when they had supported the last cease-fire proposal at the UN, but on January 19 both the House and Senate approved by voice vote similar resolutions calling on the United Nations to declare China an aggressor in Korea. About the only opposition to these resolutions was made by Democratic Representative John E. Rankin of Mississippi, who said he was unwilling "to turn over to the so-called United Nations the right to declare war for the United States or to tell us where to go and fight whose battles." Under these circumstances it would have been risky business indeed for an already embattled administration to have defied both liberal and conservative sentiment in Congress by following the dictates of diplomats at the UN wanting a modified version of the American resolution or no resolution at all. For this reason the White House was not being entirely disingenuous when it warned its NATO allies that their votes at the UN could determine the level of congressional aid they might receive in the future.[65]

Nevertheless, the American resolution of condemnation accomplished little except perhaps to appease some of the administration's harshest opponents. And even this had a price, for by its action at the UN and its position on such other matters as four-power talks with the Soviet Union, the administration also demoralized many of its strongest backers at home, including those who sought a peaceful end to the Korean War through a more flexible policy toward China, meaning a resolution of the China question favorable to Peking. By the spring, in fact, the

White House was under siege by well-wishers and foes alike. Advocates of a broad international policy based on a rapprochement with the Soviet Union and a peaceful solution to the Korean War, including recognition of the PRC, charged the administration with embracing a "spirit of negativism." Traditional White House allies in Congress accused Secretary of State Acheson of following an increasingly intransigent foreign policy in response to the attacks on him by such right-wingers as Senators McCarthy, Taft, and Wherry. One writer for the *Nation* even went so far as to maintain that America's resolution of condemnation "represented the grim presumption by both the United States and Russia that a third world war is inevitable, and was a play for stakes related to that eventuality."[66]

Even more serious, the administration, by its seemingly reckless, provocative, and intractable foreign policy, raised new doubts overseas about American leadership. Indeed, by late winter a substantial number of Europeans—and Canadians— including many committed to a strong Atlantic alliance, were accusing Washington of insipid self-righteousness and challenging its claim that, almost alone, the United States was containing Communist aggression in the Far East. "In one theatre of war, Korea, American troops predominate," wrote one such British critic. "But there is also a second major theatre, Indo-China, a secondary theatre, Malaya, and armed non-belligerency on a third frontier, that of Hong Kong."[67]

This did not mean, of course, that the western coalition was about to be shattered or the United States abandoned by its allies. As one American observer pointed out after the UN had approved the American resolution of condemnation, "the vote was a tribute . . . to the goodies our industries provide and to the realization that while it may be hard at times to get along with the United States, it would be even harder to get along without her."[68] Nor did it even mean that America's allies would try to reach a new accommodation with the Communists at the expense of the United States, although Europe's interest in four-power talks and its unhappiness at American opposition to such discussions indicated just how anxious many European leaders were to resolve outstanding differences with the Soviet Union. But European and Canadian displeasure with America's conduct of foreign policy did mean significant strain in the Atlantic alliance that made it even harder for Western heads of government to explain and defend their support for the United States.

Lastly, by pushing through the resolution of condemnation at the UN while ignoring Peking's counterproposals, the Truman administration effectively eliminated any chance for an early end to the Korean War. Whether Peking would actually have come to the bargaining table and fulfilled its promise of reaching a cease-fire in Korea before taking up other Far East issues is difficult to say, but there is reason to believe it would have. In the first place, China had launched its massive invasion of Korea with apparent reluctance and only after repeated warnings to UN forces to stop their march to the Yalu River. Less than eighteen months had passed since the PRC had been established, and it still had to contend with pockets of resistance to its authority. Its invasion of Tibet, begun in October, was running into trouble. Also China was a predominantly agricultural state that had just begun to industrialize. It had gone to war with obsolete military equipment (only later did the Soviets begin to sell the Chinese modern arms). The possibility that the United States would use the bomb against her could not be ignored. The Chinese had already achieved a significant victory by driving UN forces from North Korea, a victory which added greatly to its prestige among Asian nations and made a highly favorable impression on Moscow. At the same time, the war had already begun to stabilize by the end of January. China's superiority in manpower was matched by UN superiority in fire and air power. China was deficient in planes, tanks, and heavy artillery. China's supply lines were overextended. Lacking transport, China was forced to rely on about 300,000 conscripts to carry some 500 tons of supplies daily to meet the bare minimum of its forces in Korea. Even then, they were forced to move only at night, for UN air attacks were having a crippling effect in North Korea, freely bombing and strafing every visible target.[69]

In other words, there were compelling reasons, both in terms of the gains already achieved and the military dangers ahead, why Peking might have been anxious to find a solution to the Korean War acceptable to the West when it made its counterproposal to the UN—just as India and other Asian nations had told the United States. But the Truman administration turned down their advice, not because it was needlessly rash or provocative, as even some of America's closest allies had suggested. After all, the administration had reevaluated its war aims, after the initial shock of the Chinese invasion in November, to exclude the political unification of Korea by military means. But the administration remained convinced that Korea was a test of America's will to resist Communist aggression, that to make concessions to Peking in return for a cease-fire in Korea was a form of appeasement, which would only invite further aggression, and that America's credence as a world leader was at issue in the Korean War.

Not only that, the administration had to contend with domestic politics and with the realization that any concessions to the Chinese, apparent or real, would complicate and further inflame the political dialogue already under way in the United States and hamper even more its conduct of foreign policy. *Commonweal* described well the political realities and dilemma facing the White House when it remarked at the beginning of February, "[t]he pressure on Washington to punish the Chinese Communists is hard to withstand. Resentment over Chinese intervention in the war in Korea and their turning of a striking UN–US victory into a bitter defeat is nationwide. . . . The Administration is pushed more and more towards an unyielding and retaliatory policy in the UN by its political opponents. Mr. Acheson and his confreres are attacked constantly as appeasers."[70]

In a real sense, then, while the complexion of the Korean War had changed dramatically since the Chinese invasion in November, the basic issue before the administration had returned to what it had been at the time President Truman committed American military forces in June 1950. No longer did the White House envision the rollback of Communist expansion. Once more the central issue had become one of credibility, both American credibility in the world and the administration's credibility at home. There was an irony in all this. Just as concern with "saving face" had traditionally been an important consideration to the Chinese, it had become no less important to top administration officials in the United States.

NOTES

1. David Rees, *Korea: The Limited War* (New York, 1964), 155–64; T. H. Fehrenbach, *This Kind of War: Korea: A Study in Unpreparedness* (New York, 1964), 320–413; James F. Schnabel, *Policy and Direction: The First Year* (Washington, D. C., 1972), 274–83.
2. *Life,* 29 (December 11, 1950), 38; *ibid.* (December 18, 1950), 26.
3. National Security Council Meeting of November 28, 1950, Box 72, Elsey Papers. See also Cabinet Meeting of November 20, 1950, *ibid.;* Meeting of the President with Congressional Leaders, December 1, 1950, Box 73, *ibid.; FR,* 1950, VII, 1242–49.
4. *Ibid.*
5. *New York Times,* November 30, 1950.
6. *New Yorker,* 26 (December 9, 1950), 67–70; *New Republic,* 123, (December 11, 1950), 5; *Time,* 56 (December 11, 1950), 17; *Nation,* 171 (December 9, 1950), 520.
7. The President's News Conference of November 30, 1950, *Public Papers of the Presidents of the United States: Harry S. Truman,* 1950 (Washington, D. C., 1965), 724–28; Dean Acheson, *Present at the Creation: My Years in the State Department* (New York, 1969), 472.
8. *New Yorker,* 26 (December 16, 1950), 78–90; *Nation,* 171 (December 9, 1950), 520; *FR,* 1950, VII, 1291–96, 1322–23, and 1339–40; "Analysis of Public Comment Contained in Communications to the President Received December 4 to 8, 1950," Box 73, Elsey Papers. See also Joseph Goulden, *Korea: The Untold Story of the War* (New York, 1982), 395–98.
9. *Nation,* 171 (December 9, 1950), 521–22.
10. *Ibid.*
11. *FR,* 1950, VII, 1276–81, 1291–96, 1308–10, and 1323–24. See also Robert J. Watson, *The History of the Joint Chiefs of Staff, III, The Korean War* (unpublished manuscript, National Archives, 1978), 347–48 and 378; Acheson to Robert Lovett, December 3, 1950, Box 8, Selected Records Relating to the Korean War; *New Yorker,* 26 (December 23, 1950), 44–46.
12. *FR,* 1950, VII, 1361–74, 1392–1408, 1449–64, and 1468–72.
13. *Ibid.,* 1382–86.
14. *Ibid.,* 1472–79; *Life,* 29 (December 18, 1950), 32.
15. Loy Henderson to the Secretary of State, December 2, 1950, Box 8, Selected Records Relating to the Korean War; *FR,* 1950, VII, 1359–60, 1486–88, 1509–12, and 1518–20; *Yearbook of the United Nations: 1950* (New York, 1951), 242–43.
16. *Time,* 56 (December 11, 1950), 29–30.

17. *Yearbook of the United Nations: 1950* (New York, 1951), 243–49; *FR*, 1950, VII, 1298 and 1524–26; Warren Austin to the Secretary of State, December 4, 1950, Box 8, Selected Records Relating to the Korean War.

18. Memorandum for the Files, December 11, 1950, Box 8, Selected Records Relating to the Korean War; *FR*, 1950, VII, 1524–26, 1529–31, 1532–34, 1549–50, and 1554–62. See also Kenneth R. Mauck, "The Formation of American Foreign Policy in Korea, 1945–1953" (unpublished Ph.D. dissertation, University of Oklahoma, 1978), 304–305.

19. Quoted in Goulden, *Korea: The Untold Story of the War*, 422–23.

20. Trygve Lie, *In the Cause of Peace* (New York, 1954), 351–55; *FR*, 1950, VII, 1540–41 and 1549–50.

21. *FR*, 1950, VII, 1594–98; UN General Assembly, January 2, 1951, Box 8, Selected Records Relating to the Korean War.

22. Memorandum for Mr. Murphy, December 7, 1950; Economic Mobilization Meeting, [December 11, 1950?]; Meeting of the President on the Economic Situation, December 11, 1952; Memorandum for the Chairman of the Joint Chiefs of Staff, December 13, 1950, Box 73, Elsey Papers. See also *Public Papers of the Presidents of the United States; Harry S. Truman*, 1950, 741–45.

23. Meeting of the President with Congressional Leaders, December 13, 1950, Box 73, Elsey Papers.

24. *FR*, 1950, VII, 1570–76; *ibid.*, 1951, VII, 66–67.

25. *Ibid.*, 1950, VII, 1588–90 and 1625–26.

26. *FR*, 1950, VII, 1630–33.

27. *Ibid.*, 1951, VII, 41–43.

28. Harry S. Truman, *Years of Trial and Hope: Memoirs* (New York, 1956), 492–93; Acheson, *Present at the Creation*, 515.

29. *FR*, 1951, VII, 68–70. See also Mauck, "The Formation of American Foreign Policy in Korea, 1945–1953," 312–13.

30. Schnabel and Watson, *The History of the Joint Chiefs of Staff*, III, *The Korean War*, 414–19.

31. *Commonweal*, 53, (December 29, 1950), 291; *Time*, 56, (December 18, 1950), 17; David S. McLellan, *Dean Acheson: The State Department Years* (New York, 1976), 301.

32. *Life*, 29, (December 4, 1950), 42.

33. Truman, *Years of Trial and Hope*, 458; Acheson, *Present at the Creation*, 482.

34. Joan Hoff Wilson, *Herbert Hoover: Forgotten Progressive* (Boston, 1975), 261–63; *Time*, 57, (January 1, 1951), 9; *Life*, 30, (January 1, 1951), 18.

35. *New Republic,* 124 (January 1, 1951), 6; *Life,* 30 (January 8, 1951), 112.
36. *Nation,* 172 (January 6, 1951), 2; *Commonweal,* 53 (January 5, 1951), 315.
37. *Time,* 56 (December 11, 1950), 17; *ibid.* (December 18, 1950), 21; *ibid.,* 57 (January 15, 1951), 18–19; *Life,* 29 (December 18, 1950), 78; *Atlantic Monthly,* 187 (January 1951), 12.
38. *Life,* 30 (January 8, 1951), 10–13; James T. Patterson, *Mr. Republican: A Biography of Robert A. Taft* (New York, 1972), 477.
39. Ronald Steel, *Walter Lippmann and the American Century* (Boston, 1980), 473–76; *New Republic,* 124 (January 22, 1951), 5–6; *Atlantic Monthly,* 187 (February 1951), 27–29; *Nation,* 172 (January 20, 1951), 52.
40. *Life,* 30 (January 1, 1951), 18; *ibid.* (January 8, 1951), 14; *ibid.* (February 5, 1951), 27.
41. Patterson, *Mr. Republican,* 475; David M. Oshinsky, *A Conspiracy So Immense: The World of Joe McCarthy* (New York, 1983), 132–33.
42. Patterson, *Mr. Republican,* 453 and 475–76. See also *Time,* 57 (January 15, 1951), 12; *Life,* 30 (January 15, 1951), 26.
43. Patterson, *Mr. Republican,* 477–78; *New York Times,* January 6, 1951. For Taft's views on the constitutional issues involved in the formulation of foreign policy, see also Robert A. Taft, *A Foreign Policy for Americans* (New York, 1951), 23.
44. Patterson, *Mr. Republican,* 477.
45. *New York Times,* January 6, 1951; *Congressional Quarterly Almanac,* VII (1951), 220–21.
46. *Life,* 30 (January 15, 1951), 24; *Nation,* 172 (January 13, 1951), 21; *ibid.* (January 20, 1951), 52.
47. "Power of the President to Send the Armed Forces Outside the United States," February 16, 1951, Box 33, Elsey Papers.
48. Patterson, *Mr. Republican,* 480–81.
49. *Congressional Quarterly Almanac,* VII (1951), 223–32.
50. *New Republic,* 124 (January 8, 1951), 9.
51. *New Yorker,* 26 (January 13, 1951), 46; *Atlantic Monthly,* 187 (February 1957), 6; *Commonweal,* 53 (March 2, 1951), 514–15. See also *Nation,* 172 (January 20, 1951), 57; *Life,* 30 (January 22, 1951), 32–33.
52. *Nation,* 172 (January 6, 1951), 6 and 8; *ibid.* (January 13, 1951), 26–27; *ibid.* (February 3, 1951), 99–100; Acheson, *Present at the Creation,* 551.
53. *Yearbook of the United Nations: 1951,* 207. See also "Intervention of the Central People's Government. . .," January 17, 1951, Box 8,

Selected Records Relating to the Korean War. See also *FR*, 1951, VII, 3–4.

54. Department of State, "For the Press," January 17, 1951, Box 8, Selected Records Relating to the Korean War; *FR*, 1951, VII, 7–9, 74–76, and 83–85; Dennis Stairs, *The Diplomacy of Constraint: Canada, the Korean War, and the United States* (Toronto, 1974), 160–61.

55. *FR*, 1951, VII, 9–12, 18–21, and 37–39. See also Unsigned Memorandum of Conversation, January 24, 1951, Box 66, Papers of Dean Acheson, Harry S. Truman Library (Independence, Missouri); *New Yorker*, 26 (January 27, 1951), 58; Stairs, *The Diplomacy of Constraint*, 160–61.

56. Acheson, *Present at the Creation*, 513.

57. *FR*, 1951, VII, 44–47, 53–54, and 64.

58. *Time*, 57 (January 22, 1951), 13; *Nation*, 172 (January 27, 1951), 76.

59. *Nation*, 172 (January 27, 1951), 76–77; Stairs, *The Diplomacy of Constraint*, 165.

60. *Yearbook of the United Nations: 1951*, 207–25; *FR*, 1951, VII, 91–92; Warren Austin to the Secretary of State, January 20, 1951, and United Nations General Assembly, "Intervention of the Central People's Government. . .," January 31, 1951, Box 8, Selected Records Relating to the Korean War.

61. UN General Assembly, "Provisional Summary Record of the Four Hundred and Twenty-Ninth Meeting," January 23, 1951, and "Memorandum of Conversation," January 27, 1951, Box 8, Selected Records of the Korean War; *Nation*, 172 (January 27, 1951), 72–74; Stairs, *The Diplomacy of Constraint*, 168–69.

62. Acheson for Sebald, January 23, 1951, and Statement by Warren R. Austin, January 27, 1951, Box 8, Selected Records of the Korean War; *FR*, 1951, VII, 123–25 and 127–29.

63. Stairs, *The Diplomacy of Constraint*, 171–72.

64. *New Yorker*, 26 (February 10, 1951), 83; *Nation*, 172 (February 3, 1951), 103–104.

65. *Congressional Quarterly Almanac*, VII, 1951, 238; *Time*, 57 (January 29, 1951), 19; *Nation*, 172 (February 3, 1951), 102–103.

66. *New Yorker*, 26 (January 27, 1951), 70–78; *ibid.* (February 10, 1951), 85; *Nation*, 172 (February 17, 1951), 15. See also *New Republic*, 124 (January 1, 1951), 6; *Commonweal*, 53 (February 9, 1951), 438.

67. *Commonweal*, 53 (February 16, 1951), 463.

68. *New Yorker*, 26 (February 10, 1951), 83.

69. Adam Ulam, *Expansion and Coexistence: Soviet Foreign Policy* (New York, 1974), 530; Joseph Camilleri, *Chinese Foreign Policy:*

The Maoist Era and Its Aftermath (Oxford, England, 1980), 38–39; Allen S. Whiting, *China Crosses the Yalu: The Decision to Enter the Korean War* (Stanford, Calif., 1960), 165; *Time,* 172 (February 12, 1951), 25.

70. *Commonweal,* 53 (February 2, 1951), 411; Edgar O'Ballance, *Korea: 1950–1953* (London, 1969), 80–81 and 96–98.

CHAPTER 5

The Recall and the MacArthur Hearings

During the late winter and early spring of 1951, the immediate military crisis facing the UN Command (UNC) was overcome successfully when the Chinese offensive was halted south of Seoul and UN forces were able to launch a counteroffensive, which took them above the 38th parallel once more. But in the United States a crisis of an entirely different, but equally dangerous, kind developed after General Douglas MacArthur directly challenged the constitutional authority of the President as commander in chief. Although President Truman, in one of the most courageous acts of the modern Presidency, reaffirmed his power by recalling MacArthur from active duty, the political fallout was a repudiation of his administration by the overwhelming majority of the American public.

China's logistical weakness was already evident when Matthew B. Ridgway assumed command of the Eighth Army at the end of December, succeeding Walton Walker, who had been killed in a freak traffic accident. But it had become even more apparent in the next several weeks. Throughout this period Communist forces had remained on the offensive. Moving in close formations and striking in overwhelming numbers against the flanks and rears of UN troops, they recaptured Seoul on January 4 and then proceeded to take Osan about fifty miles to the south. At Kimpo Airfield outside of Seoul, Americans were forced to burn 500,000 gallons of fuel and 23,000 gallons of napalm to prevent them from falling into enemy hands, so rapid was the UN retreat. At Inchon the last two LSTs, carrying thousands of civilians and troops to ships offshore, left just ahead of

JANUARY, 1951 TO JULY, 1953

U.S.S.R.
Vladivostok

C H I N A
(MANCHURIA)

Chongjin

Yalu R.

Hyesanjin

Chosan

Iwon

Sinuiju

N O R T H
K O R E A

Hungnam

SEA OF
JAPAN

Pyongyang ★

Wonsan

Tongchon

Iron
Triangle

Truce talks Oct 10, 1951
to July 27, 1953

Armistice line
July 27, 1953

38th parallel

Panmunjom

Seoul

--- U.N. advances
///// Controlled by U.N.
▓▓▓ Controlled by
Communists

Ridgway counter-offensive
Jan 25-April 21, 1951

YELLOW

Kunsan

S O U T H
K O R E A

Pohang

SEA

Mokpo

Sunchon

Pusan

JAPAN

0   300
Miles

the Chinese, who crowded into the port area. Once Osan was evacuated, the road to Taejon became clogged with refugees fleeing southward, making the withdrawal of American forces difficult. In the east, the town of Wonju, an important rail and road center, was attacked from three sides by North Koreans before being abandoned by UN forces twenty-four hours later. By the time the Communist offensive was halted on January 24,

UN forces had withdrawn to defensive positions running eastward across Korea from north of Ansong in the west, to just
below Wonju in the center, and to just north of Samchok along
the east coast, or a line approximating the 37th parallel. The
Eighth Army had completed the longest retreat in American
military history, more than three hundred miles.[1]

The Communist offensive, however, had been neither an
unqualified victory for the Chinese nor an unmitigated disaster
for the Americans. Because of such inherent difficulties as prim-
itive communications and problems of supply, the Chinese
were not always able to exploit their opportunities. They were
forced to stop every five or six days to regroup and be resup-
plied, thereby allowing UN troops to withdraw rapidly but in
orderly fashion. This had been the case before the Chinese had
moved on Seoul, and it was the case after they had taken the
capital city. During the retreat American planes had also engaged in close and effective air support, inflicting high casualties on the Chinese and easing some of the pressure on UN
forces. As the Chinese advanced south after taking Seoul, moreover, they encountered stiff resistance and were subjected to
some of the heaviest artillery firing of the war. Below Wonju the
U. S. Second Division, aided by French and Dutch battalions,
carried out the first counterattack since the fall of Seoul, briefly
fighting their way into the town before withdrawing under
small arms fire. Although a horseshoe salient just south of Wonju
was subsequently given up in order to shorten and straighten
the UN line, artillery and air protection prevented enemy interference with the withdrawal.[2]

Finally, on January 25, UN forces launched a combat reconnaissance mission, designated OPERATION THUNDERBOLT,
which turned into a major counteroffensive that would last for
the next three months and would, by February 10, result in the
capture once again of Kimpo and Inchon and the neutralization
of Seoul. Marching north, UN forces attacked the Chinese with
tanks, heavy guns, napalm, and naval gunfire from ships just
offshore. Using coordinated artillery, infantry, armor, and air
power, they left more than 4200 Chinese dead in just one phase
of the advance while suffering only 70 losses themselves. As UN
troops below Seoul closed in on the Han River, *Time* reported
that the fire from tanks and artillery "reached such a furious

volume that some Chinese who surrendered had blood stream-
ing from nose and ears because of concussion."[3]

Much of the credit for reversing the direction of the war
belonged to Ridgway. A tough field commander who had led
the 82nd Airborne Division during World War II and had
jumped with the division at Normandy and later with XVII
Corps at Nijmegen and the Ardennes, Ridgway was known for
his trademark of a single grenade and first-aid kit hooked to a
web harness that he wore over his trench coat. Brought to the
Pentagon in 1949 as deputy chief of staff, he quickly earned a
reputation as a hard-driving administrator, demanding preci-
sion from his staff and boiling into rage when someone gave an
evasive answer. At the time he was ordered to Korea to succeed
Walton as commander of the Eighth Army, he was regarded by
many insiders at the Pentagon as a likely candidate for Army
chief of staff.[4]

Arriving in Korea on December 26 after being briefed in
Tokyo by MacArthur, who gave him total authority over the
Eighth Army, Ridgway's purposes were to clean house, rebuild
his forces, and inflict maximum casualties on the enemy. He was
eminently successful in all these respects. On orders from the
Pentagon, X Corps was merged into the Eighth Army, thereby
unifying the command of all ground forces in Korea. Convinced
the principal problem before his newly reorganized command
was the low morale of his troops after an extended retreat,
Ridgway sought to fire their enthusiasm and rekindle their spirits. To restore their confidence and fighting vigor he emphasized stern discipline, tough training, a sense of esprit de corps,
and professional pride. Similarly, he adopted a "meat grinder"
strategy of seeking out the enemy and striking at him again and
again while making maximum use of tanks and fire power. By
the time UN forces approached the Han River about February
10, they had inflicted a grueling punishment on the enemy,
whose toll of battle casualties since January 25 was estimated at
more than 80,000.[5]

Meanwhile, troop morale under Ridgway's command had
improved markedly. Indeed, a Pentagon team headed by General J. Lawton Collins, which had been sent to Korea in mid-
January to assess the morale problem after MacArthur had
described it as dismal, reported that conditions in Korea were,

in fact, encouraging. "On the whole," Collins told the Joint Chiefs, "Eighth Army is now in position and prepared to punish severely any mass attack." Henceforth, the JCS and President Truman increasingly bypassed MacArthur, choosing instead to deal directly with Ridgway.[6]

On February 11 the Communists launched a counterattack against the relatively weak center of the UN line that now stretched north of Hoengsong, forcing Ridgway to withdraw his troops once more to Wonju. Two days later the Chinese struck farther west, aiming at the vital crossroads town of Chipyong. The battle around Chipyong raged for three days, as the Chinese smashed against the UN forces with repeated human wave attacks. But UN forces responded with artillery salvos and aerial bombardment, and by week's end an armored force had relieved Chipyong and driven toward Wonju. The counteroffensive had been contained at a cost to the Communists of an estimated 33,000 casualties. "We have defeated the Communist counter-offensive in the central sector," Ridgway boasted to reporters. "The Communists have taken a fearful beating, and have disengaged."[7]

Seizing the initiative as the Chinese withdrew to defensive positions farther north, Ridgway launched OPERATION KILLER on February 21 in an effort to eliminate all pockets of resistance south of the Han River. A week later the mission was essentially completed. During the next month and a half UN forces conducted a series of operations, beginning with OPERATION RIPPER in March, whose purpose was to destroy as many Chinese personnel as possible and to establish a strong defensive line in the vicinity of the 38th parallel. Although Seoul was reclaimed on March 24, the UN advance proved slow and difficult. Most of the Chinese forces were able to escape the several pincer movements aimed at trapping them and to retreat to safety. But by April 22, when the Chinese launched their great spring offensive, UN forces had established a new defensive line, LINE WYOMING, which again took them above the 38th parallel and which, in the center, reached almost to the "Iron Triangle," a heavily defended area encompassed by a triangle with Pyonggang (not to be confused with the capital city of Pyongyang) at the northern angle, Chorwon at the left angle, and Kumhwa at the right angle.[8]

Considerable wrangling had preceded the decision allowing Ridgway to send his troops so far into North Korea. The State Department had been against the idea. Technically, UN forces still operated under the October 7, 1950, directive to establish a "unified, independent, and democratic Korea." But after the Chinese invasion and the retreat of UN forces in late November and December, few State Department officials considered that realistic. Nor, for that matter, did most top military leaders at the Pentagon. What caused difficulty, however, was the State Department's reluctance to define precise war aims without an assessment of America's military capabilities, which, in the opinion of the JCS and Defense Department, was a case of the tail wagging the dog.[9]

In general, the State Department's new—or, more accurately, reconstructed—aim in Korea was reasonably clear. It was to achieve a cease-fire agreement followed by UN negotiations leading to the restoration of the status quo ante June 25, 1950. Enough military pressure should be applied against the enemy and enough casualties inflicted on him to bring the Communists to the negotiating table. UN forces might even be allowed to cross the 38th parallel in order to interrupt enemy offensive operations. Under no circumstances, however, should UN forces engage in a general offensive into North Korea without the clearance of America's coalition partners, something which the State Department realized was highly unlikely.[10]

In the opinion of the JCS, the State Department's position was imprecise and amounted to determining future military decisions without stating the political objectives on which these decisions should be based. By prohibiting UN forces from moving above the 38th parallel in any major way, the State Department would also give the Communists impunity to regroup and rebuild in order to launch their own attack across the parallel. Until America's political objective in Korea was more clearly defined, UN troops should not be limited in crossing into North Korea to provide for their own safety.[11]

Seeking to scale down the war in Korea or to withdraw entirely, the Pentagon thus advocated policies that, in fact, could escalate the fighting considerably. The State Department, anxious to maintain military pressure against the Communists, nevertheless proposed limits on military action that might endanger American forces. Implicit in this conundrum of paradoxes and cross-purposes were some fundamental questions having to do with fighting a limited war in a nuclear age, particularly when the enemy could find sanctuary adjacent to the principal theater of military operations. Could a neat separation between political objectives and military means be sustained any longer? Was Karl von Clausewitz's famous epigram that war is the continuation of politics by other means always applicable? The war in Korea suggested a negative response to both these questions. It indicated, first, that any military planning had to take into account the ever-present danger of global escalation and nuclear war. In the case of Korea, the State Department's fear that a deep penetration of North Korea would increase the danger of a larger conflict, possibly involving the Soviet Union, was complicated by its concern that such a drive might fragment allied unity. But that only underscored the need for integrating political considerations into military planning.

Second, the Korean War suggested very strongly that any major policy decisions involving military power could not be made in a political vacuum. Rather, they had to reflect the military's basic concern for the safety of its forces and its awareness of such domestic constraints as public opinion and budget restrictions. Indeed, the Korean War even indicated that while the military needed to be more sensitive to the political implications of military planning, it could no longer function in its historic role as a mere executor of foreign policy. Instead, it had to be more articulate in explaining to civilian authorities the limitations inherent in the nation's military capabilities. With respect to the State Department's position favoring only limited forays across the 38th parallel, the Pentagon worried about the safety of UN forces if they could not attack the enemy's sanctuary in North Korea. It also firmly believed that fighting a war of attrition near the 38th parallel, as the State Department proposed, would seriously jeopardize America's ability to defend Japan, a nation strategically far more important to the United States. Lastly, the Pentagon was afraid that an extended war of attrition might turn an already war-weary American public even more against the conflict.

These larger issues involved in defining the proper relationship between political objectives and military means and the role of the military in the decision-making process were largely ignored. Instead, the Pentagon and State Department patched over their fundamental differences with a series of inadequate compromises. Although Assistant Secretary of State Rusk emphasized the impossibility of separating political from military objectives in Korea, Secretary of State Acheson decided not to press the department's position with the President, and the White House made no official pronouncement on whether UN forces would be allowed to cross into North Korea.[12] Following the success of OPERATION RIPPER and the advance of the UN Army to the vicinity of the 38th parallel, Truman told a reporter at a news conference on March 15 that a decision to cross into North Korea was up to the field commander. "A commander in chief 7000 miles away does not interfere with field operations," Truman said.[13] But on the same day that the President made these comments, the State Department completed the draft of a new statement on the Far East, which was generally satisfactory to the JCS and represented a new understanding with them. There was thus to be no forceful attempt to unify Korea. Military and political objectives were to be distinguished. The right of the theater commander to operate across the 38th parallel was recognized within limits. A prospective wider war, including operations against China, as had been urged by General MacArthur in January, was ruled out. In other words, the 38th parallel was not to be an artificial barrier to essential military operations, but any military action that might unnecessarily widen or extend the war was to be avoided.[14]

As UN forces began to hold against and then turn back the Chinese penetration of South Korea, some of the despair and sense of crisis evident among its allies, particularly since the Chinese invasion of November, began to diminish. As UN armies approached the 38th parallel and then crossed into North Korea again, public commentators remarked on a new optimism in Washington and overseas. Some lamented this change of attitude as unwarranted. Others frowned on the apathy they saw growing at home and abroad. But as these observers sensed, even as early as the middle of March a new feeling existed in the United States and overseas that the time was favorable to end what had become a costly and highly unpopular war.

One can easily overstate this shift in national and international temper. Although the tide of battle appeared to be turning in favor of the UN once more, it was recognized that the Chinese still had immense reserves of manpower. Real uncertainty remained as to what the Chinese might do in Korea in the next few weeks. In Washington reports circulated that they and the North Koreans were massing for another major push south. There were also unsubstantiated rumors of a heavy concentration of Soviet airplanes in Manchuria. The conviction that Korea was just one battleground of an ongoing struggle against Communist aggression, which could explode at any time into a nuclear war with the Soviet Union, continued to be shared by many Americans. In California there was even a run on bomb shelters. One contractor reported orders for 54 shelters at a cost of $500 to $1800 apiece. *Life* published four pages of photographs of backyard shelters being built in California, ranging from a wood-covered dirt hole put up by a local chamber of commerce for eight dollars to elaborate $5500 shelters complete with telephones, water, radios, and inside and outside Geiger counters. One photograph even showed a boy in "atomic-wear" that also covered his dog and was intended to protect both against radiation burns.[15]

Confidence in the administration slipped to an all-time low. A Gallup poll conducted in March showed that only 28 percent of the American voters approved the way President Truman was doing his job. This was four percentage points lower than his previous bottom in October 1946, just before the Democrats' drastic drubbing in the congressional elections. Reports of scandal within the White House staff and at the Reconstruction Finance Corporation (RFC) fueled charges of corruption and provided Republicans with a campaign slogan for 1952—K_1C_2 (Korea, Communism, and Corruption).[16]

Among America's allies doubts and skepticism continued to be expressed as to the maturity, consistency, and wisdom of American foreign policy. Europeans criticized both Washington's reluctance to engage in a serious dialogue with Moscow over German rearmament and the general "sterility" of American anti-Communism. Distrust of General MacArthur and others in the United States who would escalate the Korean War into a larger conflict against China itself remained widespread. The China question stayed a sore point, particularly in England, where "Peace with China" councils began to spring up all over the country. In England a serious split developed within the ranks of the ruling Labor Party as Prime Minister Attlee was attacked by more radical Laborites for adhering too closely to the dictates of Washington and for allowing Great Britain to be "dragged into a war with China by the Americans." Partly to mollify the opposition within his own party, Attlee had to reassure them that in no way would he support the recrossing of the 38th parallel without full consultation at the United Nations.[17]

In other words, both in the United States and abroad there remained considerable concern about future prospects in Korea, and fear of a nuclear confrontation between the United States and the Soviet Union stayed very much alive. At the same time, there was an ambivalence of attitudes, so that coexisting with anxiety in a paradoxical relationship was a new mood of hope now that the Chinese invasion in Korea had been stopped. Indeed, for many Americans and Europeans the world struggle against Communist aggression seemed to be improving in other places as well. For one thing, the success against the Chinese in Korea was widely regarded as having a beneficial effect throughout Asia. By throwing back the last two Communist offensives, UN forces, a number of military experts believed, had saved not only South Korea from the Communists but probably Indochina and perhaps the rest of Southeast Asia. They maintained that the Chinese had taken such a dreadful mauling in Korea that they had been rendered incapable of undertaking any further aggression for some time. In Indochina a brilliant new commander of French forces, General Jean de Lattre de Tassigny, added to the optimism that the struggle against the Communist Vietminh might yet be won.[18]

In Europe, too, the outlook appeared far more promising than it had even a few months earlier. Notwithstanding the concerns that Europeans continued to express about American policy and despite the fact that NATO's military strength remained negligible, the alliance seemed to be firmer politically than ever before. Although the China question still rankled in

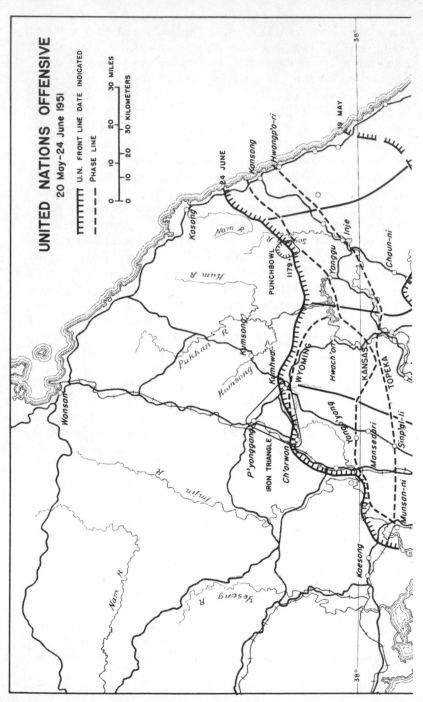

UNITED NATIONS OFFENSIVE
20 May–24 June 1951

┌┬┬┬┬┬┐ U.N. FRONT LINE DATE INDICATED

– – – – PHASE LINE

30 MILES

30 KILOMETERS

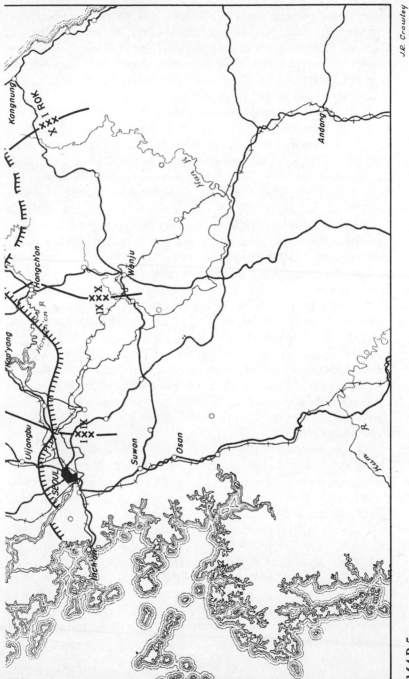

J.R. Crowley

MAP 5

many quarters, the issue of German rearmament, which had threatened to tear NATO apart, had been adroitly set aside, and General Eisenhower's eleven-nation tour of Europe as a salesman of collective security had been a thundering success. Important defections from the Communist parties in France and Italy also raised democratic morale.[19]

Still another reason for lifting the spirits of Washington was that the war mobilization program, which at first had been dogged by inefficiencies having to do with poor organization and planning, mismanagement, and wastefulness, had finally been cranked up. By March it was even making believers out of pessimists who had earlier predicted that it would be the end of 1951 or the beginning of 1952 before any impact could be made on the nation's military power. Between June 1950 and the spring of 1951, America's military establishment actually grew from 1.4 million personnel, of whom 600,000 were in the Army, to a force of more than 2.5 million, of whom 1.1 million were in the Army. Not counting the six divisions fighting in Korea, America's combat strength had been increased by 80 percent. During this same period the Air Force grew from forty-eight groups to about seventy, while naval manpower increased 60 percent and the number of combat ships ready for service increased by 50 percent. As one reporter pointed out, "At the time of Pearl Harbor, after a year of mobilization, the total of all our forces was 2,100,000; we now have a few hundred thousand more men than that and more, it is said, of just about everything else."[20]

The new confidence generated by such developments as these worried and even alarmed a number of observers, some because they feared Americans would let their guard down at a time when the danger of Communist aggression remained as great as ever, others because they were also afraid that a general apathy within the western coalition endangered the very principle of collective security. By the beginning of April, in fact, the complacency of the American public had become so disconcerting to the White House that Defense Secretary Marshall warned at a news conference that the situation in Korea was "more serious now than in November" and lashed out at the mass media for contributing to the lightheartedness.[21]

Yet the prevailing national mood of optimism penetrated

the White House as well, convincing Truman to undertake a major peace initiative. The rationale for a negotiated settlement was fairly simple. Because most of South Korea had been liberated from the Communists and UN forces had inflicted heavy casualties on the Chinese, it would be in the interests of both sides to end hostilities. But the United States was also under considerable pressure at the UN, where Secretary General Trygve Lie urged Washington to make a diplomatic approach directly to the North Koreans, bypassing China and the Soviet Union.[22]

Both the State and Defense departments approved of the idea of a peace initiative, although they felt the President should appeal directly to the Chinese. Secretary of State Acheson also believed that if the President's message was rejected by Peking, it would clear the way for whatever additional military action might be necessary in Korea by "convincing our allies that the [Chinese] were unwilling to settle for the status quo *ante bellum.*"[23] The State Department drafted a message by which Truman would announce that the UNC was ready to enter into arrangements for a cease-fire. The statement offered no concessions to the Chinese, but it held out the possibility of subsequent negotiations on broader issues affecting the Far East. The JCS then informed General MacArthur on March 20 of the planned announcement, asking him what authority he needed to protect his forces and to maintain contact with the enemy for the next few weeks. They also told MacArthur of the strong feeling at the UN for another peace effort before making a major UN advance above the 38th parallel.[24]

MacArthur was irate at the limitations he felt the JCS had placed on his forces. Although he had participated only marginally in planning the recent advance by the Eighth Army, he took much of the public credit for it. On March 7 he predicted a military stalemate in Korea unless he could strike at the enemy's war-making potential. A week later he defied a Presidential order prohibiting unauthorized statements to the press by giving one to the United Press in which he criticized stopping the Eighth Army's advance at the 38th parallel or short of "accomplishment of our mission in the unification of Korea." MacArthur simply could not reconcile himself to a war whose object had become less than total victory, particularly after the

Chinese had been stopped and a rollback of Communist forces had begun. If only he was permitted to take advantage of his superior fighting power on land and his greater mobility in the air and on the sea, he could unite Korea, drive the enemy out of the country, and inflict a huge military and political defeat on China.[25]

Responding to the JCS's message of March 20, therefore, MacArthur recommended that no further military restrictions be imposed on his command in Korea. The existing prohibitions should not be increased. The military disadvantages resulting from the restrictions placed on America's air and naval operations, together with the differences in size between his command and the enemy's ground potential, made it completely impractical to attempt to clear North Korea of enemy forces.[26] Had MacArthur stopped with this rejoinder to the Pentagon, President Truman almost certainly would have gone ahead with his announcement offering a cease-fire. Whether this would have led to early negotiations is impossible to say, although it may be significant that the Communists were already beginning to mass for what would be their greatest military effort of the war. Perhaps the Chinese had to await the outcome of this operation before deciding on whether to come to the bargaining table.

However, President Truman never made his announcement. On March 24 MacArthur issued a statement so contrary to the administration's purpose that Truman believed it would have only confused the world if he had gone ahead with his peace offer. In his statement MacArthur portrayed China as an overrated military power on the brink of destruction should it continue its war in Korea. Only the UN's decision to limit its conflict with China to Korea had kept China from being annihilated. Should the UN expand its military operations to China's coastal areas and interior bases, it would "doom Red China to the risk of imminent military collapse." This being the case, "there should be no insuperable difficulty arriving at decisions on the Korean problem if the issues are resolved on their own merits, without being burdened by extraneous matters not directly related to Korea, such as Formosa and China's seat in the United Nations." As commander of UN forces in Korea, MacArthur stood ready to meet the commander in chief of the enemy's forces in order to consider carrying out the political objectives of the United Nations in Korea without further bloodshed.[27]

In delivering this ultimatum to the Chinese, MacArthur had not known the full content of the proposed Presidential message. Also, there was precedent for his offer to confer with the enemy within "the area of [his] authority as military commander" and "to find any military means" for realizing the political objectives of the United Nations in Korea. Soon after the Inchon landing of the previous September, when the possibility of a North Korean surrender seemed real, the Department of State had told the Defense Department that a "cease-fire should be a purely military matter and accordingly they [the North Koreans] should communicate their offer to the Commanding General of the Unified Command . . . who is the appropriate representative to negotiate any armistice or cease-fire agreement." On the related issue of crossing the 38th parallel, while MacArthur had intended to move the Eighth Army above the parallel unless ordered not to by Washington, he instructed General Ridgway on March 22 not to advance above the parallel until specifically authorized to do so.[28]

Nevertheless, Truman was infuriated—and understandably so—at MacArthur's statement to the Chinese to surrender on the battlefield or face total destruction. To spread the war to China and risk a global war with the Soviet Union, as implied by MacArthur's ultimatum, was totally contrary to the thrust of the administration's policy of limiting the war to Korea and negotiating its peaceful end. In addition, Truman was incensed by MacArthur's violation of the Presidential directive of December 6 to coordinate with Washington all public statements concerning Korea, by MacArthur's implicit criticism of national policy, by the adverse reaction among America's allies that his statement was bound to produce, and, above all, by MacArthur's tacit preemption of Presidential authority. "[O]nce again," Truman later wrote, "General MacArthur had openly defied the policy of his Commander in Chief, the President of the United States."[29]

MacArthur must have known how little chance there was that China would simply lay down its arms and admit defeat, especially when it still controlled more than half of the Korean peninsula. To ask China to surrender under these circumstances was to ensure the rejection of any peace overture and the continuation of the war. Surely this was MacArthur's real purpose in issuing his statement. By prolonging the war, it seems clear, MacArthur hoped to create a situation of public frustration in the United States so great that the administration would have to increase its military effort against the Chinese, including liberating North Korea from Communist control.[30]

Less than twenty-four hours after he received the news of MacArthur's pronouncement, Truman summoned to the White House Deputy Secretary of Defense Robert Lovett, Assistant Secretary of State Rusk, and Secretary of State Acheson. Lovett was furious, The general must be removed and removed at once, he told Acheson. Acheson and Truman agreed. But there were problems. In the first place, Truman was afraid that firing MacArthur might upset negotiations then under way for a peace treaty with Japan. Second, he feared that recalling MacArthur would break up his multiplicity of commands and cause great logistical difficulties.[31]

Most important, however, the administration was perfectly aware of the tremendous popularity that MacArthur enjoyed in the United States and the overwhelmingly favorable support that his March 24 statement received. While longtime critics of the general responded to his remarks by demanding that he resign or be fired, far more typical were the views of *Life*, which defended MacArthur by asking its readers what he had done that "was so really awful." Indeed, Lovett warned Acheson that all the press reaction he had read indicated that MacArthur's remarks were "probably the most popular public statement anyone has ever made." It offered peace and held out the hope of getting out of Korea. "If the president challenged it, he would be in the position at once of being on the side of sin."[32]

Instead of firing MacArthur or demanding his resignation, therefore, Truman merely reminded him of his December 6 directive against making public statements without first consulting Washington and ordered him to seek instructions from the Joint Chiefs in case the Communists sought an armistice. Still, there is little doubt that after March the President was on a collision course with the general that could only result in

MacArthur's firing. As Secretary Acheson later explained, "MacArthur's career as an independent spokesman to the public or the enemy was obviously coming to an end." Already, in fact, MacArthur had sent a telegram to the House minority leader, Republican Joseph Martin of Massachusetts, which would lead to MacArthur's removal from command and to the most serious domestic upheaval of the entire Truman administration.[33]

MacArthur wrote his telegram to Martin in response to a copy of a speech the minority leader had sent to him, along with a letter inviting his comment "on a confidential basis or otherwise." In his address, which he had delivered a month earlier in New York, Martin attacked the President for preventing "800,000 trained men" on Formosa from opening "a second front in Asia" even though MacArthur and other military leaders at the Pentagon supported such an operation. "If we are not in Korea to win," the congressman had stated, "then this Truman administration should be indicted for the murder of thousands of American boys."[34]

MacArthur's reply, which was sent on the same day he released his ultimatum to the Chinese, seemed to challenge existing national policy. "It seems strangely difficult for some to realize that here in Asia is where the Communist conspirators have elected to make their play for global conquest," the general told Martin. In Asia, we fight Europe's war. Lose the war in Asia, Europe is doomed. "[W]in it, and Europe would most probably avoid war and yet preserve freedom. As you pointed out, we must win. There is no substitute for victory." In other words, the administration was wrong to fight a limited war in Korea for fear of weakening American strength in Europe. Unless the White House resisted Communist aggression in Korea with adequate military power, both Europe and Asia would fall to the Communists.[35]

Because MacArthur had not indicated that he wanted his remarks kept confidential, Martin decided to read them on the floor of the House, explaining that he felt he "owed it to the American people to tell them the information I had received from a great and reliable source."[36] As soon as Truman read what MacArthur had said, he scheduled a White House meeting for the next day with Defense Secretary Marshall, Secretary of

State Acheson, General Omar Bradley, and Ambassador Averell Harriman. At the meeting Harriman stated that MacArthur should have been dismissed two years earlier. Acheson also believed MacArthur should be fired, but he cautioned the President that the general's dismissal would trigger "the biggest fight of your administration." Marshall wanted more time before making a decision on what to do with MacArthur. Bradley, too, wanted to wait in order to consult first with the Joint Chiefs.[37]

The meeting at the White House was held on Friday. The President conferred again with his advisers the next day and with Acheson alone on Sunday morning. By this time a consensus had been reached among Truman's top aides that MacArthur should be recalled to the United States. On Monday, April 9, Marshall told the President that the Joint Chiefs unanimously recommended that MacArthur be relieved of all his commands. Truman then had the necessary orders drawn up. The President intended to notify MacArthur of his dismissal through Army Secretary Frank Pace, who was on an inspection tour of Korea. Pace was to fly to Tokyo to meet MacArthur. But because of a breakdown in communications and out of concern that the Chicago *Tribune* was about to leak the story, Truman decided to break the news at a press conference called for 1 A.M. April 11—before the general had received official word that he had been fired. To replace MacArthur Truman named Ridgway. On the night of the eleventh the President went on radio to explain the administration's Korean policy, including why it had become necessary to relieve MacArthur.[38]

Europeans overwhelmingly supported Truman. They had been dismayed by MacArthur's earlier ultimatum to the Chinese, which the Norwegian ambassador to the United States had referred to as the general's "pronounciomento" and which the pro-American London *Economist* regarded as a piece of unmitigated "mischief."[39] When word was received, therefore, that Truman had fired MacArthur because the general had made still another defiant statement challenging the President's authority and posing the danger of a military escalation in Asia, they made clear their relief that they would not have to contend any longer with a megalomaniac like MacArthur.

In England the *Manchester Guardian* thus remarked that

Truman was "in the right" in firing MacArthur and predicted that "in every domestic country except his own his action will be received with almost unmixed approval and relief." Reporting from London, Howard K. Smith noted that the British press had reiterated that there was only one question at issue; "whether generals may make foreign policy." In France judgment was more reserved as a number of Frenchmen waited to see if MacArthur's dismissal would bring the end of the Korean War any nearer. But important papers like *Le Monde, L'Observateur,* and *Franc-Tireur* emphasized the great danger that MacArthur might have created by bombing Manchuria. Devoting its entire front page to the news of MacArthur's firing, *Le Monde* called for negotiations to end the war in Korea and remarked that such talks could not succeed as long as General MacArthur held "in his hands the means of preventing any results."[40]

In the United States, however, the vast majority of Americans expressed outrage at the news that Truman had relieved MacArthur of his commands. In fact, the public furor caused by the firing of MacArthur stands out as one of the singular events in modern American political history. Although not entirely unexpected, the way in which the general was fired (MacArthur first learning of his dismissal secondhand) only added to the public outcry against a deeply unpopular President whose failure in China and "no-win" policy in Korea contrasted sharply with MacArthur's formula for victory in Asia.

No less important to many Americans than the policy issues separating MacArthur from Truman, however, were issues of character. If MacArthur stood as an authentic national hero, whose probity, stature, bearing, and even elegance were legend, Truman seemed in so many ways to demean the office he served. Furthermore, the President's problems stemmed beyond the charges of corruption and scandal that tainted his administration or even beyond other domestic issues, such as his unpopular imposition of wage and price controls in January. They also involved matters of personal style and taste. In contrast to MacArthur, Truman was known to cuss and use salty language, to enjoy barnyard humor, to engage sometimes in heavy drinking, and to play poker with his political cronies. Even for a President, he was unusually combative and testy with the press, snapping at such respected journalists as Arthur Sulzberger, David Lawrence, Marquis Childs, and the Alsop brothers, whom he referred to as the "Sop sisters." His public antics, such as lambasting the Washington *Post*'s music critic for his "lousy review" of his daughter Margaret's singing voice, sometimes made him look ridiculous. Alone, none of these matters made Truman unpopular. Together, they left an image of a President who remained little more than an ordinary machine politician from Jackson County, Missouri, serving by an act of fate in an office for which he was unfit and threatening by his firing of MacArthur to jeopardize the very security of the United States.[41]

Throughout the country, therefore, Americans lashed out at the President in a variety of ways. In Illinois the state legislature expressed its "unqualified confidence in General MacArthur and vigorously condemn[ed] the irresponsible and capricious action of the President in summarily discharging him from command." The legislatures of Michigan, California, and Florida passed similar resolutions. Patriotic organizations, ladies' clubs, preachers from their pulpits, and newspaper and radio editorials all made known their support for the now martyred general. In San Gabriel, California, students hanged an effigy of Truman from a flagpole. Effigies of Truman were also hung in the hills of Tennessee. In Ponca City, Oklahoma, a homemade dummy of Secretary of State Acheson was soaked in oil and burned. Flags were lowered in protest in Oakland, California; Little Rock, Arkansas; Zanesville, Ohio; and Eastham, Massachusetts. Thousands of letters poured into the White House and Congress demanding President Truman's resignation or impeachment. A news photo showed Senator Richard Nixon of California displaying some of the more than six hundred telegrams he received in the first day following the news of MacArthur's firing. "It's the largest spontaneous reaction I've ever seen," said Nixon.[42]

Talk of impeachment was not confined to the general public. On Capitol Hill the issue was raised at an emergency caucus of the House and Senate Republican leaders. Senator McCarthy said Truman's decision to dismiss MacArthur was fogged with "bourbon and benedictine" and that he should be fired. On the Senate floor Jenner of Indiana charged that the United States "was in the hands of a secret inner coterie which is directed by agents of the Soviet Union. Our only choice," he concluded, "is to impeach President Truman." Few took McCarthy and Jenner very seriously, and no organized effort was made to bring charges against the President. But the House and Senate invited MacArthur to address a joint meeting of Congress. Plans were also made for a full-scale investigation into the administration's Far East policy, including the reasons for MacArthur's recall.[43]

Familiar critics of MacArthur, like the Washington *Post,* the *Nation,* and the *New Republic,* did voice their support for the President. Most Democrats, and even a few Republicans, also defended Truman. In the Senate Democrat Robert S. Kerr of Oklahoma remarked that MacArthur's removal greatly lessened the chances of an expanded "all-out struggle" between the United States and Communist China. Saying that the general had previously made "tragic mistakes," Kerr declared that "all the mistakes he has ever made rolled into one" would not equal the "awful blunder" such an all-out struggle would represent. The chairman of the Senate Foreign Relations Committee, Democrat Tom Connally of Texas, stated that there could "be no competing spokesman for our government." Similarly, the two Republican senators from Massachusetts, Leverett Saltonstall and Henry Cabot Lodge, Jr., also supported the dismissal. The President had no alternative, Saltonstall remarked, "but to take some affirmative action against General MacArthur." "To permit a continuous dispute," Lodge added, "is unthinkable."[44]

Nevertheless, when MacArthur returned to the United States on April 17, he met a hero's welcome unsurpassed in American history. Landing at San Francisco, he was greeted by a crowd so big that it took the general and his entourage two hours to travel the fourteen miles to his hotel. On the eighteenth he traveled to Washington to address the Congress. Arriving at National Airport shortly after midnight on the nineteenth, he was met by twelve thousand well-wishers who broke through the police lines and made a shambles of the greeting ceremonies that had been planned by Secretary Marshall, the Joint Chiefs of Staff, and virtually the entire Republican membership of Congress.[45]

Twelve hours later MacArthur entered the House chamber where he was widely and wildly cheered by the assembled senators and representatives as well as by the public in the galleries, which were filled to overcapacity. Eloquent, charismatic, unhurried, resonant of voice, sometimes austere but always in control, the deposed commander delivered a thirty-minute address that even his foes in the Senate and House admitted was deeply moving and highly effective. Restating his major premises for a victory in Korea, the seventy-one-year-old general laid the basis for future controversy by declaring that these aims "have been fully shared by practically every military leader, including our own Joint Chiefs of Staff." More generally, he reiterated his conviction that foreign problems were "global and interlocked" and that neither Asia nor Europe could be considered separately. Under no condition, he warned again, must Formosa fall under Communist control, and those who would appease Red China he called "blind," adding that it was unlikely that the Soviet Union would enter the conflict in Korea if it was pressed more vigorously. Closing his remarks, he referred to a refrain about old soldiers never dying but just fading away. "And like the old soldier of that ballad," he concluded, "I now close my military career and just fade away—an old soldier who tried to do his duty as God gave him the light to see that duty. Good-bye."[46]

The reaction to the address, carried on national television, was sensational. Although Democratic Representative Thomas E. Morgan of Pennsylvania called the message "a war speech," and Majority Leader John McCormack of Massachusetts warned that "a commitment to war in China would be dangerous," MacArthur was applauded time and time again as he delivered his remarks. Afterward James Reston of *The New York Times* wrote that the general had heated political passions already near the boiling point and had divided "Washington more profoundly than it has ever been divided at any time since the start of the cold war." Following his speech, MacArthur received the key to the city of Washington and then led a motorcade down Pennsylvania Avenue as a quarter of a million people watched and as jet fighters and bombers flew overhead. The next day, in New York City, seven and a half million people (nearly twice the number that had watched General Dwight

Eisenhower return from Europe in 1945) turned out to see and cheer the soldier-turned-statesman.[47]

Considering the emotion that MacArthur's return to the United States generated, the Democrat leadership on Capitol Hill had little choice but to agree to Republican plans to hold a full-scale investigation of the administration's Far East policy. But while the Republicans wanted open hearings, the Democrats succeeded in obtaining a compromise whereby the sessions would be closed but a copy of the transcript, censored to eliminate classified material, would be made available to the press every evening.[48]

The hearings, which were conducted by the Senate Armed Services and Senate Foreign Relations Committees and which lasted seven weeks, began on May 3. Even before the hearings opened, the Senate panel stirred controversy by releasing the "Wedemeyer Report" on China and Korea and a transcript of the Truman-MacArthur talks at Wake Island the previous October; both these documents had been made available to the panel by the Pentagon. The first contained the conclusions of a Presidential mission to China and Korea by Lieutenant General Albert C. Wedemeyer in 1947. In his report Wedemeyer cited the "potential military threat" even then of "a Soviet inspired invasion of South Korea by troops of the North Korean Peoples (Communist) army." To cope with the threat Wedemeyer urged creation of an American-officered South Korean scout force. Critics of America's Far East policy used the report to lambast the administration. Republican Representative Gordon Canfield of New Jersey echoed the sentiments of other congressmen when he said that "the whole Korean war might have been avoided had the Congress been given the facts" contained in Wedemeyer's report at the time it was submitted. Some senators raised old complaints about "suppression" of the report between 1947 and 1951. In contrast the Wake Island transcripts supported the administration by substantiating what had earlier been reported—that at Wake Island MacArthur had assured President Truman that there was "very little" chance of Communist China's entry into the Korean fighting.[49]

At the hearings the first witness was General MacArthur, who answered questions for twenty-one hours during a three-

day period. The general brought no prepared statement, saying
that he had commented fully in addressing Congress. He then
sat back to await the first questions by Richard Russell of
Georgia, the chairman of the Armed Services Committee.
Democrats on the Senate panel had prepared well for MacArthur's appearance before them. In an earlier memorandum
they had pointed out the dangers—and opportunities—that the
general's testimony offered. "Properly handled," they had
stated, "it can be the turn in the tide." It could offer the public
an opportunity to evaluate the firing of MacArthur on the merits of the case rather than on the basis of emotion. "Improperly
handled, it can result at the minimum level in adding to the
present confusion and at the maximum level in building MacArthur up to the point where *anything* is his for the asking."[50]

To prevent this from happening, the Democrats decided to
handle MacArthur with great deference and to limit questions
to a minimum. As they explained, the record would be very
voluminous at best, and the Republicans would "try to load it
with everything but the battleship *Missouri.*" "The record
could easily end up as a huge indigestible mess which no one
can understand." At the same time, however, the Democrats
prepared a series of questions designed to pinpoint MacArthur's
views on foreign policy and military matters in order to make
clear to the American public just how fuzzy and fraught with
danger his position really was; in this way they also hoped to
reveal the vast gap between the general and most of his supporters.[51]

The questions the Democrats prepared, therefore, touched
on such matters as the implications and consequences of a bombardment of Manchuria, the effectiveness of a blockade of
China, and the likely results of an invasion of the Chinese mainland by the forces of Chiang Kai-shek, all of which MacArthur
had advocated in his speech to Congress. What evidence did
MacArthur have, for example, that the Soviet Union would not
go to war if the United States should bomb Manchuria? Did he
believe that the United States could hold its allies together
while following his program? To what extent did MacArthur
believe his policy of aerial bombardment of Manchurian bases
should be carried out? Should it be mere tactical bombing of
troops and supply concentrations? Or should it involve strategic

bombing of Manchurian and Chinese cities? Lastly, how much additional military power would be required in the Far East to carry out MacArthur's programs? These and other similar questions comprised a substantial list, which the Democrats, notwithstanding their desire for brevity, believed would pin down MacArthur politely but firmly to precise details.[52]

As in his speech to Congress MacArthur remained supremely confident in his testimony. In the three days he appeared as a witness, the general made a number of major points. "The dreadful slaughter" caused by "indecisive fighting" in Korea, he said, was "too expensive" as a means to buy time to prepare for a possible World War III. "Thousands of lives" would have been saved in Korea if the use of Nationalist forces on Formosa had even been threatened. China could have been forced to the bargaining table if his proposals for all-out air attacks had been accepted. The Joint Chiefs of Staff had recommended to the Defense Department on January 12 that air operations be authorized over Manchuria, that the Chinese Nationalists be given "logistical" or supply support, and that a naval blockade be instituted against China. It was these recommendations that he had in mind when he told Congress earlier that the JCS agreed with his position. Furthermore, he had never advocated the use of American, as opposed to Chinese Nationalist, forces on the Chinese mainland; to do so would be a "master folly." His policies would not materially affect U. S. manpower commitments to other parts of the world such as Europe. In fact, the United States could follow his policies, step up air offensives in Korea, and defeat Communist China with only a "relatively small fraction" of America's overall military strength. Finally, he never believed the theory "that the bringing of the Korean problem to a close would necessitate bringing the Soviets into the war [against the United States]." He was persuaded that, whatever happened in Korea and Asia, it would not be the deciding factor as to whether the Soviet Union attacked the United States.[53]

In essence what MacArthur said was that victory, not prolonged indecision, must be the objective of war and that once the United States engaged in conflict in Korea, it had no choice but to do what was necessary to bring about victory. There was no substitute for victory. Although it was possible that his strategy might bring the Soviet Union into the war, that was highly unlikely, considering America's superior industrial and military power; in any case, the possibility of Soviet intervention had been discounted in America's original decision to fight in Korea. Furthermore, MacArthur concluded, his views were "fully shared" by the military commanders in the field and by the Joint Chiefs of Staff, as indicated by their recommendations of January 12.[54]

Articulate, voluble, courteous, and patient, MacArthur was in many ways a model witness as he portrayed himself as a humble theater commander merely trying to carry out his orders and instructions as he interpreted them even when he believed them dangerous and potentially disastrous. Quite effectively and with little difficulty he fielded the first group of questions asked him. No, he did not believe it was in the Soviet's capacity to mass a major attack from the Asiatic continent. Yes, if the Navy and Air Force could operate at their full efficiency and prevent the buildup of enemy supplies and forces, it would not take a large increase in UN forces to end the war in Korea. Yes, if he had been permitted to use his air power when the Chinese entered the war in November, he had not "the faintest doubt" they would have been thrown back. No, one could not draw an easy line all the time between the military and political sides of a foreign policy matter. Nevertheless, when locked in battle, there "should be no artifice under the name of politics, which should handicap [one's] own men, decrease their chances of winning, and increase their losses."[55]

Despite MacArthur's virtuoso performance, as the hearings continued into the afternoon of the first day and then into the second and third days and as the more junior members of the Senate panel had their turn at the general, the questions became harder and more probing and MacArthur more testy. Perhaps the most damaging testimony for his case against the administration was his admission on a number of occasions that he was only a theater commander who was not qualified to comment on questions outside his field of command. Democratic Senator Brien McMahon of Connecticut pressed MacArthur particularly hard on this issue. What would happen, he asked the general, if his estimate of the world situation was wrong and if the United States was plunged into an all-out war?

"That doesn't happen to be my responsibility, Senator," MacArthur replied. "My responsibilities were in the Pacific, and the Joint Chiefs of Staff and the various agencies of this Government are working day and night for an over-all solution to the global problem." That was exactly right, McMahon responded. The President must consider all matters on a global basis. "You as a theater commander by your own statement have not made that kind of study, and yet you advise us to push forward with a course of action that may involve us in that global conflict." MacArthur must have realized the mistake he made in casting himself in the role of "only a theater commander," because the next day he tried to make the point that a general knowledge of global problems was, of course, necessary by all theater commanders to coordinate the demands of their own theater with larger global problems. But the point about his limited knowledge of other areas had already been made part of the record.[56]

On another matter the general repeated a statement that clearly was not true. This was his assertion that the Joint Chiefs of Staff, in their memorandum of January 12, had agreed with the course of action he recommended to them, namely an economic and naval blockade of China, the end of restrictions on air reconnaissance of China's coastal areas and of Manchuria, and the end of restrictions on the operations of the Chinese Nationalist forces against the Chinese Communists. As the next witness, Defense Secretary Marshall, would point out, these proposals were only part of a series of options which the JCS considered when it appeared that the Chinese might attempt to drive the UNC from Korea. But MacArthur maintained throughout his testimony that the JCS approved his recommendations, which they did not.[57]

Upon the completion of MacArthur's three days of testimony, a series of witnesses, including Secretary Marshall, Secretary of State Acheson, Chairman of the JCS Bradley, and the rest of the JCS took the stand in order to support the administration's Far East policy and to defend the firing of MacArthur. Marshall testified for several days, stating that there had never been any disagreement between the President, himself, and the JCS, but that there had been "basic differences" between MacArthur, on one hand, and the President, secretary of defense, and the JCS, on the other. Marshall then turned to the

January 12 memorandum, which, MacArthur claimed, showed that the JCS were in agreement with his recommendations regarding an economic and naval blockade and other measures against Communist China. First Marshall made the point that MacArthur's proposals were only four of sixteen options which were put forward when the military situation was bleak in Korea and the JCS had to consider the possibility of an evacuation. Furthermore, as the military situation in Korea improved toward the middle of January, it became "unnecessary to put into effect all the courses of action outlined in the Joint Chiefs' memorandum of January 12."[58]

Having disposed of the JCS memorandum, Marshall then touched on a number of other salient points. He especially criticized MacArthur's ultimatum of March 24 to the Communists. This action aborted negotiations at the diplomatic level, "thus losing whatever chance there may have been at that time to negotiate a settlement of the Korean conflict." In addition, Marshall stated that MacArthur would have the United States carry the war against the Communists beyond Korea and would take the risk of all-out war not only with Communist China but with the Soviet Union. "He would have us do this even at the expense of losing our allies and wrecking the coalition of free peoples throughout the world. He would have us do this even though the effect of such action might expose Western Europe to attack by millions of Soviet troops poised in Middle and Eastern Europe."[59]

Through their questioning of Marshall, Democratic members of the joint hearings and Republicans sympathetic to the administration's position, such as Lodge and Saltonstall of Massachusetts and Wayne Morse of Oregon, laid out the administration's argument with respect to its Far East policy and its firing of MacArthur—that MacArthur's proposals improperly challenged the President's authority and could result in a two-front war, which the administration was not prepared to undertake. During his testimony Marshall also stated emphatically that the United States would veto any effort to give Communist China UN membership or turn Formosa over to the Peking government, and he referred to the troops-for-Europe debate that had recently ended in Congress. Admitting that the House and Senate were entitled to be kept advised of military strategy, he also remarked that "under the constitution, Congress does not command armies." He implied that giving Congress the right to pass on the movement of troops could even lead to demands to "determine the strategy of battle."[60]

The most forceful spokesman for the administration, however, was not Marshall, but General Omar Bradley, who followed the defense secretary to the witness stand. The JCS had "global responsibilities," he said, and were "in a better position to assess the risks of a general war than a theater commander." The Soviet Union and not China was the United States' chief opponent. Getting further involved with Communist China would not guarantee a Korean victory, but could mean leaping from a smaller conflict "to a larger deadlock at greater expense." Indeed, Korea was just one phase of the battle to contain Communist expansion under Soviet leadership. The United States was not in a position to seek a showdown with the Soviet Union. MacArthur's plans would put the United States "in the wrong war, at the wrong place, at the wrong time and with the wrong enemy." In addition, the policy the government was following was recommended by the JCS and, in Bradley's opinion, was the most prudent course for the United States to follow in Korea, even though he could not guarantee that it would produce decisive results. Refusing to enlarge the fight to the point where America's global capacities were diminished was certainly not appeasement; rather it was a militarily sound course under the present circumstances. Like Marshall, Bradley also stressed the importance of maintaining America's friendly relations with its allies and noted the disadvantages that would follow the loss of their approval.[61]

By the time Bradley finished his testimony, it had become increasingly clear, even to the Republicans on the Senate panel, that MacArthur had stepped out of line and that Truman had acted within his authority in firing him. Republicans sought, therefore, to abbreviate the hearings. On May 24 Senator Bourke Hickenlooper of Iowa said that since other members of the JCS were in full agreement with Bradley, their testimony should not be solicited until Secretary of State Acheson had been called as a witness. Each of the JCS should be given a copy of the previous testimony and be asked simply whether they agreed with it. But Chairman Russell rejected that idea. The

Republicans had demanded the hearings, and he intended to call every relevant witness. This would not only strengthen the administration's case on relieving MacArthur, but the seemingly unlimited flow of testimony from Washington would tire a citizenry already growing bored with the details of the hearings. The Hickenlooper proposal was defeated by an 11 to 14 vote along party lines.[62]

Each of the JCS who then followed Bradley reaffirmed, on strictly military grounds, their approval of the decision to fire MacArthur. Of the Chiefs, the most important testimony came from Air Force General Hoyt Vandenberg who, better than anyone else, dispelled the notion that the JCS had allowed personal animus rather than strictly professional considerations to color their views on MacArthur. Bombing Manchuria, Vandenberg stated, would have committed a "shoestring" air force and left the United States "naked" in other areas that needed protection. Nor would bombing have guaranteed a decisive outcome to the Korean War. Actually, the United States had "reasonable chances" of gaining peace in Korea without bombing China. Besides, MacArthur's proposal required twice as many strategic bombing groups than the United States possessed.[63]

The emotional climax of the hearings came on Friday, June 1, when Secretary of State Acheson took the witness stand. For nine days the senators bore in with questions for Acheson. On trial was not simply the firing of MacArthur but the administration's entire Far East policy. Even as Acheson began his testimony, in fact, a group of senators led by William Knowland of California gained committee approval to release a classified State Department document of December 1949 concerning Formosa. The document's import was that the Department of State should emphasize Formosa's military incompetence in case it should fall to the Communists, as seemed likely in 1949. The Senate panel released this document despite Acheson's statement that it "would have a very damaging effect" on America's Far East policy. By the second day of his testimony Acheson had become so fearful "that a hash would be made of this complex matter [of America's China policy] if it was covered only by hit-or-miss questions and answers" that he asked for, and obtained, permission to postpone questions on China

until the following Monday, when he would make a full statement.[64]

Meanwhile, Acheson used the hearings to send a message to
the enemy. Under no circumstances would the United States
consider discussing, in cease-fire negotiations, the admission of
the Peking government into the United Nations or a settlement
of the Formosa question. But a cease-fire agreement might be
reached if there could be a "real settlement" of the Korean War
at the 38th parallel. In effect, Acheson was telling the Chinese
what had been America's policy since the end of 1950. The
United States was no longer seeking reunification of Korea by
military means. It was willing to accept a division of the country
at the 38th parallel.[65]

As he promised, the secretary of state delivered on Monday,
June 3, a three-hour statement on America's China policy,
which amounted to a diplomatic history of Sino-American relations from before World War II. The crux of his remarks were
the intricacies of Chinese politics and the complexities of discussions on China. If there was a central theme to Acheson's
commentary, it was, as he later said, "the century-long disinte-
gration of China's ancient institutions and ways of life from
collision with the Western world." The United States, according
to Acheson, did not "lose" China; it was the corruption of the
Chiang Kai-shek regime and its failure to broaden the government that accounted for that.[66]

During the rest of his testimony Acheson tried to amplify on
these points and to deflect some of the stinging attacks against
him and the administration. He repeated that the United States
opposed China's admission into the UN. He remarked that the
Communist regime in China was secure; that the existence of
a Sino-Soviet mutual security pact would justify Soviet intervention if the Korean War was extended to the China mainland;
that America's allies opposed such an extension; and that the
methods proposed by MacArthur "were likely to produce
greater loss and suffering than what is being done." In this
respect, he disagreed emphatically with the contention by
Ralph E. Flanders of Vermont that bombing Manchuria would
pose only a "minimum risk" of touching off World War III.
Acheson said that it would invite "catastrophe." Similarly, the
secretary rejected comments by Democrats Walter George of

Georgia and Harry Byrd of Virginia that America's decision to withdraw its troops from Korea in 1949 had been a "grave error." This had not been an act of appeasement but was the result of a UN recommendation. ("That doesn't make it an accurate or proper recommendation," Byrd responded.) On several occasions Acheson denied that there were Communist sympathizers in the State Department, although he admitted that two diplomatic aides in Hong Kong had been relieved for security reasons. Finally, in response to contrary suggestions, he stressed again and again that no connection existed between the Far East settlement worked out at the Yalta Conference of 1945 and the Communist victory in the Chinese civil war. The Nationalist defeat, he made clear, was due in good measure to economic collapse despite huge credits extended Chiang Kai-shek by the United States before the war.[67]

By the last two days of Acheson's testimony, the questions had become increasingly repetitive and had to do mostly with the issue of China's internal condition in 1945. All sides had become so tired of the hearings that on June 18 they voted to hear only four more witnesses from a prospective list of more than a hundred. Three of these were high military officials who had served in the Far East. The fourth was retired General Patrick Hurley, who had been ambassador to China from 1944 to 1945. They added little to what had already been said, although Hurley remarked that Acheson's earlier statement that Chiang Kai-shek had not been unhappy over the Yalta agreement was tantamount to saying that "China really liked the fact that we betrayed it in secret at Yalta."[68]

The hearings over, the Senate panel decided to issue no final report. As Dean Acheson later explained, Chairman Russell believed that a majority report would invite a minority report, which would be divisive and serve no useful purpose. Russell chose instead to deal "with those gloriously broad generalities to which the wise and just could repair, thus turning the committee from unhappy differences to universal agreement."[69] But eight of the twelve Republicans on the panel did issue a series of "conclusions" in which they took the administration to task on a number of accounts. They criticized the manner in which MacArthur had been relieved of his duties, the lack of a plan for victory in Korea except as MacArthur advocated, and the fact that the White House had been more concerned with conciliating the other members of the UN than advancing the security of the United States. They also attributed Chiang Kai-shek's defeat in China solely to the fact "that he did not receive sufficient support, both moral and material, from the United States." But on the central question of Truman's decision to relieve MacArthur, the Republicans remarked that the "removal of Gen. MacArthur was within the constitutional power of the President." On that note one of the most dramatic and politically important confrontations of the postwar era ended.[70]

Following the hearings, MacArthur traveled throughout the country, speaking out ever more strongly against the administration than he had during his testimony before the Senate panel, but always to diminishing audiences. In June the general traveled to Texas for a four-day, six-city tour. Elaborate preparations preceded his visit, and in each city he went to thousands of spectators lined the route from the airport into town. State and local dignitaries jockeyed for position near MacArthur. In Houston, the Shamrock Hotel, where he was staying, greeted him with a huge electric sign, "Welcome General Douglas MacArthur," and a seventeen-gun salute. The next day downtown businesses were closed at four o'clock so that employees could hear MacArthur later that day. Free shuttle service was provided to Rice Institute's new stadium where he was to speak. But when the general delivered his address, only about 20,000 of the stadium's 70,000 seats were filled. At the Cotton Bowl in Dallas, MacArthur attracted an equally small crowd of about 27,000. By the time he had finished his tour, in fact, fewer than 100,000 Texans had bothered to hear him speak. The general had simply become old news, and the American public had tired of the controversy surrounding his firing.[71]

As for Truman, a Gallup poll in June showed that his popularity had slipped even more since March. Only 24 percent of those polled now approved of his handling of the Presidency.[72] Even many of those who had stood firmly behind Truman in his decision to fire MacArthur and who had generally supported his conduct of the war were now wondering aloud about his effectiveness as President. Partly this concern reflected their fear that the White House was trying to preempt the opposition by adopting a more inflexible anti-Communist position. Here they

had mainly in mind the firm stand against UN membership for
Communist China or discussion of the Formosa question that
Secretaries Marshall and Acheson had taken in their testimony
during the MacArthur hearings. But they were also concerned
by a White House decision in May to tighten the economic
blockade of China and even to bomb Manchurian air bases in
the event of a massive Chinese air attack on UN forces from
Manchuria. The Washington *Post* was so sure that the administration was going to do just that that it called for Acheson's
resignation on the grounds that he was betraying his own policies and becoming indistinguishable from MacArthur.[73]

Beyond their concern about administration policy, however,
even these critics came to share some of the same doubts about
the President's leadership that Truman's more strident opponents were expressing. If they were less engaged in character
assassination than the latter, their conclusion was often much
the same—as President, Truman was a disaster. "Nothing like
the present collapse of Administration control in Congress has
been seen since Hoover's day," the *New Republic* thus remarked toward the end of May. "All that was happening in
1933 was the collapse of the banks, but today a war is on.
. . . Truman's prestige is near bottom; what exists is a stalemate,
a sit-down strike . . . the Ship of State drifts. Nobody is in
control."[74]

Unquestionably, Truman's firing of MacArthur had been
one of the most courageous and important actions by any President in the twentieth century. By his peremptory dismissal of
a figure who, for many, had become a symbol of national destiny, Truman had reaffirmed the fundamental principles of executive control over foreign policy and the President's role as
commander in chief of the armed services. But with twenty-one
months left before Truman would leave office and with the
Korean War dragging on from month to month, only a relatively few Americans sensed the long-term implications of what
the President had done.

As the Korean War entered its second year, in fact, the
optimism of February and March, when UN forces had contained the Communist drive in Korea and begun an offensive
of their own, had largely disappeared. By this time, the war had
turned into a military deadlock without an apparent end. In the

minds of many Americans the one military genius who might have snatched victory from disaster had been relieved of his command by one of the nation's most inept Presidents. The national mood was thus one of dissatisfaction and disillusionment. Yet even before the MacArthur hearings had ended, new hope for a negotiated end to the war developed when the Soviet delegate to the United Nations, Jacob Malik, indicated that the Soviet Union was ready for a cease-fire in Korea. From this first intimation would follow the opening of peace talks in July.

NOTES

1. James F. Schnabel, *Policy and Direction: The First Year* (Washington, D. C., 1972), 326–27 and 333–34; *Time*, 57 (January 15, 1951), 21–23.
2. *Time*, 57 (January 8, 1951), 15–16; *ibid.* (January 29, 1951), 28–29; Edgar O'Ballance, *Korea: 1950–1953* (London, 1969), 73–76.
3. David Rees, *Korea: The Limited War* (New York, 1964), 184–91; Schnabel, *Policy and Direction*, 333–39; *Time*, 57 (February 5, 1951), 19; *ibid.* (February 26, 1951), 28; *Life*, 30 (February 19, 1951), 25 and 34.
4. *Life*, 30 (February 19, 1951), 25; *Time*, 57 (March 5, 1951), 26–28.
5. O'Ballance, *Korea*, 82–83; *Time*, 57 (February 19, 1951), 34; *ibid.* (March 5, 1951), 28.
6. James F. Schnabel and Robert J. Watson, *The History of the Joint Chiefs of Staff*, III, *The Korean War* (unpublished manuscript, National Archives, 1978), 439–40.
7. Schnabel, *Policy and Direction*, 339–40; *Time*, 57 (February 26, 1951), 28.
8. Schnabel and Watson, *The History of the Joint Chiefs of Staff*, III, *The Korean War*, 466; Schnabel, *Policy and Direction*, 354–64; *Time*, 57 (March 26, 1951), 28–29; Rees, *Korea: The Limited War*, 191–93.
9. *FR*, 1951, VII, 152–53 and 165–67; Dean Acheson, *Present at the Creation: My Years in the State Department* (New York, 1969), 517; Schnabel, *Policy and Direction*, 350–51.
10. Schnabel, *Policy and Direction*, 351–53; *FR*, 1951, VII, 190–94.
11. "Memorandum for the Secretary of Defense," February 27, 1951, Box 16, Selected Records Relating to the Korean War.
12. "Memorandum of Conversation," March 6, 1951, Box 3, Selected

Records Relating to the Korean War; *FR*, 1951, VII, 202–203 and 211–13.

13. *Public Papers of the Presidents of the United States: Harry S. Truman*, 1951 (Washington, D.C., 1965), 188.

14. Schnabel and Watson, *The History of the Joint Chiefs of Staff*, III, *The Korean War*, 477.

15. *Life*, 30 (March 12, 1951), 64–68; *ibid.* (April 16, 1954), 44–45; *Nation*, 172 (March 24, 1951), 264; *New Republic*, 124 (March 26, 1951), 3–4.

16. *Time*, 57 (March 19, 1951), 25; *New Republic*, 124 (March 26, 1951), 5–6 and 13–16.

17. *Nation*, 172 (March 10, 1951), 218 and 223; *Commonweal*, 53 (March 9, 1951), 534; *Atlantic Monthly*, 187 (March 1951), 13.

18. *New Yorker*, 27 (March 24, 1951), 88–89.

19. Stephen Ambrose, *Eisenhower: Soldier, General of the Army, President-Elect, 1890–1952* (New York, 1983), 500–504; *New Republic*, 124 (April 2, 1951), 9.

20. *New Yorker*, 27 (March 24, 1951), 90–91; *Atlantic Monthly*, 187 (March 1951), 6–8. See also *Commonweal*, 53 (March 16, 1951), 555.

21. *New Republic*, 124 (March 26, 1951), 3–4; *Time*, 57 (April 9, 1951), 19; *New Republic*, 124 (April 16, 1951), 5–6.

22. *FR*, 1951, VII, 223–26; Harry S. Truman, *Years of Trial and Hope: Memoirs* (New York, 1965), 497.

23. David S. McLellan, *Dean Acheson: The State Department Years* (New York, 1976), 310.

24. *FR*, 1951, VII, 246–47, 251, and 264–65; Schnabel, *Policy and Direction*, 357; Truman, *Years of Trial and Hope*, 498–99.

25. Acheson, *Present at the Creation*, 517.

26. *FR*, 1951, VII, 255–56.

27. *Ibid.*, 265–66.

28. *Ibid.*, 731–32 and 785–86; Schnabel, *Policy and Direction*, 359.

29. Truman, *Years of Trial and Hope*, 501.

30. John W. Spanier, *The Truman-MacArthur Controversy and the Korean War* (Cambridge, Mass., 1959), 201–202; Schnabel, *Policy and Direction*, 358–59.

31. Unsigned Memorandum, March 24, 1951, Box 66, Acheson Papers; Acheson, *Present at the Creation*, 519.

32. *Ibid; Life*, 30 (March 9, 1951), 36.

33. Acheson, *Present at the Creation*, 519; *FR*, 1951, VII, 267.

34. William Manchester, *American Caesar: Douglas MacArthur, 1880–1964* (Boston, 1978), 638.

35. *FR*, 1951, VII, 299.

36. Richard H. Rovere and Arthur Schlesinger, Jr., *The MacArthur Controversy and American Foreign Policy* (New York, 1951), 172.
37. Acheson, *Present at the Creation*, 521.
38. *Ibid.*, 522–23; Truman, *Years of Trial and Hope*, 508–509; Rovere and Schlesinger, Jr., *The MacArthur Controversy and American Foreign Policy*, 175–76.
39. Rovere and Schlesinger, Jr., *The MacArthur Controversy and American Foreign Policy*, 170; Trumbull Higgins, *Korea and the Fall of MacArthur: A Précis in Limited War* (New York, 1960), 110.
40. *New Yorker*, 27 (April 21, 1951), 66; *ibid.* (April 28, 1951), 70; *Nation*, 172 (April 21, 1951), 363–65.
41. Cabell Phillips, *The Truman Presidency: The History of a Triumphant Succession* (Baltimore, 1969), 336; Robert J. Donovan, *Tumultuous Years: The Presidency of Harry S. Truman, 1949–1953* (New York, 1982), 311–12; Robert H. Ferrell, *Harry S. Truman and the Modern American Presidency* (Boston, 1983), 188–89.
42. Spanier, *The Truman-MacArthur Controversy and the Korean War*, 211–12.
43. Donovan, *Tumultuous Years*, 358–59; *Time*, 57 (April 23, 1951), 26; David M. Oshinsky, *A Conspiracy So Immense: The World of Joe McCarthy* (New York, 1983), 194; Cabell Phillips, *The Truman Presidency: The History of a Triumphant Succession* (New York, 1966), 345.
44. *Nation*, 172 (April 4, 1951), 337; *New Republic*, 124 (April 23, 1951), 5–6; *New Yorker*, 27 (April 21, 1951), 106; *Congressional Quarterly Almanac*, VII (1951), 243.
45. Phillips, *The Truman Presidency*, 347–48; Spanier, *The Truman-MacArthur Controversy*, 217; *Nation*, 172 (April 28, 1951), 388.
46. Rovere and Schlesinger, Jr., *The MacArthur Controversy and American Foreign Policy*, 179–82.
47. *New York Times*, April 20, 1951; Spanier, *The Truman-MacArthur Controversy*, 217; Phillips, *The Truman Presidency*, 348; *Nation*, 172 (April 28, 1951), 388.
48. Rovere and Schlesinger, Jr., *The MacArthur Controversy and American Foreign Policy*, 179–82.
49. *Congressional Quarterly Almanac*, 1951, 244.
50. "Memorandum on Questions for MacArthur Hearings," Box 341, Lyndon Baines Johnson Papers, U. S. Senate, 1949–1961, Lyndon Baines Johnson Library (Austin, Texas).
51. *Ibid.*
52. *Ibid.*
53. U. S. Congress, *Military Situation in the Far East*, Hearings Before

the Joint Senate Committee on Armed Services and Foreign Relations, 82nd Congress, 1st Session, 11–13, 22–26, 29–30, 39–40, 54–55, 67–68, and 136–37.

54. *Ibid.*, 13, 15–16, 25–26, and 47–48.
55. *Ibid.*, 11–20 and 45–46.
56. *Ibid.*, 76, "Some General Observations on the Hearings," n.d., Box 341, Johnson Papers, U.S. Senate, 1946–61. See also Higgins, *Korea and the Fall of MacArthur,* 160–61.
57. *New York Times,* May 5, 1951.
58. Senate Hearings, *Military Situation in the Far East,* 324–25.
59. *Ibid.*
60. *Ibid.*, 354–70, 439–90, and 571–609. See also "Analysis of Testimony of General Marshall, May 7–14 Inclusive," n.d., Box 341, Johnson Papers, United States Senate, 1949–1961.
61. Senate Hearings, *Military Situation in the Far East,* 730–44. See also "Analysis of May 15 Testimony," n.d., Box 341, Johnson Papers, United States Senate, 1949–1961.
62. Joseph C. Goulden, *Korea: The Untold Story of the War* (New York, 1982), 541.
63. Senate Hearings, *Military Situation in the Far East,* 1375–90.
64. *Ibid.*, 1673–1714 and 1765–66; Acheson, *Present at the Creation,* 525.
65. Senate Hearings, *Military Situation in the Far East,* 1756.
66. *Ibid.*, 1837–85; Acheson, *Present at the Creation,* 525.
67. Senate Hearings, *Military Situation in the Far East,* 1891, 1945–47, 1994–96, and 2008–10.
68. *Ibid.*, 2338–42 and 2827–56.
69. Acheson, *Present at the Creation,* 526.
70. "Individual Views of Certain Members . . . ," Senate Hearings, *Military Situation in the Far East,* 3567–75.
71. *Time,* 57 (June 25, 1951), 21–22; *New Republic,* 124 (June 25, 1951), 6; *Life,* 30 (June 25, 1951), 40–42.
72. *Time,* 57 (June 25, 1951), 18.
73. *New Yorker,* 27 (May 19, 1951), 71; *New Republic,* 124 (May 21, 1951), 5–6; *Nation,* 172 (May 26, 1951), 481; *New Republic,* 124 (May 28, 1951), 5. See also *Life,* 30 (May 14, 1951), 40.
74. *New Republic,* 124 (May 21, 1951), 3; *Atlantic Monthly,* 187 (June 1951), 4; *Nation,* 172 (March 31, 1951), 300–301; *ibid.* (April 14, 1951), 341.

CHAPTER 6

The Opening of Negotiations

Although the Soviet Union originated the series of events that led to the opening of cease-fire talks in July 1951, pressure on the Truman administration to arrange a cease-fire in Korea had been mounting among America's European allies and at the United Nations since the President fired General MacArthur in April. While the White House and State Department generally agreed that the United States should undertake a peace initiative following the lines of the statement the President had intended to issue in March, before MacArthur had torpedoed the plan, they also felt strongly that no peace proposal could be made until after the outcome of a military offensive that the Communists had launched on April 22. Otherwise, it would appear the United States was merely acting from a position of military weakness.[1]

Begun in the early evening of the twenty-second, after a four-hour artillery barrage whose intensity surprised American intelligence officers, the Chinese attack turned out to be their greatest military effort of the war. Striking in massive numbers and employing their now familiar tactic of human wave assaults accompanied by shouting and loud bugle blowing, they sought to envelop and isolate Seoul from the north and northeast. But the heaviest fighting was just south of the Imjin River, about twenty-five miles northwest of Seoul, where the heavily outnumbered British Twenty-ninth Infantry brigade and a smaller contingent of other UN forces beat back the enemy for almost three days before being ordered to withdraw toward Seoul. By the time the fighting was over, only 39 officers and men were left of the 622 men comprising the famed Gloucestershire Regiment, which had been in the most advanced of the brigade's three echelons when the attack began. In all the Twenty-ninth had suffered more than a thousand casualties.[2]

Fighting in other sectors along the front was also fierce. To the right of the Twenty-ninth, the American Third Division, which had retreated to the Imjin River, came under heavy attack by Chinese forces, many of whom had been newly outfitted and rearmed. Farther east, in the Marine and ROK zone of IX Corps, two ROK artillery units were overrun after losing all their equipment. To preserve his forces, General James Van Fleet, who had taken over the Eighth Army after President Truman had named General Ridgway as MacArthur's replacement in Tokyo, ordered a withdrawal of up to twenty-five miles to a new line, NO NAME, running roughly from Seoul along the north bank of the Han River.[3]

The withdrawal of UN forces, however, was much different from the disorderly retreat of the previous winter. In the first place, the attack had been expected. Although its scope and intensity had not been predicted, military intelligence knew that the Chinese were building up their forces for a spring offensive. As a result, UN forces were better prepared when the Chinese did strike. Second, even though they were forced to give ground before the sheer numbers of the enemy, they retreated in good order, fighting at favorable spots and inflicting maximum casualties on the Chinese through superior air and fire power. Although the British Twenty-ninth Brigade had suffered major casualties before breaking contact with the enemy, it left an estimated 10,000 to 15,000 Chinese dead. Also, it had held the enemy up long enough to disrupt its timetable all along the front.[4]

By the end of April the Communist offensive had spent itself. Efforts to outflank Seoul failed. On April 29 UN air power broke up a final Chinese attempt to ferry 6000 troops across the Han Estuary in order to advance on Seoul from the west. The historic capital remained in UN hands. General Van Fleet had his army intact at the NO NAME line and was even holding back some reserves. Its food and ammunition exhausted, the enemy withdrew in the face of UN firepower. For a maximum gain of thirty-five miles, the Chinese had suffered an estimated

70,000 casualties, as opposed to 7000 casualties for UN forces.[5]

On May 16 the Chinese launched a second phase of their spring offensive, but this too failed. Suffering enormous losses as they moved against defenses heavily protected with mines, barbed wire, interlocking machine gun fire, and drums of napalm that could be detonated electrically, the Chinese were able to cut a hole in the eastern sector through two South Korean divisions and, for a short time, to threaten the U. S. Second Division. But the Americans held their ground, and after four days of heavy fighting the enemy achieved only a relatively narrow penetration on a secondary front. The carnage was the worst of the war. Chinese losses were estimated at 90,000 for the week of May 17 to May 23 alone and in excess of 200,000 for both phases of the spring offensive. Instead of having his men dig in after beating back the enemy, furthermore, Van Fleet went on the offensive. Within five days UN forces and tanks had once more crossed the 38th parallel. In every sector the Chinese were falling back, their spring offensive having been routed.[6]

How far above the 38th parallel UN forces might have advanced had they been permitted to do so is difficult to determine. On one hand, the Chinese were disorganized and demoralized. For the first time in the war they were surrendering in large numbers—more than 17,000 in the last two weeks of May. Certainly Van Fleet was dismayed when the JCS ordered him not to go much beyond the vicinity of the KANSAS line, which ran along the base of the Iron Triangle. Although that order was modified somewhat and Eighth Army was permitted to advance to line WYOMING in order to iron out a bulge running from the Imjin River through Chorwon and Kumhwa, to the Hwachon Reservoir, Van Fleet felt that his forces should have been allowed to move farther north. "[W]e had the Chinese whipped," Van Fleet later remarked. "They were definitely gone. They were in awful shape."[7]

On the other hand, more than one million Communist troops still remained in North Korea, and as the UN armies moved north toward the Iron Triangle, enemy resistance stiffened considerably. The Chinese defended the approaches to the Triangle with particular tenacity. Many were holed up in bunkers and dugouts protected with eight or ten feet of logs and earth, which had been constructed by the North Koreans before they invaded South Korea the previous summer. The Chinese also laid down some of the heaviest artillery barrages of the war, using captured American 155s and Soviet-made 150s. Although UN forces were able to drive most of the enemy from their fortifications with grenades, flamethrowers, and bayonets, a move into the Iron Triangle would almost certainly have meant enormous UN casualties.[8]

Political considerations even more than military factors, however, were responsible for the decision to limit the UN offensive into North Korea. Responding to mounting world opinion against prolonging the war and believing that it could now negotiate from a position of strength, the Truman administration decided to halt the UN advance in order to test the chances for peace. It did so despite opposition from some within the administration who maintained that the enemy had given no indication that it had changed its military and political objectives in Korea.

The White House's decision to undertake a peace initiative was in sharp contrast to its first reaction to the Chinese offensive. Its initial response had been to ask the United Nations for a select embargo on war goods for China, involving both petroleum products and materials used in the production of weaponry, and to authorize General Ridgway to institute retaliatory bombing of Chinese bases in Manchuria in the event they were used for a massive attack against UN forces. On both these issues the United States gained the support of its coalition partners in Korea, but not without considerable skepticism and hesitation on their part.[9]

At the UN the American resolution for a select embargo against China was approved easily at the end of May, but even America's closest ally, the British, had been reluctant to vote for it. Although they went along with the United States after Secretary of State Acheson explained the American position to British Foreign Secretary Herbert Morrison, they made clear their opposition to a complete embargo, which the administration would have preferred, and they indicated their reservations about even a partial embargo. Not only would such trade restrictions cause grave hardship for its colony of Hong Kong, through which passed much of the world's commerce with

China, it would create considerable resentment among Asians, who would raise charges of racial discrimination by industrial countries against Third World nations.[10]

As for the possible use of American air power against Chinese air bases in Manchuria, that was even a more touchy issue with the British, although once again they yielded to the Americans. General Ridgway had first raised the question of bombing the Manchurian air bases in March when he asked the JCS for authority to retaliate against the bases if they were used to attack his forces. By this time the Chinese were far along in building a considerable force of MIG-15 jets and other fighter planes in Manchuria that threatened UN air operations over North Korea. Since February MIG fighters had been intercepting B-29s on bombing missions near the Yalu River, and military intelligence reported a significant Chinese air buildup in preparation for their spring offensive. Ridgway wanted to be able to destroy this air power if it threatened to be a major factor in the war.[11]

Although the Joint Chiefs had approved a draft order granting Ridgway the authority he requested, no final action had been taken when, on April 12, an attack by eighty MIGs operating from Manchuria against forty-eight B-29s and seventy-five escort fighters underscored just how significant China's air force had become.[12] Once again the Far East commander asked for authority to retaliate against the Manchurian air bases if the Chinese launched a major air attack against UN forces, and this time President Truman approved Ridgway's request. When informed of the President's decision, the British agreed to go along with it "in principle"; in case of heavy air attacks on UN forces in Korea from bases in Manchuria, they would "associate themselves with the policy of retaliatory action against these bases in order to prevent further attacks and to minimise casualties to United Nations forces in Korea."[13]

Throughout the months in which the question of bombing Manchuria had been under review, however, the British had made clear their serious reservations about attacking Manchuria. First they contended that any decision for retaliation against China should be made by the President and not the JCS. When General Bradley of the Joint Chiefs and Paul Nitze of the State Department tried to reassure them on this point, they insisted on the right to participate in the making of such a momentous decision. Even after they agreed to the principle of retaliatory bombing, Foreign Secretary Herbert Morrison reiterated the British position that the consequences of bombing Manchuria, "which may be general war," were so grave as to warrant London's prior approval.[14]

England's reluctance to go along with the United States on the bombing issue and on an embargo against China added to the larger malaise that characterized America's relations with its European allies in the spring of 1951. Washington and London remained extremely close allies, of course. While the occasion for much heated language both in England and the United States, the conflict over Far East policy was part of what the respected British economist John Cleveland referred to as the "growing pains of Anglo-America." Cleveland made the point that "only because both countries have felt the overriding security that their alliance provides have they been able to indulge in the healthy exercise of mutual and self-criticism."[15]

Yet it was not only on the issues of the Korean War and America's Far East policy that substantial differences had developed between London and Washington. Almost as important was the issue of European rearmament. In fact, the Labor Party had split over the costs of rearmament. In April Aneurin Bevan, the leader of the Labor left, even resigned from the Cabinet because of that issue. In explaining to Parliament the reasons for his resignation, Bevan bitterly assailed the United States. "We have allowed ourselves to be dragged too far . . . behind the anarchy of American competitive capitalism," he told the House of Commons. "The fact is that the Western world has embarked upon a scale of arms production so quickly and of such an extent that the foundations of political liberty and parliamentary democracy will not be able to sustain the shock."[16]

Other Europeans expressed similar sentiments. Indeed, opposition to the costs of rearmament was even greater in France than in England. The French believed that they had still not recovered sufficiently from the shattering economic effects of World War II to divert as large a proportion of production for defense as the United States or even England. French workers feared that a heavy military load would cut even more deeply into their already low standard of living. In a country where a skilled metals worker might hope to make thirty or thirty-five cents an hour and a university professor about forty-five dollars a month, the cost of the military program proposed by the United States seemed too much even if Washington was offering to pay most of the bill. Many Frenchmen also complained of undue American pressure to rearm. In elections in June Charles de Gaulle's Rassamblement du Peuples Français received the second largest bloc of votes, about 20 percent (finishing behind the Communists, who received about 25 percent of the vote), and gained the largest share of deputy seats in the National Assembly, 117 of 627, on a program that included resistance to American demands.[17]

Nevertheless, the Korean War remained the outstanding issue in world politics. Like the British, America's other coalition partners in Korea and most neutral and Third World nations at the United Nations opposed any military action that might continue, or even escalate, the war indefinitely. Although America's allies understood the symbolic importance of Korea in terms of resisting Communist expansion, most of them did not impute the same sense of crisis to the conflict as Washington did. Furthermore, they had to weigh other problems and commitments. The European powers continued to worry especially about becoming further mired in an Asian conflict while the Soviet Union had the capacity to strike somewhere in Europe. Neutral and Third World nations also remained concerned that the Korean War could escalate into a much larger nuclear confrontation involving the world's two superpowers.[18]

To prevent this, representatives at the UN from Sweden and Mexico met with the American delegation to discuss a proposal for ending the war by which UN forces would agree not to advance north of the 38th parallel if North Korea and China indicated that they would not move south of the parallel. Although the proposal was similar to his own plan for bringing about a cease-fire, Secretary of State Acheson rejected the UN initiative, telling the American delegates that he did not consider a General Assembly resolution the best vehicle for achieving peace. Efforts to end hostilities were far more likely to succeed, he said, if done through other available diplomatic channels and later confirmed by the General Assembly.[19] Nevertheless, the Swedish and Mexican proposal emphasized the general feeling at Lake Success that the United States should make a greater effort at reaching a cease-fire. As the American delegate to the UN, Warren Austin, told Washington, diplomats at Lake Success were disturbed by what they considered "the lack of a clear statement of aims [in Korea] beyond the military objective of repelling aggression and killing as many aggressors as possible."[20]

Responding to this growing pressure of world opinion and confident that it could negotiate from a position of military strength, the Truman administration decided to make a new effort at arranging a cease-fire in Korea. Most of those who urged that the United States undertake such a peace initiative assumed that Washington would have to deal directly with the Chinese. But an alternative which the State Department also pursued was to work through the Soviet Union, believing as it did that Moscow was the mastermind behind the Korean War. In Paris the Soviet expert, Charles Bohlen, thus approached a high-ranking Soviet official about ending the war, and for a while at the UN it looked as if the Soviet Union might be interested in the American offer. Reports to that effect even circulated in *The New York Times*. But the Soviets squashed these rumors, calling them mere fabrications.[21]

In mid-May the State Department decided to approach the Soviet Union once more, this time through George Kennan, the government's foremost Kreminologist, who was on leave at the Institute for Advanced Study. Kennan was instructed to arrange a meeting with Jacob Malik, the Soviet ambassador at the UN, in order to impress on him the dangerous world situation as a result of the Korean War and to make clear the United States' desire to arrange an armistice or cease-fire. Carrying out his instructions, Kennan met with Malik on May 31 and then again on June 5. At the second meeting Malik told Kennan that since the Soviet Union was not a belligerent in Korea, the United States should more appropriately approach the North Koreans and Chinese. Nothing was then heard from the Soviets for more than two weeks.[22]

On June 23, however, Moscow made a surprise move. Perhaps the Kremlin sensed a softening of the American position regarding the 38th parallel as a dividing line between UN and Communist forces in Korea (by this time Secretary of State

Acheson had remarked at the MacArthur hearings that the
United States was willing to consider a cease-fire around the
38th parallel and the removal of all foreign troops from Korea).
The Soviet Union was also undoubtedly anxious to end a war in
which casualties were enormous and chances of victory had
grown slim. Malik thus delivered a speech on a UN radio broadcast in which he said that the Soviet people believed the Korean
conflict could be ended. "[A]s a first step discussions should be
started between the belligerents for a cease-fire and an armistice providing for the mutual withdrawal of forces from the
38th parallel."[23]

By speaking in terms of the "Soviet people" rather than the
Soviet government and by remarking that discussions were
only "a first step" toward ending the Korean conflict, Malik
seemed to hedge a little in his speech. But from Moscow Ambassador Alan G. Kirk reported that Malik's remarks represented
a "significant new turn in [the] Soviet approach to Korea." No
longer did Moscow demand a withdrawal of foreign troops from
Korea or discussions on the China question as preliminaries to
peace talks on Korea. In Kirk's view, therefore, the United
States should not summarily dismiss Malik's statement as another Soviet ploy, but rather pursue it, albeit cautiously.[24]

This view was widely shared in the United States. In a carefully worded editorial, the Philadelphia *Inquirer* observed that
Malik's proposal "needs elaboration and careful consideration.
That is an olive branch in Malik's hand to be sure. But in reaching for it we cannot forget that experience with the USSR has
shown us we are not immune to poison ivy." Similarly the St.
Louis *Post-Dispatch* remarked, "The UN and the US certainly
cannot afford to dismiss the proposal out of hand nor can they
accept it in blissful naivete," while the Richmond *Times-
Dispatch* observed that "an end to the Korean war is fervently
to be desired, provided it can be had on honorable terms, and
provided, too, that if it comes, it doesn't lull us into a feeling of
false security." Finally *Commonweal* argued that the Soviets
sought peace because they believed the United States would
bomb Manchuria if the Chinese threw their air power into the
war. "What Mr. Malik has done is to propose a cease-fire not
because the Soviets seek peace in Korea," *Commonweal* maintained, "but because the Soviets do not want to be maneuvered

into a position of having to join the Chinese in an all-out war at this time against the superior atomic and industrial power of the West."[25]

Secretary Acheson agreed that while the United States should act with great care, it should enter into negotiations. Earlier Kennan had warned him that if the United States continued to advance into North Korea without making an effort to achieve a cease-fire, the Soviet Union would "see no alternative but to intervene themselves [in Korea]." Remarks in Chinese newspapers indicating that Chinese authorities approved of Malik's statement strengthened the argument for pursuing this apparently new opportunity to end the war.[26]

The question that faced Acheson and others within the administration was how to proceed with negotiations. In Moscow Deputy Foreign Minister Andrei Gromyko told Ambassador Kirk that military commanders in Korea should conclude an armistice limited to military matters. Political or territorial issues should not be raised. The State Department and Pentagon also concluded that it would be best for the military commanders in the field to arrange a cease-fire. Not only would that avoid the thorny question of negotiating with two governments not recognized by the United States, China and North Korea, it would make it easier to exclude sensitive political questions from the talks.[27]

On June 29 Assistant Secretary of State Rusk informed America's allies in Korea that early that evening General Ridgway would deliver a statement whose purpose was to discuss whether the enemy would be interested in meeting in the field to arrange a cease-fire. "We felt," Rusk remarked, "that it was important to continue with the idea that the other side had taken the initiative in this matter but not to say that they were suing for peace, thereby raising prestige obstacles. But we did desire to put the responsibility on the communists, to get the idea across that they had brought the topic up."[28]

On June 30, Tokyo time, General Ridgway broadcast his message to the Chinese, stating that if, as reported, they and their North Korean allies desired to negotiate a cease-fire and armistice, he was prepared to appoint a representative to meet with them aboard a Danish hospital ship in Wonson Harbor. Two days later China and North Korea replied that they were prepared to confer with Ridgway's representative but suggested that the two sides meet on July 10 at Kaesong near the 38th parallel. A leery Washington examined their proposal with care. It was couched in courteous language and stated that they wanted a meeting. But it also said that the purpose of the negotiations was the "cessation of military action and establishment of peace," whereas Gromyko had led the United States to believe that the negotiations would involve only military issues and not political or territorial matters.[29]

General Ridgway was against any proposal to halt hostilities prior to reaching an armistice agreement. Otherwise he believed the battlefield advantage which the UN forces had gained after five months of rebuilding the Eighth Army would be wiped out. He told the Joint Chiefs of Staff that he would reject an immediate cease-fire "unless otherwise instructed" and, pointing to intelligence reports of a Chinese military buildup in Korea, he stated that if he had to negotiate, the date for starting the talks should be moved up. The JCS agreed with Ridgway that hostilities should continue until an armistice agreement was reached, but they ordered Ridgway not to ask for an earlier meeting or to do anything else that might cause the enemy to change its mind about beginning negotiations.[30]

Carrying out his orders, Ridgway agreed to both the time (July 10) and the place (Kaesong) recommended by the Communists for the beginning of talks. But in another appeal to the JCS he urged that UN forces not be required by any final cease-fire agreement to withdraw farther south than the KANSAS line. "Any position taken by our government," Ridgway told the JCS, "which would compel me to abandon the Kansas line or deny me a reasonable outpost zone for its protection would vitally prejudice our entire military position in Korea."[31]

News that negotiations to end the war would soon begin in Korea created new hope in the United States and overseas. "Russia's initiative and the quick response of the Chinese and North Korean commanders to General Ridgway's truce proposals [is] implicit acknowledgment that the aggression of June 1950 has been defeated," the *Nation* thus reported. The *New Republic* was less sanguine, pointing out that "in Korea as in Germany and Japan there is likely to be an armistice but no formal peace settlement." In Congress a number of Republicans did express reservations and suspicions about the administration's efforts to begin cease-fire talks. But attempts to cut foreign spending and eliminate all wage and price controls began almost immediately after it was learned that Communist and UN negotiators would soon meet at the negotiating table. Overseas one journalist reported from London that the "moves toward peace in Korea [had] filled Londoners with hope as bright as the deep, blue mid-summer skies that are now arching over the city," while another commentator wrote from Rome that the Italians, tied as they were to the inflated American dollar, hoped that "international financial tensions [would] abate with a Korean truce."[32]

In contrast, South Korea expressed alarm at the prospect of an armistice with the Communists that would leave Korea divided. At the time arrangements were concluded to hold peace talks, the ROK government was faced with enormous economic and social problems. Much of South Korea had, of course, been ravaged by the fighting, but along with the war had also come a large refugee problem, major concerns about health and sanitation, and a skyrocketing inflation. In the first weeks of the Chinese invasion, close to one million refugees had fled south from Seoul and its environs. By June there were probably between three and six million displaced persons in South Korea. Cities in the south, like Pusan and Taegu, became overcrowded with double and triple their prewar populations. All over the south refugee camps were set up to provide shelter for the homeless, but they were not enough. Clinging to the sides of the hills that rose in the center of Pusan were hundreds of shanties and shacks built by refugees unable to find more suitable housing elsewhere. Although a number of relief organizations, such as the World Health Organization and the Red Cross, were effective in inoculating refugees against such killers as smallpox and typhus, medical facilities in most refugee camps were inadequate to handle the huge number of cases resulting from overcrowding and poor living conditions. Finally, the war contributed to a serious inflation. Prices were more than eight times what they had been three years earlier, the tax system was inefficient and poorly administered, and the government was deeply in debt.[33]

President Syngman Rhee also remained despotic and unpopular. Political opponents continued to be arrested on charges of being Communists and subversives, and Rhee stayed out of touch with most South Koreans. In a conversation with the Korean president, American Ambassador John Muccio warned him in April that for more than two years he had been "looking for indications of greater confidence of Koreans in one another and between the Government and the people and of improvement in the ability of Koreans to live and work together" and that he "could not satisfy [himself that] there had been substantial progress" in any of these respects. Less than two weeks later Muccio said much the same thing, pointing out to Rhee that no country was "militarily defensible unless it [was] in good health socially, economically and politically" and that South Korea met none of these conditions.[34]

Despite Rhee's personal unpopularity, however, and the desperate problems of economic and social dislocation, most South Koreans seemed to agree with Rhee's opposition to any plan that divided Korea at the 38th parallel. To reestablish the 38th parallel, Muccio thus told Secretary of State Acheson, "would bring a violent explosion from all Koreans and we would have [the] greatest difficulty keeping them within bounds and controlling ROK forces." Rhee wanted nothing less than to continue military operations once more to the Yalu River, and his government made clear to Washington that anything less would invite another invasion of South Korea by the Communists. His government's security would become impossible, and the Korean people would become demoralized and disillusioned with the United Nations.[35]

Anticipating the Korean reaction to the news of cease-fire negotiations, Acheson sent Muccio a virtual shopping list of points that he should use in presenting the American position regarding talks with the Communists. All of them indicated the hard line the administration intended to take toward any South Korean resistance to peace. They also underscored just how far the United States had traveled from the heady days of late October and November 1950, when the military reunification of Korea seemed all but assured.

Thus Acheson instructed Muccio to make clear to Rhee that his government never had any international recognition north of the 38th parallel. The American ambassador should also point out that while an independent and unified Korea had been American policy since 1941 and a UN aim since 1947, neither the United States nor the United Nations had ever assumed that unification should be achieved by force regardless of the circumstances. He should state that although the Security Council resolutions of June 25 and 27 related to repelling North Korean aggression and restoring international peace and security in Korea, the General Assembly resolution of October 7 authorized, but did not require, the pacification of North Korea and the unification of the country by military means. Similarly, he should note that the situation in Korea had changed dramatically since October 7 when the North Korean armies were falling apart and the presumption could be made that neither the Soviet Union nor the PRC would intervene in Korea; the Chinese intervention and "increasingly menacing attitude" of the Soviet Union, he should stress, had created a situation involving global power relationships that required the United States, in the interests of its own national security, to reassess its position and reconsider the proportion of its military resources it could commit to the Korean peninsula.[36]

After explaining why the United States had changed its policy on Korean unification, Muccio was further instructed by the secretary of state to point out to Rhee the increased dangers of a world war that a march north would bring and their likely consequences for Korea. He should make the South Korean leader realize that the outbreak of a world war would be disastrous for his country and that the future of his nation would be a prolongation of the horrors of war and probably its total destruction. Likewise, he should make Rhee aware that his hope for the future rested on the free world, which needed to end the war in order to rebuild its strength and defenses. Lastly, in a thinly veiled threat, he should emphasize to Rhee that if, by his intransigence, provocations, and inflammatory statements, he jeopardized an acceptable peace settlement, he could "expect a revulsion of feeling" against Korea by the American people, who had saved his country from destruction at a cost of nearly 100,000 battlefield casualties.[37]

Nothing that Muccio told Rhee did much to deter the aged president from his conviction that the war in Korea had to continue until the Communists were defeated and the country was unified under his leadership. Nevertheless, the United States went forward with its plans to hold talks with the Communists, and, bowing to American pressure, the South Korean government agreed to be represented at the negotiations, which both the UN and Communist sides said would begin at Kaesong on July 10.[38]

A preliminary skirmish two days before the talks were to begin indicated some of the trouble that UN negotiators might expect in their meetings with the Chinese and North Koreans. A UN liaison party, sent to Kaesong to make arrangements for the talks, was surrounded by enemy soldiers waving machine guns before Communist reporters and photographers, even though Kaesong was supposed to be a neutral site. The reporters pictured the UN forces as defeated and suing for peace and portrayed Kaesong as a Communist-held city to which UN truce teams in jeeps bearing the white flag of surrender had been summoned.[39]

The first two meetings on July 10 and 11 also revealed the considerable differences in negotiating positions between the two sides. The UN delegation, headed by Admiral C. Turner Joy, commander of naval forces in the Far East, sought to limit the talks to purely military matters, to obtain a militarily defensible cease-fire line, and to establish a Military Armistice Commission to supervise the truce. These aims were incorporated into a lengthy nine-point agenda, which the UN team handed to the Communist delegates.[40]

The North Koreans and Chinese, led by General Nam Il of the Korean People's Army and General Hsieh Fang of the Chinese People's Volunteers, responded with a much shorter four-point document calling for a cease-fire line at the 38th parallel (in other words, a return to the status quo ante bellum) and the withdrawal of all foreign forces from Korea. Joy rejected both items, maintaining that the first amounted to a conclusion that should be the subject of negotiations, not a preliminary to them, and that the second involved a political issue beyond the scope of the talks.[41]

Very quickly the talks broke down over fundamental issues of protocol and procedure. First, the Communists attempted to confine the UN negotiators to a house in Kaesong and a well-guarded pathway from there to the conference building. Then they raised a question of the UN delegation's freedom to communicate with its base at Munsan, located a short distance from Kaesong, when they refused to allow a UN courier to pass through their lines. Finally, they challenged the UN's right to decide the composition of its own delegation by refusing to permit a group of American newsmen to come to Kaesong, even though they allowed a number of their own photographers to take pictures of the conference room over the protests of the UN delegation.[42]

Responding to these provocations, Admiral Joy broke off negotiations on July 12, telling the Chinese and North Koreans that if the talks were to continue both sides would have to receive equal treatment at Kaesong, which would have to be demilitarized. The next day Ridgway broadcast a message to the Communists outlining the new terms for resuming negotiations. Not only did they agree to Ridgway's demands, but once the talks resumed on July 17, they made a major concession by consenting to eliminate from the agenda any reference to the 38th parallel.[43]

The opening of the negotiations and the agreement by the Communists to Ridgway's terms for resuming the talks after they had been broken off fed rising expectations in the United States that the war would soon end. "It appeared that the Reds —or their masters in Moscow—urgently wanted negotiations to continue," *Life* even explained in reporting the Chinese decision to return to the bargaining table. At the same time, *Commonweal* chided *Life* for arguing earlier that it was impossible to bargain with the Chinese and North Koreans. "General Ridgway has established the fact that the Communists can say 'yes' after all," it remarked.[44]

Even on the issue of withdrawing all foreign forces from Korea, the Chinese and North Koreans seemed remarkably flexible. At first they were *inflexible,* insisting on a mutual troop withdrawal despite the UN delegation's insistence that this was a political matter beyond the scope of a military armistice agreement. Indeed, the possibility that the Communists might break off armistice talks on this very question deeply troubled the Truman administration. Faced with the expectations at home that the war would soon be over, it was anxious to continue the discussions at Kaesong. So, too, the JCS stressed the importance of keeping the talks going, and when Ridgway informed them that he was planning to recess the negotiations unless the Communists altered their position, they ordered him not to do so. "You are not authorized, without further instructions," they told Ridgway, "to recess talks indefinitely, to be reconvened on condition of Communist concessions." Once again, however, the Chinese and North Koreans showed how tractable they could be by agreeing not to make the withdrawal of foreign troops from Korea an agenda item. Instead, they consented to a new item, which allowed issues like foreign troop withdrawals to be included as recommendations that the negotiators would make "to the governments of the countries concerned."[45]

As a result of this substitution, the agenda for the rest of the talks was completed. It had taken ten meetings and long hours of staff negotiations, but now the negotiators could get down to the first substantive issue between them, fixing a cease-fire line. As far as the UN delegation was concerned, prospects for a successful conclusion of the war seemed good. Morale was high, the Communists had indicated a surprising willingness to compromise on the agenda, and UN forces held a strong defensive position. In many respects the need to keep their troops alert and their guard up when peace seemed so near was the most difficult problem facing UN officers.[46]

But there were other problems as well. In the first place, the enemy was being reinforced constantly, thereby increasing its capacity for launching still another offensive against South Korea. General Ridgway cautioned his commanders that an attack could come at any time the negotiations broke down or during the Japanese peace conference scheduled for September. Chinese air strength was also growing, so that for the first time they had effective control of the air over northwest Korea. Second, the South Koreans remained highly disturbed at the prospects of a permanently divided Korea, and President Rhee agitated openly against any compromise with the Communists. The South Korean president even seriously considered withdrawing his representatives at Kaesong, and he supported massive public rallies against the peace talks. Angered by these demonstrations and by Rhee's plan to withdraw from the negotiations, President Truman warned the Korean leader of "the most serious consequences" that would follow any attempt on his part to undermine the talks. Finally, while the Chinese and North Koreans had made several concessions on the agenda for negotiations, they were certain to bring up again the issues of the 38th parallel as a cease-fire line and the withdrawal of all foreign forces from Korea. And the UN negotiators were as certain to reject the Communist position on both these matters.[47]

Indeed, as soon as the substantive talks began, the Chinese and North Koreans insisted on the 38th parallel as the demarcation line. The UN negotiators responded by advocating a line north of the battle line to compensate for the cessation of air and naval activity as far north as the Yalu River that would take place after a cease-fire. The UN position remained that any cease-fire agreement had to provide for a demilitarized zone that was militarily defensible. UN negotiators also contended that there was no military logic for a demarcation line along the 38th parallel. Admiral Joy declared that the 38th parallel had only political significance, and he reminded the Communists that the line had been crossed four times already during the war. Several times he offered to discuss lines other than the 38th parallel, but each time the Chinese and North Korean delegates argued that the 38th parallel was the only acceptable line for ending the conflict.[48]

Weeks passed without any progress toward ending the war. Newspaper and radio reports became increasingly more pessimistic as to when a breakthrough in the talks would come. Some previously optimistic government leaders issued their own gloomy forecasts about the prospects for peace. A few observers did attempt to challenge these prophets of doom. "Obviously anything can happen," one journalist thus remarked, "but a dispassionate observer would discount omens of disaster, keeping firmly in mind that the Communists, especially the Chinese and Russians, quite evidently want an end to war."[49]

Increasingly, however, Americans began to lose interest in the truce negotiations. More and more, attention was focused on other news. Major domestic stories included a Senate investigation of racketeering in the United States, new charges of corruption and malfeasance in the Truman administration, the national myopia of McCarthyism, and the Presidential elections still more than a year away. One might have expected the last two of these items to have been tied closely to the administration's conduct of the war, including its handling of the peace negotiations. A year earlier Korea had figured prominently both in the attacks against the administration by McCarthy and his followers and in the congressional elections. In addition, the Republicans' likeliest nominee for president, Robert Taft, was also one of the leading critics of Truman's handling of the war.[50]

For the most part, however, the Korean War was incidental to both of these stories. With respect to McCarthy, he and his stalwart supporters, such as Pat McCarran of Nevada, continued to figure prominently in the news. A Senate committee investigating the Maryland campaign of 1950, in which Millard Tydings had been soundly defeated by John Marshall Butler, portrayed McCarthy's involvement in the election as dishonest and malicious. McCarthy responded by calling the committee's report a "left-wing smear and character assassination" and by referring to the Democratic Party as "a party of Communists and crooks." As chairman of the Senate's Internal Security Subcommittee, McCarran repeated what had become routine charges that China had been "lost" to the Communists by the State Department and accused such authorities on the Far East as Owen Lattimore of Johns Hopkins University, whom a year earlier McCarthy had called the "top Russian espionage agent" in the United States, of being "a conscious articulate instrument of the Soviet conspiracy."[51]

Besides these familiar but still sensational accusations on Capitol Hill, there were other indications that the Red Scare had not yet run its course in the United States. For example, several leaders of the small and politically inconsequential Communist Party in the United States were arrested for violating the 1940 Smith Act, which forbade Americans to teach or advocate the overthrow of the government by force and violence. Other Americans suspected of being "Communists" or just "leftists" were also persecuted and prosecuted. A number of states even passed loyalty programs to ferret out such state employees. The territory of Hawaii adopted a particularly drastic loyalty program, authorizing the creation of a loyalty board with the power to oust any employee whose loyalty was in "reasonable doubt."[52]

But if fear of Communist infiltration and internal subversion was still very much in the news in the summer and fall of 1951, only rarely was the Korean War included in the list of charges against the administration by those who shared these beliefs. In fact, the administration's conduct of the war and its firm policy on matters like the China question, loyalty checks for federal employees, and the containment of Communist expansion were cited by even some of its harshest critics as reasons for abandoning McCarthyism. McCarthy's charges of internal conspiracy, *Life* thus remarked in October, might have seemed plausible a year ago, but not anymore. *"Communist infiltration of government is no longer a legitimate worry." (Life's* italics.)[53]

Similarly, the Korean War had not yet become an issue in Presidential politics in the same way that it had been involved in the congressional elections of a year earlier. By no means, of course, was Korea forgotten or deemed irrelevant to the forthcoming Presidential campaign. The Republican Party's leading candidate for President, Senator Taft, had been among those Republicans in Congress expressing dismay at rumors in June that peace negotiations might soon begin. On the Senate floor he had joined other Republicans in berating the administration for seeking less than total victory in Korea. "Apparently the President is willing to get out of the present war as best he can," Taft had told the Senate in June. "The Administration has moved to be somewhat more emphatic against the Chinese because of the protest against MacArthur's dismissal, but they still look longingly to such a peace. If such a peace is made, we have wasted 140,000 casualties and billions of dollars."[54]

Subsequently, the Ohio senator described the war in Korea as "useless and expensive," accused President Truman of lacking "the guts" to win in Korea, and charged Secretary of State Acheson with abandoning Chiang Kai-shek and relishing the Communist victory in China because "in the State Department there's been a strong Communist sympathy, as far as the Chinese Communists are concerned." But Korea was simply not a central theme in most of Taft's public speeches, which had to do more with such domestic issues as excessive military spending, federal aid to medical schools, and a proposal for a federal sales tax that Taft opposed. Also, when Senator McCarthy accused Defense Secretary and former Secretary of State George

Marshall of taking part in a "conspiracy so immense, so black, as to dwarf any in the previous history of man," Taft dissented. Although he agreed with McCarthy that as secretary of state in 1947 and 1948 Marshall had followed "the most stupid possible policy" in the Far East, he stated publicly that he did "not agree with Senator McCarthy's accusations of conspiracy or treason."[55]

Also in terms of foreign news, there were a number of recent developments, particularly in the Middle East, that competed with Korea for national attention. Of these the most important was the Iranian seizure of the Anglo-Iranian Oil Company (AIOC), a wholly owned firm of the British government that had a monopoly on oil production in Iran. A result of AIOC's failure to negotiate fairly with the Teheran government about increasing its royalty payments to Iran, the nationalization of AIOC's properties took place after Mohammed Mossadegh, leader of an Iranian nationalist movement, became prime minister in April.[56] Describing the obstreperousness of AIOC officials in their dealings with Teheran, former Secretary of State Acheson later commented, "[n]ever had so few lost so much so stupidly and so fast."[57] But in the summer of 1951 the nationalization of AIOC properties was widely perceived in the United States as part of a much larger problem involving a growing tide of nationalism in the Middle East that threatened such vital Western interests as access to the region's oil and control over the Suez Canal and which posed the additional danger of Soviet expansionism. The assassination in July of two pro-Western Arab leaders, King Abdullah of Jordan and former Premier Ali Razmara of Lebanon, only magnified these concerns.[58]

At the same time, the fact that the Soviet Union did not take advantage of the dispute between Iran and AIOC to attack London or to interfere in Iran's internal affairs was seen by some as part of another development, a Soviet peace campaign, which was also much commented on in the summer and fall of 1951. Indeed, following Malik's cease-fire speech in June, the Soviets issued a new English language magazine in which they emphasized the conciliatory nature of Soviet foreign policy. More important, the president of the Soviet presidium, N. M. Shvernick, wrote President Truman asking for a five-power conference, while Soviet diplomats began to be more visible in official circles, appearing at social gatherings at Western embassies they had formerly boycotted and emphasizing their country's desire to improve relations with the West. All this seemed to fit an even larger pattern. "Russia's apparent readiness to leave Iran alone," journalist Alexander Werth remarked in August, "its willingness to preserve the status quo in Korea, its feeling that Vietminh's 'just' war in Indo-China may only lead to new complications—all these things suggest that the Kremlin's real purpose in desiring a conference of the Big Five is to draw some kind of demarcation line between the two worlds, even if it means leaving some of Russia's friends in the lurch."[59]

Such stories as these and others still less connected with the war in Korea diverted public interest away from the tedious negotiations at Kaesong. Even so, the Truman administration strove to break the impasse. Despite the fact that the peace talks seemed to drag on endlessly through the hot summer months of July and August, the JCS continued to instruct Ridgway not to terminate negotiations. "If armistice discussions fail," they told the Far East commander, "it is of the greatest importance that clear responsibility for [their] failure rest upon the Communists."[60]

Notwithstanding their best efforts, however, the UN negotiatiors were unable to break the deadlock, and in August the talks were actually suspended for more than two months following a series of accusations by each side that the other had violated the neutral zone around Kaesong. In fact, as early as the middle of July the Communists had charged UN soldiers in the neutral zone of firing in the direction of the nearby village of Panmunjom. Five days later they claimed that UN forces had strafed one of their supply trucks near Kaesong. Denying the first charge, the UNC acknowledged the second when Ridgway instructed Admiral Joy to tell the Communists that without advance warning by them, enemy vehicles were liable to attack wherever found.[61]

During the following weeks both sides continued to exchange charges about violations of the neutral zone. In one instance the UN negotiators claimed that a company of armed Chinese passed through the area, within a hundred yards of the house assigned the UN delegation. Had General Ridgway had

his way, the talks would have been suspended indefinitely. But
Washington insisted that the negotiations continue, and although they were broken off for five days, they were resumed
after the Chinese acknowledged their "mistake" and assured
the UN negotiators it would not happen again. In another incident the Chinese maintained that UN forces had ambushed one
of their police patrols in the neutral zone, killing the platoon
leader. Finally, on August 24, after accusing the UN command
of bombing the conference site at Kaesong and displaying evidence, which, they alleged, proved their claim, the Chinese and
North Koreans suspended the cease-fire talks indefinitely.[62]

Why the Communists chose to break off the truce talks at
that time is not entirely clear. One possible reason is, of course,
that the bombing took place as they alleged. But the evidence
they produced to substantiate their charges, including so-called
bomb fragments that actually appeared to be part of an aircraft
oil tank and an engine nacelle, was ludicrous. Perhaps, as General Ridgway suggested, they broke off negotiations because
they wanted more time to rebuild their forces or sought a propaganda ploy for internal Communist consumption.[63]

More likely, however, was a third possibility that Ridgway
suggested. This was that the Chinese and North Koreans suspended the talks because they wanted to mesh the resumption
of negotiations with the forthcoming Japanese peace treaty
conference in San Francisco in the hope of gaining more bargaining leverage, particularly in terms of preventing Japanese
rearmament and alignment with the United States. Of all the
non-Communist areas of the Far East, Japan was strategically
the most threatening to the Soviet Union and Communist
China. Not only did it possess the only significant industrialized
economy and skilled labor force in the region, it was the principal operational base for carrying on the war in Korea. But the
danger from Japan extended far beyond Korea, for as a CIA
intelligence estimate concluded in November, "from operational bases in Japan, anti-Communist forces [could] dominate
the approaches to the Soviet Far East and northern China and
could attack by air or sea all major industrial and military targets in the Communist-held areas of the Far East."[64]

For this reason, Peking and Moscow attached great importance to preventing the rearmament of Japan and any military

ties it might develop with the United States. For the same reason, the United States was bent on making sure that this did not happen. Even more, Washington was determined to prevent Japan from coming under Soviet control, which, while considered highly unlikely, was not regarded as being impossible. Thus, the same intelligence estimate that commented on the potential threat of Japan to Communist interests in the Far East also pointed out that "under Communist control, Japan would pose the greatest threat to the US position in the Western Pacific."[65]

Because of Japan's strategic importance in the Far East, a major thrust of America's occupation of the country after 1948 had been to assure that a reconstructed Japan would align closely with the United States. This had not always been the case. At the end of World War II, Washington had not intended Japan to play a major role in the future balance of power in Asia (that role was reserved for China). Instead, the aim was, in the words of General MacArthur, to make Japan into the "Switzerland of the Pacific," basically neutral, weak, and nonaligned. But as it became increasingly clear by 1948 that China would fall to the Communists, Washington's policy toward Japan changed. The United States now undertook to convert a former enemy into a dependable ally. As part of that process, Washington placed new emphasis on rehabilitating Japan's economy and social structure and curbing leftist and Communist elements that had been allowed to develop in the country. At the same time, it decided to move forward with a peace treaty formally concluding the state of war that had existed with Japan since 1941.[66]

To negotiate the treaty, Secretary of State Acheson, who preferred to devote his energies to European matters, turned in April 1950 to the leading Republican spokesman on foreign policy, John Foster Dulles. The negotiations that followed were long, complex, and not entirely satisfactory to the Japanese, but the final agreement, along with an accompanying security pact, firmly tied Japan's security to the United States. American troops and air bases would remain on Japanese soil. Additionally, Japan would "increasingly assume responsibility for its own defense against direct and indirect aggression." In other words, Japan was to rearm, and, although no precise figures were determined, Dulles mentioned an army as high as 350,000 men.[67]

Not only the Soviet Union and Communist China, but also Australia, New Zealand, and other nations of Asia and the Far Pacific protested against the remilitarization of Japan. Australia and New Zealand insisted upon a mutual security pact with the United States—the so-called ANZUS treaty—before they would agree to sign the peace treaty. As for Moscow and Peking, which had been excluded from the negotiations, they interpreted the treaty as a warlike measure. The Sino-Soviet Treaty of 1950 had provided for joint action in case of Japanese aggression, and the Soviet newspaper *Pravda* accused the United States of rearming Japan for aggressive purposes. At the UN and elsewhere Soviet diplomats declared that they considered the rearmament of Japan "intolerable." Peking took a similar line and, along with Moscow, charged that the rearmament of Japan was already under way and that Japan was being used by the United States to support the "war of aggression against the Korean people."[68]

By breaking off talks at Kaesong until the opening of the San Francisco Conference, therefore, the Communists probably hoped to achieve one of several alternatives. At the very least they could justify a harder bargaining position on Korea as an appropriate response to America's plans for rearming and garrisoning Japan. But by making concessions at Kaesong while the San Francisco conference was taking place, they could argue that they were seeking world peace, which could be achieved more expeditiously if threats of strategic alliances and Japanese rearmament were put aside.[69]

If, however, the Communists' purpose was to gain bargaining leverage by suspending the talks at Kaesong until the convening of the San Francisco conference, they were unsuccessful. At San Francisco the Soviets, who had decided to attend the conference in order to present their own proposals for peace with Japan, were caught off balance on a number of occasions. An attempt by Deputy Foreign Minister Andrei Gromyko to have Communist China invited to San Francisco failed miserably. If anything, Gromyko's presence at the conference, along with representatives from Poland and Czechoslovakia, caused delegates from the other forty-nine countries represented at San Francisco to close ranks and muffle their own reservations about the peace treaty for fear of being identified with the Soviet opposition. An incidental result of the gathering was the considerable plaudits that Secretary of State Acheson received from even his critics for the firm and skillful way in which he presided over the meeting and dealt with Soviet efforts at obstruction. As *Time* reported in a halfhearted slap at the secretary's gentility and breeding, "Urbane and unruffled, [Acheson] dealt with the Communists as a Groton football coach with a bunch of interloping ruffians who don't know the rules of the game."[70]

Nor did the San Francisco conference have much effect on the negotiations at Kaesong, except, perhaps, to delay the resumption of talks a little. While the San Francisco conference was under way, Peking radio announced that the fate of the armistice negotiations might hang on events in San Francisco, and, to be sure, the discussions in Korea were not resumed for another seven weeks after the San Francisco gathering had adjourned. But the delay was a mutual one, involving the UN command as well as the Communist negotiators, and both before and after the resumption of talks the North Koreans and Chinese indicated their considerable flexibility, even on such a basic issue as a cease-fire line.

General Ridgway was determined not to resume peace talks until the Communists agreed to a new location for negotiations, one where incidents of the kind that had led to the suspension of talks at Kaesong would not reoccur. Militarily, the UN commander felt he could be firm with the enemy. Although the North Koreans and Chinese were being reinforced with new troops, and China was becoming an increasingly dangerous factor in the air war over northwestern Korea, UN troop strength was also growing. In addition, Ridgway's forces were by now seasoned veterans, their position along the KANSAS line was becoming stronger each day, and the war was turning into a protracted stalemate. The Eighth Army under General Van Fleet began a limited offensive in several areas along the front, and in the eastern sector some heavy fighting took place at Bloody Ridge and Heartbreak Ridge, in an area known as the Punchbowl. But neither the UN forces nor the Chinese undertook any major offensive. Lastly, the Chinese were believed anxious to avoid having to spend another winter in the battlefield. They were reported short of food and clothing, and China's industry was understood to be suffering severely from the Western embargo. Ridgway was convinced, therefore, that he could force the Communists to make concessions.[71]

The White House disagreed with Ridgway. Its purpose remained to avoid a total breakdown in the peace process, and it considered the question of a new site for negotiations a relatively minor matter, certainly not one that justified a delay in resuming talks. In conversations with America's allies in Korea, therefore, Assistant Secretary of State Rusk remarked that the United States did not intend to make a major issue over the location of negotiations or over any other "non-essential topic." The JCS instructed Ridgway very much along these lines. Even after General Bradley and State Department Counselor Charles Bohlen, whom the administration had sent to Korea on an inspection tour, returned home recommending a postponement in negotiations because the war was going so well, the White House remained opposed to any action that could destroy the chances of peace. The cease-fire talks should be kept alive not only to satisfy foreign pressures, but because a real breakdown might push the American people into demanding new and stronger military action.[72]

Once again, the Chinese and North Koreans, who clearly wanted to end a war that had become extremely costly to them without much chance of victory, proved willing to make concessions. On October 7 they agreed to change the location for negotiations, just as Ridgway had predicted they would. Instead of Kaesong, they proposed that the new site for the talks be the village of Panmunjom, about five miles to the east. Further delays in resuming negotiations were caused by new incidents in the neutral zone around Kaesong and by the need of both sides to work out new security arrangements around Panmunjom. But on October 25 UN and Communist negotiators met at Panmunjom for the first time since discussions had broken off two months earlier.[73]

Once the talks were resumed, an agreement on a cease-fire line was reached fairly rapidly. No longer did the Chinese and North Koreans demand that the 38th parallel be the line of demarcation; instead they acknowledged the UN's claim that the cease-fire line be the military front, or point of contact, between the two forces at the time hostilities ended. This still did not settle the matter entirely, for the UNC then insisted that Kaesong be under its control or within a demilitarized zone to be determined by both sides. Lying south of the 38th parallel, this ancient capital of Korea not only had symbolic importance, it was strategically located across the approaches to Seoul. Ridgway had given up efforts to take Kaesong in June only because of the approaching armistice negotiations and because he assumed that, as the location for negotiations, the city would be completely neutralized. Once the talks were moved to Panmunjom, therefore, he insisted that Kaesong come into UN hands or be effectively neutralized.[74]

No less than the Communists, however, the administration refused to go along with Ridgway. In what was already a familiar pattern, the JCS again warned the UN commander against being too inflexible. In his reply to the Pentagon, Ridgway referred to a "final offer" on a demilitarized zone that he had worked out with Bradley and Bohlen during their visit to Korea. It was his understanding, he said, that the Joint Chiefs had also approved the agreement, but the JCS denied it. Instead, they told Ridgway, with the President's approval, that the UN's minimum position remained the security of the KANSAS line. Everything else having to do with a cease-fire line was negotiable.[75]

Simply put, the administration was under intense pressure both at home and abroad to reach a peace settlement. Earlier the London *Times* had even urged the UN command to "recognize the Thirty-eighth Parallel as the frontier" between North and South Korea. In subsequent weeks the British suffered a series of major setbacks, particularly in the Middle East, that made them all the more eager to end the war in Korea. First, Egypt announced that it would break the treaty under which the British garrisoned the Suez Canal. A few days later the Baghdad government served notice that it planned to renegotiate the agreement by which Britain maintained air bases in Iraq. On the same day the prime minister of South Africa demanded that London hand over a group of native protectorates in Africa to his antinative government. And, finally, at the UN, Iran informally rejected a Security Council proposal that might have saved England at least part of its biggest foreign investment—the oil refineries at Abadan. Howard K. Smith reported from London that "[o]ne stunning blow after another has shocked the people into an awareness that the nation's fortunes are at the lowest ebb since 1776." Such a climate was hardly conducive to foreign adventures of any kind, particularly with England's ailing economy, and with new elections called for the end of October, both the Labor Party and the Conservative Party campaigned as the party of peace.[76]

In the United States there was also a rapidly growing demand to end the Korean War soon. The *New Republic* maintained that the resumption of talks at Kaesong indicated that the Chinese were anxious to "liquidate" the war and that a "fluid policy [by the UN negotiators] might still detach [Peking] and cancel out Moscow's single biggest victory since World War II." In an editorial on November 11, Armistice Day, *The New York Times* stated that it could not understand why the UN delegation was making an issue "over a seeming trifle," such as Kaesong, when it had already won agreement on the "big issues" involved in a cease-fire line. Pointing out that public opinion opposed any disruption in the cease-fire negotiations, particularly in view of the concessions already made by the other side, the JCS instructed Ridgway to accept the present line of contact as the demarcation line for a demilitarized zone, with the understanding, however, that it would be renegotiated if other issues were not settled within a reasonable time—a month or so.[77]

Despite this last provision, the Joint Chiefs were compromising perhaps even more than they realized. In effect, they were agreeing to a thirty-day *de facto* cease-fire, since neither side in the war would be willing to risk military action when any gains they might achieve would have to be given up at the end of a thirty-day period. This was a substantial change from the JCS's previous position that the demarcation line must be the final line of contact at the time fighting stopped. Ridgway's response to his latest orders from the Pentagon was immediate. "I feel there is substantial possibility," he told the Joint Chiefs, "that announcement to the Communists of the course you have directed will increase Communist intransigence and weaken our future p[o]s[itio]ns on every substantive point. . . . We stand at a crucial point. We have much to gain by standing firm. We have everything to lose through concessions. With all my conscience I urge we stand firm."[78]

But the UN commander's arguments got him nowhere. Pressure continued to mount worldwide for an end to the fighting in Korea. At the new session of the General Assembly, which opened in Paris on November 6, the Soviet Union called for an international conference on banning the atomic bomb, a peace meeting that would include Communist China, and a Korean armistice along the 38th parallel. Not only did the administration feel compelled to respond to the Soviet peace initiative with its own gestures toward peace in Korea, but in London and elsewhere, America's allies urged the United States to reach a cease-fire agreement along the lines already agreed to by the Chinese and North Koreans.[79]

Responding to world opinion and to its own desire to end the war soon, the White House instructed Ridgway to accept the current line of contact as the cease-fire line, provided an armistice was signed within thirty days. On November 17 the UN presented its proposal to the Communist negotiators. After considerable haggling as to where the line of contact was on a map, both sides reached an accord on November 27, part of which provided that both sides would establish a demilitarized zone by withdrawing their forces two kilometers from the demarcation line.[80]

Thus the UN command accepted a cease-fire line very much like the one the Chinese and North Koreans had proposed after they dropped their demands on the 38th parallel. This was done despite General Ridgway's warnings that UN concessions would increase Communist recalcitrance on other issues yet to be decided. One can speculate on whether a firmer stand by UN negotiators on such matters as Kaesong and a cease-fire line, along with sustained military pressure against the Communists, would have ended the war earlier. Certainly the UN command had the military advantage. Writing in 1957, Harvard Professor and future Secretary of State Henry Kissinger sharply criticized the administration's decision in 1951 to halt military operations at the moment cease-fire negotiations began. "[T]he decision to stop military operations, except those of a purely defensive nature, at the very beginning of the armistice negotiations," Kissinger wrote, "reflected our conviction that the process of negotiation operated on its own inherent logic independently of the military pressures brought to bear. But by stopping military operations we removed the only Chinese incentive for a settlement."[81]

What followed was a thirty-day *de facto* cease-fire that, from all military reports, worked to the advantage of the North Koreans and Chinese. For example, General Ridgway instructed General Van Fleet to assume the "active defense," limiting offensive operations to the seizure of ground necessary to protect his position and to establish an outer zone of three to five thousand yards. Meanwhile, the Communists began construction of a fourteen-mile defensive network, deeper than any on the Western Front in World War I, which protected their armies for the rest of the war.[82]

Certainly there were legitimate reasons why the Joint Chiefs agreed to a *de facto* cease-fire. Not only was the administration under tremendous pressure, particularly from its European allies, to negotiate an end to the war, but the Chinese and North Koreans had made several important concessions at the negotiating table, such as over the demarcation line at the time of a cease-fire and the withdrawal of foreign troops from Korea after the fighting ended. Any negotiating process involves a certain amount of give-and-take, and it was not unreasonable for the administration to agree to an effective halt in the fighting for a limited time if that might hasten a cease-fire agreement.

Nevertheless, Ridgway's frustration at the restrictions placed on him and the UN team at Panmunjom in bargaining with the enemy is understandable and, at least to a certain extent, justifiable. "[T]he delegation and indeed General Ridgway never knew," Admiral Joy later commented, "when a new directive would emanate from Washington to alter our basic objective of obtaining an honorable and stable armistice agreement. . . . It seemed to us that the United States Government did not know exactly what its political objectives in Korea were or should be. As a result, the United Nations Command delegation was constantly looking over its shoulder, fearing a new directive from afar which would require action inconsistent with that currently being taken." General J. Lawton Collins of the Joint Chiefs admitted much the same thing by also acknowledging later that instructions from Washington were sometimes "vacillating" and showed "a lack of firmness" that distressed Ridgway and the UN delegation.[83]

The exasperation of the UN command, then, in fighting a limited war, which it could not win in any conventional military sense, was compounded by political constraints imposed upon it by Washington. The uncertainty that followed, even as to the full political dimensions of the conflict, bewildered and confused UN negotiators even as they turned to the next item on the agenda—arrangements for a cease-fire and an armistice in Korea.

NOTES

1. Memorandum for Mr. Murphy, April 24, 1951, Box 76, Elsey Papers; *FR*, 1951, VII, 291–92 and 296–98.
2. David Rees, *Korea: The Limited War* (New York, 1964), 247–51.
3. T. R. Fehrenbach, *This Kind of War: A Study in Unpreparedness* (New York, 1964), 473–90.
4. *New Yorker*, 27 (May 5, 1951), 94; *ibid.* (May 26, 1951), 64–68; *Life*, 30 (May 7, 1951), 33–34.
5. Rees, *Korea: The Limited War*, 245–51; *Time*, 57 (May 7, 1951), 29.
6. *Life*, 30 (June 4, 1951), 27–28; *Time*, 57 (May 28, 1951), 30; Rees, *Korea: The Limited War*, 251–55.
7. Rees, *Korea: The Limited War*, 258–59; *Life*, 30 (June 4, 1951), 27–28; *ibid.* (June 11, 1951), 43; *Time*, 57 (June 11, 1951).
8. *Time*, 57 (June 18, 1951), 30.
9. Briefing of Ambassadors on Korea, May 1, 1951, Box 3, Selected Records Relating to the Korean War; Acheson to Certain Diplomatic Officers, May 1, 1951, Box 11, *ibid.*
10. *FR*, 1951, VII, 390–94 and 427–31; *Yearbook of the United Nations: 1951* (New York, 1952), 226–28.
11. James F. Schnabel and Robert J. Watson, *The History of the Joint Chiefs of Staff*, III, *The Korean War* (unpublished manuscript, National Archives, 1978), 338–42.
12. Rees, *Korea: The Limited War*, 193–94.
13. *FR*, 1951, VII, 385–87 and 427–31; Livingston Merchant to the Secretary of State, May 5, 1951, and Memorandum for General Bradley from Mr. Acheson, May 12, 1951, Box 11, Selected Records Relating to the Korean War.
14. *FR*, 1951, VII, 338–42.

15. *Commentary,* 11 (May 1951), 407–14. See also *Commonweal,* 28 (May 11, 1951), 113–14.
16. *New Republic,* 124 (May 28, 1951), 10; *Atlantic Monthly,* 187, (June 1951), 16–17.
17. *Ibid; Nation,* 172 (May 12, 1951), 440–43; *New Yorker,* 27 (June 30, 1951), 42.
18. Walter G. Hermes, *Truce Tent and Fighting Front* (Washington, D. C., 1966), 14.
19. *FR,* 1951, VII, 433–37 and 472–73; Warren Austin to the Secretary of State, May 5 and June 1, 1951, Box 8, Selected Records Relating to the Korean War.
20. Gross to Secretary of State, June 5, 1951, and Acheson to U. S. Delegation at UN, June 5, 1951, Box 8, Selected Records Relating to the Korean War.
21. Dean Acheson, *Present at the Creation: My Years in the State Department* (New York, 1969), 532; *FR,* 1951, VII, 447–60; Joseph C. Goulden, *Korea: The Untold Story of the War* (New York, 1982), 549.
22. Acheson, *Present at the Creation,* 532–33; *FR,* 1951, VII, 460–62, 483–86, and 507–11.
23. *New York Times,* June 24, 1951.
24. *FR,* 1951, VII, 551–52 and 579–80.
25. Daily Opinion Summary, Department of State, n.d., Box 76, Elsey Papers; *Commonweal,* 54 (July 6, 1951), 300–301.
26. *FR,* 1951, VII, 536–38, 553–54, and 560–61.
27. *Ibid.,* 577–78 and 593–95; Acheson, *Present at the Creation,* 533–34.
28. *FR,* 1951, VII, 593–95.
29. Message to the Commander in Chief, Communist Forces in Korea, June 30, 1951, Box 3, Selected Records Relating to the Korean War; Briefing of Ambassadors on Korea, July 3, 1951, Box 8, *ibid.*
30. *FR,* 1951, VII, 610–12.
31. Ridgway to Joint Chiefs of Staff, July 4, 1951, Box 243, Korean War File, President's Secretary File, Truman Papers.
32. *Nation,* 173 (July 7, 1951), 4; *ibid.* (July 14, 1951), 21; *New Republic,* 125 (July 9, 1951), 6; *New Yorker,* 27 (July 14, 1951), 62.
33. *New Yorker,* 27 (June 30, 1951), 60–65.
34. *FR,* 1951, VII, 416–19.
35. *Ibid.,* 496–97.
36. *Ibid.,* 610–12.
37. *Ibid.*
38. Message to the Commander in Chief, Communist Forces in Korea,

June 30, 1951, Box 3, Selected Records Relating to the Korean War; Briefing of Ambassadors on Korea, July 3, 1951, Box 8, *ibid.*

39. Department of State, "Far East: Progress in the Korean Truce Talks," Box 76, Elsey Papers.

40. *Ibid.; FR,* 1951, VII, 649–56.

41. *Ibid.*

42. *Ibid.,* 658–65.

43. Department of State, Far East: Progress in the Korean Truce Talks, Box 76, Elsey Papers; Briefing of Ambassadors on Korea, July 18, 1951, Box 8, Selected Records Relating to the Korean War; *FR,* 1951, VII, 671–73, 682–84, 687–88, and 704–706.

44. *Life,* 31 (July 23, 1951), 17; *Commonweal,* 54 (July 27, 1951), 5.

45. *FR,* 1951, VII, 711–18 and 735–37; Hermes, *Truce Tent and Fighting Front,* 31–34.

46. Hermes, *Truce Tent and Fighting Front,* 34.

47. *Ibid.; FR,* 1951, VII, 738–39, 745–47, 763–65, and 774–76.

48. Briefing of Ambassadors on Korea, August 1, 1951, Box 3, Selected Records Relating to the Korean War; *FR,* 1951, VII, 753–60.

49. *Nation,* 173 (August 4, 1951), 81.

50. *New Republic,* 125 (September 24, 1951), 5; *Atlantic Monthly,* 188 (September 1951), 8 and 11.

51. David M. Oshinsky, *A Conspiracy So Immense: The World of Joe McCarthy* (New York, 1983), 214–17; *New Republic,* 125 (August 13, 1951), 10; *ibid.* (August 20, 1951), 5; *Nation,* 173 (September 1, 1951), 166–67.

52. *New Republic,* 124 (June 18, 1951), 5–6; *Nation,* 172 (June 30, 1951), 598; *ibid.,* 173 (July 14, 1951), 21–22; *ibid.* (August 11, 1951), 106.

53. *Life,* 31 (October 1, 1951), 32.

54. Ronald J. Caridi, *The Korean War and American Politics: The Republican Party as a Case Study* (Philadelphia, 1968), 170–71; James T. Patterson, *Mr. Republican: A Biography of Robert A. Taft* (Boston, 1972), 488–92.

55. *New Republic,* 125 (July 16, 1951), 3; *ibid.* (July 30, 1951), 3; *Commonweal,* 54 (August 3, 1951), 397; Patterson, *Mr. Republican,* 503–504; Robert A. Taft, *A Foreign Policy for Americans* (New York, 1951), 56.

56. *Life,* 30 (May 21, 1951), 38.

57. Acheson, *Present at the Creation,* 503–11.

58. *Life,* 31 (July 30, 1951), 18 and 26; *Nation,* 173 (August 11, 1951), 112–13; *Atlantic Monthly,* 188 (August 1951), 4–7.

59. *Commonweal,* 54 (August 17, 1951), 445; *Nation,* 173 (August 18, 1951), 122–23 and 131–32.
60. *FR,* 1951, VII, 811–12.
61. *Ibid.,* 795–98.
62. *Ibid.,* 789–90, 801–10, and 850–54.
63. William H. Vatcher, Jr., *Panmunjom: The Story of Korean Military Armistice Negotiations* (New York, 1958), 66–67.
64. *FR,* VII, 1951, 993–1001. See also *Atlantic Monthly,* 187 (April 1951), 11; *New Republic,* 125 (August 27, 1951), 15.
65. *Ibid.; New Yorker,* 27 (September 1, 1951), 44–46; Michael Schaller, "Securing the Great Crescent: Occupied Japan and the Origins of Containment in Southeast Asia," *Journal of American History,* 69 (September 1982), 392–414.
66. Charles E. Neu, *The Troubled Encounter: The United States and Japan* (New York, 1975), 207–13.
67. *Ibid.,* 214–15.
68. *Nation,* 173 (July 28, 1951), 66–68; *ibid.* (August 4, 1951), 82–83; *ibid.* (September 1, 1951), 164–65; *New Republic,* 125 (August 27, 1951), 15; *New Yorker,* 27 (September 1, 1951), 44–46; *Commonweal,* 54 (September 14, 1951), 539.
69. *New Republic,* 125 (September 3, 1951), 8; *Commonweal,* 54 (September 7, 1951), 515.
70. *Time,* 58 (September 24, 1951), 24; *New Yorker,* 27 (October 6, 1951), 97; *New Republic,* 125 (September 24, 1951), 3; *Commonweal,* 54 (September 8, 1951), 589.
71. *FR,* 1951, VII, 937–44 and 952–55; Briefing of Ambassadors on Korea, September 21, 1951, Box 3, Selected Papers Relating to the Korean War.
72. *FR,* 1951, VII, 1004–1005, 1008–14, and 1059–61; Rees, *Korea: The Limited War,* 295.
73. Briefing of Foreign Government Representatives on Korea, October 26 and November 6, 1951, Box 3, Selected Records Relating to the Korean War.
74. JCS to Ridgway, November 6, 1951, Box 16, *ibid.*; *FR,* 1951, VII, 1071–72 and 1074.
75. *FR,* 1951, VII, 1092–93 and 1126.
76. *Nation,* 173 (October 20, 1951), 319–20; *ibid.* (October 13, 1951), 300–302; *New Yorker,* 27 (October 27, 1951), 17; *ibid.* (October 15, 1951), 3; *Commonweal,* 55 (October 26, 1951), 51.
77. *FR,* 1951, VII, 1131–33 and 1186–88; Hermes, *Truce Tent and Fighting Front,* 119; *New Republic,* 125 (October 1, 1951), 3; *New York Times,* November 11, 1951.

78. *FR*, 1951, VII, 1128–30.
79. Briefing of Foreign Government Representatives in Korea, November 6 and 9, 1951, Box 3, Selected Records Relating to the Korean War.
80. *FR*, 1951, VII, 1131–33 and 1186–88; Hermes, *Truce Tent and Fighting Front*, 119.
81. Henry Kissinger, *Nuclear Weapons and Foreign Policy* (New York, 1957), 50–51.
82. Rees, *Korea: The Limited War*, 301.
83. Admiral C. Turner Joy, *How Communists Negotiate* (New York, 1955), 173–74; J. Lawton Collins, *War in Peacetime* (Boston, 1969), 331.

CHAPTER 7

Narrowing the Issues

The military stalemate that had developed in Korea during the summer of 1951 continued into the fall and then the winter of 1952. The Chinese and North Koreans continued to reinforce their defense lines, digging and fortifying a growing complex of trenches, bunkers, and caves that honeycombed the ridges looking down on the UN forces just below. In some areas the Communists made entrenchments all the way around the hills they held and burrowed tunnels through them in order to shift troops quickly and to provide impregnable fortifications against bombs and heavy artillery. They also brought up their own heavy artillery and stockpiled ammunition. By the end of January General Van Fleet was reporting that the Chinese and North Koreans had more artillery than UN forces and that their supplies of ammunition and equipment were mountainous. Although the Communists had lost an estimated 45,000 men since the end of their unsuccessful spring offensive, Van Fleet believed their units had been brought up to full strength, and military intelligence reported that they could launch a major offensive at any time.[1]

Against these well-entrenched forces UN troops were content mostly to straighten out their own defense lines and refurbish their own supplies. At the end of October an American division did capture the strategically valuable heights above Kumsong, which lay just east of the Iron Triangle, about twenty miles north of the 38th parallel. The next month fierce fighting took place over a hill near Yonchon, which correspondents dubbed "Little Gibraltar" or "Armistice Ridge." Caught by surprise, American forces were first driven off the hill by the Communists. Before reclaiming it forty-one hours later, they had to beat off an entire Chinese division at an estimated cost to the Chinese of 1500 men. American casualties were also high.[2]

For the most part, however, UN forces did not engage the enemy in any sustained action after the negotiators at Panmunjom had agreed on November 27 to a tentative cease-fire line. Instead UN commanders in the field attempted to carry out General Ridgway's orders that they assume the "active defense," engaging in no major attack above battalion strength without prior approval. In most cases Ridgway's directive corresponded with their own assessment of battlefield conditions and the likely outcome of the peace negotiations at Panmunjom. By the time agreement had been reached on a demarcation line, many of their battle-wise troops and officers, who had successfully fought off the great Chinese offensive of the previous spring and had moved to the offensive, had begun to be rotated home. While fresh reserves arrived from the United States, including the First National Guard Division in December and the Second National Guard Division the next month, they were not used to the rigors of the Korean winter; many were unsuited even for routine patrol duty. Unschooled in such basics as keeping spare dry socks on hand and changing them often, they suffered untoward incidents of frostbite and other cold-related injuries. The contrast between them and their North Korean and Chinese counterparts, who were acclimated to the seasonal harshness of Manchuria and northern Korea and were able to function routinely, was striking.[3]

Even more important, UN commanders in the field shared Ridgway's reluctance to engage the Communists in combat when any gains that might be achieved were likely to be returned to the enemy as soon as an armistice was reached. This was especially true in the thirty-day period following the agreement on a demarcation line. Indeed, as soon as he learned of that agreement, General Van Fleet instructed his commanders in the field to cut back their military operations. Although Van Fleet made it plain that hostilities were officially to continue until an armistice was signed, his orders included such items as "maintain present defensive positions," "avoid all casualties," and "avoid engaging the enemy unless he threatens our position." News swept first on the battlefield and then at home that a cease-fire had been ordered, possibly by the White House itself. President Truman became alarmed by these reports. He and his advisers realized full well how difficult it would be at the end of thirty days to start the fighting again, and they knew all too well how a relaxation of tensions in the Western world would complicate their effort to establish an Atlantic defense system. In an angry statement, therefore, the President denied the rumors of a cease-fire and condemned the press for "issuing false reports."[4]

Nevertheless, commanders in the field still hesitated to take any action that might unnecessarily endanger their forces or cause loss of life when no permanent military advantage was likely. They followed this policy even after the *de facto* cease-fire expired thirty days later without a settlement on all outstanding issues. So long as negotiations continued at Panmunjom and the chances remained strong that any gains on the battlefield would have to be forfeited once the war ended, UN commanders saw little advantage in committing their forces to large-scale military operations. For the remainder of the conflict, therefore, the war on the ground consisted mostly of routine patrol duty, probing actions, and occasional forays against strategically located enemy positions. On the ground, in other words, Korea had become a military stalemate and a war of position.[5]

In the air the situation was substantially different. On one hand, an emboldened enemy air force increasingly challenged UN supremacy of the skies over North Korea. On the other hand, enemy antiaircraft fire began shooting down with increasing accuracy UN bombers and fighter jets flying over military targets.

Almost overnight the Chinese had developed into a major air power. By the end of November they were reported to have as many as 1400 planes. Of these, about 700 were estimated to be MIG-15s, regarded by many as the finest jet fighter in the world. "In many respects," Air Force Chief of Staff Hoyt Vandenberg remarked, "the MIG can outperform our own F-86—the only airplane in production today capable of challenging the MIG on approximately equal terms." Able to maneuver at supersonic speeds and to outrun and outclimb the F-86 at 25,000 feet, the MIG was believed by a number of military leaders to be better armed and equipped than the F-86.[6]

Although still operating from bases just across the Yalu River in Manchuria and seldom venturing over UN lines, the MIG-15s were, nevertheless, changing the complexion of the air war in the north. "Our control of the air in northwest Korea, although by no means lost, is not as firm as it was," Vandenberg even admitted in November. Indeed, General Ridgway and Far East Air Force Commander General Otto P. Weyland, who once had favored allowing American pilots to cross into Manchuria in "hot pursuit" of enemy aircraft, changed their minds. "Buildup of Communist fighter strength including available Soviet fighters makes the disregarding of the Yalu River as a boundary to fighter action meaningless," they told the JCS.[7]

Complicating the problem for American fliers over North Korea was the growing effectiveness of Chinese and North Korean antiaircraft fire. A case in point was OPERATION STRANGLE. In an effort to interdict Communist supplies from reaching the front and to sever the enemy's lines from the rest of North Korea, the UN Command (UNC) had launched the operation in the summer of 1951. Designed to strike at Soviet-built supply trucks coming down from the north and to cut road and rail communications to the front, OPERATION STRANGLE was never very successful. Almost as soon as American pilots severed lines of transportation, they were put back into operation by huge gangs of laborers. Also, the Chinese and North Koreans moved generally at night, depended heavily on human transport as thousands of men and women carried loads of supplies on their backs and engaged in clever camouflaging, which made it difficult for the fliers to carry out their mission. Eventually the operation was replaced with another strategy known as SPECIAL TARGETS SYSTEM, which involved large forces of bombers striking at selected vital targets.[8]

What was especially disturbing about OPERATION STRANGLE, however, were the losses sustained by the attacking planes. Using radar-directed searchlights and artillery, the Communists sent up huge clouds of deadly flak that sometimes struck as high as 25,000 and 30,000 feet. In January, the worst month of the air war for the UN, forty-four planes alone were reported downed by flak.[9]

By the end of January more than 600 Air Force, Navy, and Marine aircraft had been lost to the enemy either from combat in the air or, far more frequently, from ground fire. Loss of enemy planes was about half of that. In several respects the figures were misleading. Most of the losses were older piston engine planes and not the newer and faster jets being used in Korea, such as the F-86s. Particularly vulnerable were the B-29s. Originally designed as heavy bombers, they were used in Korea in tactical battlefield situations and were quite incapable of maneuvering away from incoming bursts. Also, Communist aircraft rarely came out in strength beyond "MIG Alley" in northwest Korea, so fewer downed planes were to be expected. But the growing intensity of the air war over North Korea was cause for increased concern within the UNC and among military experts and commentators in the United States.[10]

By the end of January, moreover, the hope, which had existed even within the administration just two months earlier, that peace was at hand had been largely shattered. The thirty-day period for settling all outstanding issues between the two sides at Panmunjom had passed, thereby releasing the UN from its obligation to adhere to the demarcation line agreed on earlier. Indeed, the White House was preparing to raise the ante involved in a successful conclusion of the war in Korea by approving a new policy statement that included a threat to attack China itself if the Chinese agreed to an armistice and later broke it.

The talks at Panmunjom were not going well at all. Not only had the thirty-day period for a cease-fire expired, but the negotiators had become deadlocked over the issue of the machinery necessary to administer an armistice. Discussions on this item of the agenda were almost as thorny and convoluted as those on the establishment of a demarcation line. As stated in instructions, which the Joint Chiefs of Staff had sent to General Ridgway in June, the minimum UN position was that there should be no increase in the number of military personnel in Korea and that a military armistice commission should be established with the right of inspection throughout Korea to assure compliance with the armistice. Personnel and equipment could be replaced on a one-for-one basis. On the insistence of General Ridgway—who questioned the need for unlimited inspection, which he reasoned the enemy would never accept—that provision was later modified to include the right of inspection only at selected ports and communication centers. The UN negotiators were also to seek authority to conduct aerial surveillance over all of Korea, although that item was negotiable. In response to the buildup of Chinese air power, an additional point was added that there be no construction or rehabilitation of airfields in Korea.[11]

In their response to the UN proposals, the Chinese and North Koreans once again appeared conciliatory. But as Admiral Joy, the UN's chief negotiator, pointed out, they ignored a number of important matters. For example, they agreed to the establishment of an armistice commission, but they failed to consider such basic issues as the authority and function of that body. Nor did they offer any guarantees against a resumption of hostilities. Also, when the UN delegation stated that there should be no buildup of forces after the armistice and that a military armistice commission should have "free access to all parts of Korea," they rejected these proposals. Instead, they argued that such demands constituted interference in their internal affairs and were subterfuges by the UNC, which was preparing for further aggression against North Korea and China. Rather than restrictions on a military buildup, they proposed the withdrawal of all foreign troops from Korea. Finally, they insisted on the right to construct military airfields, something which the UN negotiators now absolutely opposed.[12]

Throughout these exchanges at Panmunjom, Washington's position remained one of avoiding a breakdown in negotiations, a policy that continued to annoy and frustrate both the UN negotiating team and General Ridgway. Above all, Ridgway wanted the Joint Chiefs of Staff, from whom he received his instructions, to determine a firm negotiating position and then stick to it. Otherwise he was convinced the UN negotiators would be at a disadvantage in their talks with the Communists. When the North Korean and Chinese negotiators refused to budge from their position on the reconstruction of airfields, he even advised—as he had on previous occasions—that the UN break off the talks with them. "I yet feel," he told the JCS, "that a time must come when, if our final positions continue to be rejected, yet the Communists themselves do not break off negotiations, that the United Nations Command must do it."[13]

Even President Truman was losing patience with what he

regarded as the shilly-shally posture being assumed by the UN negotiators. In particular, he objected, as unnecessary and unwise, to a UN concession on the rehabilitation of communication and transportation facilities other than airfields, which he pointed out could be used in time of war. He asked the JCS why the United States should allow the Communists to rebuild their roads, railroads, and similar facilities. "We have expended lives, tons of bombs, and a large amount of equipment to bring these people to terms," he remarked. "They have been able to give us a bad time even in the crippled condition of their communications and they have been able to operate effectively even without air fields." A few days later he met with the JCS at the White House, where he again told them that the UN's negotiating position was too weak. The Chinese and North Koreans made all the demands and "we the concessions," he remarked.[14]

Nevertheless, the JCS remained convinced that the UN negotiators must not break off negotiations with the Communists, and they were able to convince the President they were right. Part of the reason they were able to persuade Truman was a new policy statement on Korea, NSC-118/2, prepared by the National Security Council, which satisfied the President that the UN could be conciliatory in negotiating with the enemy without increasing the chances of renewed aggression after a peace was finally concluded. The NSC document was the product of extensive deliberations within the administration for several months on the issue of what military and political actions to take against China if the armistice talks at Panmunjom failed. The paper was also an effort to resolve differences between the Departments of State and Defense on several questions, most notably whether to impose a naval blockade against China, which State believed was impractical and the JCS maintained was a "practicable military measure."[15]

According to the senior staff which prepared NSC-118/2, Korean reunification by military means would require a substantial increase in ground and air forces, a naval blockade of China, and, possibly, even the use of atomic weapons. Not only would the United States lack sufficient resources to expand the conflict in Korea well into 1952, but the deployment of forces to Korea would delay the buildup of forces in Europe and de-plete the Army's general reserves. Also, other countries would probably refuse to support an expansion of the war, which would increase tensions in the Far East and might lead even to war between the United States and the Soviet Union. For these reasons the United States should continue its limited war in Korea while seeking an armistice. But it should make clear to the Chinese that if an armistice was reached and then broken by them, China was subject to attack by the United States and its allies. "The publicly expressed determination of the United States and our principal allies to retaliate against China in case of renewed aggression would serve notice on the communist world which they would regard with the greatest seriousness," the senior staff concluded. "It thus would become the 'greater sanction,' the strongest deterrent to aggression which we could devise, and therefore worth the risk."[16]

Not all differences within the administration on courses of action to follow if the armistice failed were resolved by NSC-118/2. Disagreement between the State and Defense departments continued over such questions as a naval blockade of China, which was left for further study by the senior staff. Also, Washington's basic policy on Korean unification remained unchanged. Unification was to be achieved by other than military means. But by raising the possibility of an attack against China if an armistice was agreed to and then broken, NSC-118/2 added a new dimension to the peace negotiations at Panmunjom. In fact, an annex to NSC-118/2 even introduced the doctrine of flexibility in responding to a violation of a cease-fire agreement by stating that "the United States should make clear to the USSR and Communist China that future military aggression will result in a military reaction that would not necessarily be limited *in geographical scope or in methods of warfare employed*" [italics mine]. Here, then, was a forerunner of what became known during the Eisenhower administration as the doctrine of "massive retaliation," the threat to retaliate against Communist aggression with nuclear attack at a place of America's own choosing.[17]

Having been consulted in the preparation of NSC-118/2 and believing that a warning to Peking along the lines of the "greater sanction" statement would minimize the danger of Chinese aggression in Korea, the Joint Chiefs were convinced that the UN could be flexible in negotiating with the Chinese at Panmunjom. Because of the growing pressure, even from America's allies, to end the war, they also believed that any disruption of the cease-fire talks had to be the enemy's responsibility. They thus instructed General Ridgway to take "no irrevocable position" on the issues under discussion. Later they made clear to Ridgway just how important they considered a warning to China to be. "It is our view," they wrote Ridgway in December, "that [the] safety of UN Forces, and the major deterrent to renewal of aggression must in the last analysis be dependent upon realization by Communists that a renewed aggression in Korea would result in a new war which would bring upon China the full retribution which [the] United States and her Allies deem desirable."[18]

Considering that his administration had formulated the "greater sanction" concept and that it had his personal approval, President Truman naturally agreed with the Joint Chiefs. The President was also well aware of the currents of world opinion on reaching an armistice, and he recognized that in order to satisfy America's own allies the UNC needed to project an image of moderation and conciliation in negotiating with the Communists. After being reminded by the JCS, therefore, that a military agreement might be "the only agreement we will have for a long time" and that it "would be impossible to deny for any appreciable time" the rehabilitation of facilities essential to the Korean economy, he agreed to permit the rebuilding of these facilities in Korea other than airfields. Even in the case of airfields, he opened the way for further concessions by agreeing to reconsider the matter if it became the last obstacle to an armistice.[19]

In formulating the "greater sanction" policy, the United States had consulted closely with England, and the new policy was a principal topic of discussion when England's new prime minister, Winston Churchill, visited the United States at the beginning of January 1952. Just before leaving office the previous October after having been defeated by the Conservatives, the Labor government had agreed "in principle" that should the Chinese carry out a major attack from Manchuria, UN forces would retaliate by bombing Communist airfields in Manchuria. But they insisted that they be consulted before such an

attack was actually carried out. After assuming office, Churchill's Conservative government made it clear it would carry out
Labor's pledge on a warning statement to the Communists.
Britain's new foreign minister, Anthony Eden, told Secretary of
State Acheson as much in November while the two men were
in Paris to attend a NATO meeting and the opening sessions of
the UN General Assembly. London even consented to State
Department language that "should aggression be committed
again in Korea, the consequences would be so grave that it
would, in all probability, not be possible to confine hostilities
within the frontiers of Korea."[20]

The British agreed to such a declaration because they regarded it as the lesser of two evils, the other being a naval
blockade of China, and because they were concerned about the
buildup of Communist forces in Korea under the cover of the
truce talks. London could never accept a blockade of China,
which would threaten its tenuous hold on Hong Kong and
which, they thought, would probably be ineffective. But there
seemed sufficient cause to go along with the Americans in issuing a warning statement. At the Paris meeting of NATO in
November, General Bradley of the Joint Chiefs of Staff had
impressed the British with the need, in lieu of the right of
inspection, to let the Chinese know the dangerous consequences of breaking an armistice agreement. Since the Communists would apparently never agree to inspection in order to
assure that the terms of a cease-fire were being carried out, the
only alternative seemed to be the threat of an expanded war,
targeted at China itself, should the Chinese violate the armistice. Bradley, Secretary of State Acheson, and other Americans
at the NATO meeting also warned the British of the public
furor in America such a violation would create.[21]

Foreign Secretary Eden told the Americans that he would
consult with his government about making a warning statement and get back to them as soon as possible. That night he
wrote Churchill a summary of his conversation with the Americans in which he stressed the importance they attached to such
a declaration, even making clear that Washington would issue
it unilaterally if necessary. "[T]he Americans left me in no
doubt," he told the prime minister, "that the United States
would rise in its wrath if there was a major attack. They clearly

feel that the American Administration could not hold that position against the clamour of public opinion."[22]

Returning to London, Eden took up the American proposal with Churchill and the British Chiefs of Staffs. Together they agreed that the Chinese were increasing the size of their forces in Korea and might launch another attack on UN forces at any time. To prevent this from happening, they decided that General Ridgway should conclude an armistice as quickly as possible, even though arrangements to supervise it might not be totally satisfactory. Once the armistice was signed, the allied nations fighting in Korea should then issue a general statement warning the Chinese that a serious violation of the armistice might make it impossible to confine hostilities to Korea.[23]

By the time Churchill went to the United States in January, therefore, the British had pretty much committed themselves to support the "greater sanction" statement being advocated by the United States. But they had not agreed to—nor would they agree on—the precise steps to take against the Communists if they breached an armistice agreement. The Americans wanted to attack airfields north of the Yalu River. The Labor government had indicated its support for such bombing missions, but "in principle" only, and it expected to be advised before any military action was actually taken against China. This was essentially the same position that Churchill and Eden, who accompanied the British prime minister to Washington, insisted on in their talks with the Americans.

Churchill's visit to the United States was a personal triumph for the British prime minister, and he reached agreement with President Truman on a number of issues, including the "greater sanction" statement. But the two leaders failed to resolve important differences between their countries on a number of other matters. And to the extent that Churchill had gone to the United States hoping to ease world tensions by arranging talks between Washington and Moscow while at the same time reducing the crushing burden of rearmament, his trip proved largely unsuccessful. Indeed, the hard line adopted toward China by Truman and Churchill caused considerable consternation in the United States and raised a veritable political storm in London after the prime minister returned home.

Most of Washington had welcomed Churchill's return to

office after more than six years of being out of power. Still remembered in the nation's capital were Churchill's gallantry and heroism during World War II, his mobilization of the English people and the English language against the Nazis, his close and personal relationship with President Franklin Roosevelt, and his pivotal role as a leader of the western coalition that had defeated the Fascists. Also, a widespread feeling existed that as a symbol of unity and perseverance, Churchill might act as an antidote against growing anti-American sentiment in England and the rest of western Europe and as a force to mobilize the Western world against the threat of Communist aggression.[24]

For the most part, these expectations were never realized. In the first place, the results of the British elections were much closer than many analysts had anticipated. Despite the national humiliation in the Mideast during the past several months and the worsening economy, Labor Party candidates actually received about 224,000 more votes than Conservatives, who gained a parliamentary majority of only 18. Also, the anti-American Bevanite wing of the Labor Party did even better than the more moderate Laborites. Bevan himself was returned from Wales with a heavier majority than usual, and the rest of his backers in Parliament, including two ministers who had resigned with him in April, held their seats. Clearly, then, the British voters had not given the Conservatives a mandate—as Washington had hoped—to work more closely with the United States in strengthening western Europe against Communist aggression. If anything, the outcome of the elections showed the depth of opposition in England to massive rearmament, which was widely blamed for Britain's economic plight in the first place, and which the Bevanites had successfully made a campaign issue. If anything also, the election results underscored just how anxious the British were to substitute negotiations with the Communists for military confrontation.[25]

Despite Churchill's return to power, furthermore, western Europe remained badly split over the issue of rearmament, particularly German rearmament. Ever since the United States had decided to support the rearming of Germany following the outbreak of the Korean War in 1950, the issue had been raised time and time again. In fact, it was central to the whole argument over how best to strengthen European security. Opposed to any plan that provided for the establishment of a separate Germany army, the French had proposed the creation of a European Defense Community (EDC) that would include German forces but would not give Germany control over them or membership in NATO. Even then strong opposition remained in France against rearmament of any kind, much less German rearmament.[26]

At first resisting the concept of an EDC because it believed its development would be slow and cumbersome at a time when a speedy military buildup was needed, the United States had decided in 1951 to support a European army as a way of mollifying the opposition to German rearmament in France and throughout Europe. In September Acheson met in Washington with the foreign ministers of England and France, who were on their way home from San Francisco following the conclusion of the Japanese peace treaty. Together the three leaders agreed on the formation of a European army including German contingents. A little later NATO members meeting in Ottawa established a mechanism for allocating each member's military spending according to specific criteria rather than letting each member determine its own military contribution. In both these ways important obstacles to German and European rearmament seemed resolved. But European opposition remained strong, and "neutralism" in the confrontation between Washington and Moscow became a broad-based movement throughout Europe. Great emphasis was placed on substituting disarmament for rearmament through negotiations with the Soviet Union.[27]

This was the situation when Churchill became prime minister at the end of October. Instead of backing the EDC and seeking generally to strengthen the western coalition by encouraging European unity, the new prime minister pursued a substantially different course. Determined not to forfeit any measure of British sovereignty, Churchill made clear that he would continue his predecessor's opposition to British participation in any form of European federation, and he let it be known that he did not favor the EDC. Moreover, he emphasized the importance of negotiations with the Soviet Union in order to resolve world differences.[28]

Certainly Churchill was not against working closely with Washington. To the contrary, the main reason he decided to go to Washington was to reestablish the type of Anglo-American directorate that had governed his relations with President Roosevelt during World War II. But bent on upholding the principles of British authority and influence, he was convinced that the Labor government had been too yielding in its relations with the United States.[29]

Nor was the prime minister naïve about the prospects of peace through talks with Moscow. In later conversations with U. S. officials, he remarked that the "central factor in Soviet policy was fear; the USSR feared our friendship more than our enmity." But as he also said, he hoped that the growing strength of the West might convince the Soviets to "fear our enmity more than our friendship and . . . to seek our friendship."[30]

Another way to lessen tensions and at the same time to ease the burden that was cutting so heavily into the British economy was to reduce the enormous arms buildup already under way in England. But there were also practical political reasons for advocating arms reductions. The size of the Bevanite vote in October had made clear to Churchill no less than to other astute politicians the strength of arms reduction sentiment in England. Taking the floor of Parliament in November, Churchill even made the sensational statement that Bevan "by accident" had been right on the issue of rearmament.[31]

Churchill's opposition to the EDC and British participation in a European federation, his desire to negotiate with the Soviet Union, and his advocacy of arms reduction were at odds with Washington's own policy of "peace through strength." Not that the administration openly opposed talks with Moscow or spoke out against disarmament. In a speech to the American people on November 7, President Truman even offered to discuss international arms reductions with the Soviet Union. Referring to Moscow's "deceit and broken promises" over the previous six years, he remarked, "[n]evertheless, as responsible men and women, we must try for disarmament in spite of all difficulties." A short time later Secretary of State Acheson presented to the UN General Assembly in Paris a tripartite plan for arms reduction, which the United States had worked out with England and France.[32]

Yet the administration did not intend to rely on negotiations to prevent Soviet aggression. Nor did Acheson's proposals on disarmament, which called for a system of disclosure and verification similar to the Baruch plan of 1946 on atomic weapons, offer anything really new. Moscow had rejected the Baruch plan because of its system of free inspection, and there was no reason to believe that it had changed its mind on inspection. In fact, Acheson's vituperative language against the Soviet Union indicated that he did not expect much to happen as a result of his proposals. As one commentator later put it, "[e]ven if every harsh word he spoke about the Russians was true, it is still a fact a man does not attack a person whose agreement he is honestly seeking."[33]

The talks between the United States and England, which took place over a two-week period in January, revealed just how deep their differences were on the matters of negotiations with the Soviets and arms reductions. In his discussions with Prime Minister Churchill, Acheson thus made clear that the United States would continue to depend primarily on an arms buildup to contain Soviet expansion. The American position, he said, "was to create sufficient force to make any attempt by the Soviet Union in Europe too dangerous to be attempted."[34]

Other differences between the two countries were apparent as well. For example, the United States wanted England to be more responsive to the rising tide of nationalism in the Middle East, while the British wanted the Americans to be more understanding of their special interests in the region. Much to Acheson's annoyance, Churchill even proposed publicly that an American brigade be sent to help defend the Suez Canal, presumably without regard to Egyptian opinion. Similarly, the British and Americans disagreed sharply over the appointment of a naval commander for NATO. The British wanted this top naval position for themselves, but the Labor government had earlier agreed that an American should have the post. No final meeting of the minds was reached, and in the routine communiqué that followed the discussions no effort was made to mask the disagreement that remained.[35]

Even on the issues of European unification and the establishment of an EDC, what seemed to be considerable progress on Washington's part in winning England over to its position proved largely illusory. In conversations with the British foreign secretary, Secretary of State Acheson warned Eden that a decision to maintain American troops in Europe depended on making the EDC effective, and he strongly implied that congressional support for Europe would be badly eroded if the EDC failed. Pressured in this way by the administration, the British announced their support for EDC. But in a speech at Columbia University on January 11, Eden made clear that he remained opposed to the British actually joining the EDC or any other supranational European organization. London would support the establishment of the EDC, but only as an ally and not as a member.[36]

On matters pertaining to the Far East, however, the British and Americans were basically in agreement. This was true enough with respect to the "greater sanction" policy, to which England gave its final approval, although both Churchill and Eden again told Washington that they would first want to be consulted before reprisals were actually carried out against China. But it was also true with regard to the worsening military situation in Indochina. In response to the fighting in Southeast Asia, in fact, the British actually moved closer to the hard-line policy against Peking, which the United States had long advocated, by issuing their own warning of reprisal in case of Chinese aggression.[37]

For many Western observers the situation in Indochina was even more critical than in Korea, and there was considerable concern in both London and Washington that Peking might yet decide to intervene there, just as it had in Korea a year earlier. General Lattre de Tassigny, on whom the French had counted to defeat the Communists, had died recently after a brief illness, and there appeared no strong commander to replace him. Also, the Vietminh had resumed the offensive and were once more inflicting heavy casualties on the French. Faced with the possibility of final defeat, Paris decided to send a military delegation to Washington in order to confer with the British and Americans and to plead France's case for more military aid.[38]

Nothing immediate resulted from these meetings, and no promises of additional assistance were made. That would come later. Nevertheless, in two speeches delivered in the United States, Eden and Churchill both warned Peking against intervening in Indochina. Speaking at Columbia University on January 11, Eden remarked, "It should be understood that the intervention by force by Chinese Communists in Southeast Asia— even if they were called volunteers—would create a situation no less menacing than that which the United Nations met and faced in Korea. In any such event the United Nations should be equally solid to resist it." In a speech to a joint session of Congress six days later, Churchill was equally threatening. Referring to the possibility of a cease-fire in Korea, he warned, "our two countries are agreed that if the truce we seek is reached only to be broken, our response will be prompt, resolute, and effective." And then, turning to Indochina, the British prime minister added, "I would not be helpful to the common cause —for our evils all spring from one center—if an effective truce in Korea led only to a transference of Communist aggression to these other fields. Our problems will not be solved unless they are steadily viewed and acted upon as a whole in their integrity as a whole."[39]

Precisely because Churchill's visit to the United States appeared to give Britain's stamp of approval to Washington's hard-line policy toward China, it was praised in the United States by those who had long advocated taking more drastic action against Peking and condemned by those who sought an accommodation with the Chinese, including even recognition of the PRC. *Time* was particularly emphatic in its praise of the "greater sanction" policy, which it regarded as the major accomplishment of the trip and which, the magazine said, placed "an entirely different light on the truce talks." "Before the new policy," it added, "the U. S. had little prospect of ending the Korean war in any way favorable to U. S. interests. . . . Under the new policy, the U. N. can walk away from the Korean truce line, saying over its shoulder; 'Violate it, and the war will be brought to you.' " In contrast, the *New Republic* commented about the Churchill visit, "The fact of the matter is that contrary to what he said about British staying power, Churchill has recognized the complete supremacy of the new American empire," while the *Nation* called for public disclosure of any agreements on Asia that might have been reached in Washington "before bigger and worse wars [than Korea] are launched."[40]

In England the reaction to the prime minister's visit was much stronger. Britons were alarmed by Churchill's implied promise to back up an extension of the Korean War if a cease-fire was violated or if the Chinese invaded Southeast Asia. Leftists especially accused Churchill of "selling out" to the Americans by aligning Britain to U. S. policy in the Far East. They charged that the prime minister had given the Americans practically a blank check in an area where American policy had been, to say the least, dangerously haphazard. Nor did rumors that the U. S. Air Force was pressing for permission to bomb Chinese ports help matters. Churchill was able to quiet some of these misgivings by telling the British people that nothing new had been agreed to during his Washington trip. But doubts still remained as the Labor opposition prepared to take on the Conservatives in a debate over foreign affairs that promised to be both sweeping and unusually acrimonious.[41]

The "greater sanction" policy, around which so much of the response to Churchill's visit to the United States revolved (although, it should be pointed out, Washington never publicly acknowledged its existence), infuriated General Ridgway in Tokyo. To depend upon a warning at the time of an armistice in order to keep the peace in Korea and at the same time not to take a firmer negotiating stand at Panmunjom on such matters as the rehabilitation of airfields seemed to him the height of folly. "In my opinion," he told the JCS in early January, "the retributive potentiality of UN military power against Red China would be noneffective unless the full results of precipitating World War 3 were to be accepted, and the use of atomic weapons auth[orized]." A few days later, when sent a draft of the warning to be delivered at the time of the armistice, the UN commander added that with its "presently available resources this command would be incapable of posing a threat to Communist China sufficient . . . to deter it from renewed aggression."[42]

Privately President Truman continued to share Ridgway's desire to take a firmer stand against the Communists, and in his private journal, which he often used to vent his anger, he expressed some of his exasperation at the desultory course of the negotiations. Blaming Moscow for the stalemate in Korea, he wrote that he would serve the Soviets with an ultimatum. The ultimatum would "mean all out war," he noted. "Moscow, St.

Petersburg, Mukden, Vladivostok, Peking, Shanghai, Port Arthur, Dairen, Odessa, Stalingrad and every manufacturing plant in China and the Soviet Union will be eliminated."[43] But the White House remained committed to reaching a negotiated settlement to the war and avoiding any position that might jeopardize the peace talks. Consequently Ridgway's appeals for a stronger negotiating position were again turned down and, pointing to the "greater sanction" statement that would follow the signing of the armistice, the Joint Chiefs instructed him to proceed with a settlement on the outstanding issues having to do with administering an armistice, leaving only the question of rehabilitating airfields for later discussions. And even this issue, the UN commander was told, should not be the sole obstacle to a cease-fire agreement.[44]

One question which the Joint Chiefs could hardly have imagined would delay such an agreement for more than a year, but which had come up in the negotiations at Panmunjom and was already causing considerable difficulty involved the repatriation of prisoners of war. Simply stated, the issue was one of voluntary repatriation, whether all POWs should be repatriated regardless of their wishes or whether there were groups of prisoners who, for one of a number of reasons, did not want to and should not be repatriated. Among these were former South Korean and Nationalist Chinese soldiers who had been captured and then forced to serve in the captor's armies, and thousands of Chinese troops who wanted to go to Formosa rather than back to China. There were also thousands of South Korean civilians who had been taken prisoners by the North Koreans during the early part of the war and had been forced to work as laborers. Although they were not legally POWs, the UNC catagorized them as such.[45]

Treatment of POWs was prescribed by the Geneva Convention of 1949, which called for quick and compulsory repatriation. Intended to avoid a recurrence of the situation after World War II, when the Soviet Union kept captive a large number of German and Japanese prisoners in order to help in the country's massive reconstruction, the Geneva agreement did not provide for those prisoners who did not want to be repatriated. Although the United States did not ratify the accord until mid-1951, it announced very early in the Korean War, along with

North and South Korea, that it would abide by its provisions.[46]

As the UN forces began to take large numbers of prisoners, however, and as many of them indicated that they did not want to be repatriated, maintaining that they would be physically harmed or even executed if sent back to China or North Korea, the United States began to reconsider its position. In July 1951 General Robert A. McClure, Army chief of psychological warfare, proposed to General J. Lawton Collins that Chinese POWs who were former Nationalists be repatriated to Formosa. Collins forwarded the idea to the JCS, stating such repatriation would be legal according to the Geneva Convention since even the Communists maintained that Formosa was part of China.[47]

This was, of course, a specious argument that ran counter to the spirit and intention of the Geneva accord, and during the next few months the administration debated the merits of a policy based on voluntary repatriation. Secretary of State Acheson opposed such a policy on the grounds that it violated the Geneva agreement and that the overriding consideration with respect to the POWs should be the prompt return of all UN and South Korean prisoners held by North Korea and China. The Joint Chiefs, who, at one time, had instructed Ridgway to prepare a plan for the exchange of POWs based on the principle of voluntary repatriation, changed their minds and agreed with Acheson that the Geneva accord should be adhered to rigidly. Defense Secretary Lovett also believed that the UNC should accept an all-for-all exchange of prisoners (that is, forced repatriation) if the Communists refused to negotiate on any other basis. In contrast, President Truman, who took an abiding interest in the POW question, strongly opposed an all-for-all exchange unless it was part of a larger package that included major concessions from the enemy.[48]

Thus, as matters stood in December, when the issue of POWs was first brought up at Panmunjom, the administration had still not reached final agreement on the POW question. In accordance with the President's wishes, UN negotiators would try to obtain an exchange of prisoners based on the concept of voluntary repatriation. Also the enemy would have to make major concessions on issues still not specified before Truman would even consider an all-for-all exchange. But depending on how well the Chinese and North Koreans responded to the UN proposal and to the President's insistence on concessions, the UN might retreat to an all-for-all exchange.

Almost as soon as the POW issue was raised, trouble developed. At first the Communists even refused to exchange lists of POWs or to allow Red Cross representatives to visit their camps. And when finally on December 18 they did release their lists of names, they showed only 7142 South Korean and 4417 UN POWs (of whom 3198 were American), despite the fact that in the first months of the war alone they had reported taking 65,000 prisoners. What made the enemy figures even more shocking was the fact that South Korea reported more than 88,000 and the United States more than 11,500 missing in action, many of whom would normally have been taken as prisoners. The Communist figures contrasted sharply with the 132,000 names of enemy POWs provided them by the UNC. And this excluded another 37,000 former South Koreans recently classified as civilian internees.[49]

The UN negotiators at Panmunjom believed the fastest way to get the UN prisoners back was to agree to an all-for-all exchange. They also had serious reservations about countermanding the Geneva Convention. They questioned whether prisoners were able to make a rational decision on their repatriation, and they feared voluntary repatriation would establish a dangerous precedent in case of future wars with Communist powers. So, too, General Ridgway was concerned that the Communists would make propaganda capital out of a decision by Washington not to abide by the Geneva agreement on repatriation, and he was convinced that the American public would insist on concessions to the enemy on the release of prisoners "long before" the Chinese and North Koreans would agree to voluntary repatriation. But this was far from clear, and during the next several months at least a few commentators in the United States began to question the morality of forcing prisoners to be repatriated, especially when their fate remained uncertain and many of them had been promised UN protection.[50]

Increasingly this became the administration's view as well. Just as President Truman believed that the United States had made a moral commitment to prevent South Korea from falling to the Communists, so he felt the United States could not morally allow Chinese and North Korean POWs to be returned home against their will. "To agree to forced repatriation," he later told the American public, "would be unthinkable. It would be repugnant to the fundamental moral and humanitarian principles which underlie our action in Korea." But there were other reasons having little to do with ethical questions for not returning all Chinese and North Korean POWs. For one thing, the administration saw its own propaganda advantage in having thousands of Communist prisoners refuse repatriation. For another, the granting of asylum to these POWs might lead to wholesale defections from enemy ranks and act as a deterrent to future Communist aggression.[51]

Washington thus ordered the UN negotiators at Panmunjom to insist that the release of POWs be in accordance with the principle of voluntary repatriation. Against their better judgment, the UN team carried out their instructions, even proposing the establishment of a neutral agency, which would interview all prisoners and civilians in order to determine whether they wished to return home. The Chinese and North Koreans responded with emotional outbursts against the theory of voluntary repatriation, calling it a "gigantic trap," which would provide a pretext for holding POWs after the armistice. They also charged that the UN intended to send many of its prisoners to Formosa in order to serve in Chiang Kai-shek's army, and they characterized the UN proposal for an agency to interview POWs as interference in their internal affairs. Weeks passed in this way without any progress or significant development except that the Communists' language on repatriation grew steadily more vituperative.[52]

Yet the administration had still not finally and completely committed itself against forced repatriation. Quite clearly, the White House was moving in that direction. Hoping that the Chinese and North Koreans might yet agree to a compromise solution of the POW issue, the Joint Chiefs even raised with Ridgway the possibility of an exchange in which the UN would concede to the Communists on the rehabilitation of airfields in return for the enemy's agreement on voluntary repatriation. But for all its concern about the morality of forced repatriation and the potential advantages to be gained by rejecting an all-for-all exchange, the administration still refused to take an irrevocable stand against forced repatriation. As on other matters, the JCS instructed Ridgway on this issue to be rigid only as a last resort and only after all other possibilities had been exhausted.[53]

The Joint Chiefs' orders to Ridgway were by no means unreasonable, and there were plenty of good reasons why the administration might decide in the end to abandon voluntary for forced repatriation. Like Ridgway, the White House was concerned about public reaction at home to any delay in settling the POW question, and it was sensitive to the political fallout that the failure to end the war was already causing. As the Joint Chiefs told the UN commander, the American public was interested primarily in the return of the POWs, and public pressure might force the President to modify the UN's bargaining position in order to win the quick release of American prisoners.[54]

At times, however, the exchanges between Washington and Tokyo seemed almost ludicrous, and certainly they were demoralizing to the UN negotiators at Panmunjom, who never seemed to know just how far to go in sticking to a negotiating position one way or another. Having been opposed to the policy of voluntary repatriation, Ridgway and the UN team were, nevertheless, fully prepared—or so at least Ridgway maintained—to defend that position against the Communists just so long as it was a final position and they could take a stand on an issue confident that they would not be undermined in Washington. The orders from the Pentagon failed to provide these assurances, and they sometimes made the UN negotiating position seem unnecessarily weak and vacillating.[55]

That changed toward the end of February when President Truman decided to take a firm position on voluntary repatriation. Believing in the immorality of forced repatriation, he accepted a plan worked out within the administration for the release of those POWs in UN custody who violently opposed repatriation. By this plan, the UN negotiators at Panmunjom would offer the Chinese and North Koreans a deal in which the UN would exchange concessions on the question of rehabilitating airfields in return for an agreement on voluntary repatriation. If the Communists refused to negotiate such a quid pro quo, the JCS instructed Ridgway to screen the prisoners and to remove from the POW lists those prisoners who feared personal harm if repatriated. The Chinese and North Koreans would then be told that the UN delegation was ready for an all-for-all exchange on the basis of the revised lists. This would be "the final governmental position." In agreeing to this plan, neither President Truman nor Secretary of State Dean Acheson ever believed that their position on the prisoner of war issue would produce a lengthy stalemate in the war. They thought that by steadfast negotiations and perhaps bombing of selected targets in North Korea they could break the impasse. At most a settlement of the war would be delayed a few months, certainly not more than a year, as proved to be the case.[56]

General Ridgway strongly opposed the plan for releasing Communist POWs, which, when he had first read it, did not even include the quid pro quo that was later incorporated into it. But even in proposing a trade with the Chinese and North Koreans that included concessions on airfield reconstruction for agreement on voluntary repatriation, he did not think it had much chance of gaining Communist acceptance. Also, he was worried about the consequences the early release of Communist POWs would have on UN prisoners of war. The "premature release of POWs," he told the JCS, "could result in retaliation against our prisoners" and would constitute a "breach of faith of the principles which have guided us through the negotiations."[57]

In a real sense, Ridgway was not being true to what he had indicated earlier when he had strongly implied that he would agree to almost any proposal, be it voluntary or involuntary repatriation, just so long as UN negotiators could hold to that position. Now he was making clear that he remained opposed to the principle of voluntary repatriation because of the consequences that might have for UN POWs. Ridgway's concerns were, of course, no less real than those that had originally kept the administration from taking a firm stand on the repatriation issue. But they might have given the UN commander a deeper and more sympathetic understanding of the constraints under which Washington had to operate when formulating policy on such a complex issue as prisoner repatriation, just as the administration might have been more sensitive to the difficulties of carrying on negotiations with the enemy in a vacuum of uncertainty and indecision.

As it was, however, neither Tokyo nor Washington showed any indication of being more solicitous of each other's concerns in formulating and executing policy for Korea. Instead, they continued to rankle over a number of other matters having to do with the postwar period that the negotiators at Panmunjom were considering simultaneously with the problem of prisoner repatriation. Although the two sides had failed to reach agreement on the issue of rehabilitating airfields after the war, they continued to bargain on other postwar questions, including the rotation of troops after the war, the number of ports to handle rotation and the replenishment of troops already in Korea, the control of coastal ports, and the composition of a proposed neutral commission that would supervise an armistice. On the first three of these issues considerable give-and-take took place, but by the middle of March agreement had been reached on all of them. For example, after much bargaining, both sides consented to a rotation of 35,000 men a month and five ports for both sides. This was considerably less than the UN's initial proposal of a 75,000-man rotation with twelve ports of entry in North Korea and ten in South Korea, but it was considerably more than the 5000 men proposed by the Communists, who would also have limited both sides to three ports of entry. Similarly, China and North Korea agreed to let the UN retain control over five island groups under dispute on the west coast of Korea.[58]

On the issue of a postwar armistice commission, however, the situation was considerably different. On this vital question the Communist and UN negotiators deadlocked. In brief, while both sides had agreed in early December that there should be such a neutral peacekeeping body, the Communists wanted to include the Soviet Union as a member of that commission, while the United States absolutely refused to permit the Soviets a seat on a commission identified as "neutral." It *was* willing to allow Moscow to be represented on a commission designated by some other name, but in that case the United States would also have to be given a seat on the commission.[59]

On March 11 General Ridgway wrote the JCS asking that the United States announce its decision not to permit the Soviet Union to be a member of the armistice commission. "Removal of the USSR as an issue," he stated, "is a prerequisite to resolution of the other remaining issues, i.e., airfields and voluntary repatriation." An announcement by the United States that it would reject every effort to put the Soviets on the commission would show the Communists the UN's resolve "to stand firm on stated minimum positions" and was "imperative in order to arrest the very evident present deterioration in our negotiating position."[60]

The JCS had no quarrel with Ridgway's assertion that the time was fast approaching to take an inflexible position with the Communists on all outstanding major issues. But they told the general that a package deal would be a better way than what he proposed to present as the UN's position. It would have greater impact and offer the same, if not a better, chance of being accepted by the Chinese and North Koreans. If, on the other hand, the enemy should reject the package and subsequently break off negotiations, the UN would more likely have world opinion on its side.[61]

Accordingly, the Joint Chiefs instructed Ridgway to meet with the enemy commanders and agree to the removal of all restrictions on airfield reconstruction after the war. In return, the Chinese and North Koreans would have to agree either to eliminate the neutral designation of an armistice commission or to exclude the Soviet Union from serving on the commission. The enemy would also have to agree to a system of inspection behind their lines and a prisoner exchange based on voluntary repatriation. If the enemy refused, Ridgway should tell them it was his final and best offer and cut off any debate on individual items.[62]

The UN commander responded to his newest orders by raising doubts as to the authority of the Communist commanders to meet him on the field. He also repeated his earlier warning that the rescreening and reclassification of POWs, called for by the JCS proposal, might endanger UN POWs, and he stated again his opposition to accepting the Soviet Union in any armistice commission under any circumstances. Finally, he told the JCS that any package proposal should be presented in the form of an ultimatum, in which it was made clear that a rejection of the offer meant termination of the negotiations. The Joint Chiefs did modify their recommendations somewhat, agreeing, for example, to have the Soviet issue settled before the package was offered to the Communist negotiators. But they flatly rejected Ridgway's concept of an ultimatum, insisting as they always had that any rupture in the negotiations must remain the enemy's responsibility.[63]

By the beginning of April, therefore, the differences between the UN and Communist negotiators at Panmunjom had been narrowed to three major issues—rehabilitation of airfields, voluntary repatriation of POWs, and the constitution of a military armistice commission—and the UNC was about to offer the Communists a package proposal on these matters. Also, the two sides at Panmunjom agreed at the beginning of April, after months of disagreement, to screen their POWs in order to see how many prisoners were willing to accept repatriation. It was widely believed that any figure over 100,000 repatriates would be acceptable to the Chinese and North Koreans, since they had been informed by the UN negotiators that they could expect about 116,000 returning POWs, and previous discussions indicated that anything over 100,000 would not represent too great a loss of face for them. On April 8 UN forces began the screening process.[64]

Agreement had also been reached at Panmunjom on another issue that had been placed on the original agenda when it was worked out in the summer of 1951—recommendations to be made by the armistice negotiators to their governments. In February the Communists proposed that an international conference on Korea and "other questions related to peace in Korea" be held within three months after an armistice. Washington rejected this obvious effort by the Chinese to open talks on such problems as the status of Formosa and a seat for the PRC at the UN. But the Communists then responded by agreeing to new language calling for the conference to negotiate "the questions of the withdrawal of all foreign forces from Korea, the peaceful settlement of the Korean question, etc." The Chinese and North Koreans also said that the term "etc." did not commit the conference to anything. With this assurance the UN quickly accepted the enemy's proposal, making clear only that the term "foreign forces" meant "non-Korean forces," and that "etc." did not relate to matters outside of Korea. In essence, both sides at Panmunjom were able to reach agreement on a postwar conference on Korea within just eleven days because it was so vaguely worded that it was open to a wide range of interpretations and could later be ignored or employed as the two sides saw fit.[65]

With the issues between the UN and Communist delegations thus narrowed to only three by the beginning of April, with the process of screening prisoners of war already started, and with the UN negotiators about to make a package proposal to the Chinese and North Koreans, it seemed to some observers that a final armistice was near.[66] But for many others the mood was much more somber. In the first place, within the first three days of screening, it became apparent that far fewer than the 116,000 repatriates indicated to the Communists would choose voluntary repatriation. With about half the 132,000 POWs still to be screened, 40,000 already indicated that they would forcibly resist repatriation.[67] Second, the military stalemate that dragged on while both sides continued to negotiate at Panmunjom seemed to many Americans to favor the enemy, which was engaged in a heavy military buildup, including the continued development of a powerful air force capable of striking behind UN lines.[68] Finally, Korea remained just one theater of the ongoing struggle against Communist aggression, a struggle that seemed to be going not particularly well for the Western democracies. In addition to pessimistic reports from Indochina, there seemed to be problems throughout Southeast Asia and, indeed, throughout the Far Pacific. Beyond Asia, the Middle East, in the turmoil of nationalist uprisings and social unrest, became more and more a cause for concern. In Europe progress continued to be made on rearmament and the building of a defense force against Communist attack, but only slowly, fretfully, and in the face of increasingly well-organized resistance against German rearmament. Even in England, America's staunchest ally, Prime Minister Churchill was able to beat back a vote of no confidence on his foreign policy only by turning away from the Anglo-American solidarity on China that seemed to have been achieved during his January visit to the United States. Adding to the growing national despair was the fact that 1952 was a Presidential election year, and opponents of the administration were already playing on the unpopularity of the war for political purposes.

Politics and prisoners of war would determine much of the

dialogue over Korea for the remainder of 1952, political issues at home and the question of POWs both at home and in the truce tents at Panmunjom. In the United States and at the negotiations the discourse was at the same time elusive and elliptical. But complicating it even more was a skillfully orchestrated propaganda campaign by the Chinese and North Koreans against UN forces, as they accused the UNC of engaging in biological warfare and used a major prisoner uprising on Koje-do island to charge the UN with barbaric treatment of its Communist captives.

NOTES

1. Walter G. Hermes, *Truce Tent and Fighting Front* (Washington, D. C., 1966), 175–78
2. *Time,* 58 (December 3, 1951), 26.
3. Hermes, *Truce Tent and Fighting Front,* 178–81
4. *Nation,* 173 (December 8, 1951), 489; *Time,* 58 (December 10, 1951), 19.
5. David Rees, *Korea: The Limited War* (New York, 1964), 301–303.
6. *Time,* 58 (December 3, 1951), 19.
7. *FR,* 1951, VII, 974–75; *Time,* 58 (December 3, 1951), 19.
8. Hermes, *Truce Tent and Fighting Front,* 192–94; *Time,* 59 (February 11, 1952), 36.
9. *Time,* 59 (February 11, 1952), 36; Rees, *Korea: The Limited War,* 370–78.
10. Hermes, *Truce Tent and Fighting Front,* 199–201; *Atlantic Monthly,* 189 (February 1952), 14–16.
11. *FR,* 1951, VII, 598–600; Hermes, *Truce Tent and Fighting Front,* 121.
12. Briefing of Foreign Government Representatives on Korea, November 27, 1951 and January 18, 1952, Box 3, Selected Records Relating to the Korean War.
13. *FR,* 1951, VII, 1130–31; Ridgway to JCS, December 18, 1951, Box 16, *ibid.*
14. *FR,* 1951, VII, 1281–82 and 1290–96.
15. On the possible consequences of an embargo or naval blockade against the Chinese Communists, see CIA, "Special Estimate #20," December 15, 1951, Box 243, Korean War File, President's Secretary File, Truman Papers.
16. For the various drafts accompanying the formulation of NSC 118/2

see File NSC-118, Records of the National Security Council, Record Group 429 (National Archives, Washington, D. C.).

17. *Ibid.; FR*, 1951, VII, 1387–99.
18. *FR*, 1951, VII, 1142–43, 1290–96, and 1377–81; James Webb to Amer. Embassy Rome, November 26, 1951, Box 4267, Records of the Department of State, RG 59, 795.00/11–2651.
19. *FR*, 1951, VII, 1281–82 and 1290–96.
20. Anthony Eden, *Full Circle: The Memoirs of Anthony Eden* (Boston, 1960), 18–20; "Memorandum of Conversation at Dinner at British Embassy," January 7, 1953, Box 66, Acheson Papers.
21. Eden, *Full Circle*, 18–20.
22. *Ibid.*
23. *Ibid.*
24. *New Yorker*, 27 (November 10, 1951), 96–97; *New Republic*, 125 (November 5, 1951), 5.
25. Michael Foot, *Aneurin Bevan: A Biography*, II (2 vols., London, 1973), 350–52; *Atlantic Monthly*, 189 (January 1952), 11–14.
26. Robert McGeehan, *The German Rearmament Question: American Diplomacy and European Defense after World War II* (Urbana, Ill., 1971), 126–71.
27. *Ibid.* See also *New Republic*, 125 (November 26, 1951), 9; *ibid.* (December 17, 1951), 9; *New Yorker*, 27 (November 24, 1951), 149–50.
28. *New Yorker*, 27 (December 22, 1951), 51–52; Eden, *Full Circle*, 36–40;
29. Anthony Seldon, *Churchill's Indian Summer, The Conservative Government, 1951–1955* (London, 1981), 388–89; David S. McLellan, *Dean Acheson: The State Department Years* (New York, 1976), 357.
30. Dean Acheson, *Present at the Creation: My Years in the State Department* (New York, 1969), 599; Seldon, *Churchill's Indian Summer*, 396–97; *Nation*, 174 (January 5, 1952), 1.
31. *Nation*, 173 (December 15, 1951), 512–13; *New Republic*, 125 (December 17, 1951), 10–12.
32. *Public Papers of the Presidents of the United States: Harry S. Truman*, 1951 (Washington, D. C., 1965), 623–27; Acheson, *Present at the Creation*, 578–80; *Commonweal*, 55 (November 30, 1951), 187–88; *Nation*, 173 (December 22, 1951), 542.
33. *Nation*, 173 (November 17, 1951), 413; *ibid.* (December 8, 1953), 500; *New Yorker*, 27 (November 24, 1951), 149–50.
34. "Memorandum of Conversation at Dinner at British Embassy," January 7, 1953, Box 66, Acheson Papers; Acheson, *Present at the Creation*, 597–98.

35. Acheson, *Present at the Creation,* 600–603.
36. Eden, *Full Circle,* 40–41.
37. David Carlton, *Anthony Eden: A Biography* (London, 1981), 40; *Atlantic Monthly,* 189 (March 1952), 12–14.
38. *Life,* 32 (January 21, 1952), 28; George C. Herring, *America's Longest War: The United States and Vietnam, 1950–1975* (New York, 1979), 19–20.
39. Eden, *Full Circle,* 40–41; *Nation,* 174 (January 26, 1952), 63.
40. *New Republic,* 126 (January 28, 1952), 5; *Time,* 59 (January 28, 1952), 13 and 14; *Nation,* 174 (January 19, 1952), 49.
41. *New Republic,* 126 (January 28, 1952), 5; *Time,* 59 (February 4, 1952), 20; *New Yorker,* 27 (February 9, 1952), 59.
42. *FR,* 1952–1954, XV, 10–12 and 17–18.
43. Barton J. Bernstein, "Truman's Second Thoughts on Ending the Korean War," *Foreign Service Journal,* 57 (November 1950), 31–32.
44. JCS to Ridgway, January 27, 1952, Box 16, Selected Records Relating to the Korean War.
45. Barton J. Bernstein, "The Struggle Over the Korean Armistice: Prisoners of Repatriation?" in Bruce Cumings (ed.), *Child of Conflict: The Korean-American Relationship, 1943–1953* (Seattle, Wash., 1983), 274–75.
46. Hermes, *Truce Tent and Fighting Front,* 135–37.
47. *Ibid.,* 136–37.
48. *FR,* 1951, VII, 1073; James F. Schnabel and Robert J. Watson, *The History of the Joint Chiefs of Staff,* III, *The Korean War* (unpublished manuscript, National Archives, 1978), 687–88; Ridgway to JCS, July 21, 1951, Box 16, Selected Records Relating to the Korean War.
49. Hermes, *Truce Tent and Fighting Front,* 141.
50. *FR,* 1951, VII, 1366–72 and 1377–81; Admiral Charles Turner Joy, *How Communists Negotiate* (New York, 1955), 150–52.
51. *Public Papers of the Presidents of the United States: Harry S. Truman,* 1952–1953 (Washington, D. C., 1966), 321.
52. Briefing of Foreign Government Representatives in Korea, January 8 and 18, 1952, Box 3, Selected Records Relating to the Korean War; Ridgway to JCS, April 28, 1952, Box 18, *ibid.*
53. *FR,* 1952–1954, XV, 178–79; JCS to Ridgway, April 28, 1952, Box 16, Selected Records Relating to the Korean War.
54. *Ibid.*
55. JCS to Ridgway, January 15, 1952, Box 3, Selected Records Relating to the Korean War.
56. Hermes, *Truce Tent and Fighting Front,* 151. See also Memoran-

dum of Conversation, February 25, 1952, Box 4277, Records of the Department of State, RG 59, 795.00/2–2552.

57. *FR*, 1952–1954, XV, 66–67.

58. Briefing of Foreign Government Representatives on Korea, February 1, 1952, Box 3, Selected Records Relating to the Korean War; Ridgway to JCS, February 12 and March 28, 1952, Box 16, *ibid.*

59. Briefing of Foreign Government Representatives on Korea, February 29, 1952, Box 3, *ibid.*

60. *FR*, 1952–1954, XV, 80–81.

61. *Ibid.*, 88–91.

62. *Ibid.*

63. *Ibid.*, 95–107.

64. *Ibid.*

65. Ridgway to JCS, April 28, 1952, Box 16, Selected Records Relating to the Korean War. See also Briefing of Foreign Government Representatives on Korea, February 8, 1952, *ibid.;* Hermes, *Truce Tent and Fighting Front,* 159.

66. *Atlantic Monthly,* 189 (March 1952), 17.

67. Hermes, *Truce Tent and Fighting Front,* 169–71.

68. *New Republic,* 126 (February 18, 1952), 6.

CHAPTER 8

Prisoners, Propaganda, and Politics

Although the war in Korea remained a military stalemate as spring finally came to the country in April and May, the latest reports from the front indicated that the enemy was daily increasing in strength, particularly in terms of air power. While American ground strength dropped slightly in the six months from November 1 to April 30, declining from about 265,000 to 260,000, enemy troop strength was estimated to have grown in the same period from approximately 502,000 to 866,000. Nor was this offset by a slight increase in the contribution of the other UN countries (from about 34,000 to 36,000) and a 60,000 troop jump in ROK forces (from about 282,000 to 342,000). Also, enemy armored strength increased from practically nothing to two Chinese and one North Korean armored divisions and one mechanized division, with an estimated 520 tanks. Few if any military leaders thought the Communists had the capacity yet to sustain another major offensive. Indeed, General Van Fleet indicated that he would welcome an enemy attack. "It would be a good thing," he said, "if we could get [the Communists] out of their foxholes and dugouts, to mow them down the way we did last April and May." But the enemy buildup on the ground was worrisome all the same, and the UNC doubted that it could launch a major offensive of its own without substantial increases in troop strength.[1]

Of even greater concern to many military experts than the ground buildup was the growth of enemy air power. By April 30 the Chinese had an estimated 1250 planes in Manchuria, of which about 800 were Soviet jets. Although the jets remained

in Manchuria for the most part and were too short-ranged to
strike at UN lines from behind the Yalu River, General Hoyt
Vandenberg, the Air Force chief of staff, believed that the UN
was losing its air supremacy in Korea. Others feared that if the
truce talks dragged on and the Communists were able to complete major bases under construction in North Korea, they
could strike in force at UN lines, inflicting heavy casualties.
Some Air Force officers even proposed bombing railroads,
ports, and marshaling yards throughout China in order to force
the Communists to disperse their concentration of air power in
Manchuria. But the very strength of the Chinese Air Force
made such recommendations seem dubious even for many of
those who had earlier advocated such attacks.[2]

Still another matter that a growing number of Americans
found disturbing was their perception that the West was losing
its struggle to contain the worldwide Communist threat. Of
course, many Americans had felt the same way just before war
had broken out in Korea in 1950, and again after the Chinese
had invaded Korea in November 1950. A significant number
had continued to share this view even in the eighteen months
that followed, particularly after the war had begun to stalemate,
after the negotiators at Panmunjom had failed to reach a quick
cease-fire, and after the conflict in Indochina had turned clearly
against the French, all of which had occurred by the end of
1951. But between that time and the spring of 1952 the world
situation appeared to deteriorate even more.

In Asia Communism seemed to pose a threat not only in
Korea and Indochina but throughout Southeast Asia. In some
respects this was odd, because the internal situation in several
of the countries that concerned Americans was actually better
than it had been at any time since World War II. For example,
Burma had been torn by a Communist-led insurgency and then
by a civil war for more than a year after gaining its independence from England in 1948. But in 1952 the government of U
Nu, which had supported the UN's action in Korea in 1950,
seemed firmly in charge of the country, and Nu's party, the
AFPL, controlled about 200 of the 239 seats in the national
legislature.[3] Similarly, in the Philippines, the government of
Elpidio Quirino—thanks in large part to his secretary of defense,
Ramon Magsaysay—had restored relative stability to the nation

after more than a year of economic, political, and military crisis. A demoralized and corrupt army had been infused with a new sense of purpose and esprit de corps, most of the leaders of the Communist Party Politburo had been captured or arrested, and a degree of confidence in the electoral process had been restored because of the honesty with which the 1951 congressional elections had been conducted.[4]

Despite this progress, many Americans still remained worried that Burma, the Philippines, and the rest of Southeast Asia might yet fall to the Communists. Part of the reason for this was an early version of what later became known as the "domino theory," the theory that if Indochina was forfeited by the French, there would be nothing to prevent Communism from spreading to neighboring states, reaching eventually into Burma. Also there was a concern that China might actually invade a border country like Burma. Then, too, in the Philippines the Hukbalahap uprising, thought by many to be linked to the Communists, had still not been entirely broken, while in Malaysia, the Malayan Race Liberation Army (MRLA), also believed to be linked to international communism, was engaged in a lengthy conflict against British rule. At the same time, in Indonesia, independent from the Dutch since 1949, there continued to be deep political, ethnic, and cultural divisions, which had already led to savage fighting during an unsuccessful Communist uprising in 1948 and which would lead to significantly increased strife and a remarkable recovery for the Communist Party within the year.[5]

In fairness to the Americans, they were not the only ones concerned about a Communist threat to all of Southeast Asia in early 1952. Indeed, several correspondents thought Churchill was referring to Burma and not Indochina in his speech to Congress in January when he cautioned China against further aggression, and at the Paris meeting of the United Nations in February, the British and French certainly had Burma in mind as they joined the Americans in warning that Communist aggression in Southeast Asia "would . . . require the most urgent and earnest consideration of the U. N."[6]

Nevertheless, the fear of a Communist victory throughout Southeast Asia was most evident in the United States and contributed to the general pessimism that seemed to grip the nation in the spring of 1952. *Time* even drew a map of Asia as seen from the Soviet city of Irkutsk and remarked, "On the southern border of Red China, Russia now stands on the threshold of one of the world's greatest prizes: the rich green valleys of Communist-infested Indo-China and Malaya, and the immense unexploited riches of the islands beyond." Similarly *Commonweal* observed that beyond Indochina lay "the tin, oil and rubber of Malaya," to the south was Indonesia with "its vast production of strategic raw materials and a new and shaky government," and next door was Burma, "another highly unstable political set-up, and beyond that the great subcontinent of India." "The stakes are immense," *Commonweal* stated. Finally, the *New Republic,* reporting on a State Department review of Southeast Asia, concluded, "something had to be done [about that region] soon. Whatever is done won't be pleasant."[7]

As many of these same Americans turned to the Middle East and North Africa, they found the situation there not much better. The two largely Arab and Moslem regions remained torn by political turmoil and rampaging nationalism that continued to be hostile to the West because of the West's colonial heritage. While the French were fighting in Indochina, the British were in similar trouble in Iran, where, to the anger of the Iranian people, they maintained a complete embargo of that country's oil because of Iran's nationalization of the British-owned Anglo-Iranian Oil Company. In Egypt rioting against the British had taken place in January because London refused to withdraw its garrison guarding the Suez Canal (at least until Egypt agreed to join a Middle East defense pact) or to turn over to the Egyptians the Sudan, which Egypt claimed as its own. Although the disturbances were quickly put down by British troops, and London made efforts to resolve its differences with Cairo, they were not very successful and resentment against the British remained strong. The same was even true in Iraq, despite the support of the British by Iraq's leader, Nuri as-Said. Growing in strength against the government was the opposition Istiqlal (Independence) Party, led by an eloquent and charismatic anglophobe, Sediq Shenshal.[8]

Meanwhile, in Tunisia, situated along North Africa's Mediterranean coast about 800 miles west of Egypt, militant nationalism, which had been smoldering for more than half a century against French sovereignty, burst into flames in February following the arrival of a new French resident-general. Demonstrations and riots resulted in eight Arabs dead and twenty wounded. Nationalist discontent continued to simmer during the next two months as a group of eleven countries from the Middle and Far East attempted unsuccessfully to have Tunisia's case placed before the United Nations.[9] Even in relatively prosperous and tranquil French Morocco, where the French had invested heavily in the construction of hydroelectric plants, irrigation projects, roads, and real estate and where the United States was spending millions of dollars building five huge air bases on the country's northwest corner, Moslem nationalism and the demand for greater autonomy were beginning to pose a threat to French rule. Indeed, the Sultan of Morocco, thought to be a safe man for France, dispatched a letter to Paris in March demanding more local autonomy.[10]

Reacting to the discontent evident throughout the Arab and Moslem world, some Americans saw the long arm of Moscow reaching out to threaten Western interests in the oil-rich Middle East, along the strategically vital Suez Canal, and throughout the long coast of North Africa that faced into the all-important Mediterranean. Even Secretary of State Acheson, who generally understood the causes of the disaffection and disorder taking place in the Middle East and North Africa and who urged England and France to rid themselves of their past colonial habits, commented to Anthony Eden in February on "the new xenophobic ferment, fanned from Moscow," that was growing daily in the Middle East. Similarly, a secret report prepared in February by the North Atlantic Treaty Council presented a picture of intensified Cold War activities by the Soviet Union ranging from efforts "to prevent harmony in ideas between Western Europe and the United States" to attempts at "foment[ing] tension in Southeast Asia," sapping Western influence in the Middle East, and "encourag[ing] anti-imperialist moves in such areas as Egypt and Morocco." But even for those who did not make such links, the situation looked ominous, particularly when joined with developments in Southeast Asia and elsewhere. "The whole Middle East has ceased to be governable by the old British and French arrangements," *Life* thus commented toward the end of March. "But the Arabs hate

America too—especially Truman—on account of Israel. . . . Everywhere our policy both puzzles and alarms allies and neutralists alike. It is neither a 'strong' policy nor one of appeasement. It brings us the advantages of neither—but the penalties of both."[11]

Another problem which contributed, in *Life*'s words, to the "black[ness of the] big picture" was the uninterrupted deterioration of the British economy. Faced with a worsening balance-of-payments problem and high defense costs, Prime Minister Churchill announced that he was cutting the country's rearmament program by a third. "[It] is much more likely to be carried out in four years than in three," the prime minister told the House of Commons in March.[12] But Churchill's problems were as much political as economic and involved the growing influence within the Labor Party of its more radical Bevanite wing. Although Churchill was able to defeat the Labor challenge to his government and, in the process, further the rift within its ranks, the cost was a virtual abandonment of the Anglo-American agreement on Far East policy that had been hammered out during the British prime minister's visit to Washington in January. The cost was also increased prestige and influence within the Labor Party for Nye Bevan and his anti-American followers.[13]

Despite the fact that Churchill had been able to quiet some of the misgivings that the British people had expressed about his Washington visit, Parliament had been engaged since February in what *Time* called "the most dramatic foreign-policy debate . . . since Neville Chamberlain's rough days after the fall of Norway in 1940." At issue were the commitments Churchill had made to the United States, particularly with respect to an all-out war against China in accordance with the "greater sanction" policy. Pressured from Bevan and seeking to unite all sections of their party, Labor leaders introduced a motion of censure against Churchill. In response, the British prime minister pointed out that the Labor government before him had covertly made the very foreign policy commitment to the United States—a possible extension of the Korean War—that Labor leaders now accused him of making. "Indeed," he stated, "the right honorable gentleman, the Leader of the Opposition

[Attlee], is in the position of one who 'did good by stealth and blushed to find it fame.' "[14]

Most observers agreed that Churchill's performance had been brilliant and even reminiscent of the flair he had shown as prime minister during World War II. But as they also pointed out, the effect of his victory was to strike at the very foundation of Anglo-American solidarity in the Far East, for by denying that he had gone beyond the commitments of his Labor predecessors, he also denied that he intended to be bolder in Asia or more in accord with Washington's policy toward Peking than those before him. "The fact is," Churchill said, "that there is no change in our policy. Nothing could be more foolish than for the armies of the U. S. or the U. N. to become engulfed in the vast areas of China."[15]

By revealing the secret agreements that the Labor Party had made with Washington, Churchill also strengthened the Bevanite faction within the party. Taking the floor of Parliament after Churchill had sat down, Bevan blasted Britain's rearmament program and its alliance with the United States. "Behind the guise and facade of the United Nations," he said, "the Americans are waging an ideological war with weapons against the Soviet Union." "We do not want any differences of opinion between us and the U. S. to encourage hopes of a [Communist] military adventure anywhere," he concluded, "but we do not want such subservience to American opinion . . . that there is no hope for them except through another blood bath." Sensing the vulnerability of Labor's leadership and emboldened by their own growing strength, Bevan and his followers defied party orders a few days later by refusing to support an official Labor amendment, which combined a censure of Churchill with approval of rearmament. They then voted against Churchill's scaled-down rearmament program, even though they had been ordered by the party leadership to abstain.[16]

The next day Attlee ordered an emergency meeting of all Labor members of Parliament to consider the defiance of his leadership. At the meeting, held in early April, the differences within the party were momentarily put aside as the Bevanites promised that henceforth they would observe party discipline.

But few could dispute the fact that Bevan had emerged from the events of the last few weeks stronger than ever, and that antiwar—if not anti-American—sentiment had become a major political force in England, threatening even to capture one of the two major political parties. That prospect was hardly comforting to many Americans already disturbed by Churchill's apparent bending to Britain's political winds.[17]

Much the same was true with respect to the slow progress that was being made in rearming Europe and developing Atlantic solidarity. To be sure, there was some headway on both these matters. In February a major breakthrough occurred when a NATO defense system was ratified by the North Atlantic Council meeting in Lisbon. Prior to Lisbon, Secretary of State Acheson had commented that "no progress [seemed to have been made) toward a defense of Europe or toward European unification." The Lisbon meeting, he further warned, might be "the last clear chance" to launch the EDC. But at Lisbon the NATO foreign ministers endorsed the EDC and established future military strength levels for NATO, which could not be reached without Germany furnishing a substantial number of troops. Progress was also made on a number of other issues—such as the relative size of the French and German troop levels in the EDC and the community's relation to NATO—which had plagued efforts at establishing a European army but which had to be settled before agreement could be reached on an EDC. Commenting on the achievements of the Lisbon meeting, Secretary Acheson remarked that a "new day" was dawning for the West, while Foreign Secretary Eden referred to the meeting as the "beginning of a new era."[18]

Yet as many observers pointed out, a number of these agreements had been reached only by ignoring or glossing over major differences that still separated the European powers. Also, many of the targets set at the meeting were simply unrealistic, so that the glitter of February became the gloom of March and April. For example, no mention was made in any of the Lisbon accords about what France had always considered a basic principle of a European army—political unification within which the German danger would dissolve. In addition, the understanding reached at Lisbon to spend $300 billion for mutual defense during the next three years ignored a number of eco-

nomic and political realities, including Europe's shaky economy, Congress's growing reluctance to foot much of the bill for
European rearmament, the party differences over rearmament
in England, and the movement for disarmament growing
throughout Europe.[19]

Within a week the transparency of many of the agreements
reached at Lisbon became apparent when the French government of Edgar Faure fell after losing on a tax bill designed to
finance France's $4 billion rearmament program. The French
people also began to react very quickly against the restoration
of German power, afraid that with much of their own military
strength tied up in Indochina, Germany would have a prepon-
derance in European economic and military matters. So great
was the French opposition to the Lisbon agreements that the
new government of Antoin Pinay was forced to delay their
ratification, fearing its own collapse if it tried to push the agreements through the National Assembly.[20] In Germany, the government of Konrad Adenauer had its own trouble gaining
support for the Lisbon accords. Opponents claimed that by
making concessions on such matters as military finances, security controls to be imposed on Germany, and limits to be placed
on the production of certain war materials, Adenauer had given
away too much. The leader of the Social Democratic opposition,
Kurt Schumacher, declared that anyone who would sign the
contractual arrangements agreed to at Lisbon was not a German. In England the London *Times* referred to the European
army created at Lisbon as the "Phantom Army" and deplored
what it called "a mistaken attempt to combine military security
with political propaganda." The London *Economist* lamented,
"The decision to make Germany a participant in Western defense has imposed on the still youthful movement for European
unity a problem heavier than anyone had the right to expect its
adolescent shoulders to bear." Similarly, the view continued to
grow throughout Europe that the United States was attempting
to subvert the truly internationalist and democratic goals of
European unity with a specifically military and predominantly
American pattern of Atlantic cohesion. Complicating matters
even more, the Soviet Union offered the West a new proposal
for a neutralized and unified Germany with its own national
army. Obviously intended to prevent Germany from aligning

militarily with the West and even becoming a member of NATO, the Soviet proposal, nevertheless, enjoyed considerable support throughout Europe.[21]

Together, these developments shattered much of the optimism about a united and militarily unified Europe, including Germany, which had been evident just after Lisbon. They also contributed to the atmosphere of despair and even crisis that existed in the United States in the spring of 1952. As one highly respected political commentator, J. Alvarez del Vayo, himself no friend of the rearmament effort, remarked toward the end of May, "Once again the West finds itself in a difficult period. International problems . . . have created a situation close to crisis. Some Western observers are asking themselves whether the entire strategy of the Atlantic coalition, in the main an American concept, does not need prompt and energetic revision." Even Secretary of State Acheson later acknowledged that the three months after the Lisbon meeting "were a time of growing weakness in the [Western] alliance."[22]

Republicans in a Presidential year sought to exploit this general malaise in America for partisan purposes. Seeking his party's nomination, Robert Taft made the White House's alleged mismanagement of the Korean conflict a campaign issue. Republicans in the House and Senate, many honestly convinced that the Communists were using the peace talks at Panmunjom to screen an ever-increasing escalation of the war, pressured the administration to terminate its limited war policy. Rejecting the limited war concept and a negotiated peace for Korea, they called for a decisive military victory and the development of a deterrent power, based on increased air and sea power, to prevent further Communist aggression of the kind that had taken place in Korea.

Almost invariably, attacks on the White House's handling of the Korean War turned into renewed charges against the Democrats' entire conduct of foreign policy since the end of 1951, and this in turn rekindled old accusations of "Communists in government" and internal subversion. McCarthyism became a potent political force once more as Republicans flayed away at the administration, firing the political caldron, raising the temper of political discourse, and exacerbating the doubts and fears of many Americans.

Republicans in Congress, of course, had never stopped attacking the White House for its policies toward the war, particularly after the conflict stalemated in the late spring of 1951. In August Harry P. Cain of Washington, a Senate reactionary and a member of the infamous "class of '46," which also included McCarthy and several other of his closest allies, accused the administration of sacrificing American boys on "the altar of futility . . . in a vicious war in which American forces are prevented from utilizing their maximum strength and are required to fight with inadequate numbers." But these and similar charges were not limited to the party's right wing. Henry Cabot Lodge of Massachusetts, a party moderate, also attacked the administration's policy of limited war. "Failure to do all in our power to support our troops is a new development," he said. "It shocks our national sense of decency."[23]

Republican oratory against the administration intensified considerably, however, after Senator Taft announced in September 1951 that he would once more seek his party's nomination for President, having lost the nomination in 1948. Although Taft had been publicly attacking the administration's handling of the Korean War since the beginning of the year, at one time he had appeared to moderate his position, even telling a group of Republicans in July that a "stalemate peace at the thirty-eighth parallel [was] better than a stalemate war at the thirty-eighth parallel." But that changed once the Ohio senator began to campaign in earnest for the nomination. Now Taft denounced the administration for not following the recommendations of General MacArthur, "especially the bombing of Communist air fields and the use of Chinese Nationalist Government troops for diversionary raids on South China." Much to the annoyance of his critics, he also began referring to the UN intervention in Korea as a "useless war" and as "Truman's war." In November he published a slim volume, *A Foreign Policy for Americans,* in which he again raised questions about the constitutionality of America's police action, reminding his readers that Truman had intervened in Korea "without even telling Congress what he was doing for several weeks."[24]

Significantly, Taft also repeated familiar charges about America's failed policy in the Far East, which he linked to an internal Communist conspiracy. Communists in government, the labor unions, and "the writing fraternity in Hollywood and New York," he said, "were in a position to affect public opinion or public policy." By December, in fact, Taft was once more embracing McCarthy and seeking his support, despite the fact that he had been moving away from the Wisconsin senator since McCarthy's insinuation the previous June that former Defense Secretary George Marshall had been guilty of conspiracy or treason. To an influential Wisconsin leader, he thus wrote at the end of December that he approved McCarthy's "campaign to eliminate Communists from the government." Speaking in Beloit a few weeks later, he added that McCarthy's investigation of subversives had "been fully justified" and that the administration was "dominated by a strange Communist sympathy."[25]

Taft's new endorsement of McCarthy reflected the political importance he attached to having the Wisconsin senator on his side in the forthcoming primary in McCarthy's home state. But it also reflected the continued potency of McCarthyism in American politics. Simply stated, the Red Scare and fear of internal subversion remained very much alive in the United States and may even have influenced the outcome in 1951 of municipal elections in states like Indiana, where Republicans made "Trumanism" an issue in the local elections. Although "Trumanism" involved considerably more than accusations of Communist conspiracy, internal subversion was, nevertheless, one of the charges Republicans made against the administration. Speaking in his home state, Senator William Jenner, another member of the class of '46, thus told his constituents that a vote for a Democratic mayor was a vote for the Truman administration, for "Communists high in the State Department . . . crime and corruption in the Internal Revenue Bureau [and] creeping decay in every department of our national life." In the election Republicans won 73 of 103 Indiana cities, a gain of 25.[26]

Korea never figured prominently among the charges of internal subversion made against the administration during the 1952 campaign. Efforts to link the outbreak of the war and Communist infiltration of government had generally been dropped during the last half of 1951 because of the White House's conduct of the war, and they were never renewed. But even McCarthy himself began to attack the administration's

Korean policy. Although the Wisconsin senator much preferred to speak out on domestic rather than on foreign affairs, in February he denounced the State and Defense departments for their fear that if the United States adopted a policy of victory, it would become involved in a war with the Soviet Union. Other of his allies labeled the conflict in Korea a "treadmill war" and repeated charges that the White House was following a "nowin" policy. The attacks by the Republican right wing against the administration and their demands for victory in Asia— which clearly meant an invasion of China either by American or Chinese Nationalist forces—became so intense and shrill that Republican renegade Wayne Morse of Oregon took the Senate floor to speak out against what he referred to as a "growing war clique [who proposed] that we commit an act which constitutes for the first time in American history an aggressive act of war against a foreign power."[27]

The important point remains, however, not so much the opposition of the Republican right wing to the administration's conduct of the war or their demand for victory, neither of which was particularly new, but the fact that McCarthy and his allies promised to play a major role in the forthcoming election, particularly if Taft received the Republican nomination. In the spring of 1952 this seemed highly likely, notwithstanding a growing movement by moderate Republicans to draft General Dwight Eisenhower for President and Eisenhower's surprising victory over Taft in the March primary in New Hampshire. Furthermore, there was every reason to believe that Korea would be just one issue of a larger assault on President Truman's entire foreign policy since the end of World War II and that while the war itself might not be linked to charges of internal subversion, the administration's general conduct of foreign policy, especially in Asia, would be. For those who abhorred McCarthy as an unprincipled demagogue and saw in the Red Scare a challenge to basic American freedoms, or who were convinced an escalation of the Korean conflict might lead to World War III, the American political scene in the spring of 1952 held out the most frightening prospects of all.

Oddly enough, most Americans still did not pay the same attention to the Korean War as they had six or eight months earlier, when there still appeared a chance that a quick end to the conflict could be reached at Panmunjom. Although the war had already become an important issue in the Presidential campaign, the press did not give it that much more coverage than it did other issues, such as the war in Indochina or the nationalist uprisings in the Middle East and North Africa. Domestic matters, such as further reports of corruption within the Truman administration and growing speculation over whether Eisenhower would resign his NATO command and return to the United States in order to campaign against Taft captured far more headlines than Korea. A Roper poll conducted in May concluded that although the Korean War still topped the list of concerns expressed by the American people, there was an increasing interest in domestic events. Six months earlier the people polled mentioned international problems over domestic ones by a five-to-four margin; now the ratios were exactly reversed.[28]

Toward the end of December 1951, *Commonweal* tried to explain the disinterest in the Korean War relative to World War II that it perceived growing even then among the American people, and its remarks were almost certainly as valid in April or May as they had been in December. "[The war's] *presence,*" it noted, "has not been immediate. To the average newspaper reader, the issues are still very obscure; the meaning of this first international attempt to stand up to aggression has been somewhat hazy. . . . Somehow the idea was gathered that a 'police action' would entail only a small-scale military action," which proved not to be the case. Former Interior Secretary Harold Ickes, frequently referred to as a "curmudgeon" and very much an acerbic political commentator, seemed to be saying much the same thing when he took the administration to task for its indecisiveness in foreign policy. "As to our own State Department," he said, "one could not be sure of its announced position, since probably it would reverse its position the next day. . . . It has not taken the people into its confidence when popular support was a sine qua non to the carrying out of a policy." A New Deal Democrat, Ickes would have encountered little disagreement from Republican opponents of the administration.[29]

Still, major news stories from Korea did attract considerable public interest, and in the late winter and spring of 1952 no

news stories received more attention than Communist allega-
tions of bacteriological warfare in Korea by UN forces and a
major prison riot by Chinese and North Korean POWs on the
island of Koje-do. Although the Communists had been claiming
for months that Americans were spreading smallpox germs in
North Korea, the campaign against alleged bacteriological warfare began in earnest on February 18 when Moscow radio accused the United States of spreading smallpox and typhus
bacteria and of secretly sending lepers into North Korea. By
March 8 the Chinese Communists were charging that the
United States had dropped insects, rats, shellfish, and chicken
feathers containing disease germs on Chinese as well as North
Korean territory.[30]

On March 11 Secretary of State Acheson asked the International Red Cross to investigate the Communist accusations, but
the North Koreans and Chinese rejected such an investigation,
insisting that the Red Cross was dominated by Americans. Instead, they joined with Moscow in a stepped-up propaganda
campaign against the United States. In Moscow, Leningrad,
Kiev, and Minsk, and in other cities and villages throughout the
Soviet Union, workers were pulled from their jobs to be inocu-
lated against American bacteriological weapons. In Peking
newspapers printed photographic "proof" of weird insects and
rotting food, while Chinese radio carried its own reports of
germ warfare. According to a State Department intelligence
report, the bacteriological warfare campaign represented the
single greatest effort ever undertaken by the Communists to
discredit the United States.[31]

Speculation in the United States and in Europe as to why
the Communists decided to launch such a propaganda barrage
varied considerably. Some officials theorized that springtime
was a period of epidemic in North Korea and China, and that
the Communist leaders were merely preparing their people
for plagues, which they were unable to handle because of having to divert doctors, nurses, and medicine to the war in
Korea. Along the same lines, others speculated that China was
in very bad shape because the Korean War had drained the
country economically and an "anticorruption" campaign had
terrorized much of the country. According to this view, the
propaganda against the United States was intended to distract

the Chinese people from these internal problems. Some British diplomats even thought that since the Soviet Union was now making atomic bombs, they had to create some other dastardly form of warfare which they could claim was a Western monopoly.[32]

Whatever their purpose, the charges of bacteriological warfare were quite effective in weakening America's moral weight in Europe, particularly among neutralists, and in stirring worldwide reaction against the United States. Communist newspapers in France whipped up a demonstration against the new NATO commander, Matthew Ridgway, who was denounced as a "microbe killer." Also in France, as well as in Italy, Belgium, Holland, and West Germany, there were large Communist-led protest parades against the United States. And in Teheran Communist youths, shouting "germ warfare," touched off a large riot that left 12 dead and 250 wounded.[33]

Even more harmful to the image of the UN command than accusations about germ warfare, however, was a riot by Chinese and North Korean POWs on Koje-do island, about twenty miles southwest of Pusan. This barren and rocky piece of land, which the American guards called Beggar's Island, housed the vast majority of enemy prisoners, or about 130,000 Koreans and 20,000 Chinese troops crowded together into compounds intended to hold between 700 and 1200 prisoners but actually holding about five times that number. Conditions in the compounds made them virtually impossible to control, and by the beginning of 1952 the prisoners had organized their own government and were enforcing their own discipline in the camps.[34]

Clashes between guards and prisoners were probably inevitable, and as early as August 1951 three inmates were killed after a clash with their captors. But far more serious was the incident on February 18, 1952, when guards entering a prisoner compound were attacked by 1500 prisoners brandishing homemade weapons, including iron bars, clubs, and barbed wire. In the melee that followed, 77 POWs were killed and another 140 wounded. Similar prisoner riots took place in the weeks that followed, albeit none as serious as that of February 18, and the Communist negotiators at Panmunjom used them to accuse the UN command of barbarous treatment of POWs.

They also charged that the UN was resorting to force to prevent the POWs from choosing early repatriation.[35]

Insofar as they concerned mistreatment of POWs, these accusations contained considerable substance. Chinese Nationalist troops were sometimes used as guards in the Chinese camps, and they frequently brutalized the prisoners to "encourage" them to renounce Communist China. The UN's chief negotiator at Panmunjom, Admiral Joy, recorded in his diary that on one occasion, when prisoners were asked to decide whether they wished to be repatriated to the People's Republic (PRC), "those doing so were either beaten black and blue or killed." "[T]he majority of the POWs were too terrified to frankly express their choice," Joy said. General Ridgway, who would shortly be named to replace Eisenhower as commander of NATO, even warned the Joint Chiefs that a "potentially explosive atmosphere" existed at Koje-do, which, he said, was "capable of developing to such a point [that] it might result in heavy loss of life and great discredit to the US and the UNC."[36]

That potential turned into frightening reality when on May 7 prisoners in Compound 76 seized the commander of the island, Brigadier General Francis T. Dodd, while he was talking to them through the compound's gate, and demanded, as a condition of his release, that the UNC admit it had practiced inhumane treatment of POWs. A former deputy chief of staff in Van Fleet's Eighth Army, Dodd had been sent to Koje-do in February to prevent a reoccurrence of the bloodshed that had just taken place on the island. But conditions in the camps had gotten worse, not better. The prisoners elected their own leaders, held their own drills and classes, flew illegal Communist flags, established liaison with other compounds, and even engaged in forbidden trade with Koje natives. Prison leaders in Compound 76 and in several other compounds where the most fanatical POWs were held also refused to allow the screening of prisoners under their control. Indeed, it was to talk about the screening of prisoners in order to see which ones wanted to be repatriated that had brought Dodd to the gate of Compound 76 in the first place.[37]

Acting on his own authority, Brigadier General Charles F. Colson, who had assumed command of Koje-do following Dodd's capture, made a statement meeting most of the prisoners' demands. "I do admit," he said, "that there have been instances of bloodshed where many PW [prisoners of war] have been killed or wounded by UN Forces. I can assure in the future that PW can expect humane treatment in this camp according to the principles of International Law." Following Colson's statement, the prisoners released Dodd as they had promised. Later both he and Colson were demoted to the rank of colonel, Dodd because he had allowed himself to be seized and Colson for the unauthorized statement that he made.[38]

The whole affair, however, was a major embarrassment to the UNC, and Colson's statement affirming Communist charges of barbarous treatment of POWs on Koje-do was so much grist for the enemy's mill. Furthermore, incidents continued to take place on Koje-do as the new commander on the island, General Haydon L. Boatner, sought to reestablish his control over all the prison compounds on the island. Not until the middle of June, when UN troops, attacking behind flamethrowers and tear gas, moved against the "iron triangle" of prisoner resistance in Compounds 76, 77, and 78, was control finally reestablished. But the cost of that assault was 41 POWs killed and 274 wounded, as well as one American dead. Also, the Communists used the incidents at Koje-do to launch a second propaganda barrage against the United States, which the JCS described as equal in intensity, ferocity, and vulgarity to that directed against Germany during World War II.[39]

Together, the charges of barbarous treatment of Communist POWs and the bacteriological warfare compaign put the UNC on the defensive in its negotiations with the Communists. As a State Department intelligence report commented with respect to the bacteriological warfare charges, "[f]rom the Communist point of view, even if the BW campaign is limited to propaganda purposes, it still serves a highly useful role. In all Communist countries it provides a new approach in the constant effort to stimulate hatred of the UN."[40] In an effort to regain the diplomatic initiative and to break new ground in the negotiations at Panmunjom, the UN went ahead with the package proposal to the Chinese and North Koreans that had been in the works since the middle of March. As General Ridgway had outlined the package earlier, it represented an effort to reach an agreement on the three unresolved issues separating the UN and Communist negotiators—airfield reconstruction, the composition of a neutral armistice commission, and the repatriation of prisoners of war. By its provisions the restrictions on airfield construction and rehabilitation would be deleted; the proposed composition of the neutral nations commission would be four mutually acceptable nations, excluding the Soviet Union; and the exchange of POWs would reflect the principle of "no forced repatriation."[41]

The package was presented to the Communist negotiators on April 28 in an atmosphere of mutual distrust compounded not only by the question of UN treatment of Communist POWs and the bacteriological warfare charges, but by the Communist shock at the small number of POWs the UNC offered for repatriation. Although the UN negotiators had informed the Chinese and North Koreans before the screening of POWs had begun in April that as many as 116,000 POWs might be repatriated, after the screening was complete, it was determined that only about 70,000 prisoners wished to return home. The Communists termed this figure totally unacceptable and, for a time, even suspended talks.[42]

On May 2, however, the enemy negotiators returned to Panmunjom, where they finally responded to the UN's package proposal. They told the UN truce team that they were willing to forgo their demand that the Soviet Union be a member of the neutral nations commission, but they insisted that all Communist POWs must be repatriated. The construction and rehabilitation of airfields they took as a *fait accompli.* So now the differences between the two sides in the negotiations had been reduced to one issue: prisoner repatriation. But on this issue little progress had been made. Worse, the United States had taken a final and irrevocable position, and so, apparently, had the Chinese and North Koreans.[43]

News of the failure to break the deadlock in the talks at Panmunjom was made public on May 7. It coincided with the arrival in Tokyo of General Mark Clark, whom President Truman had named to succeed General Ridgway following the President's appointment of Ridgway as the new NATO commander. A tough field commander like Ridgway, Clark had helped plan the North African campaign in 1942, and at age forty-six had been appointed the youngest three-star general up to that time. A hero of the Italian campaign, he had fought at Anzio, Rapido River, and Cassino. Described as "straight-backed and broad-shouldered" and believing in what he referred to as the "calculated risk," he had been much criticized by his men because of the heavy casualties they had taken in Italy.[44]

Scarcely had Clark taken command when he was confronted with a major political crisis inside South Korea. Internally, that country remained in a state of economic, social, and political chaos. It is true that there were already signs of an economic turnaround and that the South Koreans had by this time taken the first steps toward reconstructing their lives and their country now that most of the war was being fought north of the 38th parallel. Although in most cities and towns food was still hard to come by because of hoarding, inflation, and the previous year's drought, the country had come through the winter (the mildest in a quarter-century) fairly well. The ROK army's winter operations had all but eliminated guerrilla activity in the countryside, and plowing and planting were well along. The UN had purchased 171,000 tons of fertilizer on world markets and had already unloaded 50,000 tons at Pusan and Inchon. Except in a few drought-stricken areas, there was enough rice seed for the current crop, and for those who could not pay or get credit, seed and fertilizer were doled out free.[45]

In Seoul U. S. Army authorities, fearful of dangerous overcrowding, had even tried unsuccessfully to keep former residents from returning to the city. By May, Seoul's population, once 1.5 million but recently as low as 150,000, was back around 800,000. Men, women, and children were busy hauling rubble away; streetcars, which had been badly damaged in the several battles for the city, were nevertheless running again—as were some of Seoul's prewar fleet of 150 buses, and a few new fire engines had even been delivered from Japan. Restaurants, pastry shops, and a few nightclubs were back in business, and vendors were everywhere selling cheap souvenirs to American GIs. Even the city's municipal politics seemed to be returning to normal. The city's mayor, under investigation for fraud by a government committee, was conducting his own investigation of the investigating committee.[46]

Despite these obvious first steps toward reconstructing a

war-shattered nation, however, the fact remained that by the spring of 1952 one out of every nine South Korean men, women, and children had been killed as a result of the war. Out of a population of 30 million before the war, at least 5 million had suffered casualties, and an equal number had been displaced. Millions of people were homeless, most of the country's factories had been leveled, its schools had been either wrecked or requisitioned by the military, inflation was spiraling, and agricultural production had fallen by a third. Seoul remained the most battle-scarred city in the world.[47]

Also South Korea was faced with its most serious political crisis since the war began in 1950 as a result of President Syngman Rhee's determination to remain in power despite widespread disaffection with his regime. Ever since the opening of peace negotiations in June 1951, the South Korean leader had remained a thorn in the side of the UNC. In simplest terms, Rhee demanded the unification of Korea by military means if necessary, even though the UNC had many months before abandoned unification as military objective of the war. By the end of February 1952 the obstreperousness of the Korean president had become such that President Truman warned him that unless he moderated his public statements in opposition to the peace negotiations at Panmunjom, South Korea would lose American support. The degree of military and economic assistance that his government could expect to receive from the United States, Truman told Rhee, would be influenced "by the sense of responsibility demonstrated by your government, its ability to maintain the unity of the Korean people, and its devotion to democratic ideals."[48]

It was precisely the devotion of the Rhee regime to democratic ideals that was in question during the spring and early summer of 1952. Political opposition to Rhee had been mounting steadily in South Korea throughout 1952, spurred on by inflation, resentment at Rhee's autocratic methods, and internal dissension within his own cabinet over various domestic issues. In March Ridgway had informed the Pentagon that the political situation in Korea was "deteriorating rapidly." The next month a special Presidential mission was appointed to work out an economic aid package with the beleaguered government. But the Rhee administration remained harassed, and when in May it appeared that the National Assembly, which elected the president, would not return Rhee to office, he declared martial law in the area around Pusan and arrested a number of his opponents in the Assembly, accusing them of treason and complicity in a Communist conspiracy.[49]

Rhee's purpose was to have a new Assembly elected, which would then change the Korean constitution so that there would be a popular election of presidents. Rhee would then have an excellent chance in a "popular vote" watched over by the police, the armed forces, and the terroristic Tae Han Youth Corps. Potential legislative opposition could be blocked by a division of the Assembly into two chambers. Rhee may even have reasoned that his proposal for the popular election of the president would have considerable appeal to the Americans, since they elected their Presidents the same way.[50]

If the South Korean president thought this, however, he was badly mistaken, for his declaration of martial law evoked widespread disapproval in Washington. Both the State and Defense departments warned of the danger of increasing political instability in Korea as a result of imposing martial law. The Joint Chiefs instructed General Clark, now settled in Tokyo, to make clear to Rhee the sharp reaction worldwide against what he had done and to point out "that those nations presently participating in [the] UN action [in Korea] may withdraw [their] support."[51]

The next day the new UN commander even raised the possibility of a military coup against Rhee. Although he hoped that Rhee would be persuaded "to listen to reason," Clark pointed out to the JCS that the "[o]nly other alternative would be to take over and establish some form of interim gov[ernmen]t." And he listed several possible developments that might necessitate a takeover—if, for example, Rhee successfully ordered the dissolution of the National Assembly and declared himself head of state; or if he accepted defeat, but organized strong opposition and resorted to strong-arm methods. "Such action on the part of President Rhee," Clark stated, "would undoubtedly cause serious internal disturbances and as a consequence might endanger the supply lines of the 8th Army and the mil[itary] situation in general. In the event that such disturbances seriously interfere with mil[itary] operations, it will be necessary for me to assume control."[52]

On June 2 Washington learned that Rhee was preparing to present the Assembly with an ultimatum—either to agree to his constitutional amendment or be dissolved—even though he lacked the constitutional authority to do that. Truman warned the South Korean president against taking such "irrevocable" action, and Rhee backed down. But the crisis remained far from over, for Rhee then organized mass demonstrations, which became increasingly vituperative and anti-American in character. In response, the Joint Chiefs issued a directive—prepared by the State Department and approved by President Truman—instructing Clark and American Ambassador John Muccio to prepare a contingency plan for military intervention against the South Korean president. "It is hoped the necessity for implementation of [the] plan can be foreseen sufficiently in advance to permit implementation [by the] highest gov[ernmen]tal auth[orit]y," the JCS told Clark. "However, in [the] event [of a] sudden outbreak of violence, civil disorder or an emer[gency] necessitating immed[iate] action, [you] will be authorized to implement the plan without further auth[orit]y."[53]

Carrying out his instructions, Clark prepared a plan by which President Rhee would be invited out of Pusan on some pretext, the UN commander would go into the Pusan area, seize ROK officials who had been leaders in Rhee's "dictatorial actions," protect the region's major installations, and take control of the martial law government, acting through the chief of staff of the ROK army. Rhee would then be informed of the *fait accompli* and be urged to sign a decree lifting martial law, restoring the National Assembly, and establishing freedom of the press and radio. If Rhee refused to sign such a proclamation, he would "be held in protective custody incommunicado and a similar proclamation w[oul]d be presented to the Prime Min[ister] Chang Taek-Saeng."[54]

The coup was never executed. Instead, Rhee cowered the National Assembly into approving a constitutional amendment on July 3 that provided for the popular election of a president and vice-president and established a second legislative chamber. First, the South Korean president broke up a meeting of fifty prominent South Korean businessmen, labor leaders, scholars, and politicians who had met to discuss ways of getting rid of him. Goon squads entered the restaurant where the meeting was taking place, upsetting tables, heaving chairs, and beating up several of those present before the police came and had the intruders arrested. Although Rhee denied knowledge of the incident, an American who was at the restaurant recognized one of the gang's leaders as a member of the feared police force of Rhee's Home Minister, Lee Bum Suk. Then, after holding martial law over the heads of the National Assembly for five weeks and having at least eleven assemblymen put in jail and others threatened by the police, he had the Assembly renew his presidency for an indefinite term. Finally, he had 600 of his supporters besiege the Assembly, catching eighty anti-Rhee members inside and demanding that they resign. For more than five hours the legislators huddled in fear until Home Minister Suk showed up and ordered his men to shove back the demonstrators. Thoroughly intimidated, the Assembly caved in the next day and gave Rhee the constitutional amendment he had wanted. In return, imprisoned legislators were released from custody. Rhee even agreed to let the Voice of America resume broadcasting, and he denounced the press censorship that had been operating for three weeks.[55]

Not until July 28 did Rhee lift martial law, but now firmly in control of the government, the South Korean leader was overwhelmingly retained in office on August 5 as the first popularly elected president of Korea, receiving more than 5.2 million of the 7 million votes cast without making a single speech. Although the UNC had not been happy at how Rhee had intimidated the National Assembly, it was pleased by the relative honesty of the election and by the fact that the immediate political crisis seemed resolved. However, its fundamental difference with the South Korean president over the military unification of Korea remained, and General Clark completed his contingency plans for a coup, which he filed "for future use if neces[sary]."[56]

While this political drama in Korea was unfolding, the war remained stalemated. Fighting a war of position, each side continued to strengthen its bunkers and interior lines. Conditions on the front came to resemble those of World War I, with deep-dug emplacements, trenches, barbed-wire defenses, and an extensive outpost line where most of the combat took place. Throughout the summer and into the fall, there were occasional bursts of activity as the enemy made fierce efforts to capture UN outposts, particularly near Chorwon and Kumhwa, two legs of the Iron Triangle. Communist artillery activity also increased markedly as Air Force and Navy planes were unable to prevent an enemy artillery buildup. On one day in September alone, more than 45,000 rounds fell on the Eighth Army's front. But heavy rains prevented any significant fighting for most of July and August, and whatever action took place hardly altered the battle line at all.[57]

In the United States there were increasing demands from Republican members of Congress and other opponents of the administration to increase the military pressure on the ground against the Communists, and the argument, frequently made during the summer, that the failure to do this removed the only Communist incentive for settling the war was by no means an unreasonable one. But as General Ridgway told the Joint Chiefs before leaving for his new command at NATO, there was little justification for launching a major military offensive when UN forces lacked the capacity to inflict a decisive military defeat.[58]

Although General Clark would soon make clear just how much he wanted the resources to launch a full-scale offensive toward the Yalu River, he shared Ridgway's general assessment that without these resources and without a major escalation of the war, a military offensive would serve little purpose. "To have pushed [the conflict] to a successful conclusion," Clark later wrote, "would have required more trained divisions and more supporting air and naval forces [and] would have necessitated lifting our self-imposed ban on attacks on the enemy sanctuary north of the Yalu."[59] But Republican calls for a decisive military victory notwithstanding, it is highly unlikely that either the American people or Congress would have gone along with such a beefing up of America's military effort in Korea even if the White House had been willing. The war had become too unpopular for that, and President Truman's effectiveness and credibility with Congress had diminished to the point, where, after his attempt in April to seize the steel industry because, he claimed, a threatened steel strike endangered the war effort, no less than fourteen separate resolutions were introduced calling for his impeachment. Reporters were even writing about the "final agony" of bipartisanship following drastic cuts in the administration's foreign aid bill.[60]

Most certainly, America's allies would never have accepted an expansion of the war involving attacks on Manchuria, which Clark stated would have been necessary to achieve a military victory in Korea. Proof of that fact was their reaction when the UNC did, in fact, expand the air war by attacking hydroelectric facilities in North Korea. Striking between June 23 and 25, American Air Force and Navy planes did serious damage to the largest of these power plants, Suiho, on the Korean side of the Yalu River and caused a blackout in North Korea that lasted for two weeks.[61] By reducing casualties American planners had hoped the air war would make the Korean conflict more palatable at home while punishing the enemy and forcing him to agree to peace. President Truman may have agreed to the attacks because of his own continued frustration with the deadlocked negotiations at Panmunjom. Once more conjuring up a situation in which he served the Communists with an ultimatum threatening them with nuclear holocaust, he ruminated privately in his diary, "[y]ou either accept our fair and just proposal or you will be completely destroyed."[62]

Whatever the reasons for the attacks or their military effect, however, the bombings infuriated opinion in England, France, and throughout Europe. For the millions of Europeans still anxious for a four-power conference with the Soviet Union to resolve the German question and to settle other world problems, including ending the Korean War, the raids along the Yalu River represented a dangerous escalation of the war that imperiled the already slim chances for world peace. The French government in particular felt that another effort should be made to bring about a Big Four Conference, and French Foreign Minister Robert Schuman expressed concern that the Korean conflict might be extended as a result of the Yalu raids. In Paris French Marshal Juin, commander of NATO's ground forces, was even quoted (although he later claimed he had been misquoted) as saying that America's Korea's policy had "often succeeded in placing the U.N. in a ridiculous posture."[63]

In no country, however, was the reaction against the bombings any stronger than in England. As *Time* reported, the British had been nursing grievances about America's conduct of the war for months (certainly since Churchill's visit to Washington in January), and their complaints and concerns had been piling up "like loose gun powder on the floor of a fireworks factory." News of the air raids was the spark that set the powder off, and the explosion which followed "belched smoke and flames through Britain's House of Commons." Particularly annoying to many prominent British officials was Washington's insistence on voluntary repatriation, which, they thought, both violated the Geneva Convention on prisoners of war and unnecessarily delayed a cease-fire. Even the London *Times* raised questions about the screening process that had determined how many POWs refused to be repatriated. "It is difficult to believe," the *Times* remarked in June, "that all of the 60,000 odd prisoners who refused repatriation are really in danger of persecution if they go back. . . . It does suggest that the screening should be done again more carefully by an impartial commission."[64]

Now the British learned that the United States had apparently expanded the war in Korea by attacking power plants on the Manchurian frontier without first consulting London, as Washington had always indicated it would do. That was too much even for the Churchill government, which had to admit to the opposition Labor Party that it had not been told of the bombings in advance. Although Churchill and Foreign Secretary Eden reluctantly supported the action, privately Eden rebuked Secretary Acheson, who happened to be in London, for his discourtesy and more or less obliged him to apologize to a group of British leaders of both parties at a private meeting at Westminister.[65]

The most far-reaching damage of the bombings, however, was not the strained relations it caused between Washington and Churchill's conservative government, as much as it was the powerful ammunition it gave to the Bevanites within the Labor opposition. By making Churchill and Eden appear as unprincipled stooges of the United States, Bevan and his followers were able to argue that this kind of undisciplined action by the United States amounted to as great a threat to world peace as Soviet aggression.[66]

Precisely because of the support it gave to the Bevanites, the pro-American *Economist* described Washington's failure to consult with London as a "capital blunder," and despite Acheson's effort at apology, his refusal to concede London's automatic right to be consulted and his suggestion that former Foreign Secretary Herbert Morrison had agreed "in principle" to such bombardments, provoked even Labor moderates. But when they then turned around and introduced a motion of censure in the House of Commons, which a correspondent for *The New Yorker* described as sounding "something like an address of appreciation to the United States for its great efforts in Korea," the Bevan group abandoned all pretense of subordination to the party leadership. Although the Bevanites still did not have the numbers to alter Labor's continued commitment to strong Anglo-American ties, their future prospects appeared more promising than ever, for as the same *New Yorker* correspondent also noted, even those violently opposed to Bevan and his views were "nevertheless genuinely alarmed by the idea that a decision could be taken somewhere, maybe without their knowledge, that would drag them willy-nilly into a third world war."[67]

Despite the enormous reaction against the United States, particularly in England, that America's bombing of the Yalu power plants had caused, the UNC continued its escalation of the air war. General Clark claimed that the Yalu raids had been a necessary military measure, and in the next few months American planes stepped up their attacks on North Korean targets, even hitting an oil refinery only eight miles from the Soviet border, as a primary means of bringing military pressure on the enemy. In July the Joint Chiefs also approved a request from Clark for a squadron of F-84s with an atomic delivery capability, which he had asked for in response to a buildup in the Far East of Soviet and Chinese air power. According to Clark, there were now approximately 1100 Communist bombers in the areas adjacent to Japan and Korea, with an additional 590 bombers in striking range of these two countries. At least some of these bombers were believed capable of delivering atomic weapons, and they were protected by an effective radar network and a fighter force now estimated to include 1500 jet and more than 2000 conventional-type fighters. The JCS doubted that the threat of an air strike against the Far East Command was any greater than against other commands. But they promised Clark a fighter squadron by August, and in the meanwhile they made available to him planes from the Strategic Air Command (SAC) in case an emergency developed requiring the use of atomic weapons.[68]

By now the UNC in Tokyo and military planners at the Pentagon were totally frustrated. The war remained stalemated not only militarily, but also diplomatically. At Panmunjom no progress was made concerning the issue of prisoner repatriation, still the only issue preventing an end to the war. At the UN, American diplomats tried to break the impasse, but without success. Occasionally there were glimmers of hope—of apparent movement by the enemy toward the UN position on repatriation of POWs—such as when China, acting through India, appeared willing to accept a version of voluntary repatriation so long as it could save face,[69] or when Constantin E. Zichenko, a high-ranking Soviet official of the UN, indicated to Ernest Gross of the American delegation that Moscow was agreeable to a scheme involving *de facto* voluntary repatriation just so long as the UN consented to the principle of general repatriation. But always promise outran reality.[70]

Discouraged by the persistent failure at the United Nations, the State Department even considered dealing directly with the Soviet Union in Moscow, but it was discouraged from doing so by George Kennan, now America's ambassador to the Soviet Union, and by General Clark, and Clark's adviser in Tokyo, Ambassador Robert Murphy. Instead, all three officials favored intensifying the bombing of North Korea, which, they believed, was undercutting North Korean and Chinese morale, even though it seemed to have no discernible effect on the negotiations at Panmunjom. The State Department then went so far as to recommend a Presidential statement offering an armistice based on the points already agreed to at Panmunjom as well as an exchange of those POWs willing to be repatriated, leaving the dispositions of the others to be resolved later. But the Pentagon argued that the issue of prisoner repatriation was too important to be left unresolved, and toward the end of September President Truman personally decided against any new approaches to the Communists.[71] Meeting with Pentagon and

State Department officials, the President stated that he was not willing to get an armistice "just to get an armistice," particularly if it would leave Communist China in a position to renew fighting. He did not want to place the United States in the same position, he said, as it had been after World War II when, "we tore up a great fighting machine."[72]

Rather, Truman directed that General William K. Harrison, Jr., who had replaced Admiral Joy as the UN's chief negotiator at Panmunjom at the end of May, offer the UN's package proposal once more to the enemy, allowing ten days for a reply. If the Chinese and North Koreans rejected the proposal, the UNC would then recess the talks indefinitely and "be prepared to do such things as may be necessary." On October 8 the Communist negotiators formally rejected the UN's package proposal, whereupon General Harrison declared the talks indefinitely recessed.[73]

Frustrated at this total lack of progress at ending the war, the Pentagon reviewed its military options. In fact, since February the Joint Strategic Plans Committee, an advisory group to the Joint Chiefs of Staff, had taken up the very question of what options to adopt in Korea in case of an indefinite prolongation or breakdown in the talks at Panmunjom. Later, in response to a new assignment to consider possible military alternatives against North Korea and Communist China, the committee had concluded that it would be necessary to authorize the use of atomic weapons in the Far East. The JCS decided that the committee placed too much emphasis on atomic weapons and asked that the question be studied more carefully.[74]

Meanwhile, the Joint Chiefs asked General Clark for his advice on military options. On September 29 Clark responded by making clear just how much of a mistake he thought it had been not to advance to the Yalu River when UN forces had had the Communists on the run in the late winter and early spring of 1951, more than a year earlier. At the same time, he conceded the futility of a military offensive without a major escalation of the war, something, he was fully aware, the administration would never permit.

The armistice negotiations had been unsuccessful, Clark thus told the JCS, not because of the prisoner of war issue but because the UNC had not "exerted suf[ficient] mili[tary] pres-

sure to impose the r[equire]m[en]t for an armistice on the
enemy." Furthermore, the UN commander distinguished between intensified military action, on one hand, and the type of
military offensive necessary to bring about a final peace in
Korea, on the other. Simply to increase military pressure on the
enemy or even to march to the narrow waist of the peninsula
(generally on a line from Pyongyang to Wonson), a possibility
raised by the JCS, would be counterproductive. Any contem-
plated course of action had to include "provision for carrying
the battle all the way to the Yalu in the event that a mili[tary]
victory cannot be achieved short of the line." Would an expansion of the war lead to Soviet intervention or possibly to World
War III? Clark did not think so. He believed "that World War
III [would] not be brought about by action on our part, that
conflict would commence only when the USSR so determines
on her appraisal, unaffected by US or UNC actions." Two weeks
later Clark told General J. Lawton Collins that while he did not
include the use of tactical nuclear weapons in his planning, he
recommended that he be given authority to do so.[75]

Yet Clark was under no illusions that the Joint Chiefs, much
less the White House, would approve the kind of military action
he had in mind, particularly the lifting of restrictions on the use
of atomic weapons. Also, he realized that under existing conditions a military offensive would serve no useful purpose. Indeed, he told Collins that it would be folly to try to win a
military victory against a numerically superior force behind a
solid defense line. In this respect he continued to agree fully
with General Ridgway, who had said precisely the same thing
before leaving for Tokyo in May. But Clark's remarks were
important, nevertheless, for in responding to the JCS and in
writing Collins, Clark expressed some of the exasperation he
and his subordinates felt in being forced to fight a limited war
with minute supervision from Washington.[76]

In fact, the sentiment was widespread at Clark's headquarters in Tokyo and among his commanders in Korea that the
armistice negotiations had constituted a colossal blunder on the
UN's part. Like the UN commander, his staff at headquarters
and his commanders in the field believed that the Communists
had been "on the ropes" after the failure of their spring offensive in 1951, and the staff and the commanders were convinced

that what had been called for was a decisive military initiative rather than a decision to seek an armistice. Similarly, Clark and his commanders, such as General James Van Fleet of the Eighth Army and General Otto P. Weyland of the Far East Air Force, expressing views similar to General Douglas MacArthur before them, emphasized that the United States had to recognize that it was a great Pacific power as well as an Atlantic power and that the Korean War was part of the global conflict being waged by the Communists against the United States so that America's security interests demanded that it win the war.[77]

Of course, most Americans shared the same frustrations that Clark and his commanders felt over a seemingly endless war that offered little hope of a battlefield victory. Many of these same Americans had also expressed the same view as they did about the need for the United States to give the Pacific region greater priority in its struggle against Communist aggression. Certainly this had been a recurring theme of the war almost since the time the North Koreans first crossed the 38th parallel in June 1950. What lent particular weight to the frustrations and grievances of so many Americans in the summer and fall of 1952, however, was that in a Presidential year the issues of ending the war and setting future directions for American foreign policy were bound to be decisive in determining the outcome of the campaign. Actually Dwight Eisenhower, the eventual Republican nominee and President-elect, offered far less in terms either of bringing peace to Korea or changing the course of the nation's foreign policy than his principal Republican rival, Senator Taft. But it was largely because he promised to be more moderate than Taft in the conduct of foreign policy while appearing to have new ideas about ending this most unpopular of all wars, that he was able to win his party's nomination in July and then go on to a relatively easy Presidential victory in November.

NOTES

1. Briefing of Foreign Government Representatives on Korea, May 13, 1952, Box 3. Selected Records Relating to the Korean War; *Time*, 59 (March 17, 1952), 26; *ibid.* (March 31, 1952), 28; Walter

G. Hermes, *Truce Tent and Fighting Front* (Washington, D. C., 1966), 198–99.

2. Hermes, *Truce Tent and Fighting Front*, 199–200; *Time*, 58 (December 3, 1951), 19; *New Republic*, 126 (February 18, 1952), 5.

3. John F. Cady, *The United States and Burma* (Cambridge, Mass., 1976), 201–205; David Joel Steinberg, et al., *In Search of Southeast Asia: A Modern History* (New York, 1971), 345–46.

4. Steinberg, et al., *In Search of Southeast Asia*, 375–76.

5. *Ibid.*, 346–47, 367–68, and 382.

6. *Life*, 32 (January 21, 1952), 28; *Nation*, 174 (January 9, 1952), 49; *New Republic*, 126 (January 21, 1952), 9.

7. *Commonweal*, 55 (January 25, 1952), 387; *New Republic*, 126 (March 10, 1952), 39–40; *Time*, 59 (March 10, 1952), 39–40.

8. *Life*, 32 (February 4, 1952), 17; *ibid.* (February 11, 1952), 19; *ibid.* (June 23, 1952), 28; *Time*, 59 (February 4, 1952), 17–18; *Atlantic Monthly*, 190 (July 1952), 4–6; Robert W. Stookey, *America and the Arab States: An Uneasy Encounter* (New York, 1975), 83–84 and 132–35.

9. *Commonweal*, 55 (February 8, 1952), 435; *New Yorker*, 27 (February 9, 1952), 98.

10. *New Yorker*, 27 (January 12, 1952), 47–49; *Commonweal*, 55 (February 15, 1952), 465; *Time*, 59 (March 31, 1952), 32–37.

11. *FR*, 1952–1954, XV, 280–88; *Life*, 32 (March 17, 1952), 36; David S. McLellan, *Dean Acheson: The State Department Years* (New York, 1976), 386–95; Dean Acheson, *Present at the Creation: My Years in the State Department* (New York, 1969), 600.

12. *Atlantic Monthly*, 189 (May 1952), 17–21; *Commonweal*, 56 (July 4, 1952), 310–12; *New Republic*, 126 (March 31, 1952), 8.

13. *Nation*, 173 (December 15, 1951), 509 and 512–13; *New Republic*, 125 (December 17, 1951), 10–12.

14. *New Yorker*, 27 (February 9, 1952), 59; *Time*, 59 (February 18, 1952), 28; *ibid.* (March 10, 1952), 32–33.

15. *Time*, 59 (March 10, 1952), 33.

16. Michael Foot, *Aneurin Bevan: A Biography*, II (2 vols., London, 1973), 361–62; *New Yorker*, 28 (March 15, 1952), 50–51; *ibid.* (March 29, 1952), 102–104; *Nation*, 174 (March 15, 1952), 247–48.

17. Foot, *Bevan*, II, 362–66; *Atlantic Monthly*, 189 (May 1952), 17–21; *New Republic*, 126 (March 3, 1952), 8; *New Republic*, 126 (May 19, 1952), 8.

18. Robert McGeehan, *The German Rearmament Question: American Diplomacy and European Defense After World War II* (Urbana, Ill., 1971), 188–98; Acheson, *Present at the Creation*, 622–27; *Time*, 59 (March 3, 1952), 17 and 23.

19. McGeehan, *The German Rearmament Question,* 192–93; *Time,* 59 (March 3, 1952), 23; *Commonweal,* 55 (March 14, 1952), 555; *New Republic,* 126 (March 24, 1952), 3.

20. *Atlantic Monthly,* 189 (April 1952), 9–12; *Nation,* 174 (March 1, 1952), 195–96; *ibid.* (March 8, 1952), 199–96; *Time,* 59 (March 10, 1952), 36; *Commonweal,* 55 (March 21, 1952), 587–88.

21. *New Republic,* 126 (March 17, 1952), 8; *ibid.* (May 19, 1952), 8–9; *Nation,* 174 (March 22, 1952), 263; *ibid.,* May 17, 1952; *Time,* 59 (March 24, 1952), 37; *Commonweal,* 55 (March 28, 1952), 604.

22. *Nation,* 174 (May 17, 1952), 466–68.

23. Ronald J. Caridi, *The Korean War and American Politics: The Republican Party as a Case Study* (Philadelphia, 1968), 182.

24. *New Republic,* 126 (February 11, 1952), 33; *Time,* 59 (February 18, 1952), 24; *Commonweal,* 55 (February 29, 1952), 509.

25. *Nation,* 174 (February 2, 1952), 98–99; *New Republic,* 126 (March 17, 1952), 11–12.

26. *Time,* 58 (November 19, 1951), 23. See also *New Republic,* 126 (January 14, 1952), 16–17; *Nation,* 174 (February 16, 1952), 151–52; *ibid.* (May 17, 1952), 473–75.

27. Caridi, *The Korean War and American Politics,* 183–84.

28. *New Republic,* 126 (May 19, 1952), 7.

29. *Commonweal,* 55 (November 21, 1951), 269–70; *New Republic,* 125 (December 13, 1951), 17.

30. *FR,* 1952–1954, XV, 79–80; Briefing of Foreign Government Representatives on Korea, March 4 and 18, 1952, Box 13, Selected Records Relating to the Korean War.

31. "Intelligence Report," March 27, 1952, Box 13, Selected Records Relating to the Korean War; *Time,* 59 (April 7, 1952), 30.

32. *Life,* 52 (April 7, 1952), 52; *Time,* 59 (April 7, 1952), 30.

33. *Time,* 59 (May 19, 1952), 23–24.

34. *FR,* 1952–1954, XV, 136–38; Ridgway to JCS, April 3, 1952, Box 10, Selected Records Relating to the Korean War; Hermes, *Truce Tent and Fighting Front,* 233–34; *Time,* 59 (January 28, 1952), 21.

35. *Time,* 59 (March 3, 1952), 34–36; *ibid.* (March 24, 1952), 30; *Life,* 32 (March 31, 1952), 92–98; Hermes, *Truce Tent and Fighting Front,* 237–39.

36. Ridgway to JCS, April 3, 1952, Box 10, Selected Records Relating to the Korean War; Barton J. Bernstein, "The Struggle Over the Korean Armistice: Prisoners of Repatriation?" in Bruce Cumings (ed.), *Child of Conflict: The Korean-American Relationship, 1943–1953* (Seattle, Wash., 1983), 284–85.

37. *Time,* 59 (May 19, 1952), 36–37.

38. Hermes, *Truce Tent and Fighting Front,* 244–45.
39. *FR,* 1952–1954, XV, 308–10; *Time,* 59 (June 9, 1952), 25; *ibid.* (June 23, 1952), 23; *Life,* 32 (June 23, 1952), 32–33.
40. *Intelligence Report,* March 27, 1952, Box 13, Selected Records Relating to the Korean War.
41. *FR,* 1952–1954, XV, 136–38.
42. *Ibid.,* 145–54.
43. Briefing of Foreign Government Representatives on Korea, April 29 and May 2, 1952, Box 3, Selected Records Relating to the Korean War.
44. *Time,* 59 (May 19, 1952), 36.
45. *Ibid.* (March 10, 1952), 29; *ibid.* (April 21, 1952), 30.
46. *Ibid.* (May 26, 1952), 30.
47. *Nation,* 174 (February 2, 1952), 107–109; *Commonweal,* 56 (June 13, 1952), 236–37; *ibid.* (June 25, 1952), 383–85.
48. *FR,* 1952–1954, XV, 74–76.
49. Ridgway to JCS, May 3, 1952, Box 16, Selected Records Relating to the Korean War; Memorandum for the Secretary of Defense from the JCS, March 26, 1952, Box 3, *ibid.;* Special Korean Briefing, June 6, 1952, Box 16, *ibid.*
50. *FR,* 1952–1954, XV, 281–85; *Nation,* 174 (February 9, 1952), 132–34.
51. JCS to Clark, May 30, 1952, Box 17, Selected Records Relating to the Korean War.
52. *FR,* 1952–1954, XV, 274–76 and 281–85.
53. *Ibid.,* 285–86, 301–305, and 358–60.
54. *Ibid.,* 377–79.
55. *Time,* 59 (June 30, 1952), 24; *ibid.,* 60 (July 7, 1952), 25.
56. Clark to JCS, August 8, 1952, Box 17, Selected Records Relating to the Korean War.
57. Edgar O'Ballance, *Korea: 1950–1953* (London, 1969), 126; Hermes, *Truce Tent and Fighting Front,* 292–96.
58. Rees, *Korea: The Limited War,* 303–305.
59. Mark W. Clark, *From the Danube to the Yalu* (New York, 1954), 80–81.
60. *New Republic,* 126 (March 24, 1952), 3; Robert J. Donovan, *Tumultuous Years: The Presidency of Harry S. Truman, 1949–1953* (New York, 1982), 382.
61. Robert F. Futrell, *The United States Air Force in Korea, 1950–1953* (New York, 1961), 451–53 and 480–87; *Time,* 59 (June 30, 1952), 24.
62. Bernstein, "The Struggle Over the Korean Armistice," 292–93.

63. *Time,* 59 (June 23, 1952), 26; *Nation,* 175 (July 5, 1952), 1; *Life,* 33 (July 7, 1952), 27.
64. *Nation,* 174 (June 14, 1952), 575–76; *ibid.,* 175 (July 5, 1952), 3–4; *Time,* 60 (July 7, 1952), 26.
65. *Time,* 60 (July 7, 1952), 3–4.
66. *Nation,* 175 (July 5, 1952), 3–4.
67. *Ibid.; New Yorker,* 28 (July 19, 1952), 64.
68. Clark to JCS, June 23, 1952, Box 17, Selected Records Relating to the Korean War; Memorandum for the Commander-in-Chief, Far East, July 9, 1952, *ibid.*
69. Memorandum of Conversation, June 25, 1952, Box 4281, Records of the Department of State, RG 59, 795.00/6-2552; John D. Hickerson to Ambassador Gross and attachments, July 7, 1952, Box 4282, *ibid.,* 795.00/7-752; Chester Bowles to the Secretary of State, July 14, 1952, *ibid.,* 795.00/7-1452.
70. *FR,* 1952–1954, XV, 364–67 and 386–98.
71. *Ibid.,* 421–27, 430–36, 446–47, and 522–25; Henkins to Kitchen, November 4, 1952, Box 4284, Records of the Department of State, RG 59, 795.00/11-452.
72. Truman to Clark, September 26, 1952, Box 17, Selected Records Relating to the Korean War. See also *FR,* 1952–1954, XV, 514–21.
73. *FR,* 1952–1954, XV, 554–57.
74. James F. Schnabel and Richard J. Watson, *The History of the Joint Chiefs of Staff,* III, *The Korean War* (unpublished manuscript, National Archives, 1978), 929.
75. *FR,* 1952–1954, XV, 548–50.
76. *Ibid.;* Schnabel and Watson, *The History of the Joint Chiefs of Staff,* III, *The Korean War,* 932–33.
77. Frank Pace, Jr., to President Truman, October 15, 1952, and attachments, Box 243, Korean War File, President's Secretary File, Truman Papers.

CHAPTER 9

New President, New Initiatives

Dwight D. Eisenhower won the Republican Party's nomination for the Presidency because a group of moderate Republicans, determined to prevent the right wing of the party from gaining the nomination for Robert Taft, saw in General Eisenhower an extremely popular alternative whose international orientation, commitment to the principles of collective security, and belief in the Atlantic alliance coincided with their own views on foreign policy. Although Eisenhower did not formally enter the Presidential race until he resigned his NATO command at the end of May, the effort to draft him, led by Senator Lodge of Massachusetts, had been going on since late 1951, and it had become increasingly clear since the March primary in New Hampshire that Eisenhower would be receptive to a draft "Ike" movement. One of the questions raised by those speculating on whether Eisenhower would be a candidate for the Republican nomination was his views on the Korean War.

As president of Columbia University at the time the conflict broke out in Korea and then as commander of NATO forces in Europe after 1951, Eisenhower had said or written very little about the war. At the outset he did state publicly his support for American military intervention, remarking that "there was no recourse but to do what President Truman did." Indeed, privately he expressed dismay that the administration was not doing enough to martial the nation's forces to resist Communist aggression in Korea. After meeting with Pentagon officials three days after the war broke out, he wrote in his diary, "I went in expecting to find them all in a dither of effort, engaged

287

in the positive business of getting the troops, supplies, etc., that will be needed to settle the Korean mess. [But] they seemed indecisive." A week later, after conferring with President Truman and Defense Secretary George Marshall, Eisenhower again left Washington disappointed, commenting that "there seems to be no disposition to begin serious mobilizing. . . . [Truman's] military advisers are too complacent." He made it clear to the administration that it needed to begin a rapid rearmament program. This enabled him to argue later that he had urged the White House to do more in Korea but had been ignored.[1]

What was noteworthy about Eisenhower's views on Korea, however, was how little he said or wrote about the war following the initial outbreak of hostilities. Convinced that Korea was part of Moscow's plan for world domination and firmly committed to the principles of international cooperation and collective security, Eisenhower remained strongly supportive of the UN action in Korea. But from June 1950 until the time he returned to the United States from Europe two years later, he concentrated almost exclusively on promoting the Atlantic alliance. In fact, had Senator Taft supported NATO, he might not have run for the Presidency. Just before leaving for Europe in 1951 to assume his duties as NATO commander, Eisenhower met with Senator Taft to discuss the European alliance. Dismayed by Taft's talk of limiting the number of American divisions in NATO and by what he sensed as growing isolationism in Congress, he concluded that Taft's advocacy of such a "fortress America" foreign policy indicated an ignorance of world affairs. He later claimed that had Taft indicated any commitment to collective security, he would have withdrawn his own name as a candidate for the Republican nomination.[2]

Not until he formally launched his bid for the nomination in June, with a speech and news conference in his hometown of Abilene, Kansas, did he begin to speak out on the Korean War. His comments differed substantially from the statements being made by Taft and his supporters, who bitterly attacked the administration's war policies and called for a decisive military victory. In contrast, Eisenhower told reporters, "I do not have any prescription for bringing the [war] to a decisive end." "I believe we have got to stand firm and take every possible step we can to reduce our losses, and try to get a decisive armistice out of it."³ Precisely because his views seemed so moderate, Eisenhower appeared to many Americans an attractive alternative to the extremism associated with the Taft wing of the Republican Party. Even those not inclined to vote for any Republican candidate could find good things to say about candidate Eisenhower while regarding Taft's candidacy as a menace to peace abroad and civil liberties at home. Largely for the same reason, Europeans also overwhelmingly preferred Eisenhower over Taft, although in the case of the Europeans, they also considered Eisenhower as having been their military savior during World War II.⁴

For groups such as these, Eisenhower's nomination in July was hailed as a victory for sound world leadership on the part of the United States. Eisenhower's moderate position on Korea —and on most other foreign policy issues—had been essential to his nomination. "Give the people what they most need," one of his advisers had told him, "the hope and the confidence that peace and security can be achieved."⁵ Even *Life* termed Eisenhower's nomination "a victory of right over wrong," while the *New Republic* commented that although there was little difference between Taft and Eisenhower on domestic issues, "the great contrast between [them] in world leaderships stands. Eisenhower accepts and inspires world leadership. Taft rejects it." In Europe also there was considerable relief that right-wing extremism had been defeated in the United States. In Paris all the city's major newspapers had preferred Eisenhower over Taft because Eisenhower appeared as the candidate of peace and Taft the candidate of war.⁶

Yet even before he won the nomination, many of the same persons who had supported Eisenhower had begun to express concern that he was not being entirely candid in his views on foreign policy and that he was even making major concessions to the Republican Old Guard. Richard Rovere thus wrote from Washington in June, soon after Eisenhower launched his campaign, that it was difficult to "smoke Ike out." "No one yet knows," Rovere remarked, "where he stands on the question of Far Eastern policy, which most people here think will be the largest question of the campaign."⁷ Indeed, during the campaign for the nomination Eisenhower sometimes sounded very much like the Republican Old Guard he hoped to defeat, such as when he deplored the "loss of China" or attacked the "secrecy" of the Yalta agreements of 1945, which these Republicans regarded as the first link in the internal conspiracy that had led to Communist domination of so much of the world. Similarly, Eisenhower also appeared to equivocate—or even cave in to the Republican right wing—on the issue of McCarthyism. When asked whether he would support Senator McCarthy's reelection, he said he would not engage in personalities but then added that he was as determined as anyone that all "Communistic, subversive or pinkish influence be uprooted from responsible places in our government."[8]

Such statements as these concerned political observers who preferred Eisenhower over Taft and recognized the need for political expediency, but began to wonder, nevertheless, about Eisenhower's commitment to moderate political principles. His endorsement of the party platform merely exacerbated these doubts, for the platform was an extremely harsh document that accused the Democrats of harboring Communists in government, called Truman's containment policy "negative, futile and immoral" (although, at Eisenhower's insistence, it endorsed NATO), and even hinted at "liberating" Eastern Europe and Asia from Communist aggression.[9] Having announced that he would campaign on that platform, Eisenhower seemed in subsequent weeks to deviate further from political moderation until finally his views and those of the political right appeared very much the same. Speaking at the American Legion Convention meeting in New York at the end of August, he remarked that there was no way to live peacefully with Communism "until the enslaved nations [have the] right to choose their own path." He also said that the United States should use its "influence and power to help" the satellite nations throw off the "yoke of Russian tyranny." Taking up another favorite issue of the political right, that of internal subversion, he told the Legionnaires that Communists had "penetrated into many critical spots of our own country, even into our own Government," and he saluted their organization for its long fight against subversion, telling them that he would enter the fight "for the duration."[10]

About the same time, the Republican nominee also began to

speak out more harshly against the Democrats' handling of the Korean War. During the Republican convention in July, numerous speakers, including the convention keynoter, General MacArthur, had made clear that the Republicans intended to hammer away at Democratic failures in Korea, despite President Truman's preconvention plea that the Korean War be left out of the campaign. In what most observers agreed was a disappointing speech that destroyed any chance he might have had to gain the Republican nomination for himself, MacArthur seemed to rise to the occasion only when, turning to Korea, he remarked, "We defeated the North Korean armies, but when the Communist armies of China struck, our leaders lacked the courage to fight to a military decision, even though victory was then readily within our grasp." MacArthur's views were echoed in the party platform, which blamed the Korean War on such previous Democratic "mistakes" as withdrawing American occupation troops in 1949 and declaring that Korea was not within America's defense perimeter in the Pacific. Charging the administration with refusing to fight an honorable war, the platform also claimed that its policies "produced stalemates and ignominious bartering [and] offer[ed] no hope of victory."[11]

At first Eisenhower rejected such an extreme view and refused to go much beyond what he had said at Abilene in June. Instead, he merely reemphasized the need to remain in the war until a cease-fire could be reached, but offered no panacea for ending the war quickly. In fact, a month before the convention met, he publicly broke with those advocating a military victory in Korea, stating that an attempt to unify Korea militarily could provoke World War III.[12] But his attitude seemed to change after he received the nomination and agreed in August that he would make foreign policy the major issue of the campaign. Speaking in Philadelphia a week after he addressed the American Legion Convention, he altered his tone dramatically. Now he blamed the war on the administration's "failure to observe some of the principles for preventing war," and tied this to its "loss" of China. "We are in [Korea]," he said, "because this Administration abandoned China to the Communists . . . [and] announced to all the world that it had written off most of the Far East as beyond our direct concern." By October the Republican nominee was even denouncing the Korean peace talks as a Communist "bear-pit" into which the Democrats had fallen and arguing that if there were to be wars in Asia, the United States should let Asians fight them.[13]

In contrast to Eisenhower, the Democratic nominee, Governor Adlai Stevenson of Illinois, appeared a model of urbanity and sobriety. Defending the very principles of moderation that Eisenhower had seemed to abandon, Stevenson charmed audiences with his wit, manner, and reasoned judgment. Forced to defend the administration's foreign policy and its conduct of the war, the Democratic candidate did so with sophistication and eloquence. Europeans were particularly won over by Stevenson's grace and good sense. Whereas Eisenhower disappointed them more and more, the Democratic candidate, largely unknown in Europe before his nomination, appeared a gratifying revelation. The London *Observer* reported that the governor's support was "mounting quite dramatically" in England, while in France he was hailed by the Paris newspapers as "the great discovery from the West."[14]

Outcomes of American elections, however, are decided in the United States and not in Europe, and despite the disappointment expressed by Europeans and many Americans at Eisenhower's campaign, the Republican nominee remained the overwhelming favorite of the electorate. Also, to the extent that the Korean War was decisive in the election, it worked overwhelmingly to Eisenhower's advantage. A Gallup poll taken in September on which Presidential candidate could best handle the Korean War found that 67 percent of the voters believed Eisenhower could do a better job than Stevenson, while only 9 percent believed Stevenson could be more effective than Eisenhower. Five percent thought there was no difference between the two men, and 19 percent had no opinion.[15]

The high point of the campaign, however, came in Detroit on October 24 when Eisenhower promised to go to Korea if elected. "Only in that way," he told his audience, "could I learn how best to serve the American people in the cause of peace. I shall go to Korea." Several of Eisenhower's advisers had been suggesting for weeks that he make such a pledge, and on the very day that he spoke in Detroit, the movie mogul, Darryl Zanuck, submitted a slogan coined by one of his associates: "Our country was founded by a general: now let's save it with one." But the person responsible for incorporating the pledge into the speech was Emmet John Hughes, one of Eisenhower's speech writers on loan from *Time,*, who wanted the candidate to remain flexible and not succumb to pressures to escalate the war. When Eisenhower saw the text of the speech, he liked it so much that he made only a few stylistic changes to highlight the pledge that Hughes had written into it.[16]

Actually neither Eisenhower nor the Republican Party had a concrete program for ending the war other than that they would end it on "honorable terms." In fact, Eisenhower's position on Korea was not that much different from the Democratic opposition, public perceptions notwithstanding, and despite the harshness of his rhetoric, the Republican candidate never altered his fundamental position that intervention in Korea in 1950 was "inescapable" and that a "stupidly aggressive attitude [in Korea would] markedly increase the risk of global war." Furthermore, critics of the Republican campaign were quick to point out that Eisenhower's promise to go to Korea had some of the quality of quicksand. Calling it a "spectacular grandstand play" that would not bring peace to Korea, the *New Republic* maintained that the failure to achieve peace would destroy the administration's prestige at its very start and tempt Eisenhower either to intensify the war or appease the Communists into ending it, which, the liberal journal said, was "exactly what the crypto-isolationist old guard backing his candidacy want."[17]

Indeed, the importance of Eisenhower's pledge to go to Korea and, for that matter, the precise relationship of the Korean War to the election's outcome remain ambiguous. For one thing, Eisenhower's personal popularity with the voters would probably have assured his victory regardless of any campaign issues. For another, the very lack of a systematic and comprehensive dialogue on the war until the final weeks of the campaign suggests that it might not have been the decisive issue of the campaign as some have maintained. As the *Nation* pointed out on the eve of the election, "it was not until the final phase of the campaign that the Korean War made its appearance, and even then it was treated obliquely rather than as a central problem for creative thought and discussion." So, too, Arthur Krock of *The New York Times* suggested a week before the election took place that America's involvement in the war, the continuing stalemate, and the events contributing to it were always "implicit" rather than explicit as a campaign issue.[18] In this respect the election involved a number of local and national issues other than Korea, including corruption within the administration and McCarthyism. Although the corruption issue faded considerably after Truman announced in March that he would not run for reelection and took measures to purge corruption from government, this issue continued to rankle many voters, while accusations of internal subversion remained an undercurrent throughout the campaign, especially after Eisenhower refused to disavow McCarthy and other Red baiters. A poll taken after the election by the Survey Research Center of the University of Michigan found that domestic issues such as these were far more important to the voters than foreign policy. The Survey Center also discovered that although only 3 percent of those voters it interviewed approved of the Democrats' management of the conflict, only 13 percent felt the Republican Party had the ability to handle the war, hardly an indication that the electorate was voting for Eisenhower in order to bring a quick end to the conflict.[19]

If, however, the Michigan organization concluded that Korea was a minor issue once the electorate actually entered the voting places, other highly respected pollsters reached just the opposite conclusion. Furthermore, while the war might not have been the decisive issue of the campaign as these pollsters maintained, it was beyond doubt of paramount importance in determining Eisenhower's *margin* of victory. Seen in this context, the Republican candidate's pledge to go to Korea if elected was a masterful political stroke, for it persuaded many Americans that only the Republicans could end the war, while Eisenhower's own prestige convinced them that concrete results would emerge from his trip to the battlefront.

Unquestionably, unhappiness with the Democratic conduct of the war figured prominently in the magnitude of Eisenhower's victory. Shortly before the election, pollster Elmer Roper concluded that Korea was "clearly Eisenhower's strongest asset." Similarly, Louis Harris, a one-time research executive for Roper, determined that Korea was the most important issue in the 1952 election. "If one were to find a single, basic root cause out of which the impatience and protest of 1952 grew,"

Harris wrote, "it would have to be the failure of the Administration to bring the Korean fighting to a successful close."[20] It was not only the inconclusive and seemingly endless nature of the war that disturbed many Americans, but also a series of related issues, such as the nation's high inflation rate that was attributed directly to the war, and the recalling of World War II reservists to active duty, particularly pilots. Many of those recalled, having to leave their families and successful civilian careers, felt they were being unfairly assigned dangerous combat missions, while their regular Air Force counterparts were being given cushy office assignments. Some reservists actually risked court-martial by refusing to fly in combat. At the same time, Americans were particularly incensed about the drafting of young men to fight in Korea, while the Republicans were able to turn to their own advantage Democratic boasts that the American people were enjoying an unparalleled prosperity by countering that the Korean War was at the root of this prosperity and that good times at home were "being bought by the lives of our boys in Korea."[21]

As for Eisenhower's pledge to go to Korea, the Stevenson strategists, sensing the damage of that promise to their own campaign, tried to devise a counterblow. Speaking in Boston, the Democratic candidate asked if Eisenhower was actually planning to escalate the war. "The root of the Korean problem does not lie in Korea—it lies in Moscow," Stevenson argued. "If the purpose of the general's trip is to settle the Korean war by a larger military challenge, then the sooner we all know about it the better."[22] But also sensing a ground swell of support because of his Detroit speech, Eisenhower highlighted his Korean pledge for the rest of the campaign. At the same time, he hammered away at the theme that he was the peace candidate. "So long as a single American soldier faces enemy fire in Korea," he remarked in Pittsburgh as the campaign was coming to a close, "the honorable ending of the Korean war and the securing of honorable peace in the world must be the first—the urgent and unshakable—purpose of a new administration." A few days later the voters delivered their verdict, overwhelmingly electing him President by a margin of almost 55 percent to Stevenson's 44.3 percent.[23]

Reaction to Eisenhower's victory followed predictable partisan lines, but even those who had opposed the Republican nominee's drift to the political right and feared he had sold his soul to win the election recognized that, unlike the Democrats, he had given the American voters hope the war could soon end. "The Democrats showed little creative initiatives in the campaign," the *Nation* thus remarked in analyzing the election results. "It was Eisenhower who broke the ice in which the key issue of Korea had been encased." Having elected Eisenhower in anticipation that he would bring peace to Korea, many Americans expected speedy results. After the President-elect appeared on the front pages of newspapers playing golf in Georgia, irate readers even phoned the papers wanting to know why he was not in Korea fulfilling his campaign pledge. Even in Washington it was widely speculated that Eisenhower might say or do something in Korea that would lead to a resumption and early conclusion of the truce talks.[24]

Such hopes were quickly shattered by developments at the United Nations, where Soviet Ambassador Andrei Vishinsky delivered an angry speech blasting an Indian peace initiative that, ironically, had also been opposed by the United States. First circulated by India's Krishna Menon toward the middle of November, the resolution provided for the establishment of a neutral nations repatriation commission to handle the repatriation problem until peace was restored in Korea. Then the political conference that was supposed to be called after the armistice would decide the final fate of those prisoners of war still resisting repatriation. Secretary of State Acheson spoke out strongly against the resolution because he believed it would leave the repatriation question unresolved at the time of the armistice. Instead, the United States pushed an earlier twenty-one-nation resolution that it had cosponsored calling on Communist China and North Korea to agree to an armistice based on voluntary repatriation.[25]

Although Acheson referred to the Indian proposal as a "dangerous idea" that was also conceptually vague, it nevertheless had the support of most of America's allies, including England, France, Canada, and Australia. Not only did countries like England and France consider the resolution a way to break the deadlock in the peace negotiations, they were also deeply concerned about what the new administration would do in Korea

once it took office. In England, it is true, Eisenhower was still
the best-liked American since Franklin Roosevelt. But Stevenson had been the favorite of most political observers and the
press, and as the Sunday *Observer* remarked after the election,
"a large part of the British public received the news of the
American election results with feelings of regret and misgiv-
ing." In France the response to Eisenhower's election was one
of almost total chagrin. The French had watched the campaign
closely, and having made Stevenson their clear choice, they
were afraid after the election that Eisenhower's planned trip to
Korea might merely be the prelude to a new policy in Korea
based on the goal of military victory. The latest news from
abroad seemed to confirm their worst fears. On top of an Associated Press story from Tokyo that an "all-out war" would
soon start in Korea, including the possible use of the atomic
bomb, had come a statement by Lewis Gough, head of the
American Legion, insisting that the bomb must be used and
that the Soviet Union would not retaliate. The French regarded
such news as evidence that the United States was about to
embark on a more aggressive—and dangerous—foreign policy.
Seen in this context, it behooved the British and French to
settle the Korean War before the new administration took over
in Washington.[26]

Other reasons also compelled the allied nations to support
the Indian resolution. In England Foreign Secretary Eden had
to consider the unity of the British Commonwealth, particularly
the demands of the so-called New Commonwealth nations, who
were gradually being added to the older White Dominions as
members of the Commonwealth and who—as in this case—
often aligned themselves with neutralist powers against the
United States. In France the pressures on the government were
more subtle but also concerned a form of anti-Americanism
generally associated with neutralism and resistance to German
rearmament, but which ran the gamut from opposition to
American high tariffs to opposition to American high ideals. At
the end of 1952 the French were particularly indignant at
America's rigid anticolonialism, especially on North Africa, and
bitterly resented America's recent decision to side with the
Asian-Arab block in putting the question of French colonialism
in North Africa on the agenda of the UN General Assembly. As

an obvious warning to Washington to mind its own business, *Le Monde* accused Americans of meddling in French affairs and prophesied critical relations between the two countries unless the United States changed its policy. By supporting the Menon resolution, the French were able to send a message to Washington that it, too, could align with the neutralist block against the interests of an ally.[27]

Aware of the widespread support for the Menon resolution and seeking to gain allied backing for America's own twenty-one-nation resolution, Acheson resorted to what he later described as a "blocking, defensive game," holding a round of talks at the United Nations with allied leaders, including Foreign Secretary Eden, who arrived in New York to attend the meeting of the General Assembly. The White House also persuaded President-elect Eisenhower to make a statement publicly backing the administration's position on voluntary repatriation to show that there would be no policy change on that essential issue after the Republicans took office in January. But the secretary of state failed to change any minds, and the Menon resolution continued to gain such widespread support after it was formally introduced on November 17 that it ceased to be a matter of whether the General Assembly would approve it. As Acheson told President Truman, the only question now was whether the Indian proposal could be amended to make it more acceptable to the United States.[28]

This proved to be just what happened. The crucial amendment in Acheson's view had to do with the question of when POWs resisting repatriation would be released. According to the Menon resolution, at the end of ninety days those prisoners not yet repatriated would be turned over to the political conference, which was to be held after the armistice. But it was not made clear how much longer they would have to remain incarcerated. The secretary of state did not like handing the POWs over to the political conference in the first place, but certainly not for an indefinite period. Applying the principle of the carrot and stick, in which he appeared conciliatory even as he warned America's European allies that their failure to support him on this issue would jeopardize American support for NATO "and other arrangements of the same sort," the secretary of state was able to bring them around to the American position. In turn, they prevailed on India to agree to amendments assuring that within three months after the armistice the repatriation process would end and the final disposition of remaining prisoners would be determined by the United Nations itself.[29]

By this time, however, Vishinsky had taken the floor of the General Assembly to assail the Menon resolution, stating that it was "designed not to put an end to the war but to perpetuate it." The Soviet diplomat's harsh remarks, which certainly did not curry favor with the neutralist block supporting the Indian initiative, took political observers at the UN by surprise. Why Moscow directed Vishinsky to reject the Indian proposal is still not entirely clear. Perhaps it feared that acceptance of the principle of voluntary repatriation would encourage mass defections from its own armies in future wars. Or perhaps it was worried about what Peking and Pyongyang would do, for China had indicated in May and July that it would permit nonforcible repatriation of North Korean POWs if all the Chinese POWs were returned, and some reports claimed that Peking was behind the Menon resolution in the first place. As for North Korea, which had suffered enormously from the war, there is evidence to suggest that it was anxious to end the war even if that meant the loss of 42,000 soldiers who preferred to remain in South Korea.[30]

Most observers agreed, however, that the Soviets' purpose in rejecting the Menon resolution was to confirm the worst fears of those countries concerned about Eisenhower's forthcoming trip to Korea. By wrecking any prospect of an imminent political settlement of the war, these observers believed that Moscow hoped to put the President-elect in the awkward position of going to Korea for no apparent purpose other than to consider means of expanding the war, a position America's allies would certainly reject.[31]

If this was in fact Moscow's purpose, the Soviets miscalculated badly, for Vishinsky's speech solidified UN support behind the American position, making it appear that Moscow and not Washington represented the roadblock to final peace in Korea. Ironically, Washington now became the driving force behind the Indian initiative, even dissuading Menon from withdrawing his resolution after the Chinese, following Moscow's lead, also turned the proposal down. With Washington fully behind it, the General Assembly approved the resolution on December 3 by a vote of 54 to 5. In this way the United States succeeded in turning an unacceptable proposal into a victory for its position on POWs.[32]

But the victory had not been without cost to the principle of allied unity. Indeed, Secretary Acheson would later refer to the allied efforts in behalf of the Menon resolution as the "Menon Cabal." And there can be no doubt that for a while at least the Indian proposal strained the united front on Korea that the Truman administration tried so hard to maintain. The fact was that since the United States bore the greatest burden of responsibility in Korea, it expected its views to carry the greatest weight in matters concerning Korea, and it deeply resented when this was not the case. "I did not believe that those who were encouraging and supporting the Indian effort really understood the full consequences of what they were doing," Acheson remarked on November 22 during the period of greatest strain between the United States and its allies, "and I felt that if their actions were continued to the point of a sharp break between those who were carrying the main brunt of the effort and those who were not, the gravest results would flow both to the United Nations and to the whole future of collective security."[33]

As the Soviets may also have hoped, their rejection of the Menon resolution just about eliminated any chance that Eisenhower's trip to Korea would produce anything tangible in the way of ending the war. Indeed, what was most noteworthy about the trip was what Eisenhower did *not* do. Keeping his campaign pledge, the President-elect went to Korea at the beginning of December under a blanket of total secrecy. During his trip he flew along the front, toured the battlefields, ate with the troops, visited the wounded, and met separately with President Syngman Rhee and General Clark. But his two meetings with Rhee, who had hoped to turn Eisenhower's visit into a week-long public display of patriotism, parades, dinners, and mass rallies, were kept brief, and Eisenhower refused to appear publicly with him. Nor did the President-elect give Clark, who had prepared elaborate plans for a military victory, an opportunity to outline his proposals. Because driving the Chinese completely off the Korean peninsula, as Clark proposed, required carrying the conflict across the Yalu River, it risked a global war with the Soviet Union, a gamble that Eisenhower was not yet prepared to make.[34]

Nevertheless, the new President's visit to Korea made some lasting and important impressions on him. Above all, he returned home persuaded that the United States "could not stand forever on a static front and continue to accept casualties without any visible result. Small attacks on small hills," he later commented, "would not end the war." A military gesture of considerable magnitude was warranted. In this sense, those who had always been nervous that Eisenhower's trip to Korea might lead to a military escalation had cause to be concerned.[35]

Following Eisenhower's return to the United States, however, a lull set in as President Truman prepared to turn over his office to Eisenhower and as the talks at Panmunjom remained recessed. Relations between the President and the President-elect had become increasingly acrimonious after Truman had begun personally attacking Eisenhower during the campaign, even suggesting at one point that he was anti-semitic. But they became downright acerbic after the outgoing President questioned Eisenhower's motives for going to Korea and took umbrage at a meeting that the President-elect held with General MacArthur following his return home. On December 5, in a speech before the National Association of Manufacturers, MacArthur stated he had a plan for ending the war in Korea, which involved no threat "of provoking universal conflict," and he offered to disclose the plan to Eisenhower. The President-elect's advisers recommended against conferring with MacArthur because of his highly publicized views on an all-out war in Korea and because of his ties with GOP extremists, but Eisenhower agreed to meet with him, hoping that just maybe he had a solution for ending the Korean quagmire.

At the meeting in New York in mid-December MacArthur proposed a summit conference between the United States and the Soviet Union in which the two nations would guarantee the neutrality of Germany, Austria, Japan, and Korea. If the Soviets refused to go along with such an agreement, America would make clear its intention to clear North Korea of enemy forces. "This could be accomplished," MacArthur remarked, "through the atomic bombing of enemy military concentrations and installations in North Korea and the sowing of fields of suitable radio-active materials, the byproducts of atomic manufacture, to close major lines of enemy supply and communication leading south from the Yalu, with simultaneous amphibious landings on both coasts of North Korea."[36]

Details of Eisenhower's meeting with MacArthur were not made public, and in any case, the President-elect was not about to adopt a scheme based on what he considered the frivolous use of atomic weapons. Instead, he merely thanked MacArthur for his proposal and said he would have to study it in greater detail. "[I]f we're going to bomb bases on the other side of the Yalu, if we're going to extend the war," he told the general "we have to make sure we're not offending the whole world."[37] Nevertheless, when Truman heard that Eisenhower was going to meet with MacArthur, he turned livid. At a news conference he shot back by doubting whether MacArthur had a feasible proposal for ending the war and by labeling Eisenhower's trip to Korea a piece of demagoguery whose sole purpose was to fulfill a campaign promise. The President's remarks stirred a nest of controversy, but although Eisenhower was infuriated by Truman's comments, he refused to break openly with the President, preferring to use the time before inauguration day on organizing his new administration.[38]

In Korea, meanwhile, the truce tent at Panmunjom stayed empty as neither side offered any new proposals to break the deadlock over prisoner repatriation and as the Communists waited to see if the new administration had any fresh approaches toward resolving this problem. In the prison camps themselves the situation remained tense and dangerous. Four months after the bloody riots at Koje-do island in February, General "Bull" Boatner, who had successfully put down the prison uprisings, had the ringleaders moved to neighboring Pongamdo Island. In this way he had hoped to control better the most recalcitrant POWs and keep them from stirring up trouble with the other prisoners. But the transfer to another camp only isolated the problem of prisoner unrest, it did not eliminate it; and on December 14 a major riot erupted at Pongamdo after a group of prisoners began to stone UN guards who had told them to break up a military drill they were conducting in violation of camp rules. By the time the skirmish ended, 85 prisoners had been killed and 113 hospitalized, the largest number of casualties reported in a POW camp since the war began.[39]

On the battlefront there was a significant increase in fighting in October and November as the Chinese apparently sought to pressure the United States out of the war in this election season. Some of the fighting was the heaviest since 1950 and involved sizable contingents of ROK troops, who performed extremely well. In October, for example, ROK forces engaged the Chinese in the battle of White Horse Hill, near the Chorwon corner of the Iron Triangle. In six days of extremely bloody fighting both sides used tanks and heavy artillery. In one day alone, the Communists fired 93,000 artillery and mortar shells—about twice their previous record for one day. The ROK forces also called in U. S. fighter bombers to provide tactical support from the air. By the time the fighting was over, ROK and other UN forces had taken more than 8000 casualties, and the hill had been reduced to a stinking shambles littered with the dead of both sides. But the South Koreans had killed or wounded an estimated 10,000 Chinese in the first six days of battle alone, and they still retained the hill. A few weeks later bitter fighting was also reported at Triangle Hill, where the Chinese took the summit and then beat back a South Korean counterattack. Elsewhere along the front, Communist probes were beaten back, and there were no signs of a major enemy breakthrough.[40]

Otherwise, there was little to cheer about. According to Pentagon figures released in November, the United States was taking casualties at the rate of more than 1000 a week, the heaviest in a year. Since the truce talks had begun sixteen months earlier, more than 44,700 American troops had been killed or wounded. The Pentagon also announced that the United States had already dropped more bombs on Korea than in the first two years of World War II. The Eighth Army had used about the same weight of mortar and artillery shells as in the whole European operation from D Day to V-E Day. And yet the enemy had gotten stronger, not weaker. By the end of 1952 its forces in North Korea totaled about 1.2 million, and its defensive lines had become virtually impenetrable.[41]

This was the dilemma facing Eisenhower when he took

office in January. Although he had not committed himself to any particular program or plan for ending the war, he was determined to take new initiatives to bring the conflict to a close. While he believed the pivot of the Cold War remained Europe and not Asia, he recognized that influential sectors of public opinion favored a more vigorous policy in the Far East. And although he had frowned on suggestions for using nuclear weapons in Korea, his secretary of state, John Foster Dulles, believed that the United States should threaten a nuclear response in case of Communist aggression, a policy that later became known as "massive retaliation."

A highly successful lawyer and diplomat, who had negotiated the Japanese Peace Treaty signed in San Francisco a year earlier, Dulles had been the recognized Republican spokesman on foreign policy for more than a year. Almost certainly he would have been secretary of state in 1949 had Governor Thomas Dewey of New York beaten Truman four years earlier. Generally regarded as a moderate Republican because of his internationalist views, he had, beginning with an article that *Life* published in May 1952, made clear his willingess to use America's nuclear power. Our present policies, he said, were "treadmill policies which, at best, might keep us in the same place until we drop exhausted." The way out of this trap was to rely on nuclear deterrence—"that is for the free world to develop the will and organize the means to retaliate instantly against open aggression by Red armies, so that, if it occurred anywhere, we could and would strike back where it hurts, by means of our own choosing."[42]

Eisenhower believed that Dulles's formulation of the doctrine of deterrence was too simple and unqualified. How, he asked his close friend, Lucius Clay, should the United States respond to minor aggressions or internal subversion in remote places? "To my mind, this is just a case when the theory of 'retaliation' falls down." Even so, the new President felt it was important for the Soviets to know that aggression against America's vital interests could produce a nuclear response. And by relying on air power and nuclear deterrence, the United States could avoid spending itself into bankruptcy, an issue that Dulles had also raised in his *Life* article. With certain reservations, therefore, Eisenhower was sympathetic to a foreign policy based on nuclear deterrence, and at no time did he eliminate as an option the use of nuclear weapons in Korea.[43]

In fact, at a National Security Council meeting less than a month after taking office, Eisenhower himself raised the nuclear option. The NSC was discussing a request from General Clark to attack the neutral sanctuary around Kaesong, which, Clark said, was being used as a staging area for Communist forces. After instructing Secretary Dulles to take up the matter with America's allies in Korea, the President stated that the administration should consider using tactical nuclear weapons in the Kaesong area. The United States could not continue fighting the war as it had in the past, he added. Its self-respect and that of its allies was at stake, and if the allies objected to the use of atomic weapons "we might as well ask them to supply three or more divisions needed to drive the Communists back." In making these remarks, Eisenhower was probably just speculating out loud, and he dropped the subject after General Bradley told him how opposed the allies would be to any form of nuclear warfare. But it is clear that as early as February, the new President was already considering adopting a nuclear strategy in Korea.[44]

It is also clear that Eisenhower was determined to end the Korean War quickly. To pressure the Chinese into signing a peace agreement and to appease Old Guard Republicans, the President announced in his first State of the Union message that the "Seventh Fleet [would] no longer be employed to shield Communist China." Eisenhower stressed that his instructions implied no aggressive intent on his part; in fact, the Seventh Fleet had been assisting the Chinese Nationalists in conducting raids along the coast for some time. But in stopping the fleet's patrolling of the Formosa Strait, Eisenhower was effectively warning Peking that if a truce was not forthcoming, Chiang Kai-shek's forces might be used against the mainland.[45]

A truce *was* coming but not as fast as the administration had hoped. In December the International Red Cross in Switzerland urged both sides to exchange their sick and wounded POWs. After conferring with Washington, Clark agreed to the swap, not because he believed the Chinese and North Korea would accept the proposal but because he thought offering an exchange of the sick and wounded would make a favorable impact on world opinion. Much to Clark's surprise, however, the Communists agreed to the exchange on March 28 and even suggested that the truce talks be reopened at Panmunjom. Two days later Premier Chou En-lai of the PRC announced over the radio that he was willing to have all nonrepatriates turned over to a neutral state "so as to ensure a just solution to the question of their repatriation."[46]

Apparently Peking made this major concession on the POW question, a concession which resembled the same Indian plan that China had rejected the previous December, at the Soviets' behest. On March 5 Soviet Premier Joseph Stalin died after suffering a brain hemorrhage. With his death ended an epoch of almost total domination of the country by a single person. Lacking his control over the governing bureaucracy, Stalin's replacement, Georgi Malenkov, sought to improve relations with the West and, for this purpose, began what reporters and other political observers referred to as a "Soviet peace offensive." On March 15 he announced that there were no disputes between Moscow and Washington "that cannot be decided by peaceful means, on the basis of mutual understanding." Shortly thereafter, the Soviet Union relaxed its controls over Eastern Europe, arrested Lavrenti P. Beria, head of the notorious KGB, and renewed an earlier offer by Stalin in 1952 to consider a reunited, partially rearmed, but neutralized Germany. Anxious to resolve some of its differences with the West, realizing that the war in Korea could escalate into a global conflict, which it wanted no more than the United States, and also apparently feeling more confident about its own military capability now that it was a strong nuclear power, Moscow probably pressured China and North Korea to end the conflict.[47]

This may not have been so hard to do, for the costs of the war to them were enormous. In 1951, for example, 60 percent of China's tax revenue went to the defense budget, and by the end of 1952 there were more than a million Chinese soldiers in North Korea. Estimates at the end of the war placed China's losses at about 900,000 men. Also, the conflict meant a drain of trained personnel who were badly needed to rebuild a country ravaged by forty years of internal strife. Since Peking had already achieved maximum prestige by driving UN forces out of most of North Korea, there was little more to be gained from continuing the conflict. As for North Korea, it suffered the loss of nearly 520,000 personnel, while unofficial estimates placed the number of civilian casualties at about a million. Food shortages had become so serious that widespread famine was prevented only by emergency food shipments from other Communist countries, and morale was extremely low.[48]

With China no longer insisting on the repatriation of all POWS, it now appeared that the deadlock on the one issue preventing an end to the Korean War had been broken and that peace was finally at hand. Once more, pressures mounted on the United States to accept Chou En-lai's offer on nonrepatriates and to reopen the armistice talks. From England Anthony Eden wrote Secretary Dulles, "I do not, however, think we should at this stage insist rigidly on conclusion of exchange [of sick and wounded prisoners of war] before resumption of main negotiations. We should retain flexibility so as to exploit developments to our best advantage."[49]

Dulles and Eisenhower were more skeptical. Before talks were resumed at Panmunjom, they believed that the Chinese and North Koreans should first make good on the other part of their proposal, an exchange of sick and wounded POWs. Indeed, the secretary of state was not even certain the White House should honor earlier agreements reached at Panmunjom. Considering how anxious the Communists now were for an armistice, he thought the UNC could obtain a much better agreement than one based on a division of Korea at the 38th parallel. Although he realized that America's allies were desperately anxious to end the fighting in Korea, he was convinced that such a divided Korea would not be economically viable and that it would be unacceptable to the South Koreans. Personally he would like to tell the Chinese and North Koreans that unless Korea was divided at the narrow waist of the peninsula that lay ninety miles north of the 38th parallel, the armistice would be called off. President Eisenhower vetoed that idea because it would mean a politically unacceptable renewal of the war in Korea. But he agreed to a National Security Council statement reserving to the United States the right to void any armistice agreement that failed to lead to a permanent political settlement in Korea.[50]

Meanwhile General Clark made contact with the enemy

about exchanging sick and wounded prisoners. Like the administration, Clark had remained extremely suspicious of the Communists, warning the Joint Chiefs that it would be "completely naïve" not to anticipate "every form of chicanery" in their proposal for a prisoner exchange. But on April 5 the Chinese and North Koreans agreed to meet the next day to work out the details for the exchange, and within the week arrangements were concluded for swapping 5800 POWs held by the UN in return for 600 POWs held by the Communists. All this created tremendous excitement and optimism at the United Nations, in Washington, and throughout Europe that peace was finally at hand.[51]

Yet a number of difficult questions remained unanswered. Which "neutral" country, for example, would take responsibility for prisoners resisting repatriation according to Chou En-lai's statement of March 30? The United States preferred Switzerland or Sweden in that order but was willing to consider Asian neutrals such as Pakistan, Burma, or Indonesia. It was resolutely opposed to the Soviet Union or any other Communist nation as a "neutral" state, and it did not much care for India, whose name was also mentioned but whose neutrality seemed to lean too heavily toward the Communists. Another question that was later raised had to do with whether these prisoners would be physically transferred to the neutral country that was to be given responsibility for them or whether they were to be left in Korea. (What, in other words, did Chou En-lai mean when he spoke of "handing over" these prisoners to a neutral nation?) The United States could find no justification for sending prisoners out of Korea to another country. A final question was what was meant by a "just solution" to the POW question that Chou En-lai mentioned in his message.[52]

To answer these questions the UNC agreed to reopen armistice talks with the Communists. So anxious were America's allies to resume the negotiations that the British warned Washington against pressing the Chinese too hard for clarifications of Chou En-lai's earlier statement. But in South Korea the government responded to the news that truce talks were about to begin again by orchestrating a series of anti-armistice demonstrations, parades, and rallies throughout the country and by pressing the United States for a security pact, which would obligate Washington to assist the South Koreans in militarily expelling the Communists from the Korean peninsula if a postwar conference failed to bring about Korea's political reunification. President Rhee even threatened to march to the Yalu River alone if necessary.[53]

Despite a personal letter from Eisenhower to Rhee in which the American President warned the South Korean leader that any effort on his part to disrupt an armistice would "nullif[y]" America's peaceful efforts in behalf of political reunification, the demonstrations continued in Seoul, Pusan, and in other cities and towns throughout South Korea. In one incident American Marines guarding the American embassy in Seoul were forced to fire a shot in the air after a group of marchers, including a Korean police band and fifty members of the Korean National Assembly, attempted to storm the building. None of this prevented the exchange of sick and wounded POWs from beginning on April 20 and ending on May 3 in an operation known as LITTLE SWITCH. But it indicated the irascibility of the South Korean president and his determination to thwart any peace agreement that did not include Korean reunification.[54]

Even as LITTLE SWITCH was getting started, negotiations were resumed at Panmunjom. Almost immediately it became apparent that the two sides at the negotiating table remained far apart over the particulars of a prisoner exchange. The Chinese and North Koreans proposed that within three months after the armistice nonrepatriates be sent from Korea to the neutral state assuming responsibility for them. They would be kept there for another six months while agents of their governments tried to persuade them to return home. Those who still refused repatriation would remain as prisoners indefinitely—or until the political conference that was to be called after the armistice could decide what to do with them. All this the United States found simply unacceptable. In addition, the State Department was afraid that the Communists would nominate India as the neutral nation responsible for the prisoners. This would place the United States in the embarrassing position of either accepting a country whose motives it distrusted or alienating a government with which it still wanted to maintain good relations, particularly since General Harrison, the UN's chief negotiator, had nominated India's foe, Pakistan, as one of the three nations acceptable to the UNC (the others being Switzerland and Sweden). As a way out of this dilemma, Secretary of State Dulles instructed the UN delegation to offer a proposal by which it would accept India's nomination by the Communists in return for their acceptance of Switzerland or Sweden as the UNC's nomination. But it was far from clear that China and North Korea would go along with this scheme.[55]

On May 7, however, the Communists offered a new proposal for settling the repatriation issue. No longer insisting that non-repatriates be sent out of Korea and cutting the screening process from six to four months, the Chinese and North Korean negotiators proposed in place of a single neutral nation a Neutral Nations Repatriation Commission (NNRC) similar to the one intended in the Indian resolution of the previous December. Composed of Poland, Czechoslovakia, Switzerland, Sweden, and India, each of which would provide equal numbers of armed personnel, the NNRC would take over custody of non-repatriates in the camps where they were being held. But the final disposition of the nonrepatriates after the screening process was complete would be determined by the postwar political conference.[56]

Although this latest proposal by the Chinese and North Koreans opened the way for a final settlement of the Korean War, few realized it at the time. Instead, there followed five weeks of delicate negotiations in which the White House had to maneuver between South Korea's absolute rejection of the Communist offer without a defense pact with the United States, and China's and North Korea's absolute refusal to offer any more concessions. Determined to end the war, the new administration responded to both its ally and its enemy with a mixture of cajolery and firmness, reassuring the Rhee government of its intentions to safeguard Korean security but preparing to seize the government if necessary, offering to negotiate with the Communists on the basis of their latest proposal but threatening nuclear warfare if concessions and peace were not forthcoming.

The administration's initial response to the Communists' latest offer was one of cautious interest. On one hand, it believed the proposal could be a positive step toward ending the war. On the other, it thought the offer could be acceptable only if provision was made for the final disposition of nonrepatriates within a fixed period. It was willing to accept Poland and Czechoslovakia as members of a five-member Neutral Nations Repatriation Commission. But it also proposed a complex scheme whereby nonrepatriates would be transferred to the custody of the NNRC within sixty days after an armistice. There they would remain for another sixty days while the Chinese and North Koreans tried to convince them to return home. Then, the political conference would have thirty more days to determine what to do with them. After that the NNRC would be disbanded and the remaining nonrepatriates would become civilians. To prevent an unfavorable split in the NNRC (that is, an alignment of the two Communist nations and India against Switzerland and Sweden), the administration insisted that all decisions on substantive matters be by unanimous vote.[57]

When he learned of this counterproposal to the Communists' latest offer, President Rhee was furious. At a meeting with General Clark on May 12, Rhee rejected the introduction of any neutral troops into South Korea, especially Poles, Czechs, or Indians, whom he referred to as political spies, saboteurs, and agitators. Rather than accept Indian troops on Korean soil, he threatened to release the nonrepatriated POWs without consulting the UNC. He also refused to turn over any Koreans to any neutral commission.[58]

Clark sympathized with much of what Rhee had to say, having earlier warned the Joint Chiefs of the violent reaction the placing of armed Communist personnel in South Korea would create in the country and having his own misgivings about the membership of the NNRC. He even got Washington to agree that, pending further consideration, all nonrepatriated Korean POWs would be released as soon as possible. But on May 23 the administration sent him new instructions, ordering him to agree to hand over all Korean as well as Chinese nonrepatriates to the NNRC and to accept the Communist demand that all disputes within the Repatriation Commission be decided by a majority rather than by a unanimous vote, thereby conceding a point on which the UNC had previously taken a firm position. Clark was also to consent to changes whereby nonrepatriates would remain in the custody of the NNRC for ninety days rather than the sixty days stipulated earlier. Clark found these new instructions particularly galling because he had formulated his own proposal, which, if implemented, would have taken a much harder line toward the Communists, including possibly releasing North Korean POWs and increasing military pressure against enemy lines.[59]

Clark also proposed that the UN negotiators at Panmunjom continue to insist on a unanimous vote on substantive matters before the NNRC, but for several reasons his recommendations were unacceptable to the administration. In the first place, the renewed talks had been dragging on for nearly a month without any resolution. The enemy had flatly rejected the UNC's counterproposal to its offer of May 7 but had not made any additional proposals of its own. Meanwhile, word came from India that among the greatest obstacles to a final peace settlement were the very points on which Clark wanted to remain firm—that is, the UNC's position on Korean nonrepatriates and its insistence on unanimity on substantive issues before the NNRC. The Indian government indicated that prospects for peace would be greater if the United States adhered more closely to its resolution of the previous December. Although India's views were always suspect, the American embassy in New Delhi believed that India had some understanding with China on its resolution. The embassy strongly suggested therefore—and the State Department agreed—that the UNC bring its proposals closer to the Indian proposal since in that way India would be better able to get Peking to accept an armistice agreement.[60]

A second reason why the administration changed its stand on the armistice talks was simply the ever-present pressure of its allies to reach a settlement of the war, even if that meant making concessions to the Communists. Indeed, in recent weeks that pressure had become unrelenting as a number of America's closest friends, including England and France, became more convinced than ever that the United States was becoming obsessed by its terror of world Communism and internal subversion and that President Eisenhower lacked the leadership either to control the saber rattling of his secretary of state or to put an end to the rantings and ravings of Senator McCarthy and his mad followers.

Having feared that Eisenhower would be dominated by the Republican right wing even before he assumed office, most

European political commentators found little reason to change their minds after he had been in the White House for several months. His order rescinding the Seventh Fleet's patrol of the Strait of Formosa with its threat of "unleashing" Chiang Kai-shek against the mainland particularly troubled Europeans, who were afraid it was the first step toward widening the war. Reaction in England to the President's announcement was typical of most other European nations. Seeking to gain political advantage from the announcement, the Bevanites stated that the British people were not prepared to sacrifice one British life in order to put Chiang back into China. But British uneasiness was not limited to one political group or party. So worried were members of Parliament that Secretary of State Dulles had to reassure them privately that the United States was not intending to change policy or to widen the war.[61]

Many European politicians and political commentators, however, distrusted the American secretary of state, whom they regarded as reckless and irresponsible. Soon after taking office, Dulles made his first European trip as secretary of state in order to push for ratification of the EDC. By this time the six countries that were to make up the military organization had all initialed an EDC treaty, but none of their parliaments had ratified the agreement, and popular opposition against it had continued to mount, particularly in France. Before leaving for Europe Dulles warned in a television speech that "if it appeared there were no chance of getting effective unity . . . then certainly it would be necessary to give a little rethinking to America's own foreign policy in relation to Western Europe." Once in Europe Dulles promoted the EDC with the zeal of a convert, telling American diplomats that ratification of an EDC treaty had to be completed within six months. Europeans objected both to the implied threat of an American withdrawal into isolationism should they not ratify a treaty and to the pressure tactics employed by Dulles in promoting the agreement, which they likened to an ultimatum.[62]

Matters between Washington and Europe did improve considerably following a major address on foreign policy, which President Eisenhower made to the American Society of Newspaper Editors. In his speech the President warned of the dangers of atomic warfare and spoke of the unacceptable costs of an arms race. Offering to devote "a substantial percentage of the savings achieved by disarmament to a fund for world aid and reconstruction" if the Soviets showed that they too were ready for peace, Eisenhower seemed to offer new hope for bridging the perilous gap between Washington and Moscow. Accordingly, his address was hailed throughout the continent with an enthusiasm unsurpassed for any American statement since George Marshall outlined his plan for European recovery in 1947.[63]

Within a month, however, the luster of Eisenhower's speech had worn thin, and the most eminent European statesman of all, Prime Minister Churchill, was calling for a Big Four Conference to settle world problems. Soon after Eisenhower made his remarks, Secretary Dulles returned to Europe, where he warned the members of NATO that Moscow's recent "peace campaign" was purely tactical and that the West must not drop its guard against the Communist menace. He also made the "liberation" of Eastern Europe a precondition for negotiations with Moscow. Europeans were taken aback by the secretary's uncompromising language, particularly when compared to Eisenhower's earlier statement. The London *Times* found Dulles's remarks "strangely hard to reconcile with the spirit of the President's speech," while *Le Monde* of Paris commented on the American system of the "Scotch douche" (cold showers after warmth) and added that the President's "conciliatory words and generosity of tone" had been followed by "a harangue in which intransigence competed with mock innocence."[64]

What worried many Europeans as much as the harshness of the secretary's comments was their conviction that the administration had been taken over by the Republican right wing and that Senator McCarthy as much as anyone else was dictating foreign policy. Europeans had long been perplexed by the phenomenon of McCarthyism, whose broad appeal they found hard to comprehend. But in the spring of 1953 they were concerned that the Wisconsin senator was powerful enough and the President weak enough to jeopardize the very structure of American diplomacy. Now chairman of the Senate's Permanent Subcommittee on Investigations, McCarthy fought the nomination of Charles Bohlen, a distinguished career diplomat and Soviet expert, as ambassador to Moscow, and he cowed the State Department into accepting his nomination of Scott McLeod, a close friend and ally, as its Personnel and Security Officer. He also launched an investigation into subversion in the "Voice of America" and sent his chief counsel, Roy M. Cohn, and a friend, David Schine, to Europe, where they upbraided American diplomats for being "soft on communism," and ordered the removal of "radical" books from United States Information Service libraries.[65]

Because the administration failed to stand up to McCarthy (except in the case of Bohlen's nomination, for which it fought hard and won), critics at home and abroad accused the White House of cowardice and even complicity in the latest round of conspiratorial mania that seemed to be sweeping the nation. But in Europe the major concern was that Eisenhower was hapless before this onslaught of hysterical anti-Communism. Commenting on the multiple leadership in Moscow of Georgi Malenkov, Lavrenti Beria, and V. M. Molotov, *Le Monde* thus asked, "Who reigns?" Then turning to the Washington triad of Eisenhower, Taft, and McCarthy, it also asked, "Who governs?" Similarly, *Franc Tireur*, which had always supported Eisenhower, said in a headline, "McCarthy Is Compromising Eisenhower's Future," and referred to the senator as a scarecrow with a bloody mailed fist.[66]

Precisely because many European leaders were concerned that Eisenhower was not in command of his own administration and that he was being dictated to by extremists within his own party, among whom they often listed Dulles, they concluded it was necessary to press even harder for an end to the Korean War. In England Prime Minister Churchill went a step further. Addressing Parliament, he berated the truce negotiators at Panmunjom for dillydallying, and he taunted Washington for its unwillingness to meet with the Soviets face to face. Expanding on this theme, he said that Stalin's death had apparently induced "a change of attitude and . . . of mind in the Soviet Union," and he called for a "conference on the highest levels . . . between the leading powers without delay." There should be no rigid agenda, he said, and the conference should be confined to the "smallest number of powers and persons possible." A few days later the leader of the Labor opposition, Clement Attlee, joined Churchill in a bipartisan effort to end the war and to hold a summit conference of world leaders. "[The] American government," Attlee remarked, "[is] not really master in [it]s own house. . . . One sometimes wonders who is more powerful, the President or Senator McCarthy."[67]

Reaction in the United States to Churchill's and, especially, to Attlee's remarks indicated that Anglo-American relations had reached a new low since the outbreak of the Korean War. McCarthy referred to the leader of the Labor Party as "Comrade Attlee" and added, "If [the British] are trying to blackmail us into accepting a Communist peace on the ground that if we do not they will withdraw, I say, 'Withdraw and be damned!' " California Senator William Knowland added that the United States was "now face to face with the problem that our chief ally has joined with certain other United Nations members in urging a Far Eastern Munich." But the outpouring against England was by no means limited to the Republican right wing. The Washington *Post,* a good friend of England, compared Attlee's speech to "Big Bill" Thompson's promise to Chicago voters that he would " 'punch King George in the snoot,' " while Democratic Senator Paul Douglas of Illinois stated that "the free world . . . should not move together in acquiescence to tyranny."[68]

It was not only England, however, which objected to the apparent inflexibility and uncompromising position of the United States. The State Department reported that it had received protests or criticisms from Canada, Australia, Belgium, New Zealand, and even Italy, among others. Ward Allen of the Bureau of European Affairs pointed out that many of these same countries were also concerned about America's failure to consult with them before making important decisions, and he recommended that the UNC be prepared to compromise with the Chinese and North Koreans at Panmunjom rather than have the talks broken off. Responding to this worldwide demand for compromise and peace in Korea, the administration decided to agree to terms on the problem of nonrepatriates along the lines of the earlier Indian resolution of December— that is, a settlement based on the transfer of all POWs to a Neutral Nations Repatriation Commission for a stipulated period of time (60, 90, or 120 days) followed either by the release of the remaining nonrepatriates as civilians or a decision as to their final disposition by the General Assembly.[69]

What most concerned the White House now was how South Korea would react to the prospects of an imminent armistice agreement, for President Rhee had continued to make clear his determination to accept nothing less than the expulsion of the Chinese Communists from the Korean peninsula and the military reunification of the country. On April 21 he even informed President Eisenhower that if Chinese troops were permitted to remain in Korea, he would withdraw his own forces from the UNC and fight on alone. Furthermore, he appeared to enjoy wide support among the Korean people, who massed in frequent anti-American demonstrations, and within the National Assembly, which adopted a resolution approving unifying Korea by invading the North.[70]

Worried that Rhee might try to sabotage an armistice agreement, the administration instructed General Clark and Ambassador Ellis Briggs in Pusan to confer with the South Korean president in order to warn him not to impede the peace process and to explain why the United States could not give him the security pact he so badly wanted. Meeting with Rhee on May 25 (the same day that the UN negotiators at Panmunjom presented their latest—and final—offer to the Communists), the two Americans tried to reassure Rhee that a bilateral defense pact was not necessary, that it would weaken the "greater sanctions" statement agreed to earlier (which together with an armistice agreement would better assure Korea's security), and that the United States was prepared to assist South Korea in developing and maintaining a twenty-division army and a marine brigade.[71]

At the same time, however, Clark and Briggs made clear to the South Korean leader that the United States would take a strong stand against any action affecting its policy in the Far East. They also told Rhee that American assistance after the war depended on his firm assurance that South Korea would cooperate with UN troops in Korea. Rhee's government had to refrain from agitating against an armistice. It also had to cooperate in implementing the agreement, and it had to keep its armed forces under the operational control of the UNC. If South Korea acted unilaterally, they said, Washington might be forced to take "all necessary measures" to safeguard the security of its forces.[72]

Rhee would have none of it. Appearing shocked by the UNC's armistice proposals and declaring them unacceptable to the ROK government, he informed Clark and Briggs that he would now have to consider making his own proposal, which would include an immediate cease-fire and the simultaneous withdrawal of all Chinese Communist and UN forces from Korea. He also suggested strongly that he would order the release of all North Korean nonrepatriates while turning the Chinese nonrepatriates over to the UNC. In a personal message to the South Korean president, President Eisenhower tried to reassure him that the United States would not abandon Korea, but Rhee remained unpersuaded.[73]

Rhee's persistent opposition to an armistice agreement and his increasingly bolder threats to pursue a unilateral course persuaded the UNC and administration officials to make plans for the worst possible contingency—a withdrawal of ROK forces from the UNC. The Eighth Army drew up Plan EVER-READY, which envisioned three different scenarios, the most extreme being a situation in which ROK forces and the Korean population became openly hostile to UN forces. Depending on the seriousness of the circumstances, the UNC would respond with an escalating series of measures up to and including the proclamation of martial law, the seizure of dissident military and civil leaders, and the establishment of military government. Both Secretary Dulles and Defense Secretary Charles E. Wilson disapproved of Plan EVERREADY as being too extreme. But they authorized Clark to take whatever measures were necessary "to insure the integrity of [his] forces," thereby giving him broad powers to act in case of a perceived emergency.[74]

At the same time that the administration considered drastic measures against the Rhee government, however, it also decided to meet one of Rhee's principal demands, a mutual security pact between the United States and South Korea. Although the White House had opposed such a pact on the grounds that it would weaken the "greater sanctions" statement and detract from the UN character of the Korean conflict, it changed its mind at the beginning of June. After receiving a communica-

tion from General Clark urging an agreement as a way of mollifying the South Koreans, Secretaries Dulles and Wilson recommended to President Eisenhower that the United States
conclude a pact along the lines of those with the Philippine
Islands and the Anzus nations (Australia and New Zealand); that
is, an agreement which provided for periodic consultations for
defensive purposes. But the offer would be contingent on the
willingness of the ROK government to accept an armistice
along the lines proposed by the UNC and to leave Korean forces
under UNC control. Eisenhower promptly approved this
recommendation, although he made it clear that he did not
want the proposal publicized for fear it might become em-
broiled in the peace talks.[75]

What the administration was doing at the end of May was
reconsidering its position with respect to the Korean War. To
be sure, its objective remained the unification of Korea by political rather than by military means, and it was searching for ways
to resolve the POW question, the last obstacle to peace if the
ROK government would agree to armistice terms. For this reason alone the administration had consented to a mutual pact
with South Korea. In order to end the war in Korea, however,
the President introduced another new element into the equation of peacemaking—the threat of atomic warfare if the Peking government did not agree quickly to an armistice.

Actually, the White House never gave the Chinese such an
explicit warning. But Eisenhower had been considering a nuclear option since at least February when General Clark had
requested permission to bomb the area around Kaesong. At the
end of March the President again raised the possibility of using
atomic weapons during a meeting of the National Security
Council. Although recognizing that America's allies would
strongly object to the use of such weapons since they would be
the battleground in an atomic war between the United States
and the Soviet Union, he and Secretary Dulles agreed that "the
tabu" which surrounded the use of atomic weapons would have
to be destroyed.[76]

In subsequent weeks the Joint Chiefs of Staff sought Eisenhower's permission to employ atomic weapons. Having determined by the end of May that military action against the enemy
should be intensified and extended to include air and naval

operations against China and Manchuria if the enemy did not agree to the UNC's latest proposal, they agreed that this would have to include "extensive strategical and tactical use of atomic bombs." The President did not give the JCS the authority they wanted, but he agreed that it might be necessary to expand the war outside Korea if the Chinese and North Koreans rejected the UN's latest offer. In that case, he recognized the atomic bomb might need to be used, although he was deeply concerned that the Soviet Union might retaliate by bombing Japan. About the same time, Secretary Dulles told Prime Minister Jawaharlal Nehru during a visit to New Delhi that in the absence of armistice agreement, the war in Korea would be broadened, a message which, Dulles assumed, Nehru would pass on to Peking.[77]

In other words, Eisenhower did not have to threaten the Chinese directly with nuclear war. Almost certainly they knew that his patience was wearing thin, that he was determined to end the Korean War quickly, that he was under pressure to widen the war, that he did not feel constrained by the policies of the previous administration with respect to any military option, including the use of nuclear weapons, and that the United States had nuclear weapons on Okinawa. The President did not have to deliver an ultimatum to Peking—peace or atomic bombs—because they understood he was thinking along these lines anyway.[78]

In response to—or in spite of—the threat of nuclear war, the Chinese and North Koreans broke the deadlock in the peace talks on June 4 by accepting the UNC's proposals of May 25 with only a few minor changes. Indeed, in some respects—for example, the formula for releasing nonrepatriates to civilian status—the Communist proposals far exceeded the administration's most optimistic expectations. According to the Chinese and North Korean plan, thirty days after the post-armistice political conference, the NNRC would release from prisoner of war status any POWs who had not been repatriated and for whom no other disposition was agreed to by the political conference. For a further thirty days the commission and the Indian Red Cross would offer assistance to those who elected to go to neutral nations, after which the commission would be disbanded.[79]

Barring unforeseen developments, then, the POW issue had

been finally resolved, and the way seemed open for concluding the armistice negotiations that had dragged on for more than two years. But the Eisenhower administration had still to contend with its South Korean ally, which had already indicated its determination to undermine the delicate peace process.

NOTES

1. Stephen E. Ambrose, *Eisenhower: Soldier, General of the Army, President-Elect, 1890–1952* (New York, 1983), 494–95.
2. Elmo Richardson, *The Presidency of Dwight D. Eisenhower* (Lawrence, Kans., 1979), 14–15; Herbert S. Parmet, *Eisenhower and the American Crusades* (New York, 1972), 46–47 and 68–69.
3. *New York Times*, June 6, 1952; *Time*, 59, June 16, 1952.
4. *Commonweal*, 56 (June 27, 1952), 286.
5. Ambrose, *Eisenhower: Soldier, General of the Army, President-Elect*, 534.
6. *New Republic*, 127 (July 7, 1952), 5; *Life*, 33 (July 21, 1952), 28; *New Yorker*, 28 (July 26, 1952), 44; *Atlantic Monthly*, 190 (October 1952), 8.
7. *New Yorker*, 28 (June 21, 1952), 98.
8. Thomas C. Reeves, *The Life and Times of Joe McCarthy: A Biography* (New York, 1982), 422–23; *Time*, 60 (July 7, 1952), 14.
9. Ronald J. Caridi, *The Korean War and American Politics: The Republican Party as a Case Study* (Philadelphia, 1968), 217–20.
10. *Time*, 60 (September 1, 1952), 9; *Commonweal*, 56 (July 25, 1952), 379; *ibid.* (September 9, 1952), 572–73.
11. Caridi, *The Korean War and American Politics*, 217–23.
12. Ambrose, *Eisenhower: Soldier, General of the Army, President-Elect*, 533.
13. *Time*, 60 (September 15, 1952), 22–23; *ibid.* (September 22, 1952), 24; *New Republic*, 127 (October 20, 1952), 3; *Commonweal*, 57 (October 31, 1952), 85–90.
14. *New Republic*, 127 (September 22, 1952), 8–9; *New Yorker*, 28 (October 25, 1952), 119; *ibid.* (November 1, 1952), 113–14; *Nation*, 175 (November 1, 1952), 402–404.
15. *Time*, 60 (September 15, 1952), 21.
16. Robert A. Divine, *Foreign Policy and U. S. Presidential Elections, 1952–1960* (New York, 1974), 75–76; Caridi, *The Korean War and American Politics*, 233–36.

17. Ambrose, *Eisenhower: Soldier, General of the Army, President-Elect,* 539; *New Republic,* 127 (November 3, 1952), 3.
18. *New York Times,* October 31, 1952; *Nation,* 175 (November 8, 1952), 417.
19. Caridi, *The Korean War and American Politics,* 212–13.
20. *Ibid.,* 210–11; *Time,* 60 (November 3, 1952), 19.
21. Caridi, *The Korean War and American Politics,* 182–208. See also Joseph B. Phillips to the Secretary, September 15, 1952, and attachments, Box 4283, Records of the Department of State, RG 59, 795.00/9-1552; *Time,* 60 (November 10, 1952), 21; *Nation,* 175 (November 11, 1952), 315–16.
22. *Time,* 60 (November 3, 1952), 19.
23. Caridi, *The Korean War and American Politics,* 235–45.
24. *Nation,* 175, (November 15, 1952), 437; *New Republic,* 127 (November 17, 1952), 7.
25. Dean Acheson, *Present at the Creation: My Years in the State Department* (New York, 1969), 700–702.
26. *New Yorker,* 28 (November 29, 1952), 164.
27. *Ibid.* (November 15, 1952), 175.
28. Memorandum of Conversation, October 29 and November 11 and 13, 1952, Box 67, Acheson Papers. Meeting with the President, November 5, 1952, *ibid.;* Memorandum for the President, November 8, 1952, Box 4284, Records of the Department of State, RG 59, 795.00/11-852; *FR,* 1952–1954, XV, 662–63.
29. *FR,* 1952–1954, XV, 662–86.
30. Barton J. Bernstein, "The Struggle Over the Korean Armistice: Prisoners of Repatriation?" in Bruce Cumings (ed.), *Child of Conflict: The Korean-American Relationship, 1943–1953* (Seattle, Wash., 1983), 304–305; *New Republic,* 127 (December 8, 1952), 6.
31. *New Yorker,* 28 (December 6, 1952), 174–76.
32. *Yearbook of the United Nations: 1952* (New York, 1953), 195–202.
33. Acheson, *Present at the Creation,* 700–705.
34. Stephen E. Ambrose, *Eisenhower: The President* (New York, 1984), 30–31; Mark W. Clark, *From the Danube to the Yalu* (New York, 1954), 233.
35. Ambrose, *Eisenhower: The President,* 31; Dwight D. Eisenhower, *Mandate for Change* (New York, 1963), 95.
36. "Memorandum on Ending the War," December 14, 1952, Box 8, Subject Series, Papers of John Foster Dulles, Dwight D. Eisenhower Library (Abilene, Kans.); William Manchester, *American Caesar: Douglas MacArthur, 1880–1964* (New York, 1978), 688–89; Ambrose, *Eisenhower: The President,* 31–32 and 34–35.
37. Ambrose, *Eisenhower: The President,* 35.

38. The President's News Conference of December 11, 1952, *Public Papers of the Presidents of the United States: Harry S. Truman,* 1952–1953 (Washington, D. C., 1966), 1075.
39. *Time,* 60 (December 22, 1952), 20; Joseph C. Goulden, *Korea: The Untold Story of the War* (New York, 1982), 598–99.
40. *Time,* 60 (October 20, 1952), 36; David Rees, *Korea: The Limited War* (New York, 1964), 385. Walter G. Hermes, *Truce Tent and Fighting Front* (Washington, D. C., 1966), 311–18; Rees, *Korea: The Limited War,* 385–86.
41. Edgar O'Ballance, *Korea: 1950–1953* (London, 1969), 127–29; Hermes, *Truce Tent and Fighting Front,* 366–39.
42. *Life,* 32 (May 26, 1952), 146.
43. Ambrose, *Eisenhower: Soldier, General of the Army, President-Elect,* 547–48; Ambrose, *Eisenhower: The President,* 51–52.
44. *Ibid;* Discussion at the 131st Meeting of the National Security Council, Box 4, Ann Whitman Files, National Security Council Series, Dwight D. Eisenhower Papers, Dwight D. Eisenhower Library (Abilene, Kans.).
45. Ambrose, *Eisenhower: The President,* 47; David Rees, *Korea: The Limited War* (New York, 1964), 405.
46. Hermes, *Truce Tent and Fighting Front,* 411–14.
47. Robert B. Simmons, *The Strained Alliance: Peking, Pyongyang, Moscow and the Politics of the Korean Civil War* (New York, 1975), 227–28; Adam B. Ulam, *The Rivals: America and Russia Since World War II* (New York, 1971), 194–200.
48. Robert A. Scalapino and Chong-Sik Lee, *Communism in Korea,* I (2 vols., Berkeley, Calif., 1972), 422; Rees, *Korea: The Limited War,* 461; Simmons, *The Strained Alliance,* 213.
49. Memorandum for the President, April 1, 1953, Box 9, Subject Series, Dulles Papers; Memorandum to the Secretary of State from Eisenhower, April 2, 1953, *ibid.*
50. Discussion at the 139th Meeting of the National Security Council, April 8, 1953, Box 1, Ann Whitman Files, National Security Council Series, Eisenhower Papers.
51. *FR,* 1952–1954, XV, 136–38; Mark W. Clark, *From the Danube to the Yalu,* 245–47.
52. Memorandum of Conversation, April 1, 1953, Box 4285, Records of the Department of State, RG 59, 795.00/4-153; Hermes, *Truce Tent and Fighting Front,* 412–14.
53. Resumption of Korean Truce Negotiations, April 14, 1953, Box 4285, Records of the Department of State, RG 59, 795.00/4-1453; U. Alexis Johnson to the Secretary, April 8, 1953, *ibid.,* 795.00/4-853.

54. Eisenhower to Rhee, April 23, 1953, Box 1, Ann Whitman Files, International Series, Eisenhower Papers; Memorandum from Young to Robertson, Records of the Department of State, RG 59, 795.00/4-2453; Briggs to Secretary of State, April 23, 1953, *ibid.,* 795.00/4-2353.

55. "UNC in Current Korean Negotiations," April 28, 1953, Box 4285, Records of the Department of State, RG 59, 795.00/4-2853: "Personal for Murphy," from Dulles, May 4, 1953, *ibid.,* 795.00/5-453; Clark, *From the Danube to the Yalu,* 259.

56. Memorandum for the Files, May 11, 1953, Box 2885, Records of the Department of State, RG 59, 611.95A24/15-1153; Memorandum of Conversation, May 8, 1953, *ibid.,* 795.00/5-853.

57. "Korean Truce Negotiations," May 11, 1953, *ibid.,* 795.00/5-1183.

58. Clark, *From the Danube to the Yalu,* 264; Briggs to Secretary of State, May 14, 1953, Box 4286, Records of the Department of State, RG 59, 795.00/5-1453.

59. Clark, *From the Danube to the Yalu,* 264–68; Clark to JCS, May 16, 1953, and JCS to Clark, May 23, 1953, Records of the United States Joint Chiefs of Staff, RG 218, 383.21 (Korea 3-19-45) (Section 129).

60. Allen to Secretary of State, May 15, 1953, Box 4285, Records of the Department of State, RG 59, 795.00/5-1553.

61. *New Yorker,* 28 (February 14, 1953), 82; *Commonweal,* 57 (February 20, 1953), 487.

62. *Commonweal,* 57 (February 20, 1953), 487; Ambrose, *Eisenhower: The President,* 49; *Nation,* 176 (February 14, 1953), 147–48; *New Republic,* 128 (February 9, 1953), 8–9; *ibid.* (March 3, 1953), 9.

63. *Nation,* 176 (April 25, 1953), 337; *New Republic,* 128 (April 27, 1953), 5–7; *New Yorker,* 29 (May 2, 1953), 107–108.

64. *Nation,* 176 (April 25, 1953), 337; *ibid.* (May 9, 1953), 389: *New Republic,* 128 (May 11, 1953), 9.

65. *New Yorker,* 29 (March 7, 1953), 89; *ibid.* (April 4, 1953), 109–10; *ibid.* (May 16, 1953), 97–98; *Nation,* 176 (April 11, 1953), 202–203; Ambrose, *Eisenhower: The President,* 58–62.

66. *New Yorker,* 29 (May 30, 1953), 86–87.

67. *Time,* 61 (May 18, 1953), 32; *ibid.* (May 25, 1953), 28; *New Republic,* 128 (May 25, 1953), 5–6.

68. *Time,* 61 (May 25, 1953), 19.

69. Allen to Mr. Bonbright and Mr. Merchant, May 18, 1953, Box 4286, Records of the Department of State, RG 59, 795.00/5-1553.

70. Memorandum for the President, May 19, 1953, *ibid.,* 795.00/5-19.

71. Smith to Amembassy Pusan and Amembassy Tokyo, May 22, 1953, *ibid.,* 795.00/5-1853. See also John Kotch, "The Origins of the American Security Commitment to Korea," in Bruce Cumings

(ed.), *Child of Conflict: The Korean-American Relationship, 1943–1953* (Seattle, Wash., 1983), 243–44.

72. *Ibid.*

73. To Secretary of State from Seoul, May 25, 1953, and Smith to Amembassy Pusan and Amembassy Tokyo, May 27, 1953, Box 4285, Records of the Department of State, RG 59, 795.00/5-2553 and 795.00/5-2753.

74. Outline of Plan EVERREADY, May 4, 1953, Records of the United States Joint Chiefs of Staff, RG 218, 383.21 Korea (3-19-45) (Section 130); Collins to Clark, May 30, 1953, *ibid.*

75. James F. Schnabel and Robert J. Watson, *The History of the Joint Chiefs of Staff,* III, *The Korean War* (unpublished manuscript, National Archives, 1978), 993–94; Telephone Conversation with Senators Wiley and George, June 4, 1953, Box 9, Subject Series, Dulles Papers.

76. *FR,* 1952–1954, XV, 826–27; Eisenhower, *Mandate for Change,* 179–81.

77. *FR,* 1952–1954, XV, 1059–69; Ambrose, *Eisenhower: The President,* 97–98.

78. Ambrose, *Eisenhower: The President,* 98.

79. Memorandum for the President, June 4, 1953, Box 4286, Records of the Department of State, RG 59, 795.00/6-453; Telephone Conversation with the President, June 4, 1953, Box 10, Telephone Calls Series, Dulles Papers.

CHAPTER 10

Peace Without Victory

Having broken the stalemate in the peace negotiations, the administration's major concern now shifted to persuading the ROK government to accept the armistice terms that had been agreed to by the Communists and the UNC and not to attempt to disrupt the peace process. From the time agreement was reached on an armistice, the UNC was concerned that at some point South Korea would attempt to engineer the unsanctioned release of North Korean nonrepatriates. In Tokyo Robert Murphy persuaded General Clark that American personnel supervising the POW camps should be augmented by a mixture of other UN personnel, so that the United States would not be held solely responsible if ROK forces tried to free POWs. In Washington President Eisenhower wrote a letter to President Rhee on June 6, which he released to the press, urging the South Korean leader to accept the armistice terms. If South Korea agreed to the armistice, Eisenhower said, he could reassure Rhee that his administration would not renounce its efforts to bring about the peaceful reunification of Korea. The White House would also go forward with a mutual defense pact and continue to supply economic aid to Korea. But the time had now come to decide whether to seek Korean reunification through military or political means. "We would not be justified in prolonging the war," the President warned Rhee, "with all the misery that it involves in the hope of achieving by force, the unification of Korea."[1]

Still Rhee remained recalcitrant. Anti-cease-fire demonstrations organized by the government grew in intensity, as crowds gathered outside the American embassy at Pusan to sing patriotic songs and to chant anti-American slogans. In Seoul demonstrators, mainly students and members of the government-sponsored Youth Corps, paraded through the main streets, particularly in the vicinity of UN installations and the press compound. The government also ordered the immediate return of all ROK officers from the United States, took what it termed "pseudo-extraordinary security measures," and recalled the South Korean delegate from the armistice negotiations at Panmunjom. Finally, on June 16 President Rhee responded to Eisenhower's letter of June 6 with a harsh and uncompromising message. Although Eisenhower's offers of economic and military assistance were highly appreciated by the Korean people, Rhee told the President, they could not induce Korea to agree to an armistice, for "to accept such an armistice is to accept a death warrant." Then Rhee added, "We cannot avoid seeing the cold fact that the counsels of appeasers have prevailed in altering the armistice position of the United States."[2]

Despite such indications that the South Korean leader might try to undermine the armistice agreement, White House officials were shocked, nevertheless, when on June 18, the day after Rhee sent his message to Eisenhower, his government orchestrated the mass breakout of more than 25,000 North Korean POWs from four major prison camps. Korean guards simply stood aside as the prisoners broke out of the compounds. Outside they were greeted by other Koreans who gave them food, shelter, and clothes. Rhee openly acknowledged his complicity in the breakout, stating that the reason why he acted without consulting the UNC was "obvious." Even so, Rhee had acted in defiance of the UNC, and his action gave the Communists a major propaganda issue and a good excuse for breaking off the armistice talks if they were so inclined.[3]

Rhee's freeing of North Korean POWs also aggravated relations between Washington and its European allies, already sensitive to American dictation in foreign policy and its heavy-handed policy toward the Soviet Union, and increasingly alarmed by the menace of McCarthyism across the Atlantic. Indeed, by the time of the June 4 breakthrough in the armistice negotiations, Europe had become haunted by the specter of the United States in the grip of an hysterical witch-hunt and of a President cowering before the power of Senator McCarthy and his followers. As the *Atlantic Monthly* commented, "[i]t is progressively more difficult to persuade Europeans that McCarthy does not speak for the United States."[4]

Many of the same European leaders who were obsessed by the power of right-wing extremism in the United States found it hard to believe that American officials did not conspire in the release of the North Korean prisoners of war or that they were so naïve as not to know of Rhee's plot to free them ahead of time. From England Ambassador Winthrop Aldrich thus wrote that there was "widespread concern" over the freeing of the POWs, ranging from fear that the truce negotiations would be upset to insinuations that the UNC had been either "negligent, acquiescent or even directly involved" in their release. About the same time, Britain's ambassador to the United States, Sir Roger Makins, told Secretary Dulles that developments in Korea had raised a question as to the language of the "greater sanctions" statement, which might no longer be appropriate in view of the fact that South Korea and not the Communists might break an armistice agreement.[5]

In the United States the National Security Council met in an emergency session and, with the President presiding, agreed that the administration should repudiate the release of the POWs as violating South Korea's agreement with the UNC. The NSC also decided to tell Rhee that unless he agreed to cooperate with the UNC, including retaining his troops under UNC command, the United States would "have to effect other arrangements." Although the NSC never stated what these "other arrangements" might be, it later became clear that the UNC would proceed with an armistice agreement without the South Koreans and that South Korea would be cut off from American aid after the agreement was signed. One thing that the NSC never intended was that the United States would withdraw from Korea, for as Eisenhower later remarked, "[s]uch a result would be surrender to the Chinese, handing them on a silver platter everything for which they had been fighting for three years."[6]

Following the NSC meeting, President Eisenhower sent Rhee the strongest note he had written so far to the South Korean leader. Using the same language as at the NSC meeting, Eisenhower told Rhee that unless he was "prepared immediately and unequivocally to accept the authority of the UN command to conduct the present hostilities and to bring them to a close, it will be necessary to effect another arrangement." Secretary Dulles told Korean Prime Minister Paik Tu Chin, who was visiting the United States, much the same thing.[7] Dulles also sent Assistant Secretary of State Walter Robertson on a special mission to Korea in order to make clear to the South Koreans America's determination to conclude a peace with or without the ROK government. Robertson carried with him an unusually harsh letter from the secretary of state to President Rhee in which Dulles denied that the United States had ever sought the reunification of Korea by military means. The secretary also charged Rhee with breaking the principle of allied unity at a time when the enemy offered an armistice restoring South Korean authority over a territory somewhat larger than before the North Korean invasion. "It is you who invoked the principle of unity and asked us to pay the price," Dulles scolded Rhee. "We have paid it in blood and suffering. Can you now honorably reject the principle which, in your hour of need, you asked us to defend at so high a price?"[8]

As Robertson began his mission, the situation in Korea was volatile. On the positive side, the Chinese and North Korean negotiators did not use the release of the POWs as an excuse for breaking off the talks as they might have, although the UN negotiator, General Harrison, recessed the talks on June 20 until the UNC could gain assurances from Rhee that he would not disrupt the armistice. To be sure, the Communists did accuse the United States of complicity in the release of the POWs. The Chinese also sought assurances that former prisoners were not being impressed into the ROK army and that all North Korean POWs had been released. But they seemed satisfied when Washington gave them the assurances they wanted and denied participation in the release of the POWs. From the evidence that was available at the end of June, it appeared that the Chinese were willing to accept Washington's explanations even if they doubted their truthfulness.[9]

On the negative side, however, President Rhee proved unpredictable. On the day that Robertson arrived in Seoul, the South Korean president scorned acceptance of the proposed armistice agreement in an impassioned speech to a gigantic rally of about half a million persons. In private conversations with Robertson, Rhee also insisted that before he would agree to an armistice, all remaining non-Korean repatriates had to be turned over to the Neutral Nations Repatriation Commission at the demilitarized zone (DMZ) and that the postwar political conference agreed to at Panmunjom had to be limited to ninety days. Furthermore, the United States had to reaffirm its pledge to provide economic aid to South Korea and to help build up its army to twenty divisions. Finally, Washington had to conclude a mutual defense pact with his country.[10]

President Eisenhower responded quickly to these terms. He agreed in principle to all of them, although he pointed out that he could not "guarantee" (the term mistakenly used in transmitting Rhee's conditions to Washington) passage of a mutual defense pact since that was up to the Senate, and he made clear that the time limit for the political conference was up to the conferees. But he assured Rhee that if after ninety days no progress was being made at the meeting and the Communists were using the gathering for propaganda purposes, the United States would consider joining South Korea in boycotting it.[11]

Although Robertson was greatly encouraged by the news he received from Washington and was convinced that Rhee would accept a cease-fire if he could do so without losing face, more trouble lay ahead. On June 27 the South Korean leader stated that President Eisenhower had agreed to all his conditions for an armistice and asked that they be put into writing. But that very same evening he injected new conditions for an armistice agreement. He wanted a larger army than twenty divisions, and, even more unacceptable to Washington, he wanted the United States to agree that it would join South Korea in resuming military operations if the political conference failed to bring about the reunification of Korea within ninety days after the signing of an armistice.[12]

Robertson immediately rejected these new demands. Instead, the administration attempted, through thinly veiled threats and carefully planned leaks, to leave the impression in Korea that the United States would withdraw from that country if Rhee sabotaged the armistice. Robertson made clear to Rhee that his government had received Washington's final and best offer. Support for the ROK military buildup, the program of economic aid, the "greater sanction" statement, a mutual defense treaty, and the United States' pledge to "work shoulder to shoulder" with South Korea in the political conference after the war would be lost if Korea veered off on an independent and unilateral course of action. The White House also had congressional leaders and other public officials who were known to be sympathetic to the ROK cause write the South Korean president urging him to accept an armistice agreement. But Rhee remained defiant, insisting as he had before that the United States must agree to renew hostilities against the Communists if the political conference failed to bring about the unification of Korea within ninety days after the armistice.[13]

In pressing the Rhee government to agree to armistice terms, the administration remained under pressure of its own to conclude a truce without South Korea, most notably from the British and a growing block of congressional leaders. London told Washington that it was becoming increasingly difficult to remain silent while the United States attempted to deal with Rhee. At the same time, reports from Capitol Hill indicated a growing sense of frustration at Rhee's efforts to undermine a truce agreement. Even many Old Guard Republicans sympathetic to Rhee, who a month earlier had maintained that an armistice would be a blatant case of appeasement that would strip the United States of its honor and moral authority, now either remained silent or came out in support of a cease-fire. The demand in the United States for ending the war and the reaction against Rhee's unauthorized release of enemy POWs had simply become that great.[14]

At Eisenhower's request, Secretary Dulles conferred with Senate leaders of both parties. They told the secretary that they could still get a defense agreement approved provided there was no further loss of confidence in the ROK government's willingness to cooperate with the United States in the armistice and in the postwar political conference. In fact, by now Dulles was himself so frustrated by Rhee that he advised Undersecretary Robertson to return to the United States. "If, as seems probable, you can be of no further assistance," he instructed his special envoy, "you may terminate your mission at your convenience."[15]

Before leaving Korea, however, Robertson met one last time

with the South Korean leader to report on Dulles's conversations with the Senate leaders and to warn him again that arrangements agreed to by the United States were contingent upon the conduct of the South Korean government. Increasingly apprehensive now that the Senate might not ratify a defense pact, Rhee capitulated. The next day he informed Robertson that although his government would not sign an armistice agreement, neither would it obstruct its implementation. Two days later he repeated his promise in a personal letter to President Eisenhower. [16]

So the last major hurdle to an armistice agreement had been overcome—or so it seemed. Because of Rhee's persistence and obstinancy, South Korea had obtained significant concessions from the United States. Besides the promise of a mutual defense pact, there was the promise of long-term economic aid, including an initial installment of $200 million, and an implicit agreement that the United States and South Korea would withdraw from the political conference after ninety days if nothing substantial was achieved. In addition, the United States promised military assistance to help expand South Korea's army, and it agreed also to hold high-level talks with the South Korean government on joint objectives before the political conference was held. But Rhee had also made major concessions. Most important, he had abandoned his insistence on the withdrawal of Chinese troops from Korea before an armistice, and he had effectively given up his hope for the reunification of Korea, at least as an immediate outcome of the war.[17]

On July 10 the armistice talks reconvened. The most immediate question insofar as the Communists were concerned was whether the United States could guarantee South Korea's conduct in the post-armistice period. The UNC negotiators told the Chinese and North Koreans that the UNC would withdraw all military aid and support if ROK forces violated the armistice agreement. But the Communists took their own measure to assure the ROK's good conduct by launching a final military offensive against ROK forces along the main lines of resistance (MLR).[18]

Since early in the year the tempo of the war had increased significantly as the likelihood of reaching an armistice agreement improved. In fact, a direct relationship existed between stepped-up military activity by the Communists and the prospects of peace. The closer peace appeared, the more the enemy intensified its military effort. If the Chinese and North Koreans could correlate an armistice with a successful military offensive, they could argue that they had won a military victory. Such a claim would have potentially enormous propaganda value, particularly among Asians. Furthermore, the winter lull in the fighting had given the Communists time to rearm and regroup for an escalation of the war, and victory in the battlefield would improve their bargaining power at Panmunjom. Finally, as peace grew nearer, it behooved the Chinese and North Koreans to "bloody" the ROK army in order to force the Rhee government to accept armistice terms and to make it clear just how costly an independent move north would be.[19]

In March and April there had been a flurry of activity in the Old Baldy-Porkchop area, a complex of hills about twelve miles west of Chorwon on the western front. On March 23 the Chinese launched a coordinated strike against both Old Baldy and Porkchop Hill. An ugly, barren mass with a flattened top, which jutted out awkwardly in front of the Eighth Army, Old Baldy was attacked after a massive Chinese artillery and mortar barrage destroyed most of the bunkers that had already been weakened by heavy spring rains. Manned by units of the U. S. Seventh Division and a Colombian battalion, the hill was then overrun by a reinforced Chinese regiment of about 3500 men, advancing in waves through a curtain of their own fire. Despite repeated counterattacks, including the use of tanks and artillery, and air strikes from Air Force, Navy, and Marine fighters and bombers, the enemy held their positions tenaciously. Finally General Maxwell B. Taylor, who had replaced Van Fleet in February as commander of the Eighth Army, ordered that no more attacks be carried out, having decided that Old Baldy was not essential to the defense of the sector.[20]

But the heaviest fighting of the spring and, indeed, one of the heaviest battles of the entire war, began the next month on Porkchop Hill. Although attacked simultaneously with Old Baldy in March, Porkchop was still in UN hands when, on April 16, the Communists struck again. Flanked by the Chinese as a result of the loss of Old Baldy, Porkchop probably should have been abandoned along with Old Baldy, for according to the

November 1951 agreement on an armistice line, it would almost certainly be surrendered on the conclusion of a cease-fire. But as both sides understood, political prestige and a test of wills was at issue over Porkchop, not military logic. Besides, the hill did overlook an important part of the MLR northeast of Old Baldy and near White Horse Hill. As a result, both the Communists and the UNC attached great importance to holding Porkchop. Although American forces managed to hold on to the hill, in the three-day seesaw battle that took place, they engaged the enemy in hand-to-hand combat. At the same time, Eighth Army artillery set a new record for such a narrow front by firing 77,000 rounds in a single day, while each side inflicted heavy casualties on the other.[21]

Still seeking to gain a tactical advantage on the battlefield and to improve their bargaining power at Panmunjom, the Chinese and North Koreans intensified the fighting once more toward the middle of May. By the end of the month, as negotiations entered their final phase, the war had escalated considerably. Directing their attacks mainly against ROK forces, the enemy was probably attempting to remind the South Koreans of their ability to crush the ROK army should it attempt to move north again. This strategy continued well into June, when the sudden release of Korean nonrepatriates reintroduced the element of uncertainty into the armistice talks and activity on the ground slackened significantly.[22]

On July 6, however, the Chinese launched against Porkchop Hill a massive attack that was even heavier than the battle in April. Determined to take the hill, the Chinese simply overpowered the badly outnumbered American defenders. As the fighting continued into the second and third days and as casualties on both sides mounted, the stakes became higher, and each side committed more and more forces to the battle. But inclement weather prevented the UNC from launching air strikes against the enemy, and by June 11 General Taylor decided that the Chinese determination to hold the hill, regardless of the cost in casualties, outweighed any tactical advantage Porkchop might have. Reluctantly, therefore, he ordered the withdrawal of the remaining American forces from the hill.[23]

By this time peace talks had already resumed at Panmunjom, and with the approach of a final cease-fire agreement, the

Communists launched their largest offensive since the spring of 1951, once more directing the main effort against the ROK army. In the fighting that followed, ROK forces suffered enormous casualties. ROK lines along the central front were pierced. The crack ROK Capitol Division simply collapsed, and three other South Korean divisions sustained enormous losses. So intense was the enemy attack and so great were Korean losses that Generals Clark and Taylor decided to fly reinforcements from Japan to bolster the front. In all, the Chinese drove ROK forces back as much as six miles before the offensive was halted by combined American and South Korean forces. Some of the ground lost to the Communists was recovered, but before the attack ended, UNC forces had suffered more than 14,000 casualties, most of them South Korean. In General Clark's view, the main reason for the Communist offensive "was to give the ROKs a 'bloody nose' and [to] show them and the world that 'puk chin'—'go north'—was easier said than done." If this was in fact their purpose, they had succeeded well.[24]

By July 19 the Communist offensive was over. Lines were stabilized, and the enemy, having accomplished its objective and suffering large casualties of its own, was prepared to sign a final agreement. There still remained a number of details to be worked out, such as a revision of the final demarcation line, the delivery of the nonrepatriates to the DMZ, and the signing ceremony. But for the most part, these were settled without too much difficulty. Determination of the demarcation line, for example, proceeded with relatively little rancor, although both sides tried to adjust the line that had been worked out earlier in their favor as a result of the recent fighting. In the end only minor changes were made.[25]

What difficulty remained was largely with the Rhee government, which for a final few days imperiled the armistice process. On July 20 Peking radio broadcast a statement by North Korean Lieutenant General Nam Il, senior delegate to the Communist truce team, which Nam had delivered at Panmunjom the previous day. In his statement Nam referred to a number of promises that General Harrison had made to the Chinese and North Koreans over the period between July 11 and 16. These had included assurances that the United States would not support the ROK army in cases where it violated the armistice agreement, that the South Korean government would abide by the terms of the armistice indefinitely and not just for the ninety-day period of the political conference, and that any personnel who were authorized to enter South Korea in conformity with the armistice agreement would be protected.[26]

Both publicly and privately the Rhee government rejected the promises that Harrison had made. What the government still wanted was the resumption of hostilities in case the political conference failed to bring about Korean unification, American military and "moral" assistance if it resumed hostilities, and American approval of the Korean text of a draft mutual-defense treaty containing an automatic military clause in the event of an attack on Korea by another power (i.e., North Korea or Communist China). In addition, President Rhee objected strongly to the implication in one of Harrison's promises that Indian troops would be allowed on South Korean soil. Foreign Minister Pyun Tai Yung even told representatives of the American press that his government was "reconsidering her position" as a result of Harrison's statements at Panmunjom. In San Francisco Dr. Yu Chan Yang, South Korea's ambassador to the United States, said that his government would "attack" if Korean unification was not achieved within ninety days after the start of the political conference. And from Korea President Rhee remarked that the guarantees offered to him by Assistant Secretary of State Robertson during his mission to Korea had been "vitiated" by the pledges General Harrison had made to the Communists at Panmunjom.[27]

In Washington the administration responded once more to these threatening remarks with a combination of the carrot and stick. On one hand, it argued that Harrison was speaking only on behalf of the UNC and as the military commander responsible for the signing of the armistice. Neither he nor the command could commit the United States to any particular course of action, the White House said. On the other hand, Secretary Dulles and others within the administration made it clear to the South Koreans that the United States could not promise to resume hostilities automatically if the political conference broke up or in any way bind Congress to issue a declaration of war. Nor could it promise material aid to South Korea if its forces sought to unify Korea by military means. Lastly, the administration rejected the ROK government's request for a mutual defense pact with an automatic military clause in it, offering instead a standard clause that in the event of a future attack on South Korea, the United States would consult on the best means of restoring peace and would make its decision in accordance with its own constitutional procedures.[28]

In the end South Korea had little choice but to agree once more that it would do nothing to undermine the armistice terms even though it would not be a party to the truce. It was simply too dependent on American economic and military aid and too vulnerable to military attack from the North to follow its own course. For a second time, therefore, Rhee told the United States that his government would not obstruct the peace process. But his recalcitrance was rewarded again by renewed promises of support from the United States, including a defense pact, a promise of an immediate $200 million in economic assistance, and a pledge from Secretary of State Dulles that he would meet with Rhee shortly after the armistice was signed to discuss mutual problems and prepare a common negotiating position for the post-armistice political conference.[29]

In fact, in a telegram to Rhee approved by Eisenhower, Dulles told the South Korean leader, "[i]f in violation of the armistice the Republic of Korea is subjected to unprovoked attack you may of course count upon our immediate and automatic military reaction. Such an attack would not only be an attack upon the Republic of Korea but an attack upon the United Nations Command and U. S. forces within that Command." In other words, while South Korea did not get the automatic military clause that it wanted, it obtained something very closely approximating it. Indeed, as the secretary of state told Rhee, '[n]ever in all its history has the U. S. offered to any other country as much as is offered to you."[30]

Finally, July 27 was set as the date for the signing of the armistice at Panmunjom. Now General Clark threatened to delay the signing ceremony until the Chinese and North Koreans removed from the building where the signing was to take place copies of Picasso's "Dove," which had become the Communists' symbol of peace. The Communists agreed to paint over the copies. There was also a last-minute snag over the signing ceremony itself. The UNC wanted the commanders to sign the agreement at Panmunjom along with the chief negotiators at the talks. The Communists said they would come to Panmunjom only if the UNC agreed that no South Korean would attend the ceremony in any capacity and that no newsman from Formosa would be admitted into the DMZ on armistice day. The UNC rejected this demand, with the result that in the end the chief negotiators signed the agreement at Panmunjom, General Harrison for the UNC and Nam Il for the Communists, while the commanders in chief countersigned at their respective headquarters. Apropos of the entire history of the negotiations, first at Kaesong and then at Panmunjom, the signing ceremony was conducted in complete silence. Neither side spoke to the other as they left the building in which they had agreed finally to end the war.[31]

The armistice had been signed and the war ended. But what followed was not a sense of victory or euphoria on the part of most Americans, merely gratification that an unpopular war was over. Instead of jubilation a widespread feeling existed in the United States that while there was no more war, neither was there peace or victory. For the first time in its history, the United States could not claim victory over its enemies. Also for the first time in their history, Americans were told that the end of a war meant merely a cease-fire, not a return to peacetime conditions. Certainly this was the message that President Eisenhower conveyed to the American people when, in announcing the end of the conflict, he stated, "there is, in this moment of sober satisfaction, one thought that must discipline our emotions and steady our resolution. It is this: we have won an armistice in a single battleground—not peace in the world. We may not now relax our guard nor cease our quest."[32]

On the day after peace was announced, Eisenhower fulfilled one of his pledges to South Korea by sending a special message to the Congress asking the House and the Senate to authorize him to use up to $200 million for the rehabilitation and economic support of Korea, the sum to be taken from the savings in expenditures resulting from the cessation of hostilities. On August 6 Congress routinely approved the necessary legislation.[33]

Also on the day after the peace was announced, the sixteen nations with armed forces in Korea signed the "greater sanction" statement in which they reaffirmed their intention to resist any renewed attacks on South Korea from the north. The consequences of such a breach of the armistice, they declared, "would be so grave that in all probability, it would not be possible to confine hostilities within the frontiers of Korea." But the statement was not made public until August 7 when General Clark revealed its existence in a report to the UN Security Council. It was done this way because of growing allied opposition to the greater sanction concept. In brief, the allies, particularly the British, had second thoughts about issuing a declaration that appeared warlike, would be unpopular at home, might appear to tie them too closely to the Rhee government, and might poison any effort to ease world tensions.

The fact was that throughout Europe widespread disgruntlement continued to be expressed about the irresponsibility of American foreign policy and the failure of the Eisenhower administration to respond to the gestures of peace coming from Moscow since Stalin's death in March, including even the Communists' willingness to end the three-year war in Korea. For example, in May Prime Minister Churchill called for a summit meeting of the Big Four Powers. The Soviets responded by proposing a peace treaty with Germany that would include the reunification and neutralization of the country followed by the holding of free elections. Chances for a summit meeting diminished considerably after Churchill suffered a stroke in June, but Washington's well-known reluctance to meet with the Soviets irritated many European leaders, who much preferred a rapprochement with Moscow to the inclusion of a rearmed Germany in a European Defense Community and regarded the first option as an alternative to the second. At a July meeting of the foreign ministers in Washington, Georges Bidault of France thus told his colleagues that as long as French leaders saw a possibility for reaching a general agreement with Moscow, especially on the question of Germany, there was no chance of getting the French Assembly to ratify EDC.[34]

Also, in July Secretary of State Dulles rejected the Soviet proposals on Germany, maintaining that the holding of elections in that country should precede rather than follow the conclusion of a peace treaty. Once more Europeans made note of the intractability and unreasonableness of American foreign policy. By August *Time* was even commenting on "the new fluidity" in the Cold War, remarking that in Europe "old cries no longer persuaded, old decisions no longer held. . . . Increasingly, the trend is for individual nations to go their own way, consulting their friends but not being bound by them." In England the House of Commons devoted two days just before adjourning for a summer recess to a debate on foreign policy, during which considerable displeasure was expressed about Washington's reluctance to negotiate with the Soviets on such questions as the future status of Germany.[35]

Under these circumstances London was loath to follow America's lead in approving a "greater sanction" statement, which could lead to an extension of the Korean War into China itself should the armistice be broken. The British reminded Washington, therefore, that they had been uneasy about the statement since Rhee had freed the POWs on June 18, and they maintained that in terms of world opinion the declaration might do more harm than good. In response to such objections, Secretary of State Dulles agreed not to issue the statement until after the armistice was signed and then to do so without any fanfare.[36]

Still, by the time Dulles visited Korea at the beginning of August, the United States had taken several concrete steps to reassure the Rhee government that it would carry out its promises and pledges. Dulles's main business in Korea was to sign a mutual defense treaty. As the Eisenhower administration had made clear to the South Koreans, it could not agree to a treaty with an automatic military clause in it. Instead, the treaty merely provided that the United States and South Korea would "consult together" whenever their political independence or security seemed threatened. Although this was less than what Rhee had wanted, he accepted the treaty as the best he could obtain. In the final communiqué of the visit the United States assured Rhee that if the Communists attacked South Korea before the treaty was ratified by the Senate, "the UNC, including the Republic of Korea forces, would at once and automatically react, as such an unprovoked attack would be an attack upon and a threat to the UNC itself and to the forces under its command."[37]

Even as Dulles was visiting South Korea, the operation

known as BIG SWITCH began, as 75,823 POWs (of which 70,183 were North Korean and 5640 were Chinese) were returned to the Communists in exchange for 12,773 UNC POWs, including 3597 Americans, 946 Britons, and 7862 South Koreans (the remainder were from other nations). This left more than 22,600 enemy nonrepatriates (the vast majority Chinese) and 359 UNC nonrepatriates, of which 23 were American, 1 British, and 333 South Korean. As agreed in the armistice, the nonrepatriates were turned over to the Neutral Nations Repatriation Commission toward the end of September, several weeks after OPERATION BIG SWITCH had ended. During the time that the NNRC had custody of the POWs, they were given "explanations" in which they were strongly encouraged to return home, but without much success. Indeed, on a number of occasions anti-Communist POWs attacked the emissaries from China and North Korea. In the end only 137 of the former Communists elected to go back, while only 10 of the UNC nonrepatriates (2 Americans and 8 Koreans) chose to return home. The rest were eventually released the following January after the NNRC handed them back to their custodians, the period for "explanations" having expired on December 23. First, the UNC let its prisoners go after announcing that the nonrepatriates had been promised their freedom within 180 days after the signing of the armistice. A few days later the Communists, who had been against releasing the prisoners, did the same with the nonrepatriates they held. On February 1 the problem of the POWs thus having been finally resolved, the NNRC voted to dissolve itself.[38]

By this time plans for the post-armistice political conference, which was supposed to have been held within ninety days after the armistice, had been floundering for several months. The United States had begun thinking seriously about the conference—its membership and agenda—for only a short while before the armistice was signed. On one point the administration was certain, however, that the conference be arranged in such a way that those who had borne the brunt of the fighting predominate; or, in other words, that the United States would not be one among equals representing the UN position. The White House also felt strongly that representation at the conference should be limited to those countries which had actually fought in Korea—with the one exception of the Soviet Union. It was against having "neutral" nations, specifically India, represented, and while it was willing to allow the Soviet Union to participate, it wanted it to do so only as a belligerent, not as a neutral nation. As Washington interpreted the armistice agreement relating to the political conference, the agreement called for a conference of "both sides," and countries like India, which had been officially recognized as a neutral nation, would thus have no logical place at the gathering.[39]

Not all of America's allies agreed with this interpretation. The French preferred a "round-table" rather than an "across-the-table" conference, or a conference built around the concept of open discussion involving a number of nations rather than one based on the concept of confrontation between two opposing parties. They wanted to invite neutral nations like India to the conference rather than to limit it to the former belligerents only, and they wanted the meeting to discuss a number of issues, including the war in Indochina, rather than to confine discussion strictly to Korea. The British and the Commonwealth countries also favored inviting India and other neutral nations to the sessions.

At the United Nations the United States was able to round up enough votes and abstentions to prevent the two-thirds vote needed to seat India at the conference, so that the UN resolution of August 28 approving the armistice agreement limited the postwar political conference to the former belligerents only, except for the Soviet Union, which could participate "provided the other side desires it."[40] But many diplomats at the UN regarded the vote as the greatest diplomatic defeat the United States had suffered since the end of World War II, the rationale being that for the first time in the history of the United Nations the United States had isolated itself almost completely from its allies and had handed the Communists the best opportunity they had ever had to appear to the Asian masses as champions of international cooperation. The London *Times* even remarked that the United States was beginning to "look more and more like a satellite of South Korea."[41]

Preparations for the political conference did not begin, however, until the end of October, nearly ninety days after the armistice was signed. On October 26 Ambassador Arthur Dean, representing the UN side, met with representatives from the PRC and North Korea. The exchange of notes and the talks that followed had an all too familiar ring to them. Both sides disagreed over the agenda, the U. S. emissary wanting first to decide the time and place for the conference, the Communists wanting to talk first about participation by Asian neutrals, which, in their view, included the Soviet Union.[42]

In the weeks that followed, the preliminary talks remained deadlocked, and the Communists became increasingly vituperative. Ambassador Dean yielded a little to them by agreeing to allow members of the NNRC to attend the conference as nonvoting observers. He also agreed that the Soviet Union should participate in the negotiations, but not as a neutral nation. Nor would he give ground on the fundamental issues of opening the conference to Asian neutrals or to discussion of a broad range of Asian problems. Finally, on December 12, when the Chinese delegate to the talks repeatedly refused to retract his charge that the United States had conspired with President Rhee to release the 27,000 POWs on June 18, Ambassador Dean simply walked out of the meeting and returned to Washington.[43]

America's problems were not with the Communists alone, however. President Rhee continued to cause difficulty for the administration, making emotional outbursts and threatening to renew hostilities unilaterally if the political conference did not bring about Korean unification. At the beginning of November President Eisenhower wrote Rhee warning him that by his remarks he was endangering Senate ratification of the mutual defense pact that had been negotiated in August. "If I should be forced to conclude that after the coming into force of the [Mutual Defense] Treaty, you might unilaterally touch off a resumption of war in Korea," the President told Rhee, "I could not recommend its ratification and I am certain that the Senate would not ratify it." The South Korean president did muffle his remarks for the while, and in January the Senate approved the treaty with Korea. But Rhee remained a thorn in the side of the administration.[44]

Eventually, in 1954, agreement was reached to hold a conference of the Korean belligerents in Geneva in April in order to discuss Korean unification and other related matters. But the meeting deadlocked over the supervision and conduct of elec-

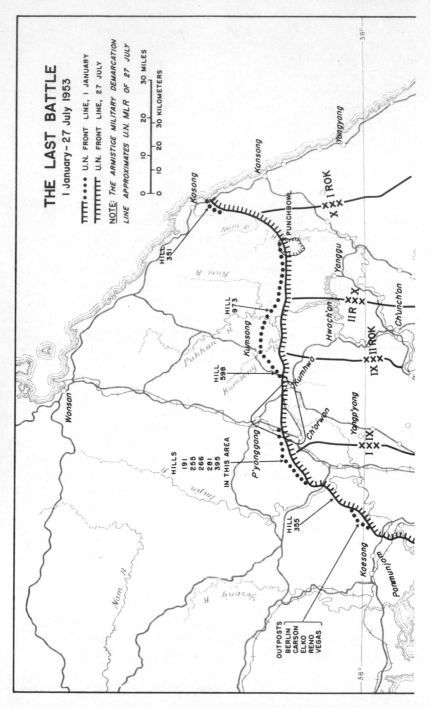

THE LAST BATTLE
1 January – 27 July 1953

⊤⊤⊤⊤ •••• U.N. FRONT LINE, 1 JANUARY
⊤⊤⊤⊤⊤⊤⊤ U.N. FRONT LINE, 27 JULY
NOTE: THE ARMISTICE MILITARY DEMARCATION
LINE APPROXIMATES U.N. MLR OF 27 JULY

0   10   20   30 MILES
0   10   20   30 KILOMETERS

HILLS
191
255
266
281
395
IN THIS AREA

OUTPOSTS
BERLIN
CARSON
ELKO
RENO
VEGAS

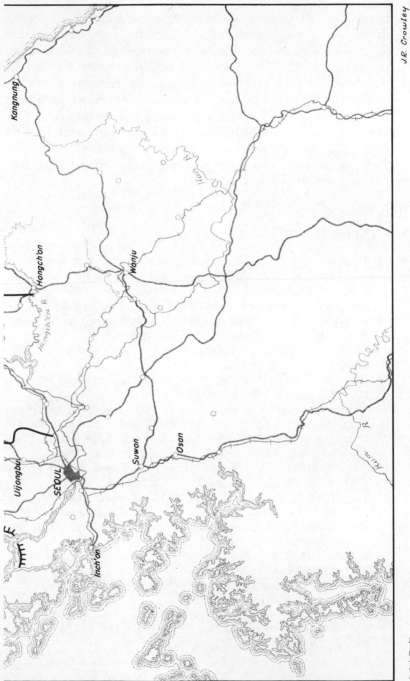

MAP 7

tions that were to bring unification about, and it finally broke up in June. As a gesture toward unification, the nations that fought in Korea and the ROK government signed a declaration reaffirming as their objective the holding of carefully supervised free elections throughout Korea. Since no agreement between the two sides had been reached, however, the armistice remained in effect, and the problem of Korean unification reverted to the United Nations, where it remains today. But by June 1954 most of the world's attention had turned to another phase of the Geneva meeting having to do with another area of the world, Indochina.[45]

NOTES

1. Memorandum for the President, June 4, 1953, Box 9, Subject Series, Dulles Papers; Letter to President Syngman Rhee of Korea, June 6, 1953, *Public Papers of the Presidents of the United States: Dwight D. Eisenhower,* 1953 (Washington, D. C., 1960), 377–80.
2. *FR,* 1952–1954, XV, 1165–67; Rhee to Eisenhower, June 17, 1953, Box 1, International Series, Eisenhower Papers.
3. Mark W. Clark, *From the Danube to the Yalu* (New York, 1954), 279–83.
4. *Atlantic Monthly,* 192 (July 1953), 9–10. See also *Time,* 60 (June 29, 1953), 12–13; *Life,* 35 (July 6, 1953), 10.
5. Aldrich to Secretary of State, June 18, 1953, Box 4287, Records of the Department of State, RG 59, 795.00/6-1853; Memorandum of Conversation with the British Ambassador, Sir Roger Makins, June 18, 1953, *ibid.,* 795.00/6-185.
6. *FR,* 1952–1954, XV, 1200–1205; Dwight D. Eisenhower, *Mandate for Change* (Garden City, N. Y., 1963), 185–86.
7. *FR,* 1952–1954, XV, 1206–10; Eisenhower, *Mandate for Change,* 185–86; Dulles to Amembassy Seoul, Amembassy Pusan, Amembassy Tokyo, June 18, 1953, Box 4287, Records of the Department of State, RG 59, 795.00/6-1953.
8. *FR,* 1952–1954, XV, 1238–40.
9. *Ibid.,* 1234–36.
10. *Ibid.,* 1276–77. See also *Time,* 61 (June 22, 1953), 29.
11. *FR,* 1952–54, XV, 1277–78.
12. "Personal for Secretary Johnson from Robertson," June 27, 1953, Box 4287, Records of the Department of State, RG 59, 795.00/6-2753; *FR,* 1952–1954, XV, 1280–86.

13. W. K. Scott to the Secretary of State, June 30, 1953, Box 4287, Records of the Department of State, RG 59, 795.00/6-3053; Telephone Conversation with Sen. Knowland (and Sen. Smith), Box 9, Subject Series, Dulles Papers.

14. *FR*, 1952–1954, XV, 1331–32; "Current Discussions with Rhee Re. Korea Truce," July 2, 1953, Box 4287, Records of the Department of State, RG 59, 795.00/7-253. See also *New Yorker*, 29 (June 20, 1953), 82–84.

15. *FR*, 1952–1954, XV, 1340; Dulles to Amembassy Seoul, July 7, 1953, Box 4287, Records of the Department of State, RG 59, 795.00/7-753. See also Telephone Conversation with Stephens and Persons, Box 10, Dulles Phone Calls Series, Dulles Papers.

16. *FR*, 1952–1954, XV, 1352–59.

17. Clark, *From the Danube to the Yalu*, 287.

18. Kenneth R. Mauck, "The Formation of American Foreign Policy in Korea, 1945–1953," (unpublished Ph.D. dissertation, University of Oklahoma, 1978), 399.

19. Walter G. Hermes, *Truce Tent and Fighting Front* (Washington, D. C., 1966), 459.

20. *Ibid.*, 393–95; *Time*, 61 (April 6, 1953), 34.

21. David Rees, *Korea: The Limited War* (New York, 1964), 409–13.

22. Hermes, *Truce Tent and Fighting Front*, 470–72.

23. *Ibid.*, 472–73; Rees, *Korea: The Limited War*, 413–14; *Time*, 61 (June 22, 1953), 28–29.

24. Clark, *From the Danube to the Yalu*, 291. See also Hermes, *Truce Tent and Fighting Front*, 473–78.

25. William Vatcher, *Panmunjom* (New York, 1958), 199–200; Hermes, *Truce Tent and Fighting Front*, 483–84.

26. *New York Times*, July 20, 1953.

27. *Ibid.*, July 22, 23, 24, 1953; *FR*, 1952–1954, XV, 1406–1407 and 1413–18.

28. Dulles to Amembassy Seoul, July 22, 1953, Box 4288, Records of the Department of State, RG 59, 795.00/7-2253; *FR*, 1952–1954, XV, 1418–20.

29. *FR*, 1952–1954, XV, 1430–32.

30. *Ibid.*

31. *Ibid.*, 1432–36 and 1442–44; Clark, *From the Danube to the Yalu*, 294–95.

32. Radio and Television Address to the American People Announcing the Signing of the Korean Armistice, July 26, 1953, *Public Papers of the Presidents of the United States: Dwight D. Eisenhower*, 1953 (Washington, D. C., 1960), 520–22. See also *New Yorker*, 29 (August 8, 1953), 53.

33. Special Message to the Congress Concerning Increased Aid to the Republic of Korea, July 27, 1953, *Public Papers of the Presidents of the United States: Dwight D. Eisenhower,* 1953, 522–24.
34. *Time,* 62, (July 27, 1953), 7–8; *New Yorker,* 29 (July 25, 1953), 48.
35. *New Yorker,* 29 (August 8, 1953), 69; *ibid.* (August 29, 1953), 64; *Time,* 62 (August 24, 1953), 16.
36. "Circular Re: Joint Policy Declaration," from Dulles, July 22, 1953, Box 4288, Records of the Department of State, RG 59, 795.00/7-2253.
37. Press Releases Nos. 424 and 426, August 8, 1953, Box 9, Subject Series, Dulles Papers.
38. Joseph Goulden, *Korea: The Untold Story* (New York, 1962), 647; Rees, *Korea: The Limited War,* 436–37.
39. Telephone Conversation with Amb. Lodge, June 20, 1953, Box 9, Subject Series, Dulles Papers; "Post Armistice Korean Problems," July 20, 1953, Box 4288, Records of the Department of State, RG 59, 795.00/7-2053.
40. "Political Conference on Korea," July 28, 1953, and Visit of Ambassador Bonnet Regarding Korean Political Conference, July 31, 1953, *ibid.,* 795.00/7-2853 and 795.00/7-3153.
41. *New Yorker,* 29, (September 5, 1953), 77–84; *Time,* 62 (September 7, 1953), 17.
42. U.S. Ambassador Seoul to Department of the Army, October 30, 1953, Box 4032, Records of the Department of State, RG 59, 795B.00(w)/10-3053.
43. U.S. Ambassador Seoul to Department of the Army, November 6, 1953, *ibid.,* 795.00(w)/11-653; U.S. Ambassador Seoul to Department of the Army, December 18, 1953, *ibid.,* 795.00(w)/12-1853.
44. *FR,* 1952–1954, XV, 1591–93.
45. Department of State, *The Korean Problem at the Geneva Conference, April 26–June 15, 1954* (Washington, D. C., 1954).

Conclusion

As United States Marines retreated from the strategic town of Hagaru after the Chinese Communists had entered Korea in massive numbers in December 1950, they broke into a parody of an old British Indian Army song:

> Bless 'em all, bless 'em all,
> The Commies, the U.N. and all:
> Those slant-eyed Chink soldiers
> Struck Hagaru-ri
> And now know the meaning of the U.S.M.C.
> But we're saying goodbye to them all,
> We're Harry's police force on call,
> So put back your pack on
> The next step is Saigon,
> Cheer up, me lads, bless 'em all![1]

Certainly the Marines could not have anticipated that American soldiers would be fighting in Vietnam, in defense of the Saigon government, less than fifteen years later. But neither was it entirely fortuitous that the song's refrain should mention Saigon as the next likely area of American combat, for one major consequence of the Korean War was to increase American military assistance to the French fighting the Vietminh in Indochina to the point where the United States was underwriting about eighty percent of the cost of the war by 1954.

At the same time, the Korean War made the United States reluctant in the 1950s to enter into another limited war, such as was being fought in Indochina. Even before President-elect Eisenhower took office in 1953, Secretary of State Dean Acheson had warned against committing American troops in Indochina. It would be "futile and a mistake to defend Indochina in Indochina," Acheson remarked. We "could not have another Korea, we could not put ground forces into Indochina."[2] Similarly, President Eisenhower, sensitive to Truman's fate in Korea, refused to intervene in Indochina in 1954, when the French were on the brink of defeat, without the support of Congress and America's allies. "[I]f the United States were, unilaterally, to permit its forces to be drawn into conflict in Indochina and in a succession of Asian wars," the President told Acting Secretary of State Walter Bedell Smith, "the end result would be to drain off our resources and to weaken our over-all defensive position."[3]

Most of America's military leaders felt the same way. In fact, many high-ranking officers found themselves on the horns of a dilemma as a result of the Korean experience. While Korea revealed much of the futility of limited war, it also made clear to a number of generals and admirals that this was the only type of war feasible in the future. Former General Matthew Ridgway thus wrote in 1967:

> Before Korea, all our military planning envisioned a war that would involve the world, and in which the defense of a distant and indefensible peninsula would be folly. But Korea taught us that all warfare from this time forth must be limited. It could no longer be a question of *whether* to fight a limited war, but of *how* to avoid fighting any other kind.[4]

Different leaders, however, drew different lessons from the experience of the Korean War. For President Lyndon Johnson, who was about to begin the build-up of American forces in Vietnam in 1965, the North Korean invasion of June 1950 was a lesson in the dangers of not meeting military responsibilities abroad. "I could never forget the withdrawal of our forces from South Korea," he later wrote, "and then our immediate reaction to the Communist aggression of June 1950."[5] To Assistant Secretary of State William P. Bundy, testifying in 1965 before the Senate Foreign Relations Committee, the Korean War taught three lessons. The first was a recognition that aggression must be met "head-on" or else it would intensify and be harder to contain. The second was that a defense line in Asia limited to an island perimeter, such as existed before Korea, did not adequately define America's vital interests in that region of the world, that what happened on the Asian mainland would bear directly on these interests. The final lesson of the Korean experience was that "a power vacuum was an invitation to aggression" and that in cases of such aggression "there must be a demonstrated willingness of major external power both to assist and to intervene if required." Thus the Korean experience did not keep the United States from engaging in another limited war in Vietnam in the 1960s.[6]

Did the Korean War offer lessons for the Vietnam conflict, which, had they been heeded, might have changed the course of the war in Vietnam? This is a question that has begun to interest a number of writers. It has even been suggested that Korea should have served as a model of how the war in Vietnam might have been won. According to this view, Korea represented not a military defeat or even a military draw for the United States but a military victory. This argument is based on the proposition that military victory is the achievement of the political ends for which a conflict is fought, a position first set forth by the military strategist Baron Karl von Clausewitz over 150 years earlier. It rests also on the point that except for the heady period between General MacArthur's amphibious assault at Inchon in September 1950 and the massive Chinese invasion across the Yalu River two months later—during which the Truman administration thought in terms of "liberating" North Korea from Communist control—Washington's political objective in Korea was to keep South Korea from falling to the Communists, which it succeeded in doing.[7]

The United States was able to achieve a military victory in Korea, this argument continues, because it tailored its political objectives to the limited military means its political leaders were willing to expend. Unprepared to make the military commitment necessary to bring about the total destruction of the enemy (in this case Communist China), the Truman and Eisenhower administrations opted instead for a limited war with limited political objectives and, within that framework, the UN command adopted the necessary military strategy to achieve a military victory. Had the United States followed a similar course in Vietnam, it could have won the war there as well.

Unfortunately, the nation's military leaders drew the wrong conclusions from the Korean War even though they had learned the right lesson—that political considerations might require wars of limited objectives. Failing to understand that military victory did not necessarily mean the total destruction of the enemy and that, therefore, it could be achieved even in a limited war, they dropped victory as an aim of war. In its place, they introduced the concept of "limited means" as a way of preventing limited war from turning into total nuclear war. Instead of being concerned with the primary task of devising a military strategy to achieve political objectives, they conceded the formulation of military strategy to civilian policymakers and concentrated essentially on questions of logistics and tactics dictated by that strategy. What the nation's military leaders should have done was to recognize that the Vietnam War was a conventional war very much like the Korean War, involving Communist aggression from the north. Then they should have devised a military strategy to achieve the limited political objective of repelling that external aggression—by isolating the battlefield and orienting the war on North Vietnam. Instead they concerned themselves with matters of internal subversion, counterinsurgency, and nation-building, issues which deflected from the real military threat posed by North Vietnam and which were better left to South Vietnamese forces.

This analysis of the lessons from the Korean War that might have been applied to the war in Vietnam rests on a number of highly dubious assumptions. Perhaps the most important of these is its attempt to portray the Vietnam War as a conventional war much like the Korean conflict, thereby emphasizing the external aggression of North Vietnam and deemphasizing the internal guerrilla activity within South Vietnam. Such an assumption runs counter to the commonly held view that while North Vietnam had infiltrated men and supplies into South Vietnam and by 1965 was lending considerable assistance to the guerrilla forces known as the Vietcong, its military role was still limited, certainly not comparable to the overt aggression of North Korea in 1950.[8]

Other major differences also existed between the Korean and Vietnam wars which further underscore the need for caution in drawing parallels between them. For example, there were no Korean equivalents of Laos and Cambodia through which supplies and equipment could flow to the enemy. So too, the politics of Vietnam and America's need to project the Saigon government as more than a pawn of the United States was in sharp contrast to the experience in Korea, where South Korean forces were placed under UN command and the war was fought largely irrespective of the Rhee government. Although Korea and Vietnam were both unpopular wars at home, furthermore, there was no antiwar crusade in the United States over Korea comparable to those over Vietnam in the 1960s and early 1970s. Undoubtedly one reason for this was that television was still in its infancy in the early 1950s, and the horrors of war were not brought home to the American people on a daily basis in quite the same way that they were in the 1960s. This point can be easily overstated. Several studies have made clear that notwithstanding the impact of television, public support for the war in Vietnam remained at a high level longer into the war than had been the case in Korea, perhaps due to the backlash against the antiwar demonstrations that were also a common feature of the nightly news. Moreover, at least until mid-1967 television coverage of the war appears to have been favorable toward President Johnson's war policies. In fact, the growing opposition to the war came first from the college educated, who were inclined to rely as much on newspapers and magazines as on television for their news.[9]

Nevertheless, television coverage of the Korean War did not present the same problem for Truman that television coverage of the Vietnam War presented for Johnson. Also, many antiwar activists in the 1960s had learned the mechanics of mass organization in the civil rights movement of the early 1960s and applied that knowledge to the struggle against the Vietnam War. Finally, opposition to the Korean War came from the political right in the United States because of what it perceived as the administration's bungling and no-win policy, while opposition to the Vietnam War came from the political left outraged at what it regarded as the moral depravity of American foreign policy.[10]

Despite these significant differences, there were also parallels between the two wars, and despite some of the questionable assumptions of those who have argued that Korea offered les-

sons for Vietnam, there were lessons that might have been
learned from the Korean experience. In the first place, Korea
and Vietnam were both limited wars whose object became less
than total victory. Second, America's leaders during the Korean
and Vietnam conflicts were guided by essentially the same purpose, although they used different terminology. Presidents
Harry Truman and Dwight Eisenhower in the 1950s and Presidents Lyndon Johnson and Richard Nixon in the 1960s and
1970s sought to extricate themselves from an unpopular and
costly conflict but to do so in a way that preserved America's
honor and prevented a victory for Communist aggression. In
essence, the Munich syndrome of the Korean War period (appeasement leads to further acts of aggression) and the domino
theory of the Vietnam War period (if Vietnam falls to the Communists then the rest of Southeast Asia would fall like a row of
dominoes) were products of the same Cold War mentality.

Truman had thus gone to war in 1950 because he saw the
world in crisis and because he was concerned with maintaining
the international credibility of the United States and his own
credibility at home. Much the same was true in the case of
Lyndon Johnson in 1965. To be sure, Johnson was not faced
with the same Red Scare and accusations of being "soft on
communism" that confronted Truman. Nor did the world seem
as much in jeopardy in 1965 as it did in 1950, just months after
the loss of China to the Communists and the Soviet detonation
of an atomic bomb. Nevertheless, in committing American
forces to Vietnam, Johnson was responding to strong and articulate sentiment in the United States against further Communist
expansion. He also decided to go to war in Vietnam because, as
he later commented, the "military campaign against South Vietnam was part of a larger, much more ambitious strategy being
conducted by the Communists" and because the action he took
with respect to Vietnam would determine not only the fate of
that country "but also the shape of Asia for many years to
come." In other words, the sense of crisis and concerns about
credibility that determined Truman's policy with regard to the
Korean War also heavily influenced Johnson's decisions with
respect to the war in Vietnam.[11]

What Korea might have taught those who were responsible
for the conduct of the war in Vietnam, both military and civil-

ian, were some of the problems of waging a limited war, particularly the unique problems of command. For example, Korea might have revealed the difficulty in sustaining popular support for a war in which total victory (the complete destruction of the enemy) was not the aim and in having constantly to reassure America's own allies of its limited purpose in the war. In fact, one of General MacArthur's problems as UN commander was his failure to understand the limitations and pressures imposed on the United States by its allies. Although Truman was largely successful in getting the British and America's other allies to cooperate with the administration in Korea and at the United Nations, this had to involve at least some political—and military —compromises on the part of the United States. MacArthur never fully appreciated this fact.

For its part, the administration often failed to appreciate the military consequences of its political decisions, with the result that seemingly contradictory orders were sometimes given to MacArthur and his successors, Generals Ridgway and Clark. This included their general instructions, irrespective of any consideration about the safety and security of their forces, to maintain maximum military pressure against the enemy without doing anything that might escalate the war into a larger conflict. For this failure on the administration's part to comprehend fully the military implications of its political actions, the Joint Chiefs of Staff have to assume a good part of the responsibility. Instead of communicating to the administration the nation's military capabilities and limitations in Korea, it violated another dictum of Clausewitz—namely that the civilian leadership had to be made aware of the imperatives of military operations.

This simply was not the case in Korea. What is striking about the war in Korea, in fact, was the generally passive role that the Joint Chiefs of Staff played in formulating political *and military* policy in Korea. The decision to limit the war in Korea after the Chinese invasion was essentially a political one reached with surprisingly little input from the Joint Chiefs. Much the same was true of the military strategy—the active defense—that was subsequently followed notwithstanding pleas from the field for a general offensive above the 38th parallel. Throughout most of the war, the Joint Chiefs largely ac-

quiesced in political decisions made without much consideration of battlefield conditions.

Had greater military pressure been maintained against the
Chinese and North Koreans after negotiations began in July of
1951, it is quite conceivable that a settlement of the war might
have been reached much earlier, long before Eisenhower
raised the threat of atomic warfare. But the longer the war
dragged on, the more hazardous a general offensive became
and the more difficult it was to follow any military strategy
other than the active defense. As General Maxwell Taylor, who
took over command of the Eighth Army from General James
Van Fleet in 1953, later commented, "Our unwillingness to
keep military pressure on the enemy during the negotiations
had been a mistake, I was sure, but by 1953 it was established
policy, and it was too late to try to change."[12] In other words,
the Korean War might have served as an example of the need
for the military to play a more prominent role in establishing
militarily obtainable political objectives, not because this occurred in Korea, as asserted by those who would make Korea
a model of the way the war in Vietnam should have been
fought, but for the very opposite reason.

Nevertheless, the Korean conflict remains one of the decisive events of recent American history. As one writer has remarked, "[i]n many ways Korea did for the [C]old [W]ar what
Pearl Harbor had done for World War II. It 'globalized' the
Cold War. Prior to Korea the only American political or military
commitment outside the Western Hemisphere had been the
North Atlantic Treaty, but by 1955 the United States had about
450 bases in thirty-six countries and was linked by political and
military pacts with some twenty countries outside Latin America. Also, the United States' foreign aid program, appropriately
named the 'mutual security program,' no longer had as its purpose economic and social reconstruction but military support
for recipient countries. Most important, the communist menace
was now perceived in Washington in broad global terms rather
than in terms of Europe alone, as had largely been the case
prior to 1950."[13]

An added significance of the Korean War was that it was
America's first war fought in the nuclear age. President Eisenhower had raised the threat of nuclear war, of course, to pres-

sure the Communists into concluding an armistice, and the threat of atomic warfare was basic to the Eisenhower-Dulles doctrine of massive retaliation. Recalling a meeting he had with the Joint Chiefs of Staff at the end of 1954, Eisenhower thus later wrote, "I stressed that the United States would not employ the same policies and resources to fight another war as were used in the Korean conflict. I saw no sense in wasting manpower in costly small wars that could not achieve decisive results under the political and military circumstances then existing."[14] Yet the very existence of nuclear weapons in the first place had dictated a limited war in Korea. And as the first war the United States fought since the advent of nuclear weapons, Korea confronted American leaders with the relative powerlessness of a weapon that, in the final analysis, was too terrible to be used.

NOTES

1. The quote is from T. R. Fehrenbach, *This Kind of War: A Study in Unpreparedness* (New York, 1973), 294–304.
2. George C. Herring, *America's Longest War: The United States and Vietnam, 1950–1975* (New York, 1979), 20.
3. Dwight D. Eisenhower, *Mandate for Change* (Garden City, N.Y., 1963), 354. See also Norman Podhoretz, *Why We Were in Vietnam* (New York, 1982), 34–35 and 51.
4. Matthew B. Ridgway, *The Korean War* (Garden City, N.Y., 1967), vi.
5. Lyndon Baines Johnson, *The Vantage Point: Perspectives of the Presidency* (New York, 1971), 152.
6. The quote is from Russell H. Fifield, *Americans in Southeast Asia: The Roots of Commitment* (New York, 1973), 150–51.
7. See, for example, Podhoretz, *Why We Were in Vietnam*, 31, and Harry G. Summers, *On Strategy: A Critical Analysis of the Vietnam War* (Novato, Calif., 1982). The following paragraphs are based largely on Summers' analysis of the Korean and Vietnam wars.
8. See, for example, Herring, *America's Longest War*, 110, and 118–119.
9. "Some Lessons and Non-Lessons of Vietnam. Ten years After the Paris Peace Accords." Woodrow Wilson International Center for Scholars, (Washington, D. C., 1963); Alonzo L. Hamby, "Public

Opinion: Korea and Vietnam," *Wilson Quarterly*, 2 (Summer 1978), 137–41.

10. *Ibid.*; see also Robert J. Donovan, *Nemesis: Truman and Johnson in the Coils of War in Asia* (New York, 1984), 140–42.

11. Donovan, *Nemesis*, 72 and 131–32; Johnson, *The Vantage Point*, 136–38.

12. Maxwell D. Taylor, *Swords and Plowshares* (New York, 1972), 137.

13. Lisle A. Rose, *Roots of Tragedy: The United States and the Struggle for Asia, 1945–1953* (Westport, Conn., 1976), 239–44; Charles E.-Bohlen, *Witness to History, 1929–1969* (New York, 1973), 294–304.

14. Eisenhower, *Mandate for Change*, 454.

Suggestions for Further Reading

Still the best overall account of United States participation in the Korean War is David Rees, *Korea: The Limited War* (New York, 1964), a balanced and judicious study amply documented by the primary material available in 1964. This should be supplemented by the more recent Joseph C. Goulden, *Korea: The Untold Story of the War* (New York, 1982). Although somewhat melodramatic and unbalanced in that more than two-thirds of the book covers the period through MacArthur's firing in April 1951, it is based on a wealth of new information, largely from the records of the Joint Chiefs of Staff. Also not to be neglected are several official histories of the war, which, too, are based on military records but which deal at length with the diplomacy of the war. These are James F. Schnabel, *Policy and Direction: The First Year* (Washington, D. C., 1972); Roy E. Appleman, *South to the Naktong, North to the Yalu* (Washington, D. C., 1961); and Walter G. Hermes, *Truce Tent and Fighting Front* (Washington, D. C., 1966).

Two important collections of essays on the origins and conduct of the war, several of which will be noted individually in the course of this essay, are Frank Baldwin, ed., *Without Parallel: The American-Korean Relationship Since 1945* (New York, 1973), and Bruce Cumings, ed., *Child of Conflict: The Korean-American Relationship, 1943–1953* (Seattle, Wash., 1983). For a broad assessment of the impact of the Korean War in terms of American foreign and domestic policy, see also the essays in Francis H. Heller, ed., *The Korean War: A 25-Year Perspective* (Lawrence, Kans., 1977). In addition consult Walter

359

LaFeber, "Crossing the 38th: The Cold War in Microcosm," in Lynn H. Miller and Ronald W. Pruessen, eds., *Reflections on the Cold War: A Quarter Century of American Foreign Policy* (Philadelphia, 1974), 71–90; John Lewis Gaddis, "Was the Truman Doctrine a Real Turning Point?", *Foreign Affairs*, 52 (January 1974), 386–402; and Arnold Wolfers, "Collective Security and the War in Korea," *Yale Review*, 43 (June 1954), 481–96.

Among other general treatments of the Korean War are Carl Berger, *The Korean Knot: A Military-Political History* (Philadelphia, 1964); Harry J. Middleton, *The Compact History of the Korean War* (New York, 1965); Edgar O'Ballance, *Korea: 1950–1953* (London, 1969); Robert Leckie, *Conflict: The History of the Korean War* (New York, 1962); T. R. Fehrenbach, *This Kind of War: A Study in Unpreparedness* (New York, 1963); Guy Wint, *What Happened in Korea: A Study in Collective Security* (London, 1954); and Martin Lichterman, "To the Yalu and Back," in Harold Stein, ed., *American Civil-Military Decisions: A Book of Case Studies* (University, Ala., 1963), 569–642. Most of these books deal with the military aspects rather than the diplomacy of the war. A contemporary account of the opening of hostilities is Marguerite Higgins, *War in Korea* (Garden City, N. Y., 1951). Much less useful is Robert B. Rigg, *Red China's Fighting Hordes* (Harrisburg, Pa., 1951).

On the period between World War II and the outbreak of hostilities in Korea in June 1950, for which the documentation is ample, there are a number of fine books and essays, which cover such matters as the nature of Korean society, American-Korean policy, and the causes of the war. On United States policy toward Korea during World War II, see especially James A. Matray, "An End to Indifference: America's Korean Policy During World War II," *Diplomatic History*, 2 (Spring 1978), 181–96. For the decision to divide Korea at the 38th parallel, see another essay by Matray, "Captive of the Cold War: The Decision to Divide Korea at the 38th Parallel," *Pacific Historical Review*, 50 (May 1981), 145–68. On Secretary of State Dean Acheson's famous statement to the National Press Club in January 1950, defining America's defense perimeter, see John Lewis Gaddis, "The Strategic Perspective: The Rise and Fall of the 'Defensive Perimeter' Concept, 1947–1951" in Dorothy Borg and Waldo Heinrichs, eds., *Uncertain Years: Chinese-American*

Relations, 1947–1950 (New York, 1980). In his essay Gaddis points out the fragility of the consensus on the defensive perimeter strategy.

A brilliant study of Korean society in the 1940s is the prize-winning *The Origins of the Korean War: Liberation and the Emergence of Separate Regimes, 1945–1947* (Princeton, N. J., 1981) by Bruce Cumings. Making use of Korean language materials as well as archival and government publications from the United States, Cumings argues that the root causes of the Korean conflict can be found in the civil and revolutionary struggle within Korea during the five years preceding the outbreak of hostilities in 1950 that led to the creation of two hostile regimes in North and South Korea. More concise statements of Cumings' thesis are Bruce Cumings, "American Policy and Korean Liberation," in Baldwin, ed., *Without Parallel: The American-Korean Relationship Since 1945,* 39–108, and Cumings, "Introduction: The Course of Korean-American Relations, 1943–1953," in Cumings, ed., *Child of Conflict: The Korean-American Relationship, 1943–1953,* 3–55. Other studies that emphasize the civil nature of the struggle in Korea include Robert R. Simmons, "The Korean Civil War," in Baldwin, ed., *Without Parallel: The American-Korean Relationship Since 1945,* 143–78; John Merrill, "Internal Warfare in Korea, 1948–1950: The Local Setting of the Korean War," in Cumings, ed., *Child of Conflict: The Korean-American Relationship, 1943–1953,* 133–62; and Okonogi Masao, "The Domestic Roots of the Korean War," in Yonosuke Nagai and Akira Iriye, eds., *The Origins of the Cold War in Asia* (New York, 1977), 299–320.

Perhaps the best study in English of the internal development of Korea that does not have as its major purpose an explanation of the causes of the Korean War is Gregory Henderson, *Korea: The Politics of the Vortex* (Cambridge, Mass., 1968). Basing his study on Korean and Japanese, as well as English, language materials, Henderson stresses the homogeneity and centralization of Korean society and argues the need for decentralization of political authority. A major study of the Communist movement in Korea is the two-volume work, Robert A. Scalapino and Chong-Sik Lee, *Communism in Korea* (Berkeley, Calif., 1972). This should be supplemented by an earlier work, Dae-Sook Suh, *The Korean Communist Movement, 1918–*

1948 (Princeton, N. J., 1967), which stresses the two conflicting societies that had developed in Korea by 1948. Other books which deal with internal developments in Korea and the growth of Communism are Koon Woo Nam, *The North Korean Communist Leadership, 1945–1965: A Study of Factionalism and Political Consolidation* (University, Ala., 1974); Chong-Shik Chung and Jae-Bong Ro, *Nationalism in Korea* (Seoul, 1979); Byung Chul Koh, *The Foreign Policy of North Korea* (New York, 1969); Chong-Shik Chung and Gahb-Chol Kim, eds., *North Korean Communism: A Comparative Analysis* (Seoul, 1950); Joungwon Alexander Kim, *Divided Korea: The Politics of Development, 1945–1972* (Cambridge, Mass., 1975); George M. McCune, *Korea Today* (Cambridge, Mass., 1950); and John Kie-Chang Oh, *Korea: Democracy on Trial* (Ithaca, N. Y., 1968). The latter is highly critical of Syngman Rhee, particularly because of his repressive government in the 1940s.

United States policy toward Korea in the five-year period prior to 1950 has received extensive attention recently. Two important monographs are William Whitney Stueck, Jr., *The Road to Confrontation: American Policy Toward China and Korea, 1947–1950* (Chapel Hill, N. C., 1981), and Charles M. Dobbs, *The Unwanted Symbol: American Foreign Policy, the Cold War, and Korea, 1945–1950* (Kent, Ohio, 1981). In his work Stueck argues that while the United States did not view Korea as being important in a military sense, the country became increasingly important in terms of America's credibility worldwide—that is, in terms of the United States playing a central role in the world. To maintain its credibility in the world, the United States went to war in South Korea's defense in 1950. Sharing much the same view, Dobbs argues that by 1948 Korea had become a symbol of the United States' determination to defend the free world against Communist aggression; the "loss" of China in 1949 made the symbolic importance of Korea even greater. An excellent essay which emphasizes the errors of policy toward Korea by the big powers in the 1945–1950 period is John Lewis Gaddis, "Korea in American Politics, Strategy, and Diplomacy, 1945–1950," in Nagai and Iriye, eds., *The Origins of the Cold War in Asia,* 277–98. On the United States' reluctant but growing ties to the Syngman Rhee government by 1948 see Lisle A. Rose, *Roots of Tragedy: The United*

States and the Struggle for Asia, 1945–1953 (Westport, Conn., 1976). An important essay on the reasons why Truman delayed a settlement of the Korean question in 1945 is Mark Paul, "Diplomacy Delayed: The Atomic Bomb and the Division of Korea, 1945," in Cumings, ed., *Child of Conflict: The Korean-American Relationship, 1943–1953*, 67–91. For the American occupation of South Korea after World War II, consult E. Grant Meade, *American Military Government in Korea*, (New York, 1951). For American assistance in training the South Korean army prior to 1950, see Robert K. Shaw, *Military Advisers in Korea: KMAG in Peace and War* (Washington, D. C., 1962).

On the outbreak of hostilities almost all writers attribute the war to North Korea's invasion of South Korea. But I. F. Stone's *The Hidden History of the Korean War* (New York, 1952) takes a different view. Based largely on his reading of *The New York Times* immediately before and after June 25, Stone argues that South Korea started the war by attacking north of the 38th parallel. Similarly, Joyce and Gabriel Kolko's *The Limits of Power: The World and United States Foreign Policy, 1945–1954* (New York, 1972), although conceding that North Korea probably began the war, attributes its invasion of South Korea, nevertheless, to the military imbalance in favor of South Korea that the United States and the Rhee government had created in 1949 and 1950. The Kolkos also argue that the United States planned to play an active role against Communist expansion even before the outbreak of the Korean War. For a critique of the Kolko thesis and a rejoinder by the Kolkos see William W. Stueck, Jr., "Cold War Revisionism and the Origins of the Korean Conflict: The Kolko Thesis," and Joyce and Gabriel Kolko, "To Root Out Those Among Them—A Response," *Pacific Historical Review*, 42 (November 1973), 537–66. Emphasizing the civil nature of the Korean conflict (like other authors already mentioned) and taking a position similar to the Kolkos', Robert R. Simmons, *The Strained Alliance: Peking, Pyongyang, Moscow and the Politics of the Korean Civil War* (New York, 1975) argues that, contrary to popular opinion (and most historical accounts) North Korea acted on its own initiative and without the approval of the Soviet Union and may have attacked South Korea in anticipation of an early South Korean attack from the other direction.

The immediate American response to the outbreak of hostilities in Korea, almost on an hourly basis, can be followed in Glenn D. Paige, *The Korean Decision* (New York, 1968). See also two articles by Paige, "Comparative Case Analysis of Crisis Decisions: Korea and Cuba, " in Charles F. Hermann, ed., *International Crises: Insights from Behavioral Research* (New York, 1972) and "On Values and Science: The Korean Decision Reconsidered," *American Political Science Review*, 71 (December 1977), 1603–1609. An interesting account of why Truman decided quickly to come to the defense of South Korea is Stephen Pelz, "U. S. Decisions on Korean Policy, 1943–1950: Some Hypotheses" in Cumings, ed., *Child of Conflict*, 93–132. Besides considerations growing out of the Cold War conflict between the United States and the Soviet Union, according to Pelz, Truman intervened so decisively in Korea because of his fear of a political attack on his administration at home, growing out of the vulnerability of his previous policies toward Korea, if he did nothing. Another important account of the first week of the war is Barton J. Bernstein, "The Week We Went to War: American Intervention in the Korean Civil War," *Foreign Service Journal*, 54 (January 1977), 6–9 and 33–35, and *ibid.* (February 1977), 8–11 and 33–35. Bernstein largely substantiates Paige's account of the opening week of the conflict. Ernest May, *Lessons of the Past: The Use and Misuse of History in American Foreign Policy* (New York, 1973) argues that Truman's effort to avoid the mistakes of the past, particularly by not repeating the failed policy of appeasement of the 1930s, influenced his decision to go to war. Alexander L. George, "American Policy-Making and the North Korean Aggression," *World Politics*, 7 (January 1955), 208–32, also agrees that Truman intervened in Korea because he feared the consequences of inaction, believed intervention was necessary to prevent the Soviet Union from other acts of aggression, and was influenced by the Munich syndrome. Morton H. Halperin, "The Limiting Process in the Korean War," *Political Science Review*, 78 (March 1963), 13–39, remarks that the defense of Korea was motivated partly by a feeling in Washington that action was necessary in Korea to convince western Europe that the United States would come to its aid if attacked by the Soviet Union. Finally, Yonosuke Nagai, "The Korean War: An Interpretative Essay," *The Japanese Jour-*

nal of American Studies, 1 (1981), 151–74, states that the Korean War afforded the United States an opportunity to draw a line of containment against Communism in East Asia.

Besides the Schnabel, Appleman, and Hermes volumes mentioned at the beginning of this essay, which deal with diplomatic as well as with military themes, two other official military histories of the war are James A. Field, Jr., *History of United States Naval Operations: Korea* (Washington, D. C., 1962), and Lynn Montrose, Nicholas A. Canonza, et al., *U.S. Marine Operations in Korea* (5 vols., Washington, D. C., 1954–1972). Other histories of military operations during the war include Robert Frank Futrell, *The United States Air Force in Korea, 1950–1953* (New York, 1961); James J. Stewart, ed., *Airpower: The Decisive Force in Korea* (Princeton, N. J., 1957); Walt Sheldon, *Hill or High Water: MacArthur's Landing at Inchon* (New York, 1968); S. L. A. Marshall, *The River and the Gauntlet: The Defeat of the Eighth Army by the Chinese Communist Forces* (New York, 1953); Robert Jackson, *Air Power Over Korea* (New York, 1975); Russell A. Gugeler, ed., *Combat Actions in Korea* (Washington, D. C., 1954); and U. S. Eighth Army, Historical Office, *Key Korean War Battles Fought in the Republic of Korea* (Seoul, 1972). For the problem of command in a limited war see D. Clayton James, "Command Crisis: MacArthur and the Korean War," *The Harmon Memorial Lectures in Military History* (United States Air Force Academy, Colorado Springs, Col., 1982). For Canada's military role in the war consult Thor Thorgrimsson and E. C. Russell, *Canadian Naval Operations in Korean Waters, 1950–1952* (Ottawa, 1966), and Herbert Fairlie Wood, *Strange Battleground: The Operations in Korea and Their Effects on the Defense Policy of Canada* (Ottawa, 1966).

On Truman's decision to cross the 38th parallel in September 1950, and on Communist China's subsequent decision to enter the war, consult James I. Matray, "Truman's Plan for Victory: National Self-Determination and the Thirty-Eighth Parallel Decision in Korea," *Journal of American History,* 66 (September 1979), 314–33; Walter LaFeber, "American Policy-Makers, Public Opinion, and the Outbreak of the Cold War, 1945–1950" in Yonosuke Nagai and Akira Iriye, eds., *The Origins of the Cold War in Asia* (New York, 1977), 43–65; and

Allen Whiting, *China Crosses the Yalu: The Decision to Enter the Korean War* (Stanford, Calif., 1960). LaFeber maintains that Truman's decision to cross the 38th parallel was made as early as July 1950. Whiting states that China entered the war reluctantly and only out of concern about the dangers to its interests in having a determined and powerful enemy at its doorstep.

On the domestic side of the war there are a number of books and articles. For a narrative on American Society in the two weeks following the outbreak of war, see David Detzer, *Thunder of the Captains: The Short Summer in 1950* (New York, 1970). See also John Edward Wiltz, "The Korean War and American Society" in Heller, ed., *The Korean War: A 25-Year Perspective,* 112–58. On the constitutional issues raised by America's undeclared war in Korea, consult Arthur M. Schlesinger, Jr., *The Imperial Presidency* (Boston, 1973). On the Truman-MacArthur controversy, see John Edward Wiltz, "Truman and MacArthur: The Wake Island Meeting," *Military Affairs,* 42 (December 1978), 168–75; Trumbull Higgins, *Korea and the Fall of MacArthur: A Précis in Limited War* (New York, 1960); Richard H. Rovere and Arthur M. Schlesinger, Jr., *The MacArthur Controversy and American Foreign Policy* (New York, 1951); and especially John W. Spanier, *The Truman-MacArthur Controversy and the Korean War* (Cambridge, Mass.,' 1959). On the impact of the war on American politics, the most complete study remains Ronald J. Caridi, *The Korean War and American Politics: The Republican Party as a Case Study* (Philadelphia, 1968). But see also the appropriate chapters in Robert A. Divine, *Foreign Policy and the U. S. Presidential Elections, 1952–1960* (New York, 1974); H. Bradford Westerfield, *Foreign Policy and Party Politics: Pearl Harbor to Korea* (New Haven, Conn., 1955); and Gary W. Reichard, "Divisions and Dissent: Democrats and Foreign Policy, 1952–1956," *Political Science Quarterly,* 93 (Spring 1978).

There are several biographical studies of Douglas MacArthur that cover his career through the Korean War. But none of these is very satisfactory, and two, written by his former aides, make no pretense at objectivity. For a satisfactory account of MacArthur's activities with respect to the conflict in Korea, the student will probably have to wait for the next volume of D. Clayton James's multivolume biography of the general.* But in the meanwhile one might consult William Manchester, *American Caesar: Douglas MacArthur, 1880–1964* (Boston, 1978), and Robert Smith, *MacArthur in Korea: The Naked Emperor* (New York, 1982). Smith describes MacArthur as an impervious individual around whom much myth has been created but who was essentially a downright liar and charlatan. The best volume on President Truman during the war is Robert K. Donovan, *Tumultuous Years: The Presidency of Harry S. Truman, 1949–1953* (New York, 1982), a balanced but sympathetic treatment. Also good is Cabell Phillips, *The Truman Presidency: The History of a Triumphant Succession* (Baltimore, 1969); the theme is evident in the book's title. A magisterial biography of Dwight D. Eisenhower are the two volumes by Stephen E. Ambrose, *Eisenhower: Soldier, General of the Army, President-Elect, 1890–1952* (New York, 1983); and *Eisenhower: The President* (New York, 1984)

Several studies deal with various aspects of the diplomacy during the war. On the role of the United Nations, consult Leland M. Goodrich, *Korea: A Study of U. S. Policy in the United Nations* (New York, 1956). In general Goodrich is critical of the United States for not following a forceful enough policy with respect to South Korea, politically and diplomatically. India's efforts at mediation are covered in Shif Dayal, *India's Role in the Korean Question* (Delhi, 1959), and Blema S. Steinberg, "The Korean War: A Case Study in Indian Neutralism," *Orbis*, 8 (Winter 1965), 937–54. Also worthwhile is J. C. Kundra, *India's Foreign Policy, 1947–1954* (Grunigen, Holland, 1955). A first-rate analysis of Canada's diplomatic role in the Korean War is Denis Stairs, *The Diplomacy of Constraint: Canada, the Korean War and the United States* (Toronto, 1974).

For the armistice negotiations and other matters leading to the end of the war, see three articles by Barton J. Bernstein, "Truman's Secret Thoughts on Ending the Korean War," *Foreign Service Journal*, 57 (November 1980), 31–33 and 44–45; "Syngman Rhee: The Pawn as Rook: The Struggle to End the Korean War," *Bulletin of Concerned Asian Scholars*, X (January-March 1978), 38–47; and "The Struggle over the Korean

*D. Clayton James, *The Years of MacArthur: Triumph and Disaster 1945–1964* (Boston, 1985) was published while this volume was in press.

War Armistice: Prisoners of Repatriation?" in Cumings, ed.,
Child of Conflict, 261–307. In these essays Bernstein describes
Truman's phantasies with respect to the use of atomic weapons
and an actual policy of increased bombing of North Korea in an
effort to bring about an end to the war. A fourth essay by
Bernstein, "The Origins of America's Commitment in Korea,"
Foreign Service Journal, 55 (March 1978), 10–13 and 34, de-
scribes America's dealings with Syngman Rhee, including plans
to overthrow the South Korean president, in an effort to win
South Korea's acceptance of an armistice agreement, in return
for which Washington agreed to a defense pact with the Seoul
government. On the United States' commitment to South
Korea, consult also John Kotch, "The Origins of the American
Security Commitment to Korea," in Cumings, ed., *Child of
Conflict,* 239–59. On other aspects of the armistice negotiations
and final settlement of the war, see Wilfred Bacchus, "The
Relationship between Combat and Peace Negotiations: Fighting While Talking in Korea, 1951–1953," *Orbis,* 17 (Summer
1973), 547–74; Edward Friedman, "Nuclear Blackmail and the
End of the Korean War," *Modern China,* 1 (January 1975),
75–91; and John Gittings, "Talks, Bombs, and Germs: Another
Look at the Korean War," *Journal of Contemporary Asia,* 5
(1975), 205–17.

For a comparative analysis of America's involvement in
Korea and Vietnam, see Robert J. Donovan, *Nemesis: Truman
and Johnson in the Coils of War in Asia* (New York, 1984). On
the same subject see also Alonzo Hamby, "Public Opinion:
Korea and Vietnam," *Wilson Quarterly,* II (Summer 1978),
137–41; and Chang Jin Park, "American Foreign Policy in
Korea and Vietnam: Comparative Case Studies," *Review of
Politics,* 37 (January 1975), 20–47.

Finally, the student of the Korean War is fortunate to have
the memoirs and recollections of a number of the participants
in the conflict, politically, diplomatically, and militarily. Among
the most important of these are Harry S. Truman, *Memoirs:
Years of Trial and Hope* (Garden City, N. Y., 1956); Robert H.
Ferrell, ed., *The Autobiography of Harry Truman* (Boulder,
Col., 1978); Robert H. Ferrell, ed., *Off the Record: The Private
Papers of Harry S. Truman* (New York, 1980); Dwight D. Eisenhower, *Mandate for Change, 1953–1956* (Garden City, N. Y.,

1963); Dean Acheson, *Present at the Creation: My Years in the State Department* (New York, 1969); Douglas MacArthur, *Reminiscences* (New York, 1964); Omar N. Bradley and Clay Blair, *A General's Life* (New York, 1983); Matthew B. Ridgway, *The Korean War* (Garden City, N. Y., 1967); Mark W. Clark, *From the Danube to the Yalu* (New York, 1954); C. Turner Joy, *How Communists Negotiate* (New York, 1955); Allen E. Goodman, ed., *Negotiating While Fighting: The Diary of Admiral C. Turner Joy at the Korean Armistice Conference* (Stanford, Calif., 1978); J. Lawton Collins, *War in Peacetime: The History and Lessons of Korea* (Boston, 1965); and John M. Allison, *Ambassador from the Prairie or Allison Wonderland* (Boston, 1973).

Other memoirs also contain matters bearing on the Korean War. For George Kennan's efforts in Moscow in 1951 to get negotiations started on Korea, see George F. Kennan, *Memoirs, 1925–1963* (2 vols., Boston, 1967–1972). For the dubious activities of India's ambassador to China to bring about a settlement of the war, consult K. M. Panikkar, *In Two Chinas* (London, 1959). In *Witness to History, 1929–1969* (New York, 1973) Ambassador Charles Bohlen, who was an active participant in State Department discussions on Korean policy, criticizes the United States for overinterpreting the Korean War and overextending its commitments. Although for the most part disappointing, in *Farewell to Foggy Bottom: the Recollections of a Career Diplomat* (New York, 1964), America's ambassador to Korea after November 1952, Ellis Briggs, chronicles Syngman Rhee's opposition to an armistice agreement. In *As It Happened* (New York, 1954) former British Prime Minister Clement R. Attlee remarks on his concern in 1950 and 1951 that the Far Eastern war be confined to Korea. He also describes his trip to Washington in December 1950 for discussions on Korea. Former Foreign Secretary and Prime Minister Anthony Eden discusses British views on the "greater sanction" statement in 1951 in *Full Circle: The Memoirs of Anthony Eden* (Boston 1960). Lastly, in *In the Cause of Peace* (New York, 1954), former Secretary-General of the United Nations Trygve Lie discusses some of the diplomacy at the UN with respect to the Korean War.

Index

A NOTE ON THE TYPE

The text of this book is set in CALEDONIA, a Linotype face designed by W. A. Dwiggins. It belongs to the family of printing types called "modern face" by printers—a term used to mark the change in style of type-letters that occurred about 1800. Caledonia borders on the general design of Scotch Modern, but is more freely drawn than that letter.

This book was composed by Com Com Division of Haddon Craftsmen, Inc., Scranton, Pa., printed and bound by R. R. Donnelley & Sons Co., Harrisonburg, Virginia.

ABOUT THE AUTHOR

Burton I. Kaufman received his B.A. degree from Brandeis University (1962) and his Ph.D. degree from Rice University (1966). He taught for seven years at the University of New Orleans before coming to Kansas State University in 1973, where he is currently professor of history. His earlier works include *Efficiency and Expansion: Foreign Trade Organization in the Wilson Administration* (1974); *The Oil Cartel Case: A Documentary Study of Antitrust Activity in the Cold War Era* (1978); and *Trade and Aid: Eisenhower's Foreign Economic Policy* (1982). In 1972 he received the Newcomen Prize from the Newcomen Society and in 1978 the Stephenson-Binkley Award from the Organization of American Historians.